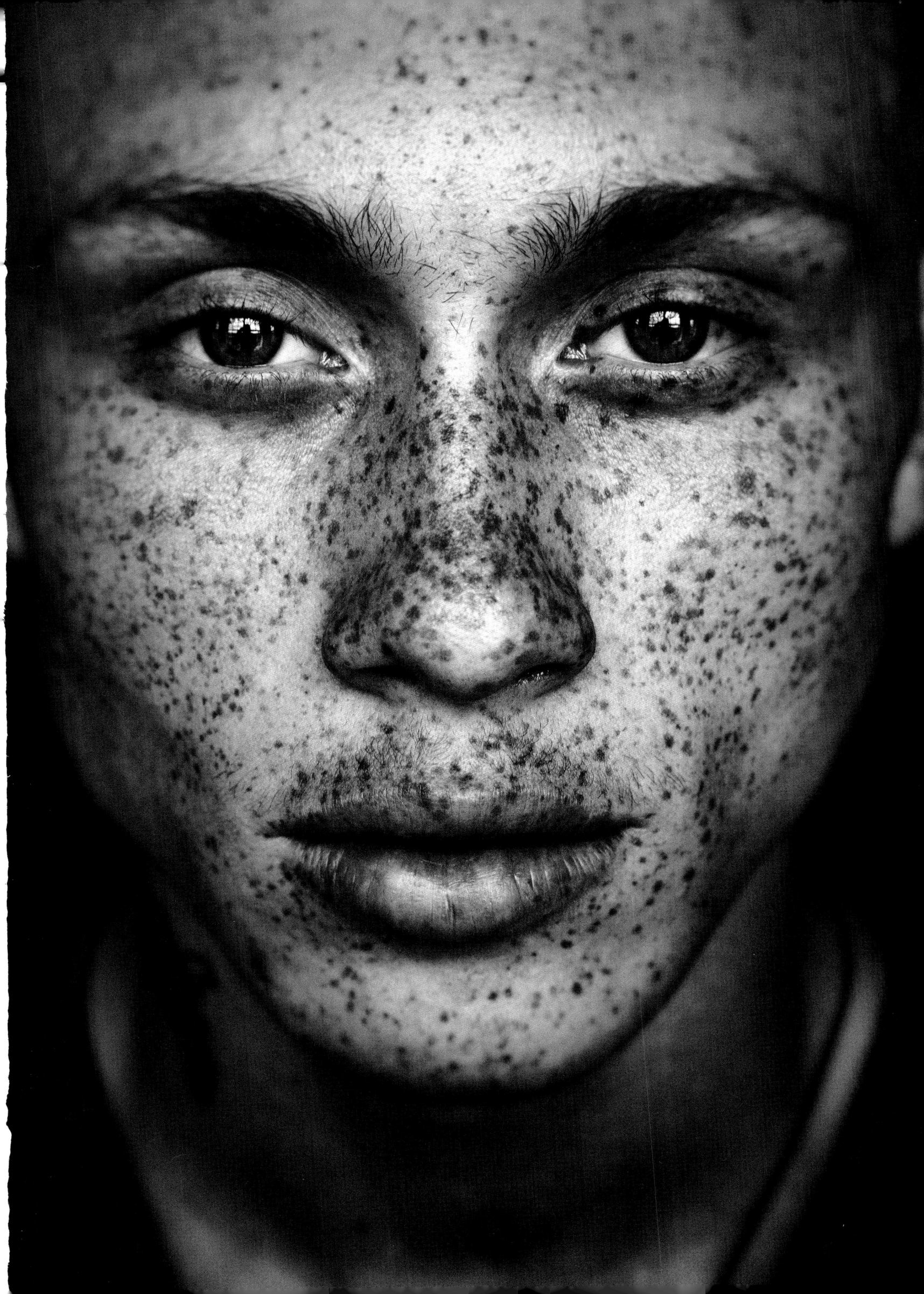

A catalogue record for this book is available from the British Library.

First Edition 2018

First published in Great Britain in 2018
by Carpet Bombing Culture.

An imprint of Pro-actif Communications

www.carpetbombingculture.co.uk

Email: books@carpetbombingculture.co.uk

©Carpet Bombing Culture. Pro-actif Communications

Words and images by: ©Derek Ridgers

ISBN: 978-1908211-69-9

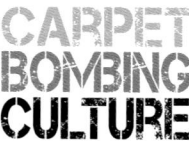

www.carpetbombingculture.co.uk

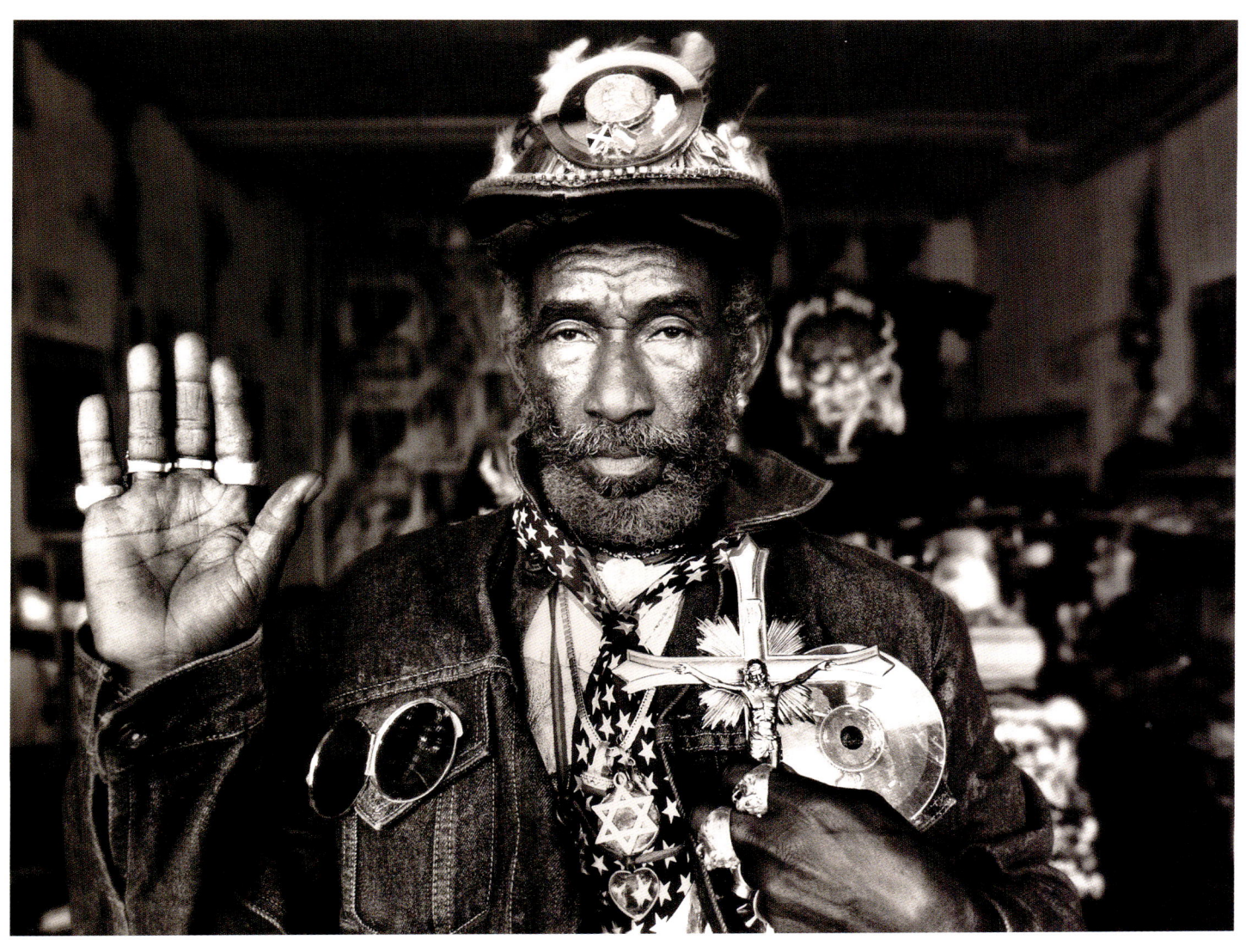

DEREK RIDGERS

PHOTOGRAPHS

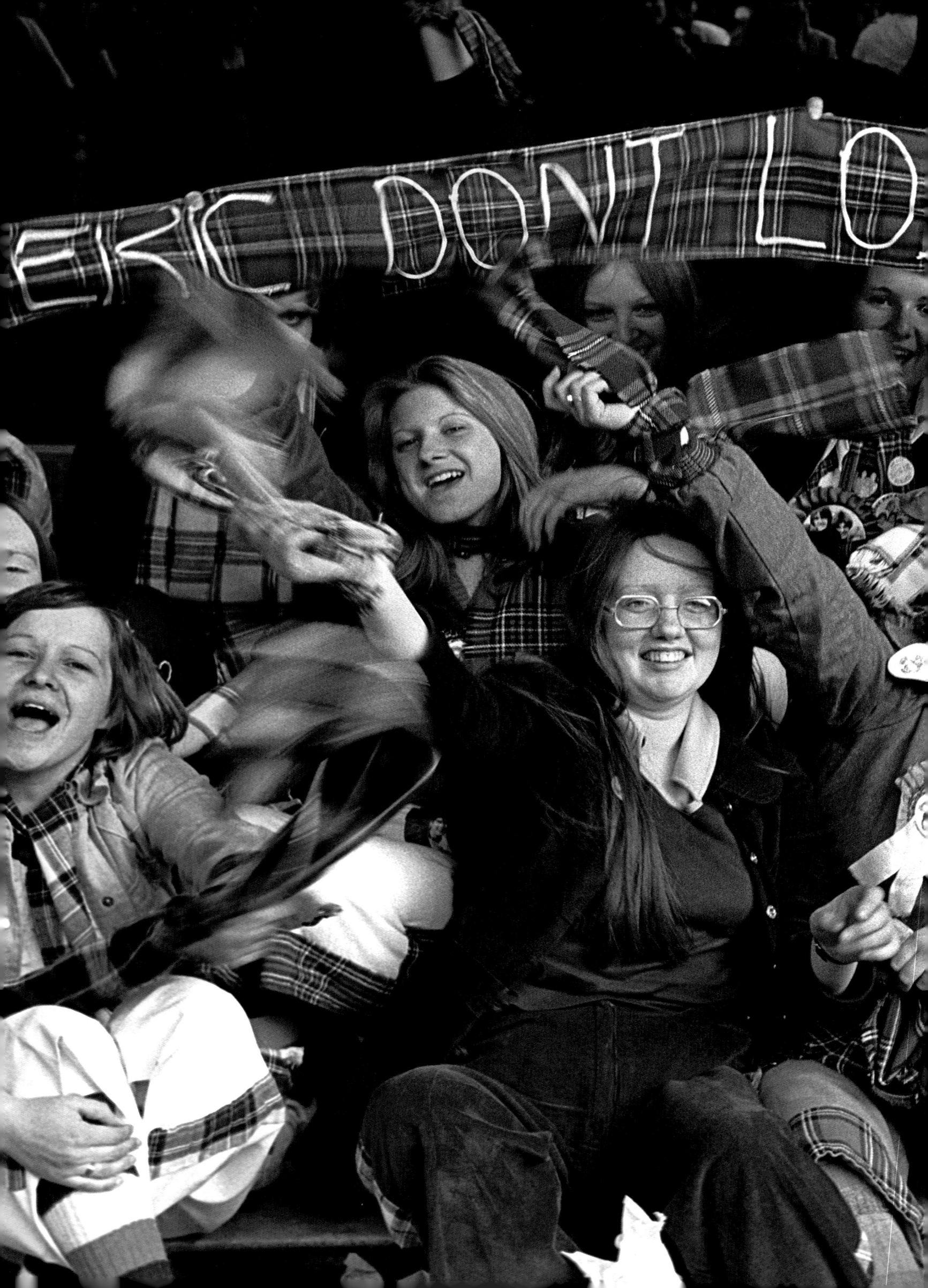

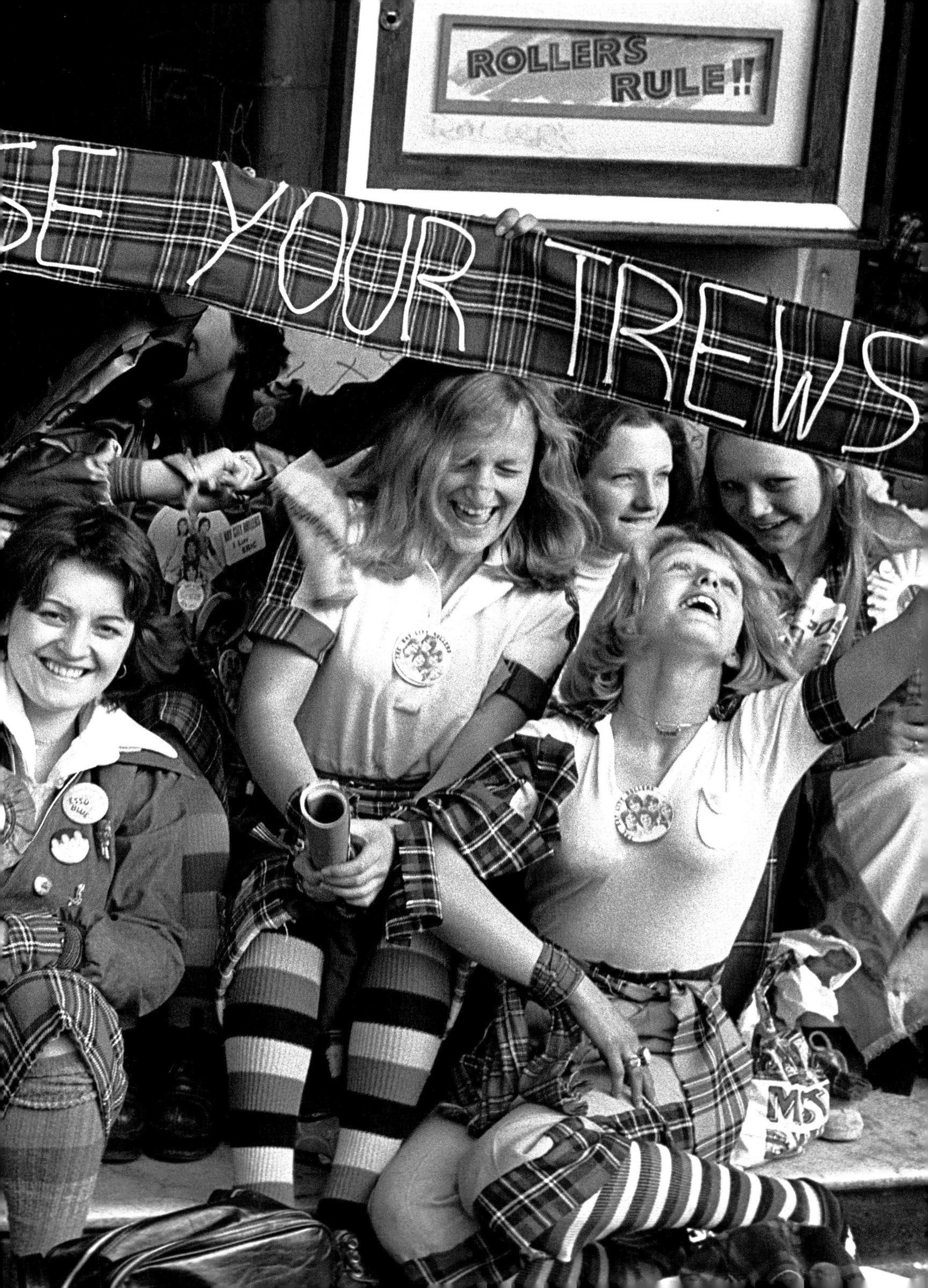

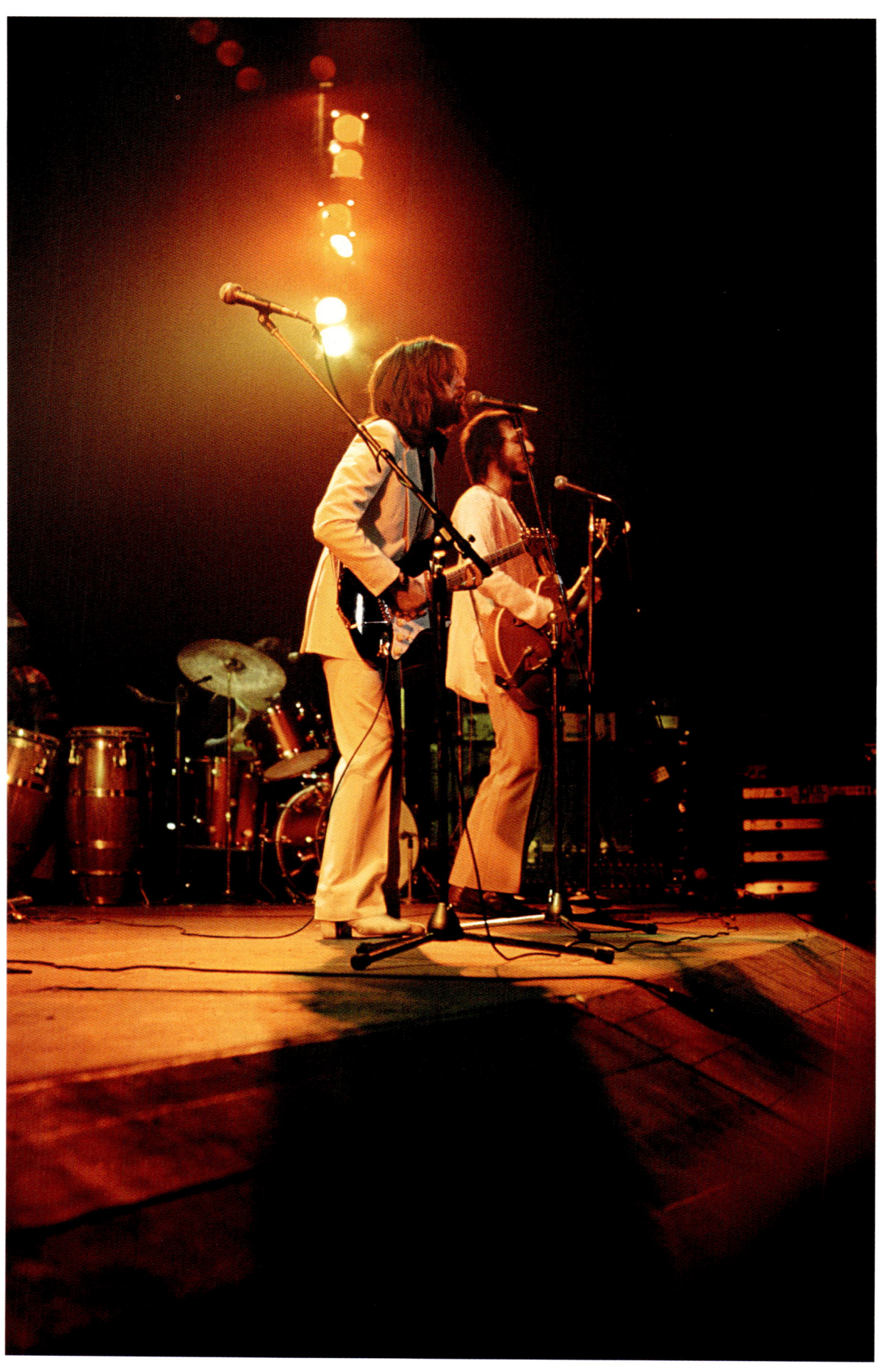

When I was young, I loved to look at photographs but I had absolutely no interest in being a photographer myself. I didn't even own a camera.

I went to Ealing School of Art; at age 16 and I was determined that one day I would become a famous painter, like my heroes Edwyn Burne Jones, John Everett Millais and Dante Gabriel Rossetti. But it was the 1960s and although the Pre-Raphaelites were very fashionable at that time, the tutors didn't see figurative art as having much of a future.

At the end of my first year, and after getting turned down for a fine art degree course at both St Martin's and The Slade, my determination evolved into wanting to become a famous ad agency art director. It was, after all, only a few years after the Mad Men era and, for a young man with plenty of hopes and ideas, the advertising world held some degree of promise.

And although that didn't quite work out as planned either, by 1973 I was at a small hot shop ad agency in Camden Town called Maisey Mukerjee Russell. The MD was a wonderfully charismatic man called Kim Mukerjee. I got put on the Miranda SLR camera account and Kim suggested I start taking one home with me to learn how to use it and familiarise myself with all its functions. I had absolutely no idea what all the little buttons and knobs did, so it was certainly a good idea.

This was why, when I went to a concert in Finsbury Park, featuring Eric Clapton playing in a band with Steve Winwood, Ron Wood and Pete Townshend, I happened to have a loaded SLR camera with me.

The concert (recorded and later released as Eric Clapton's Rainbow Concert) turned out to be something of a milestone. Wikipedia records the date as 13th January 1973. I didn't think of it as a particularly significant date at the time but it was really the night that changed my life.

When my girlfriend Jo-Anne and I arrived, we found the seats we'd booked were right at the back, in the very last row. The view was terrible.

So when the lights went down and the band came on, rather unchivalrously I got up, left Jo-Anne in her seat, ran to the front, hopped over the low wall into the photo pit and pretended to be a photographer.

Exactly how I had the balls to do this, I don't know. In those days there weren't many photographers at gigs and hardly any security. But I was putting myself in between the band and several thousand people. All of which could then see me almost as much as they could see the band.

I must admit, I felt quite exposed. But at the same time, the excitement of being only a few feet away from my musical heroes was quite compelling.

Although I only had one camera, one lens and, to the best of my recollection, only one roll of film, I did the best I could. When I got the film processed, some of the shots didn't seem too bad (see previous page). And I resolved to try to again at the next opportunity.

After which, I sort of slipped into becoming a bit of an amateur photographer. Eventually I was sacked from Maisey Mukerjee Russell but I bought myself a second hand Nikkormat and I was away. I joined a camera club and started showing my photographs to people. No one visibly recoiled.

I'd take a camera out occasionally at weekends and shoot sunsets, rusty, abandoned motorcars or painted, wooden boats in quaint looking harbours. The sort of photographic cliches that many amateurs start with. And of course, I'd be shooting every gig I went to.

When punk happened, in late 1976, something quite profound happened. Almost overnight the audience became more photogenic than the bands. At which point I started photographing the fans at gigs as well.

I had my first one-man show at the ICA in 1978. The show was called 'Some Punk Portraits'. The work was actually hung in the ICA's restaurant (a detail I don't normally remember to mention). After which I started to take my photography a little more seriously.

I don't suppose it was until 1982, after the advertising business had shown me the door for the final time and I started to work regularly for The Face and NME, that I considered myself to be a proper photographer. Or maybe I shouldn't really say "proper", because there's always been a part of me that felt like the imposter I was on the night of the Rainbow Concert; like I shouldn't really be there and I would soon get found out. As Tony Hancock put it "sorted out sometimes, then slung out".

Beyond the photographs that date from my early days as an amateur, most of the rest were taken on assignment for The Face, NME, Time Out, The Sunday Telegraph, The Independent on Sunday Review, Loaded, Vox or, more recently, 10 Magazine. I'm very grateful for the belief they showed in me. The rest were tests, shots taken for magazines I worked for only once or part of personal projects, like my ongoing series of street portraits. The book starts off with my earliest photographs and ends with some of my most recent but, apart from that, they are not really arranged chronologically.

As I say above, I never wanted to be a photographer but gradually photography drew me in and took over my life. I have to say it's been all been tremendous fun.

They do say that in life the journey is more important than the arrival. In my case that's completely true. And it was a journey along which I seemed to take lot of photographs.

Derek Ridgers, May 2018.

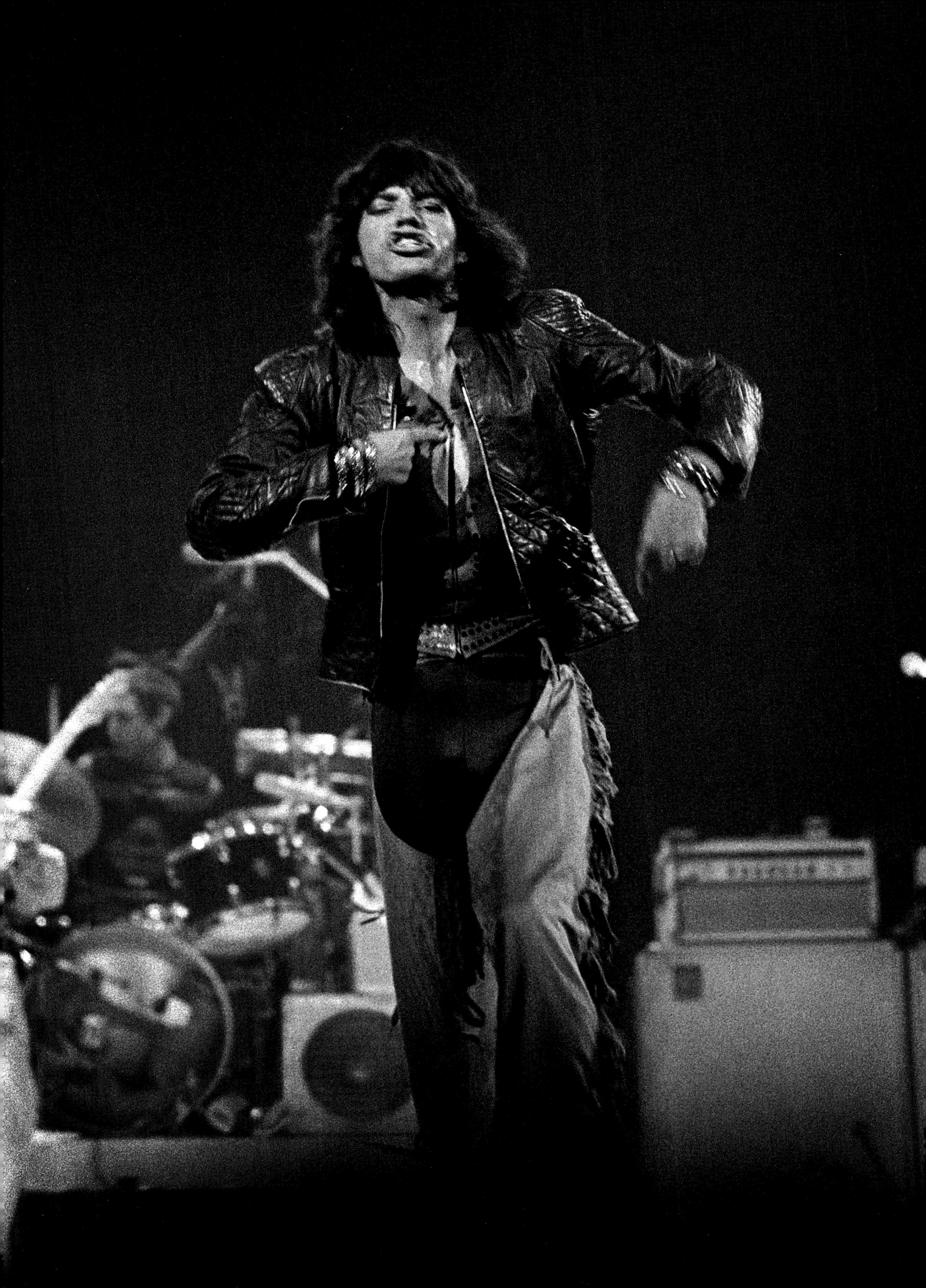

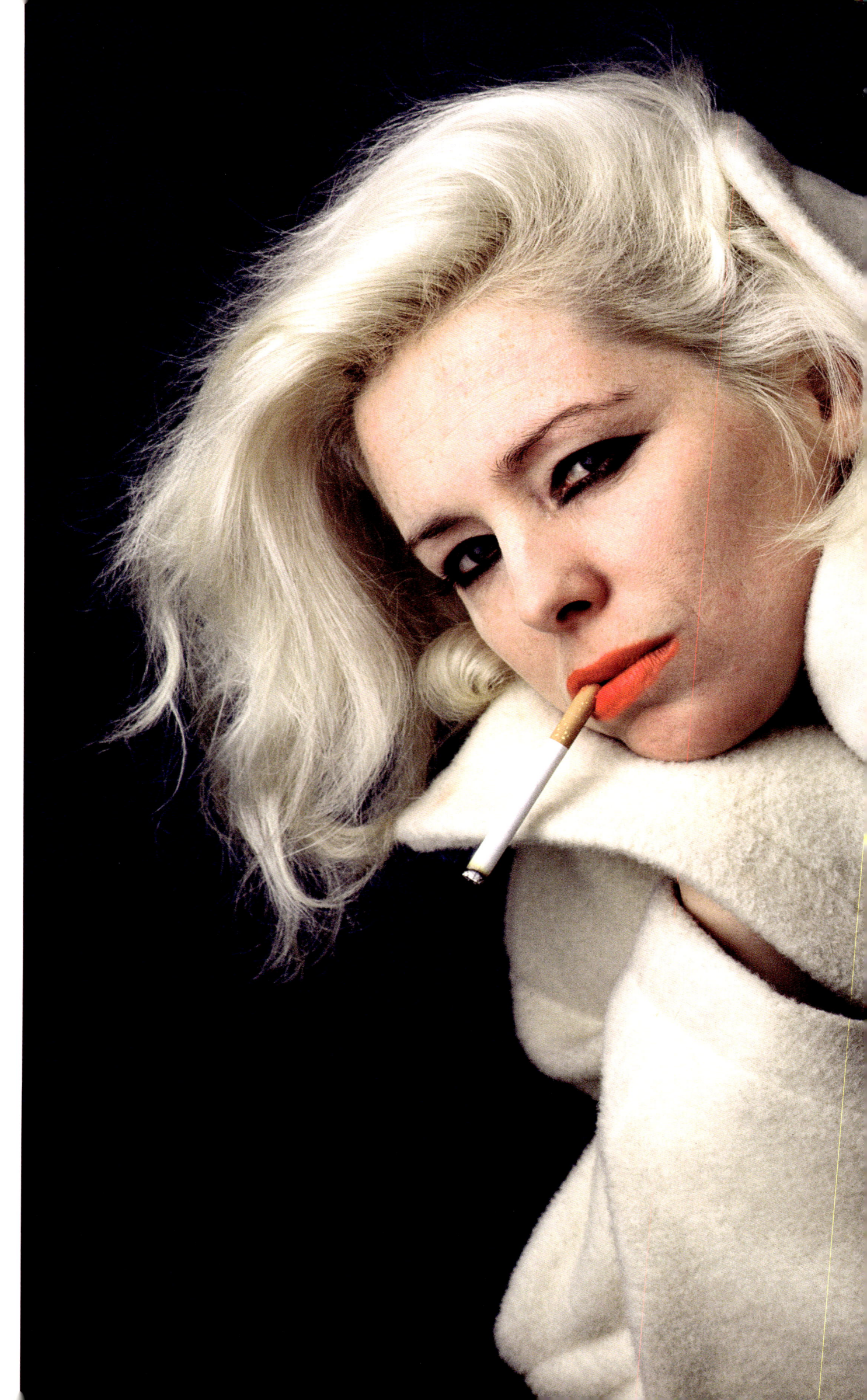

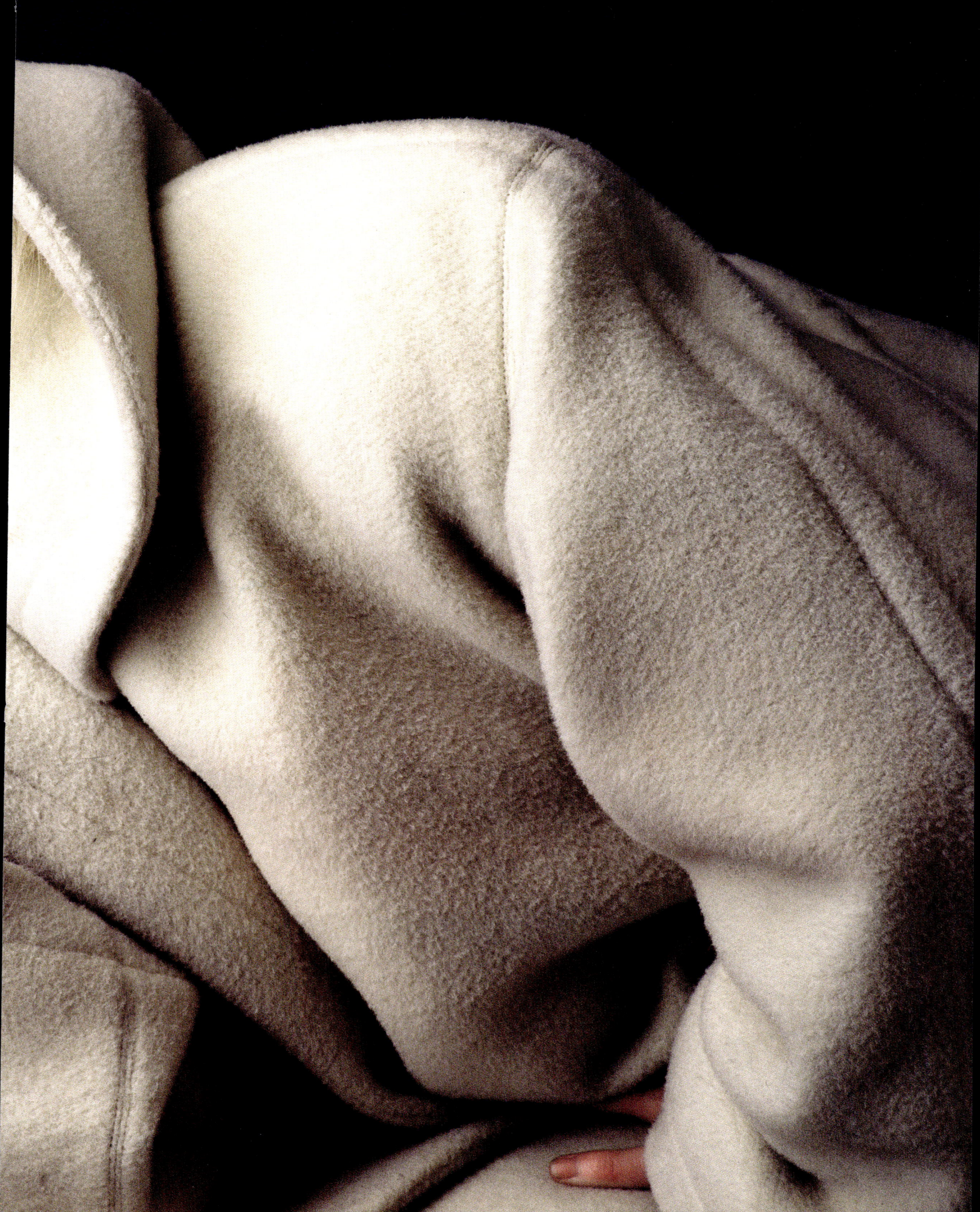

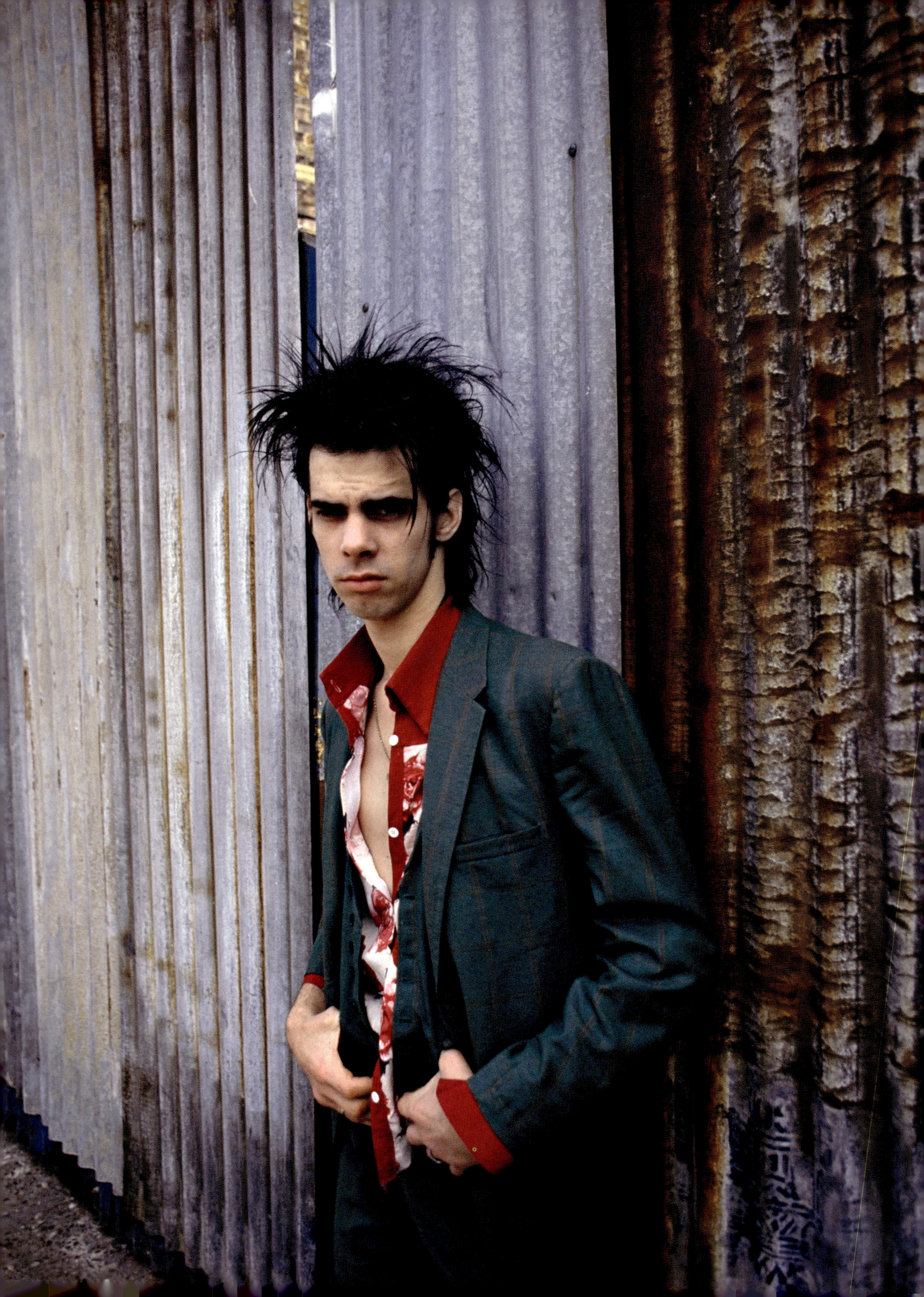

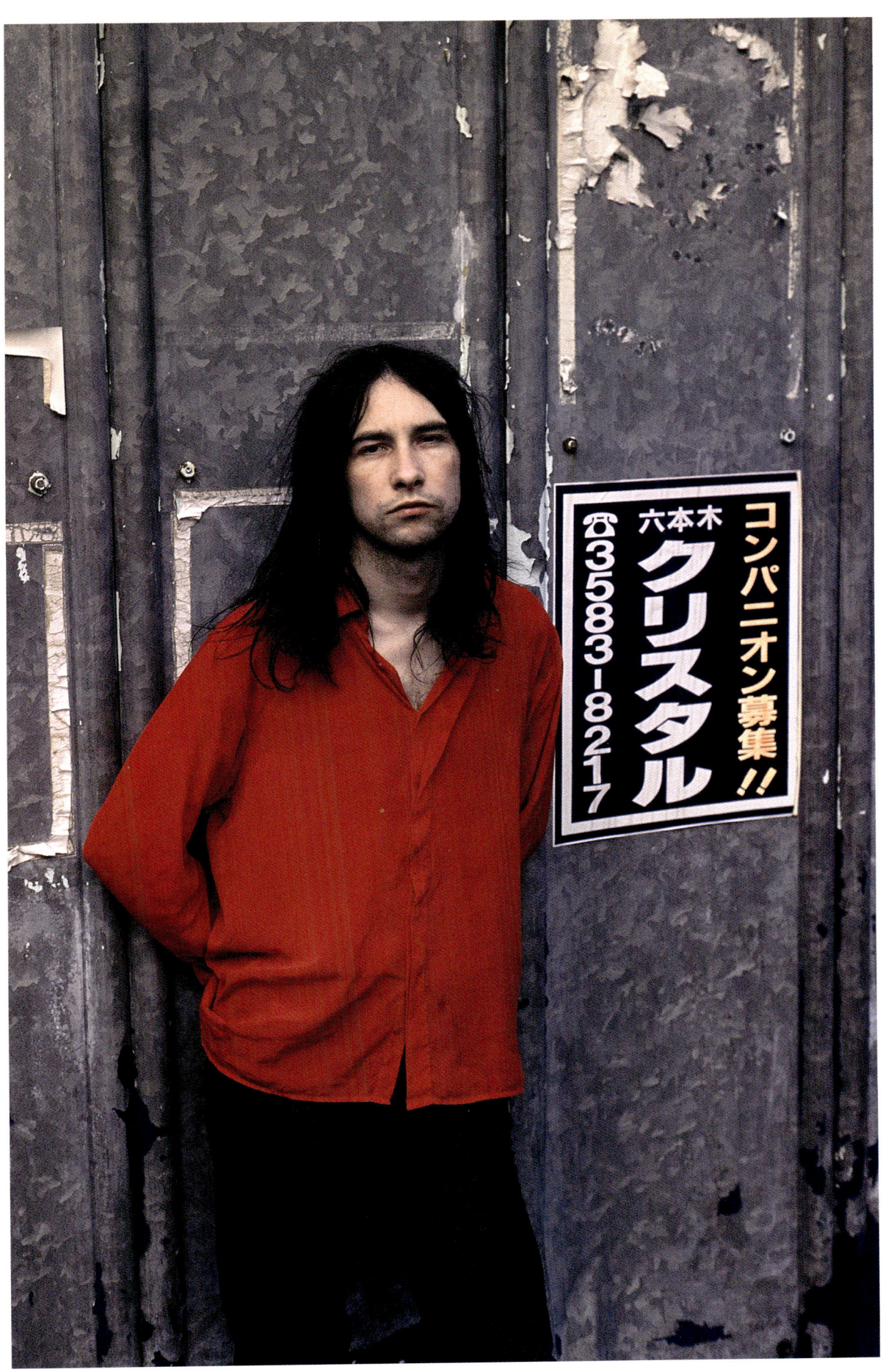

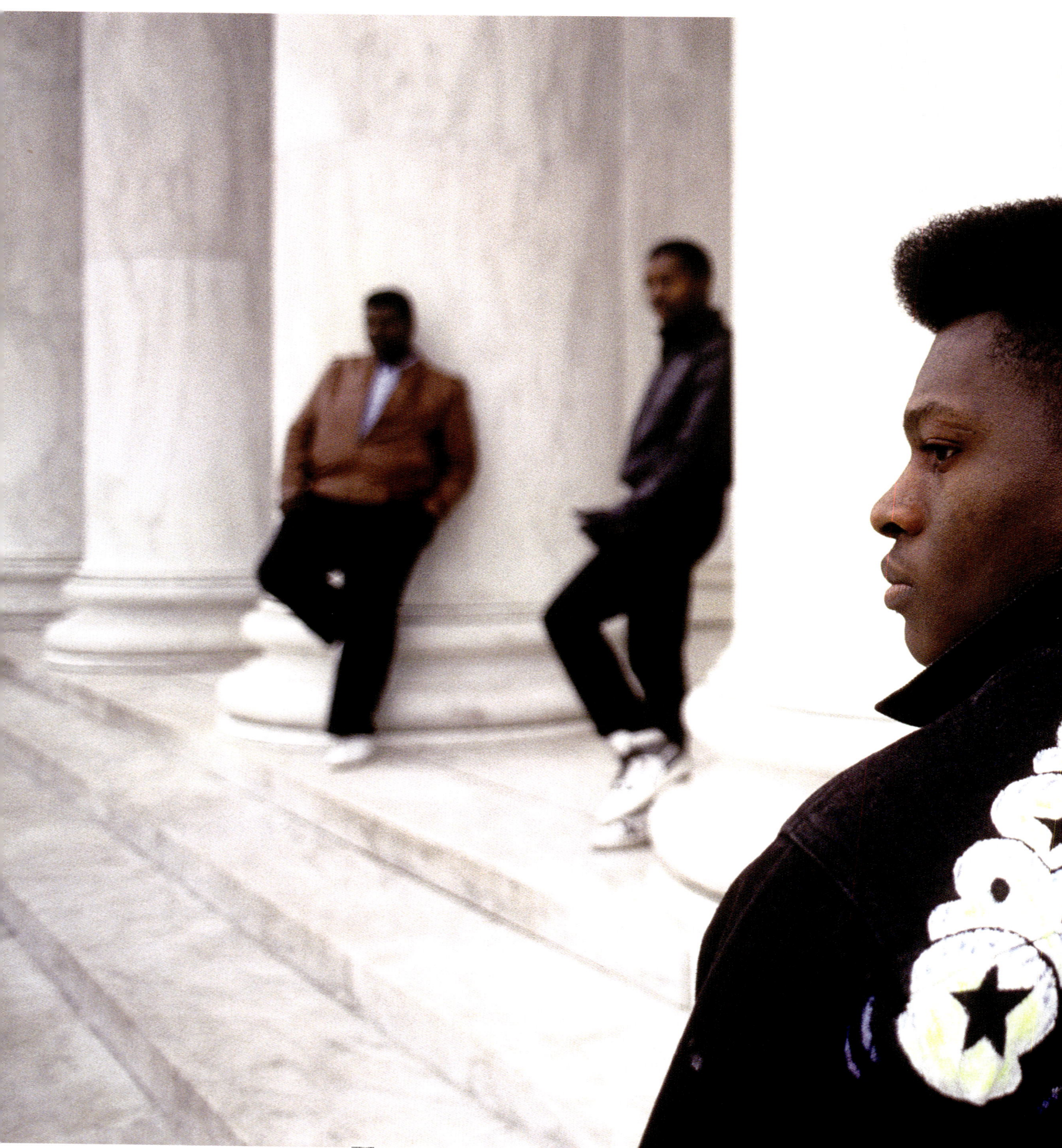

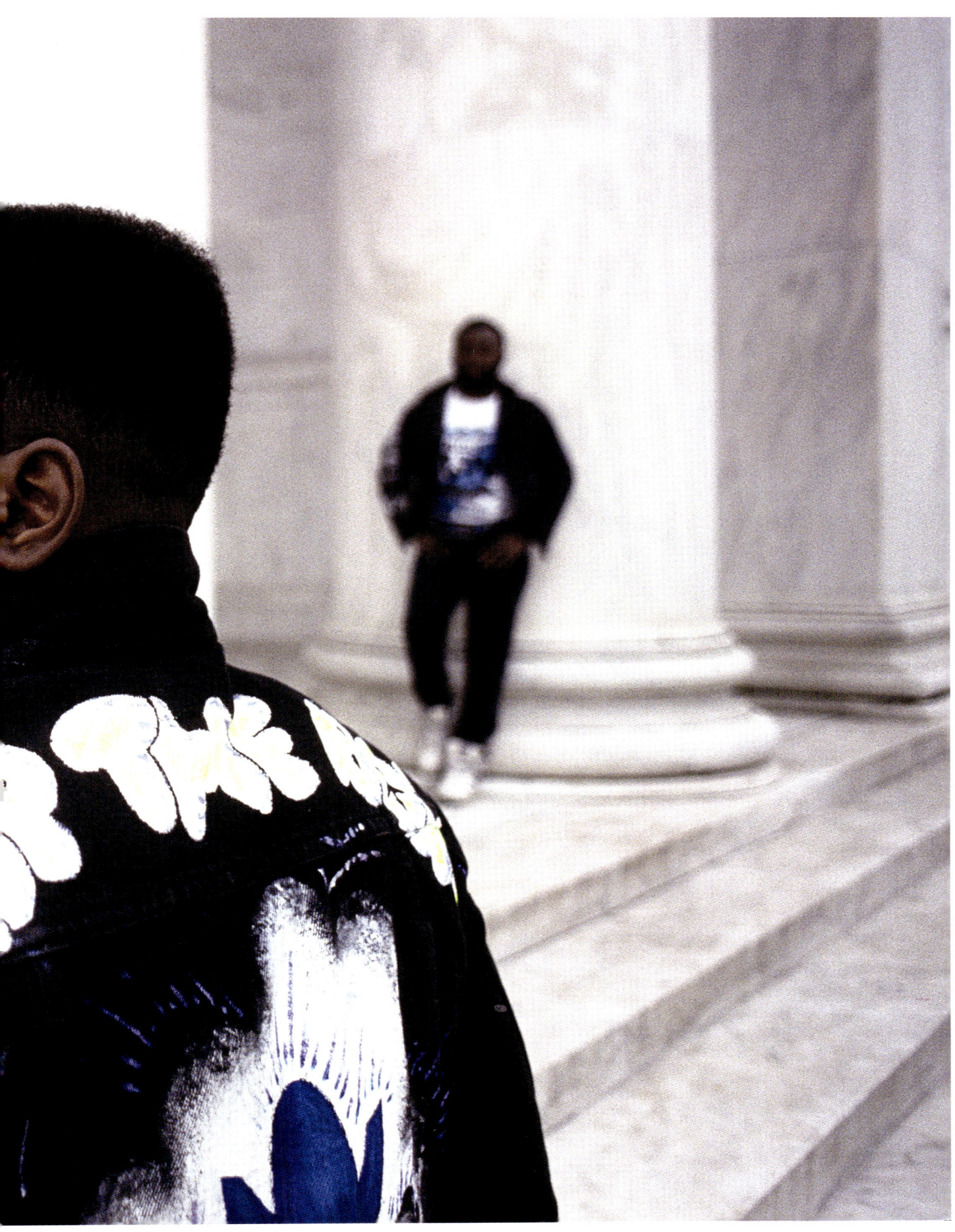

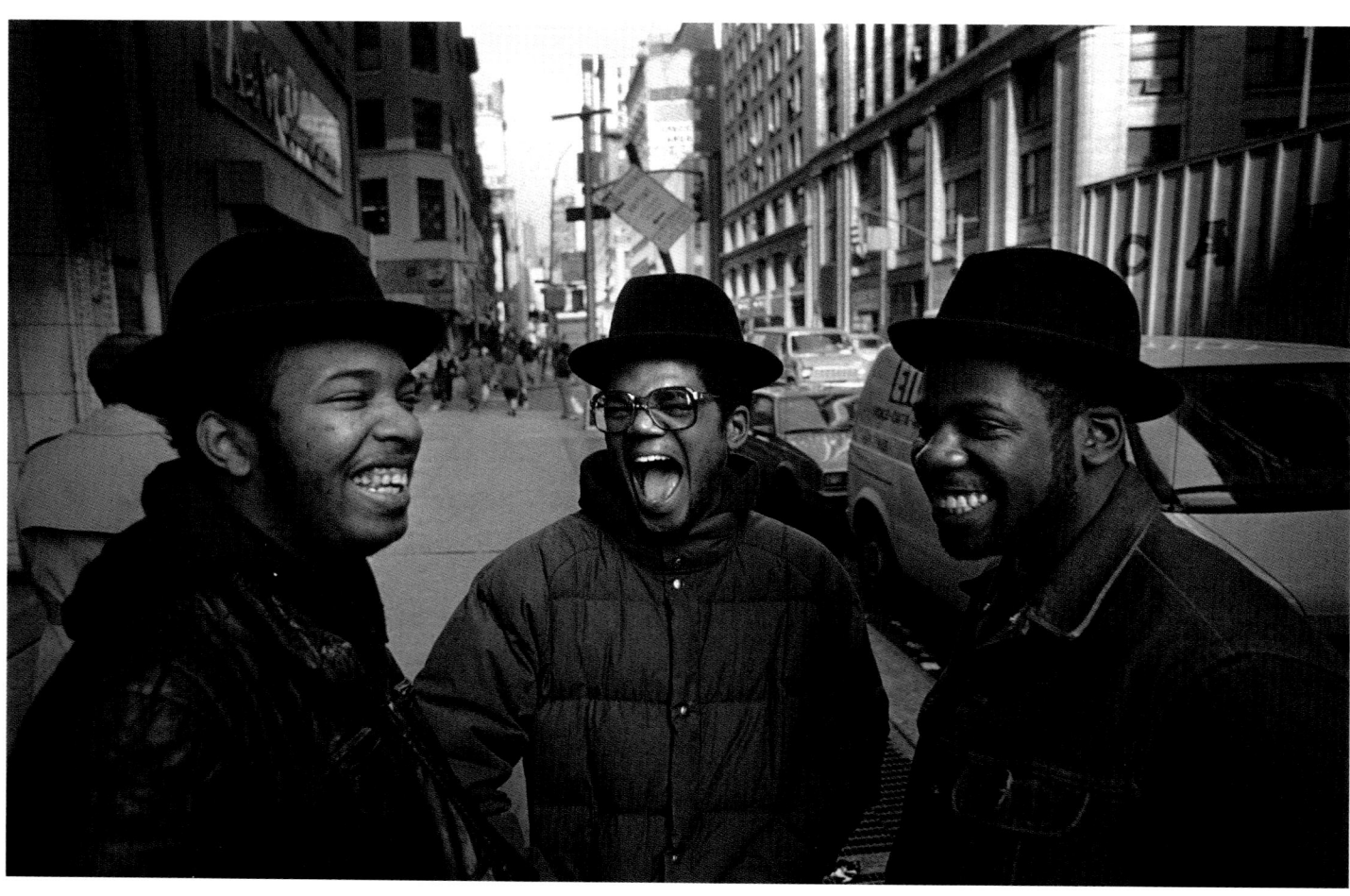

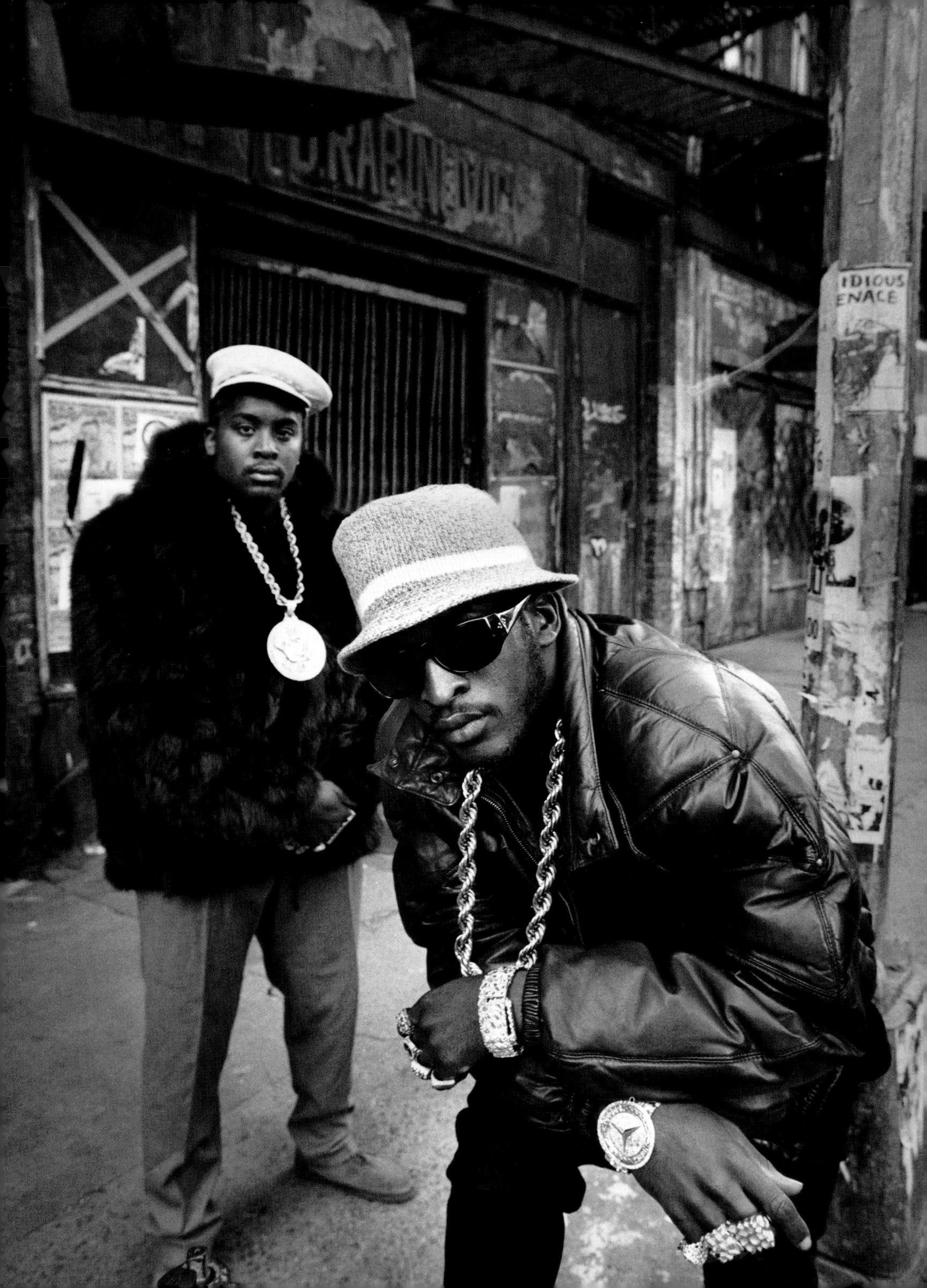

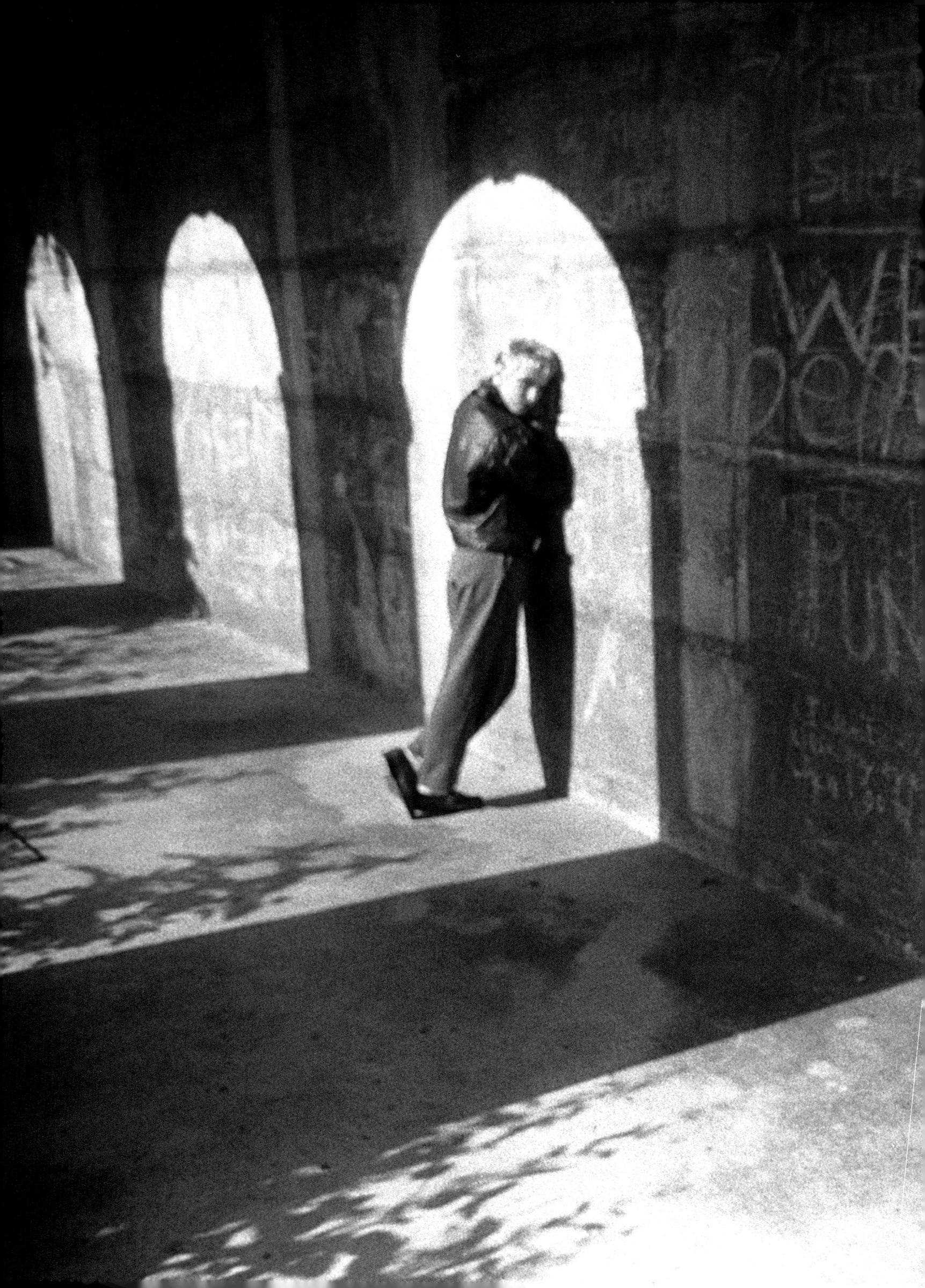

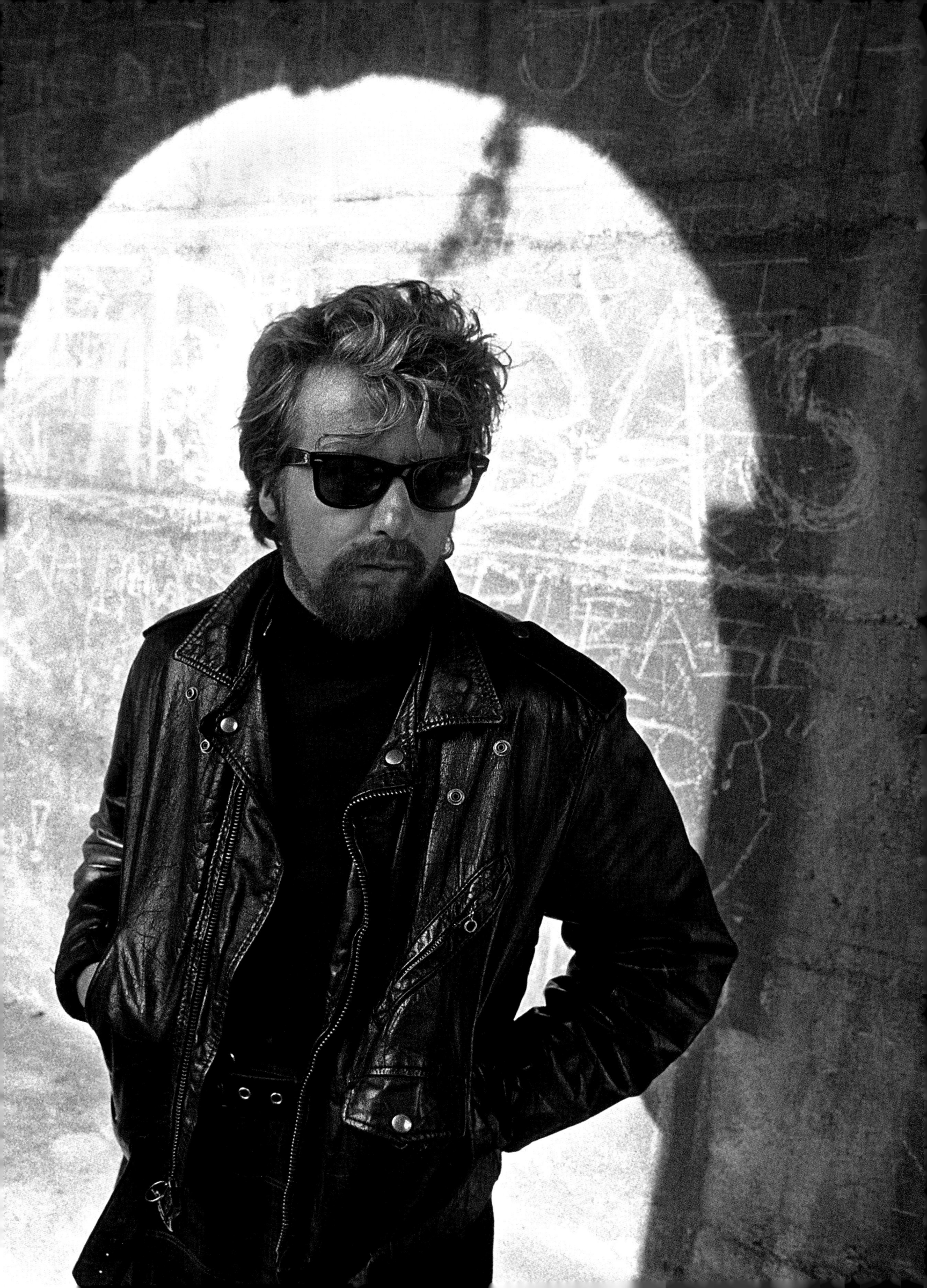

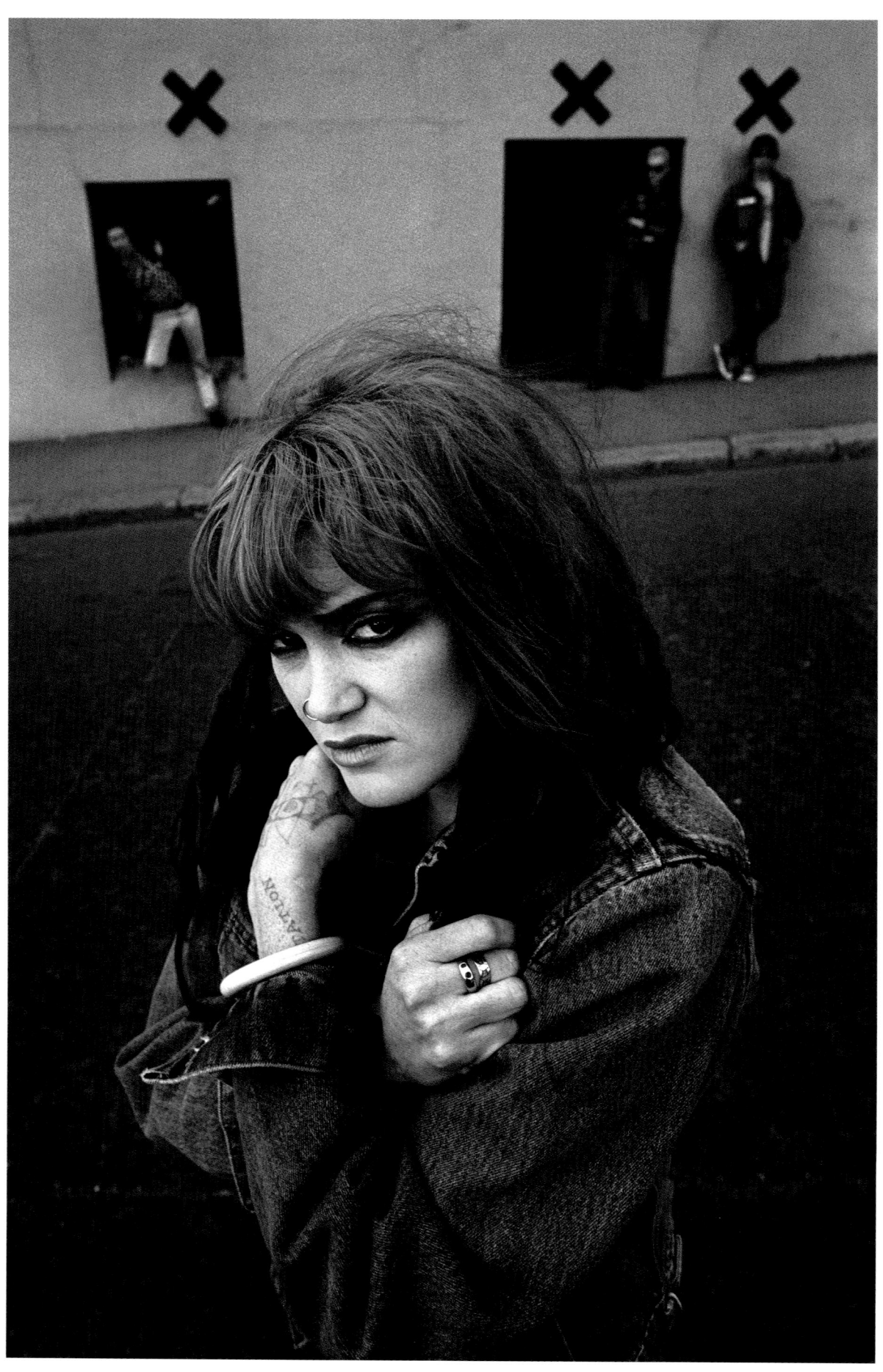

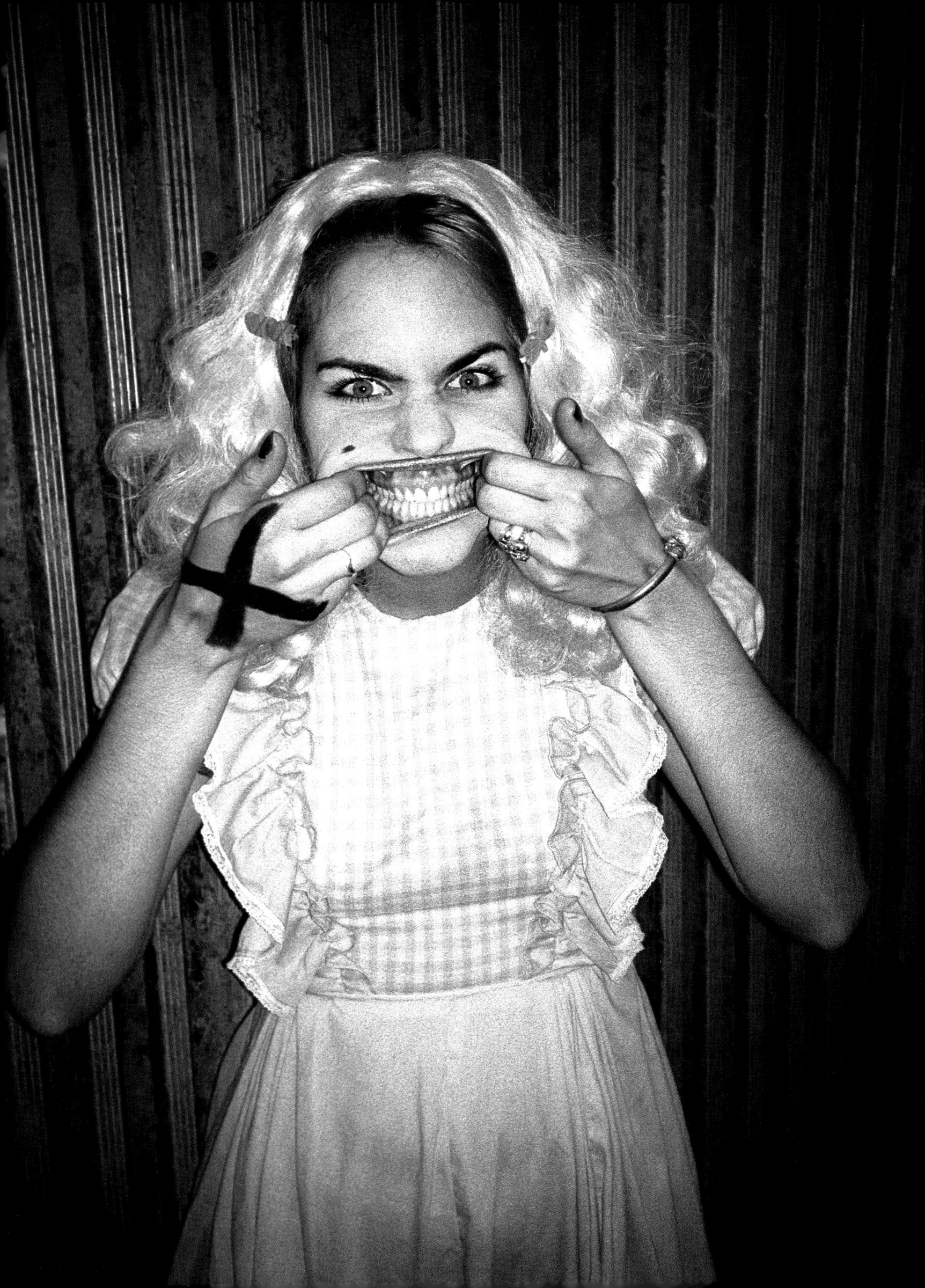

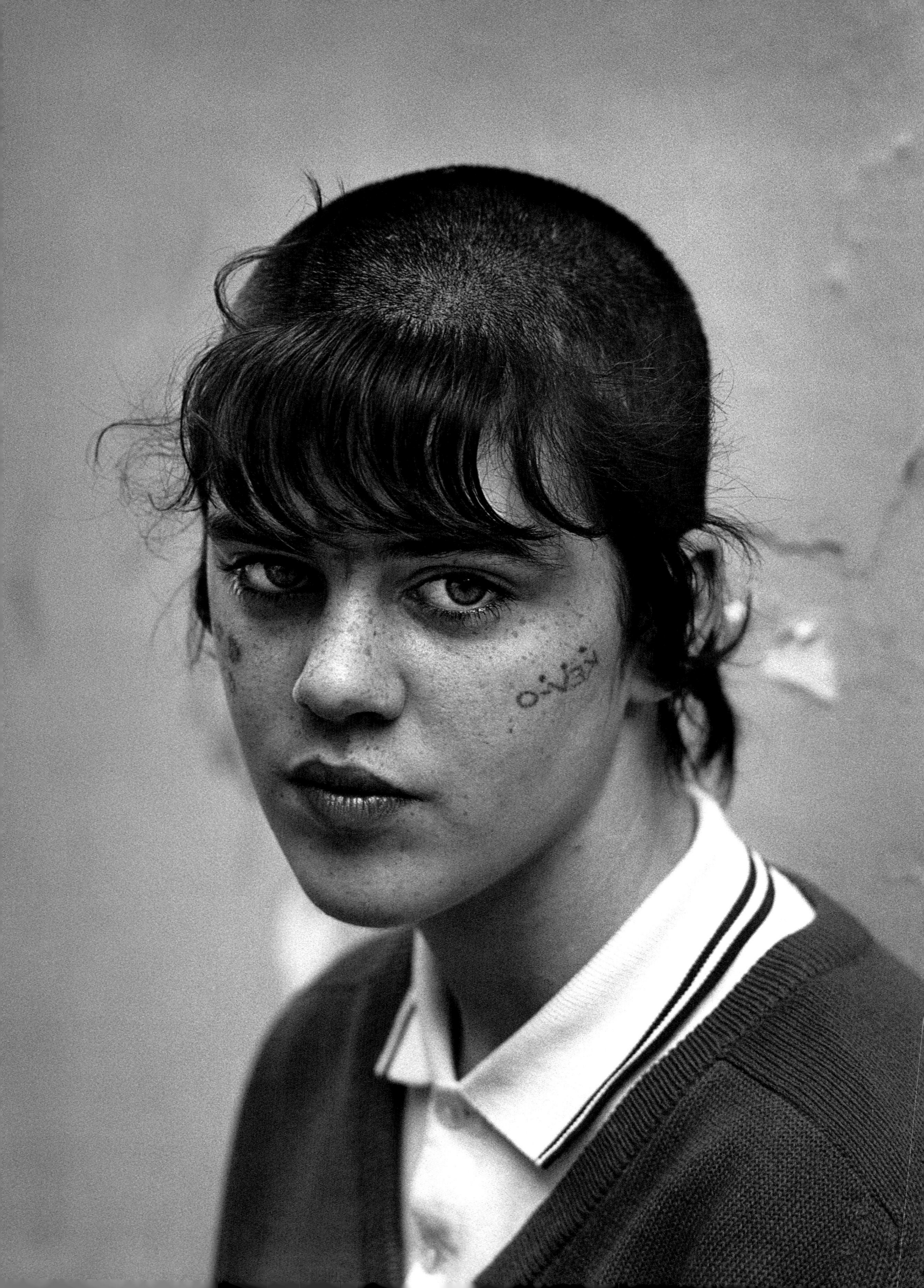

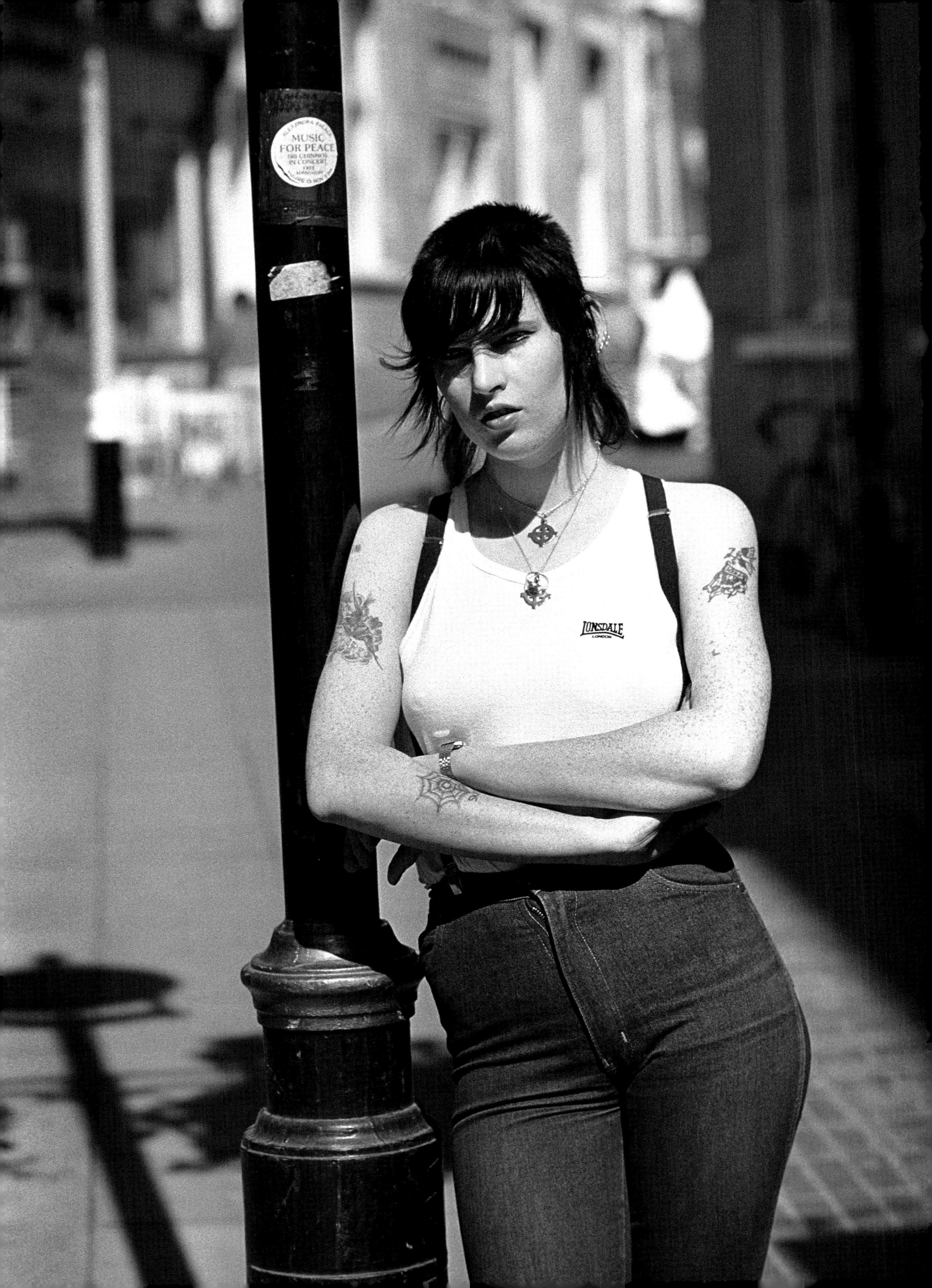

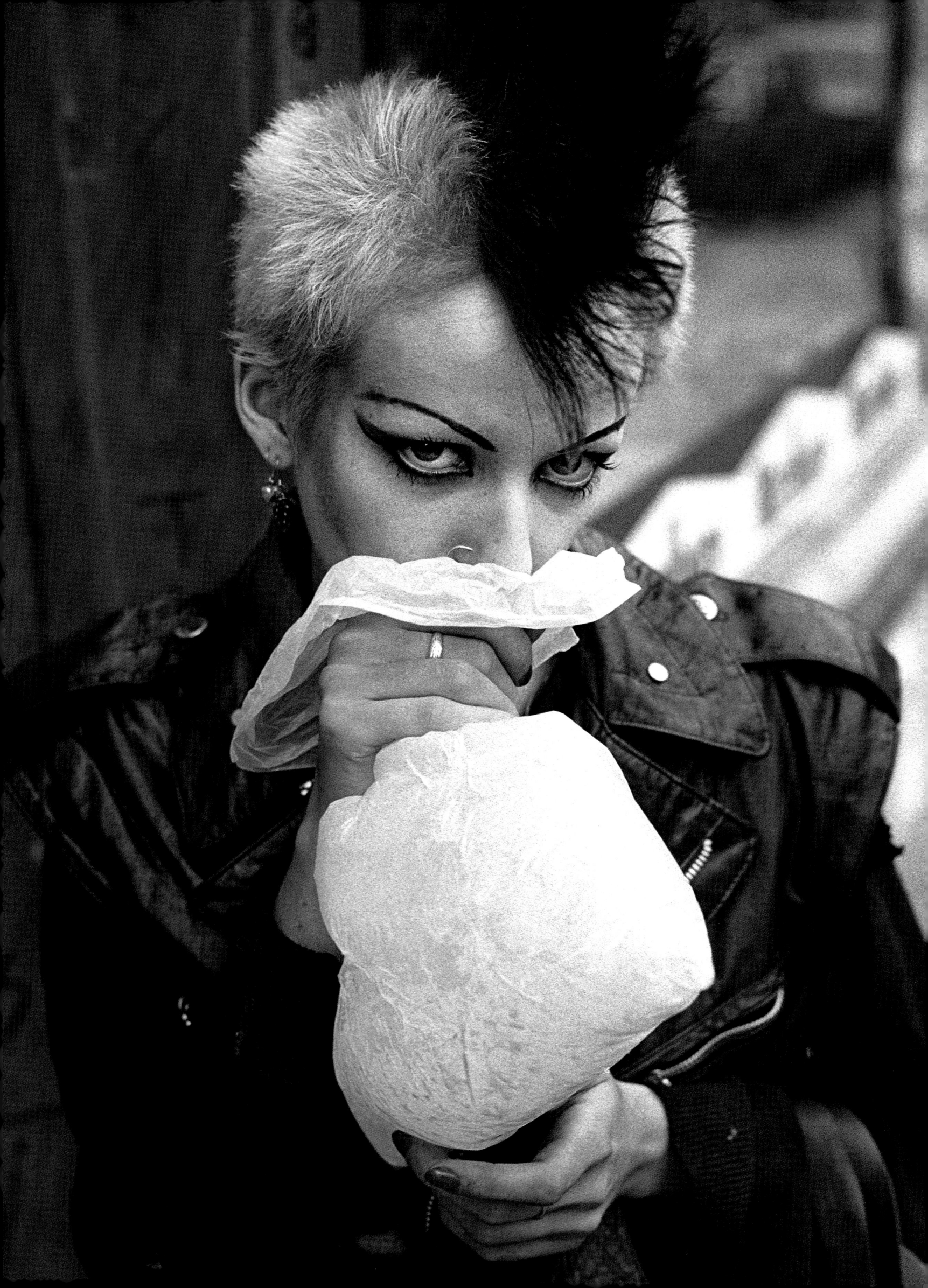

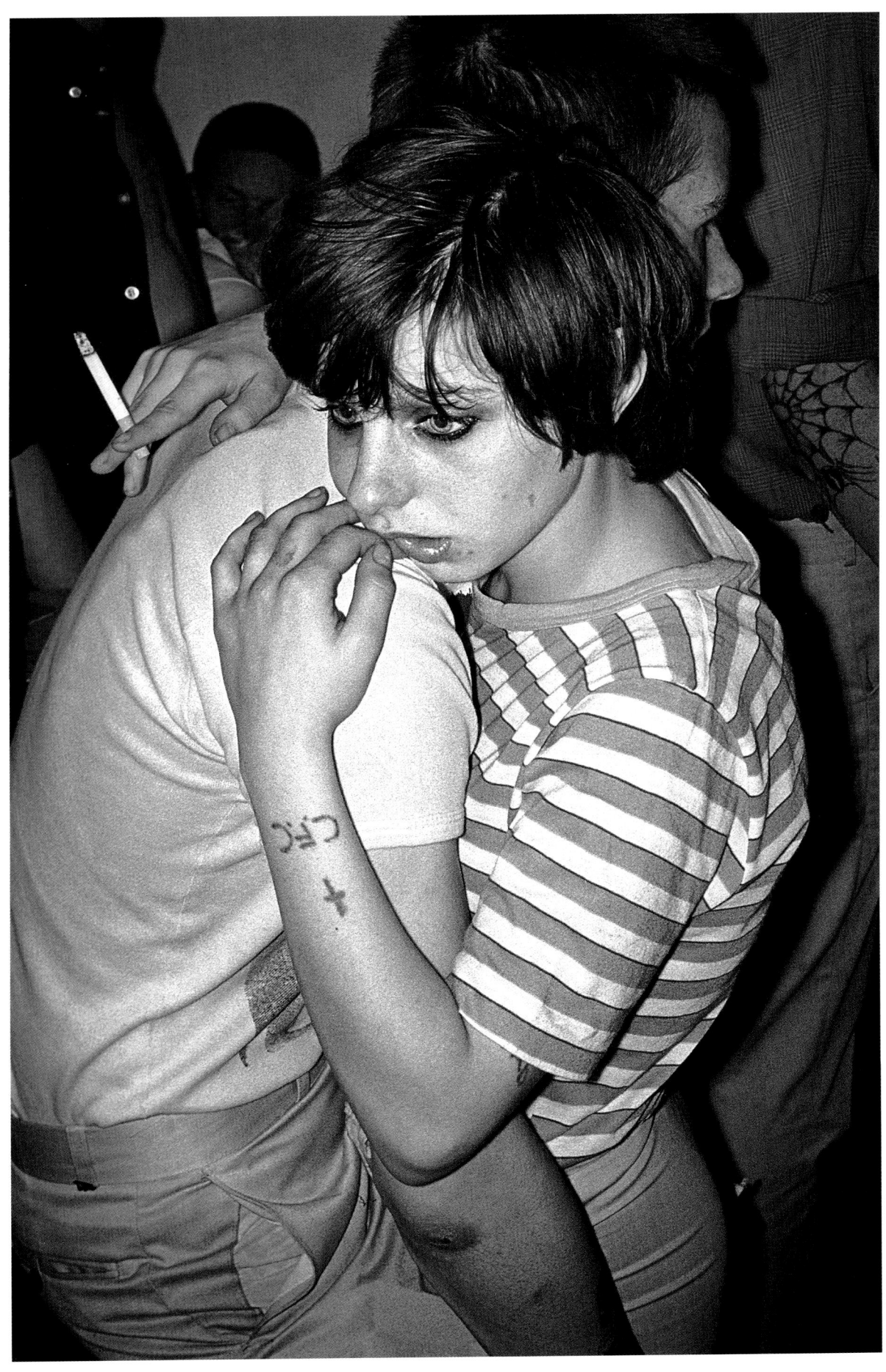

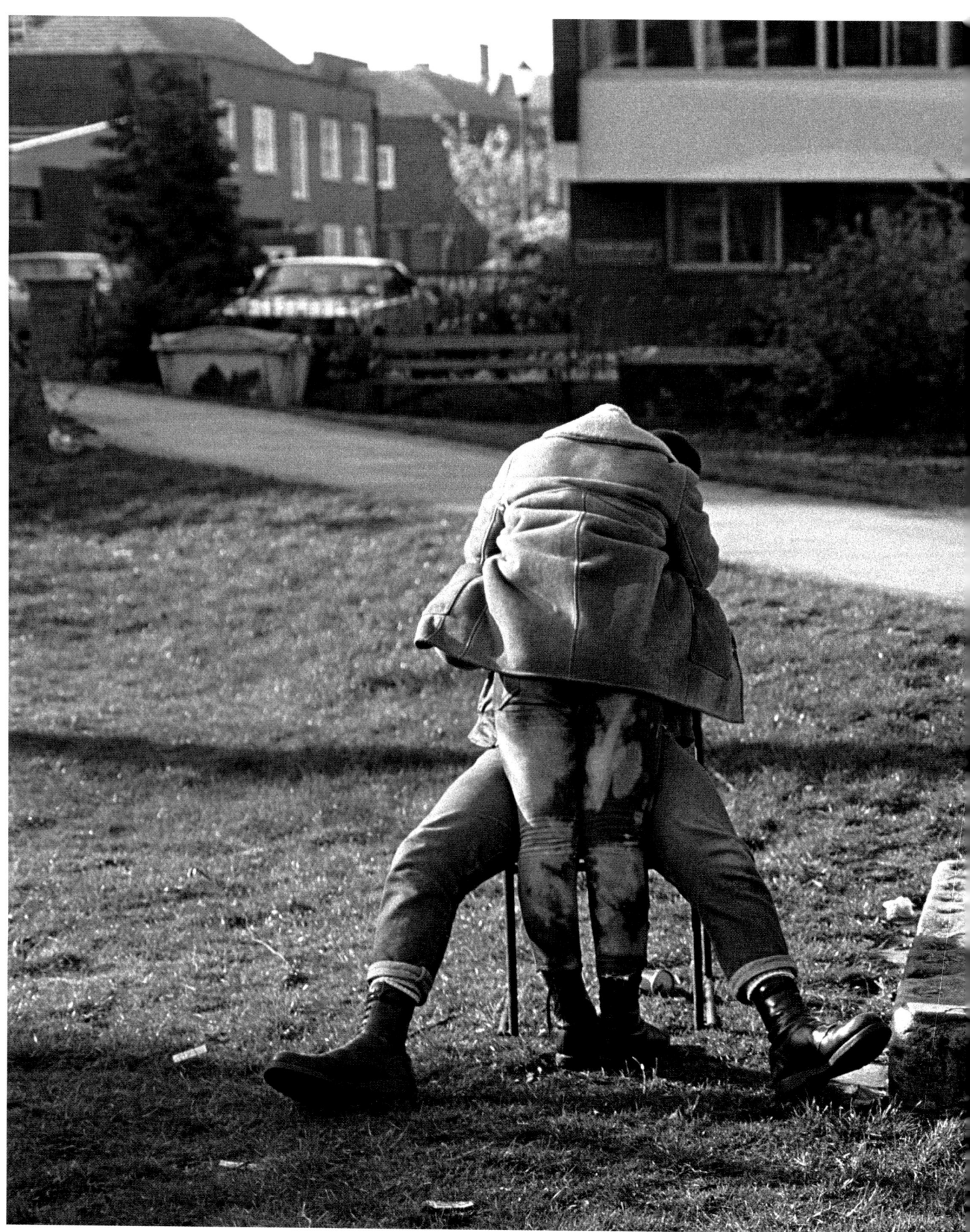

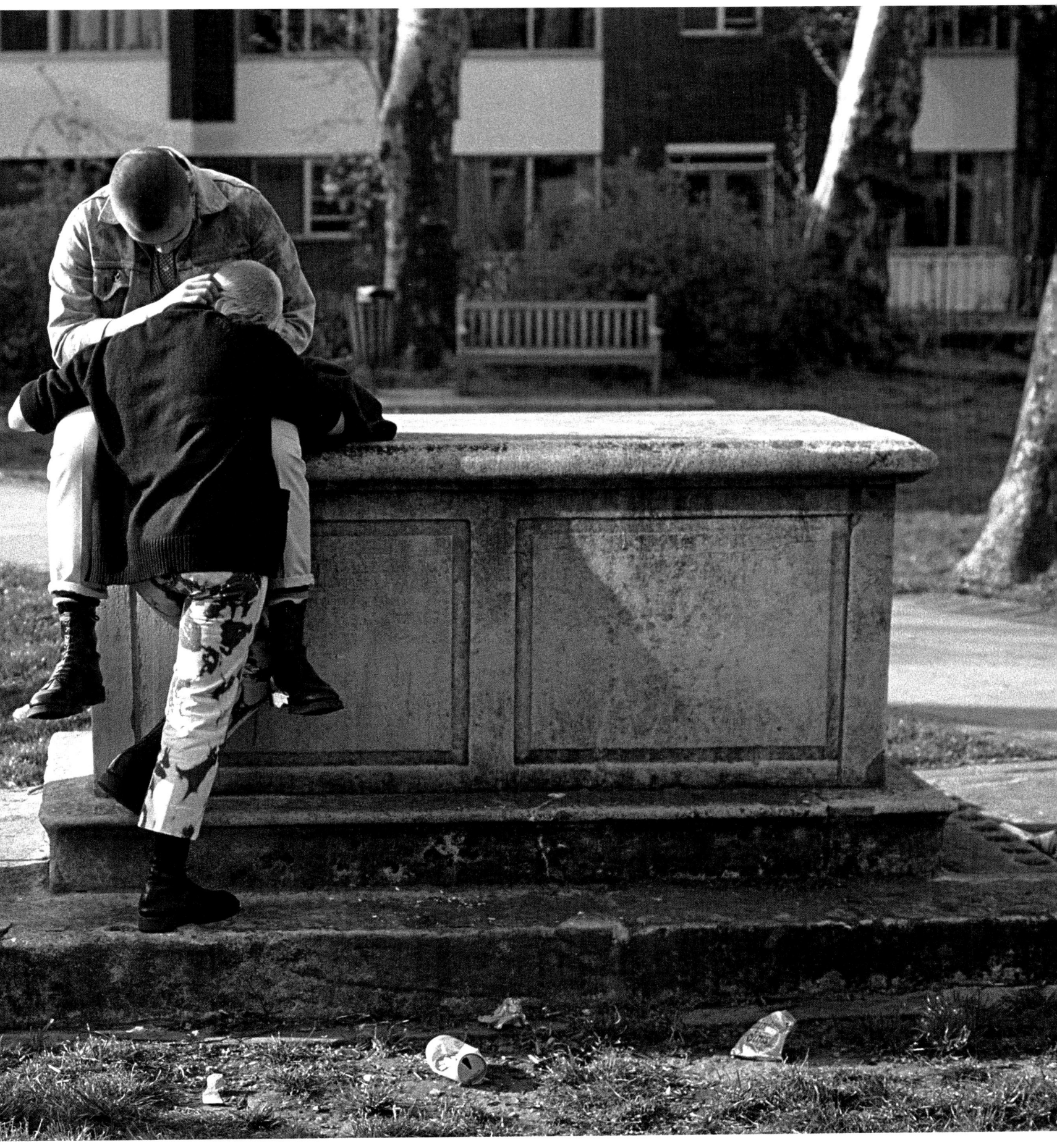

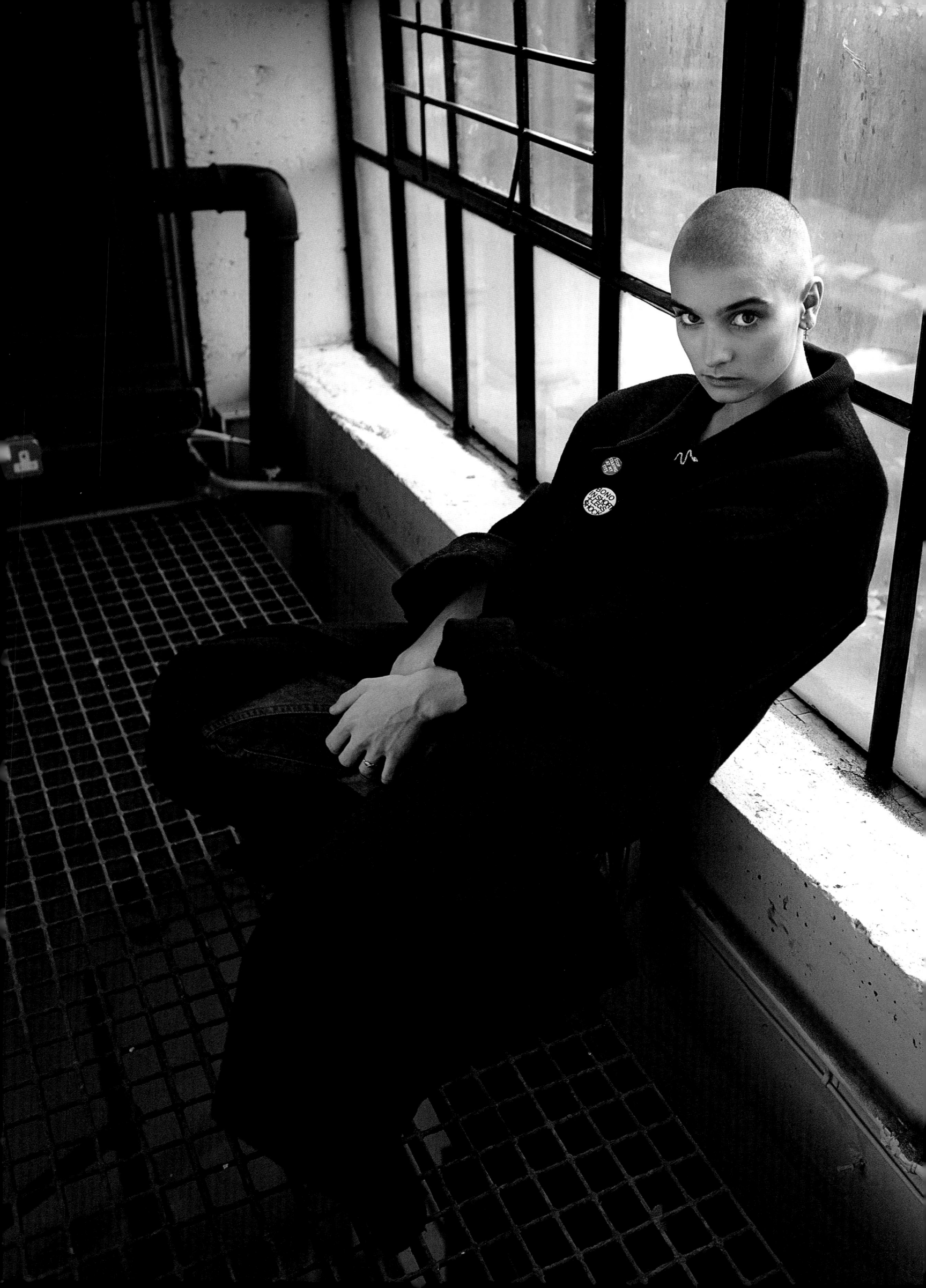

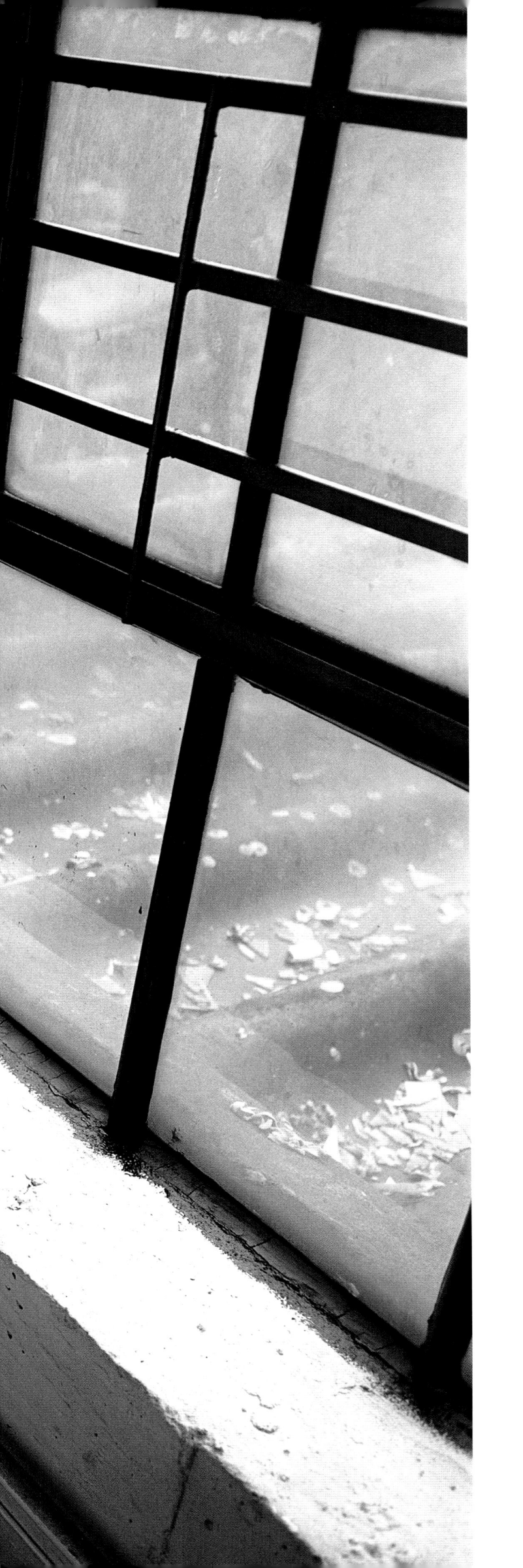

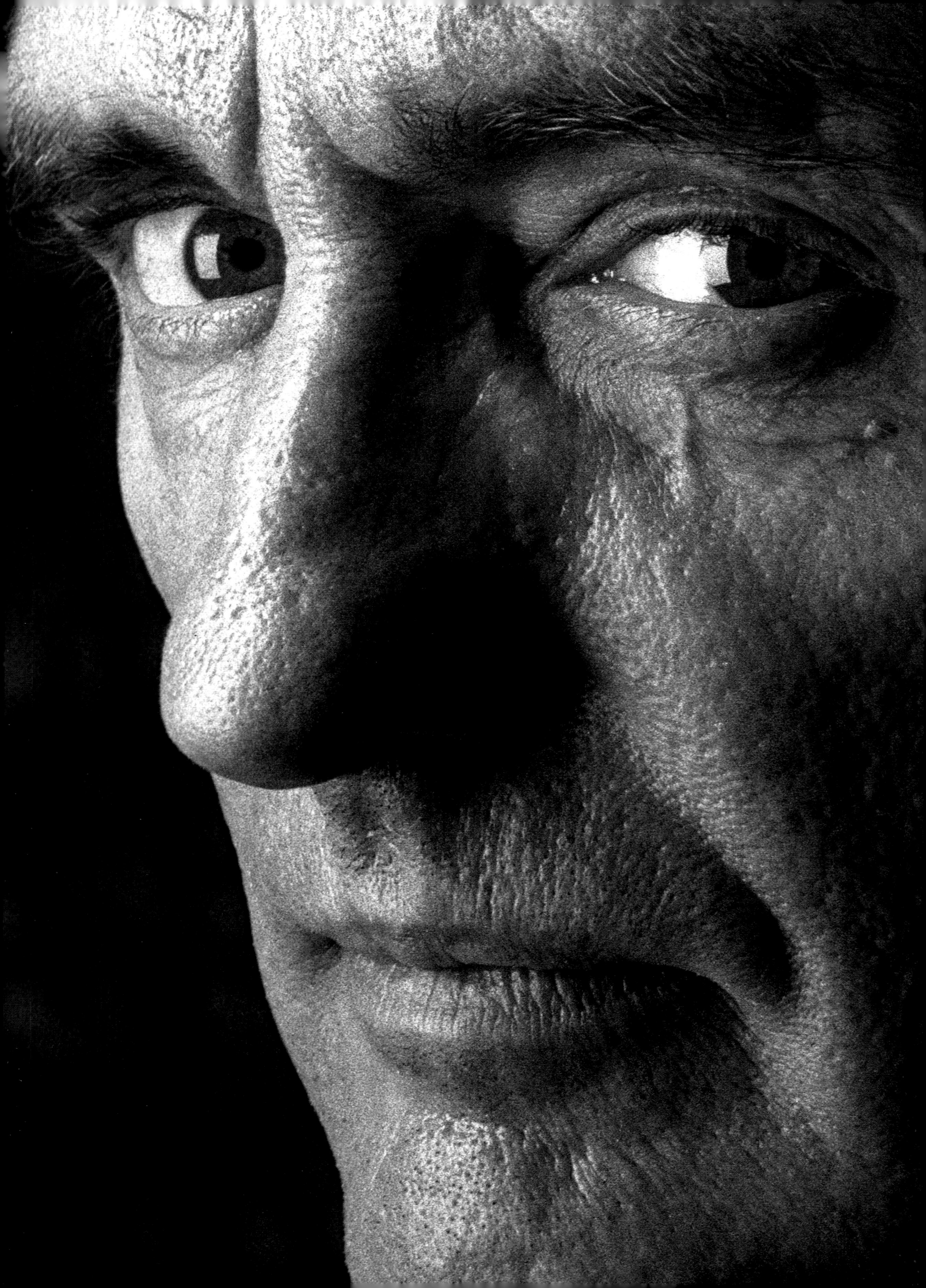

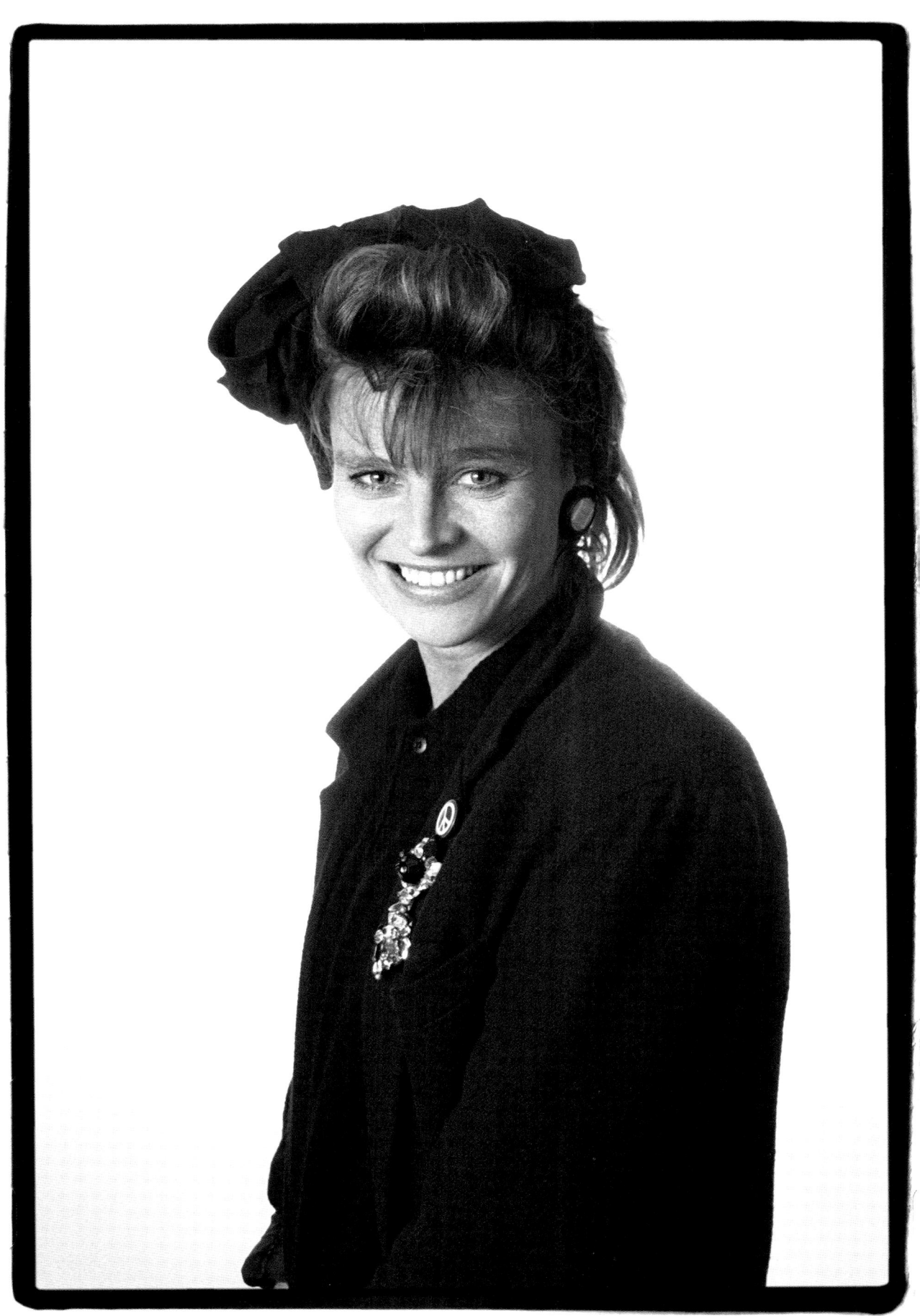

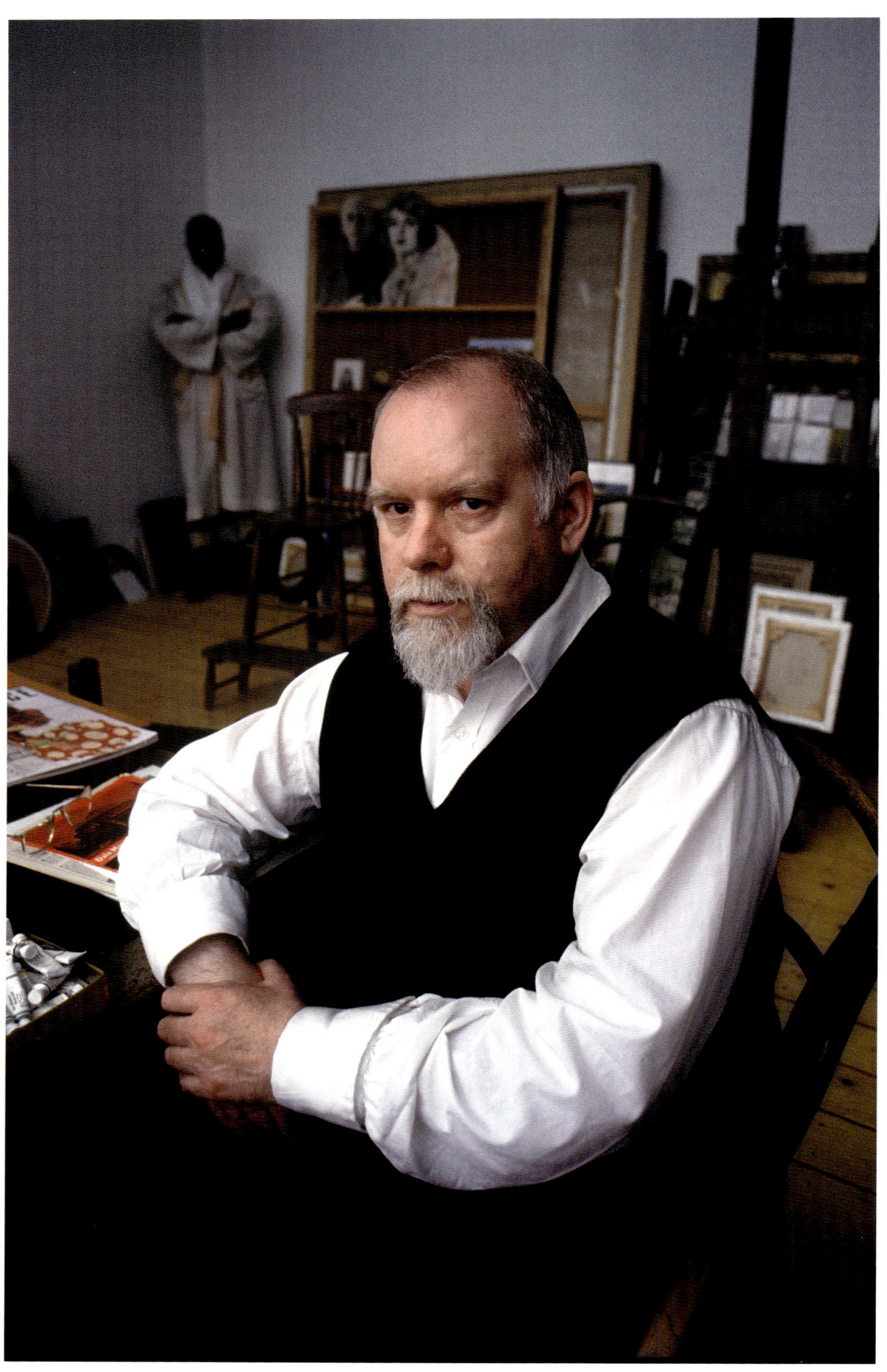

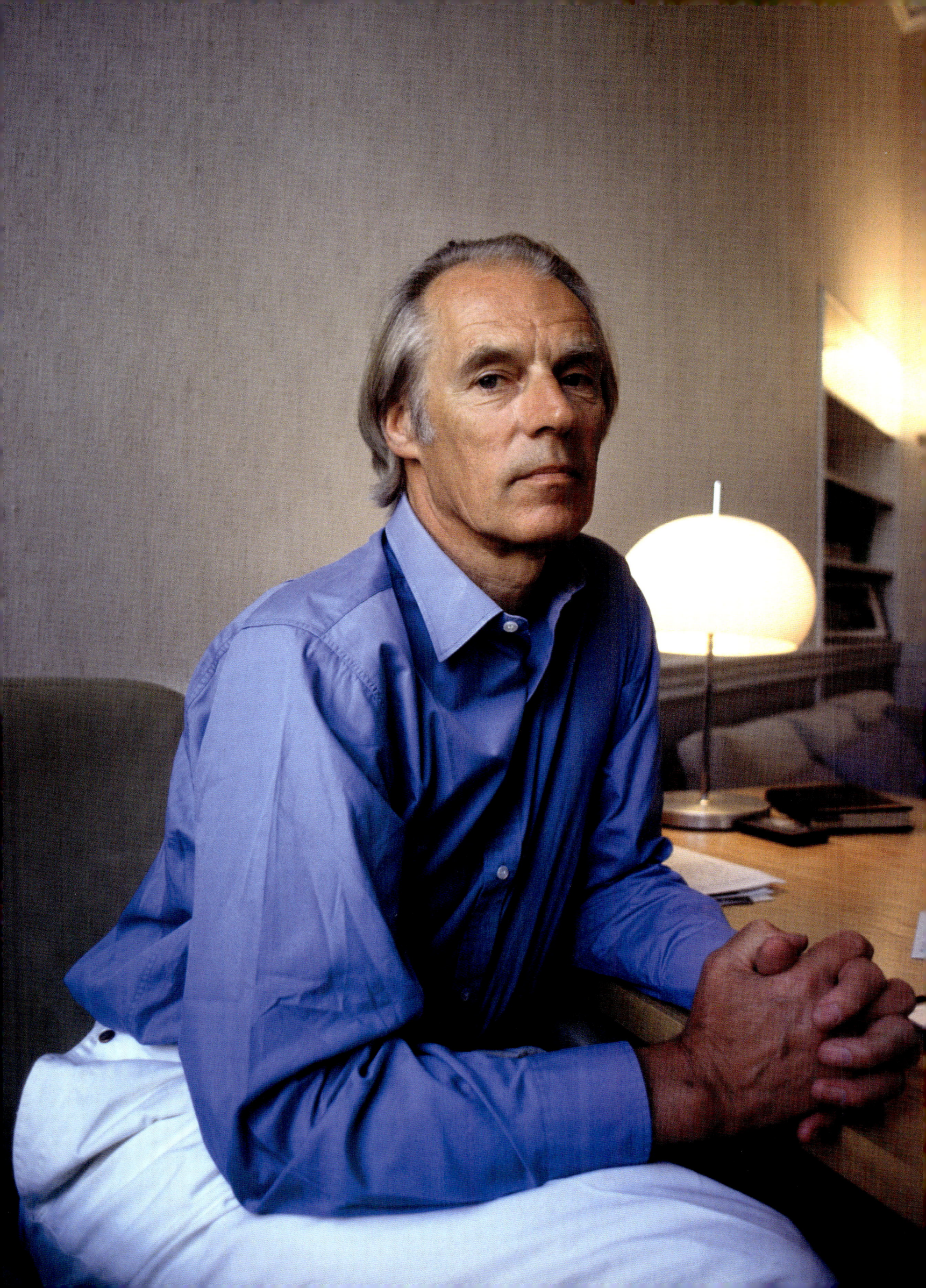

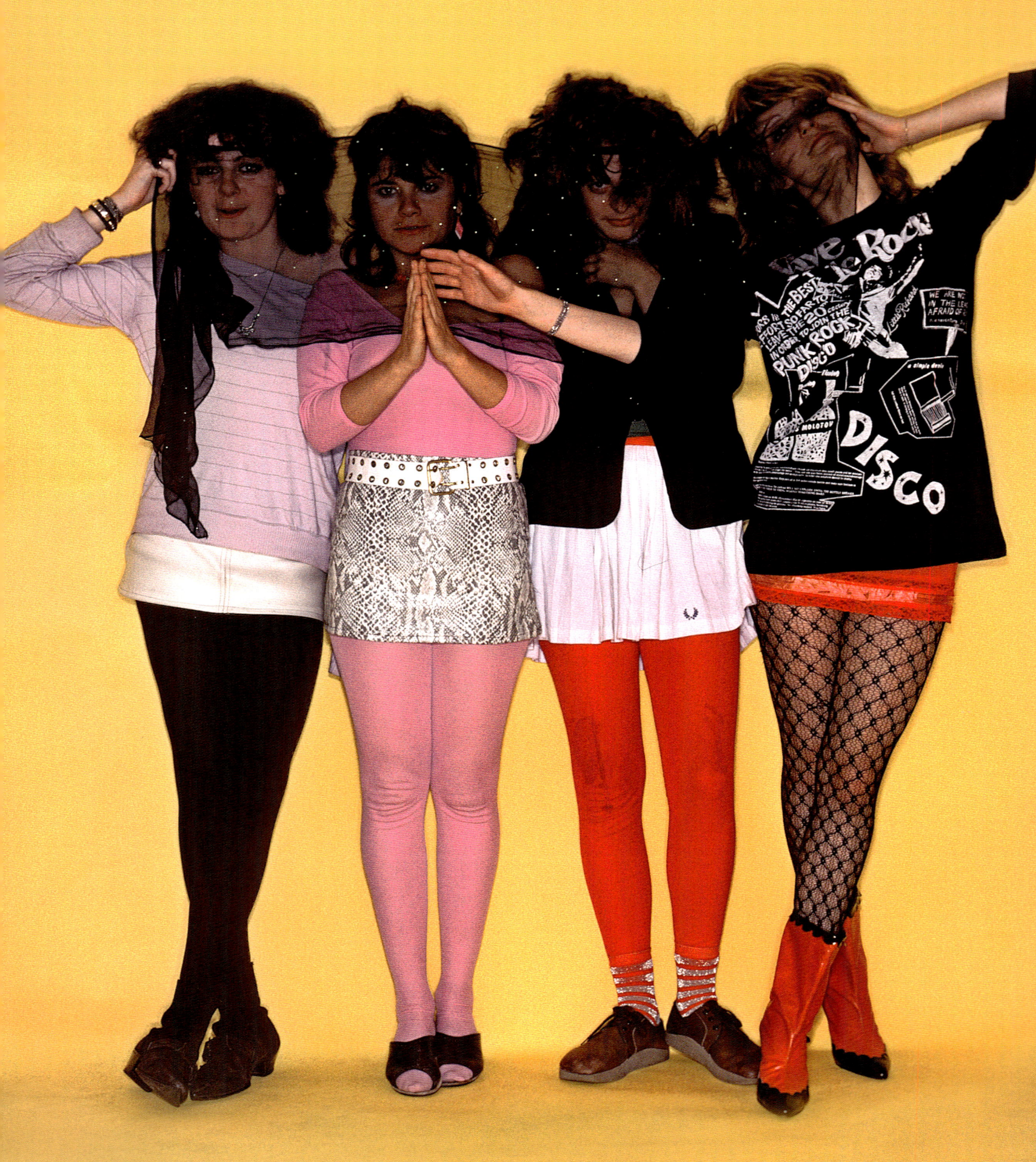

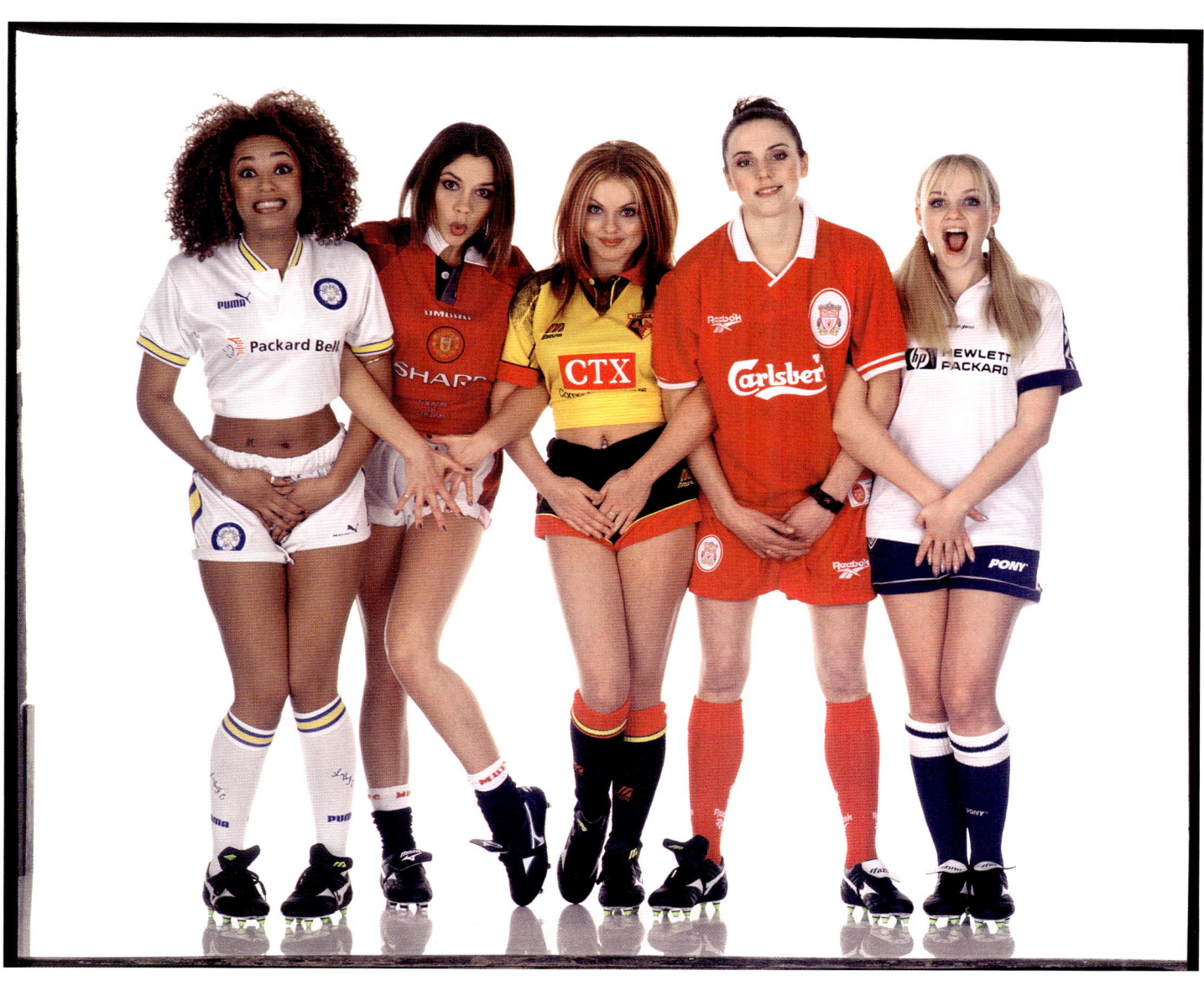

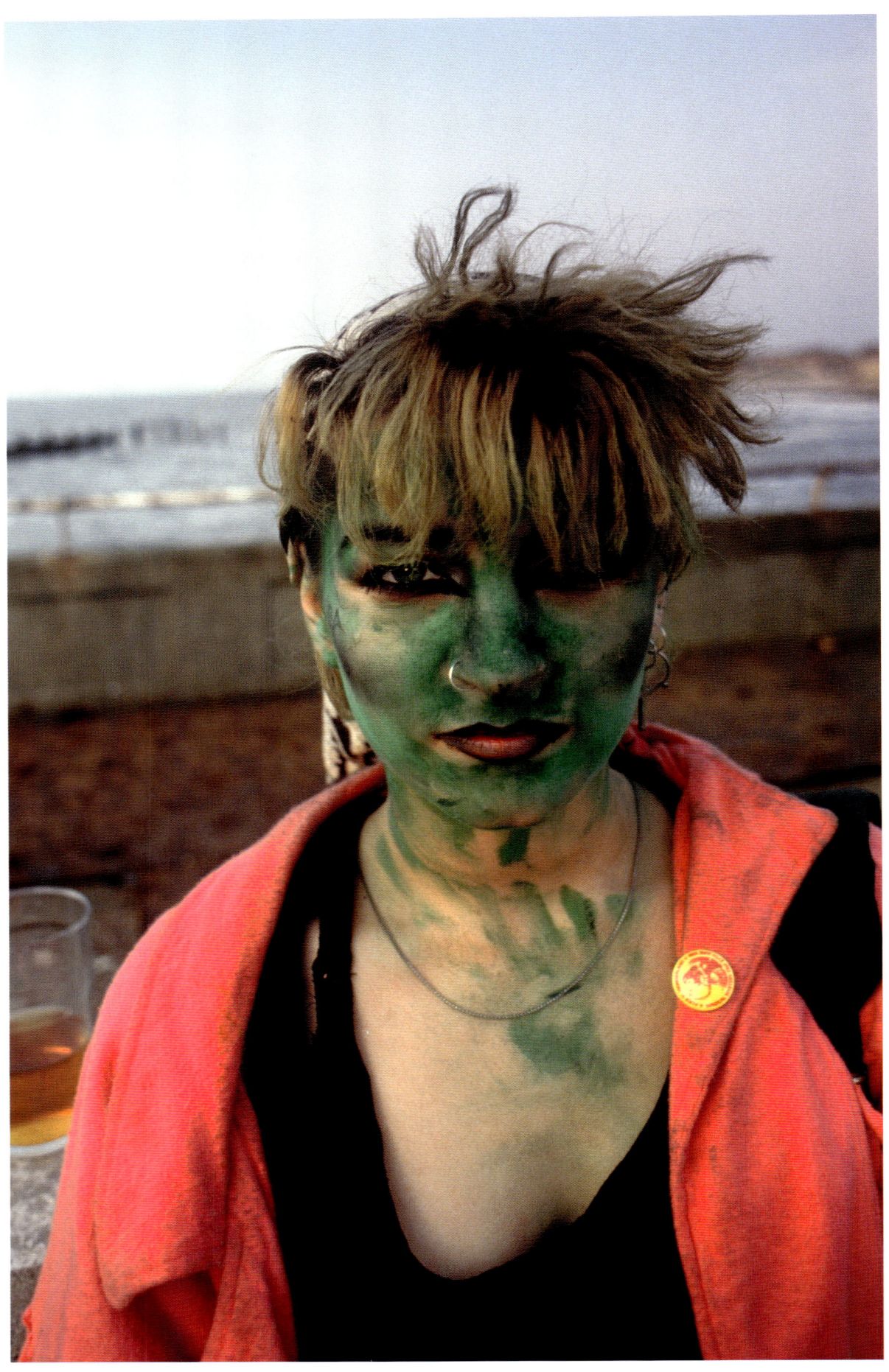

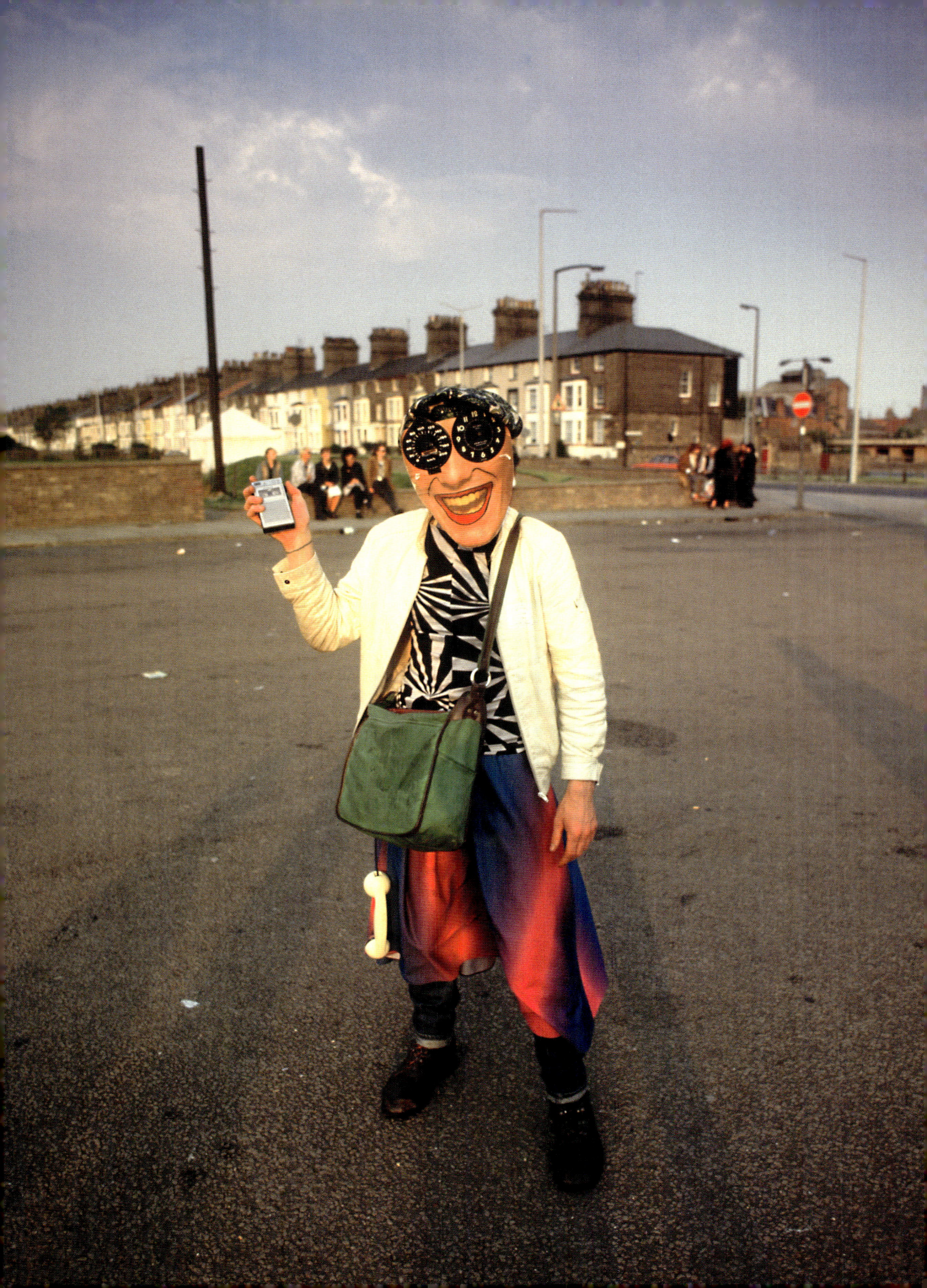

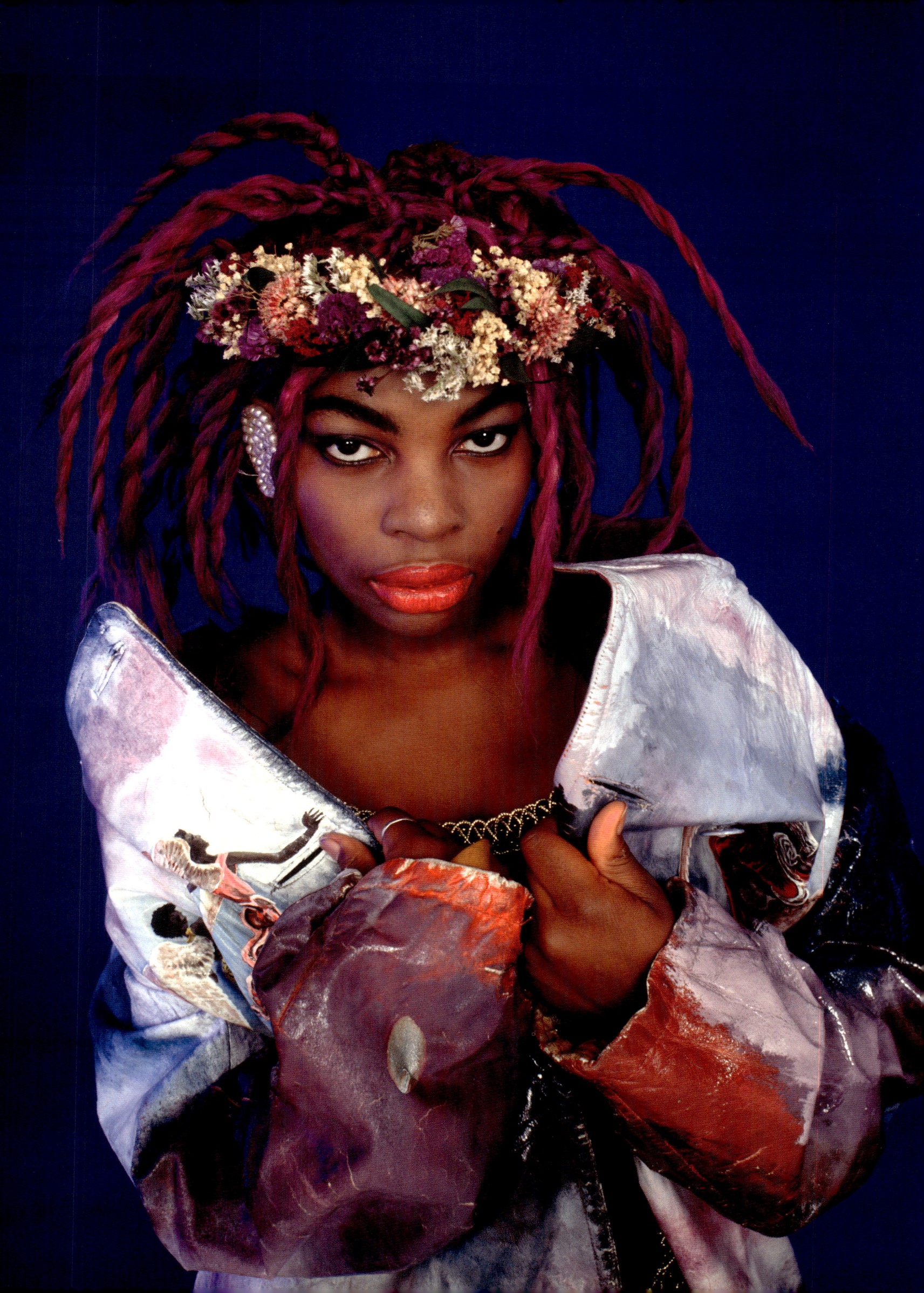

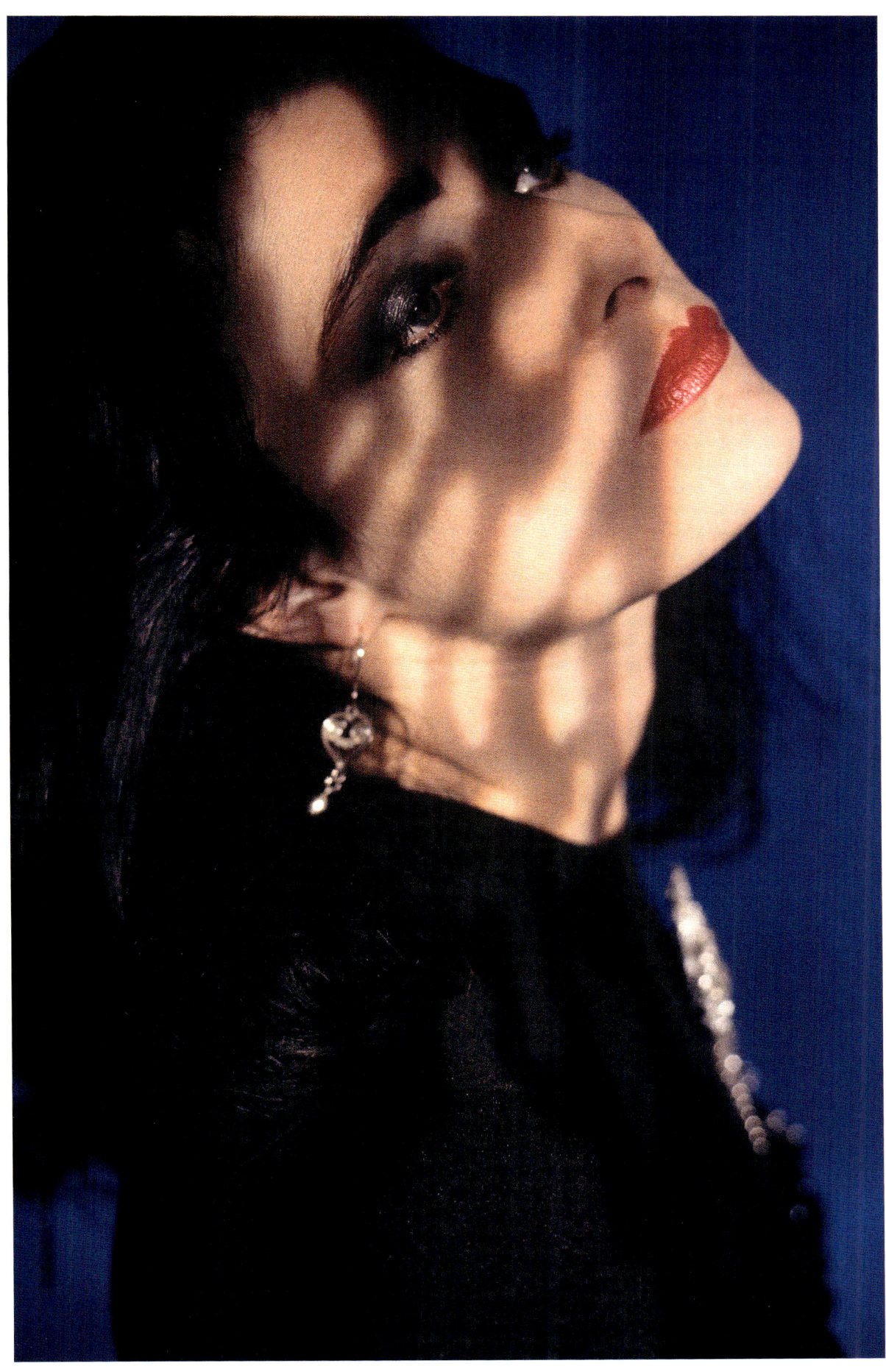

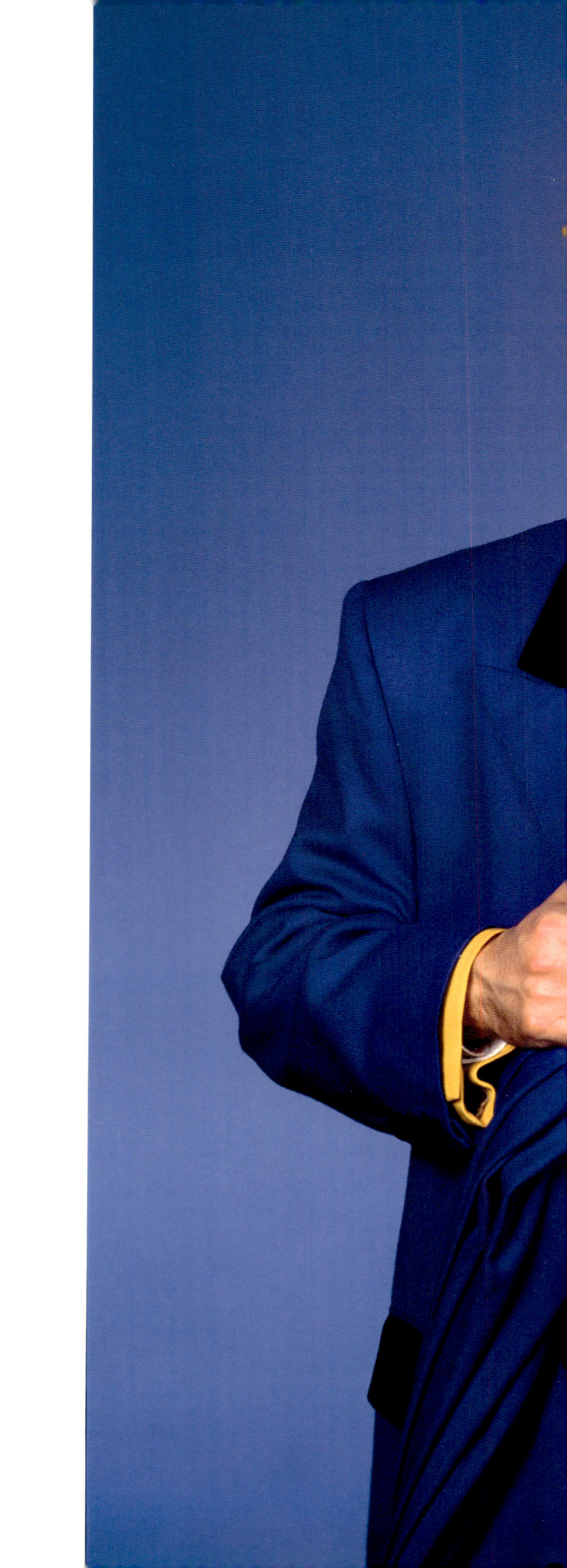

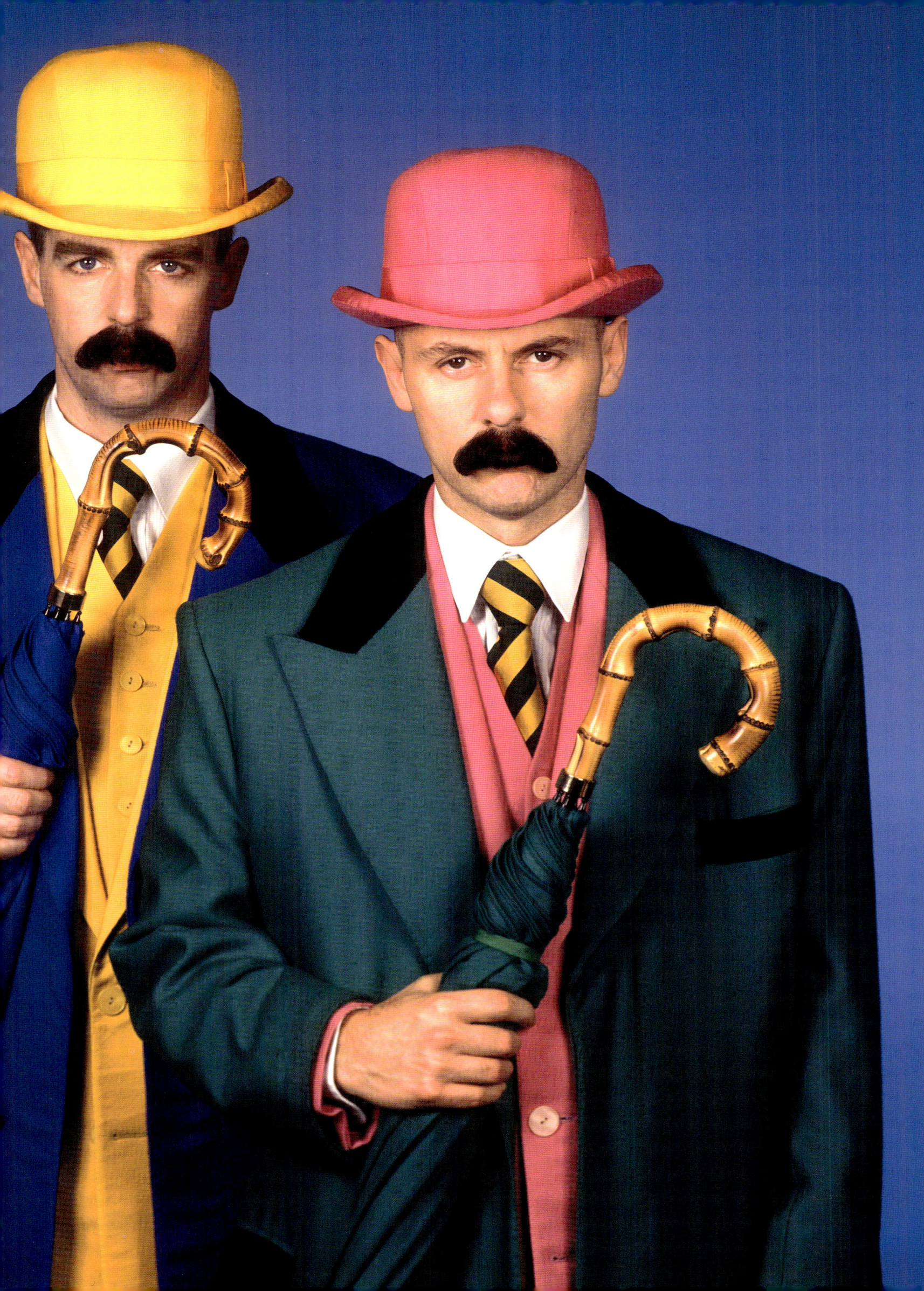

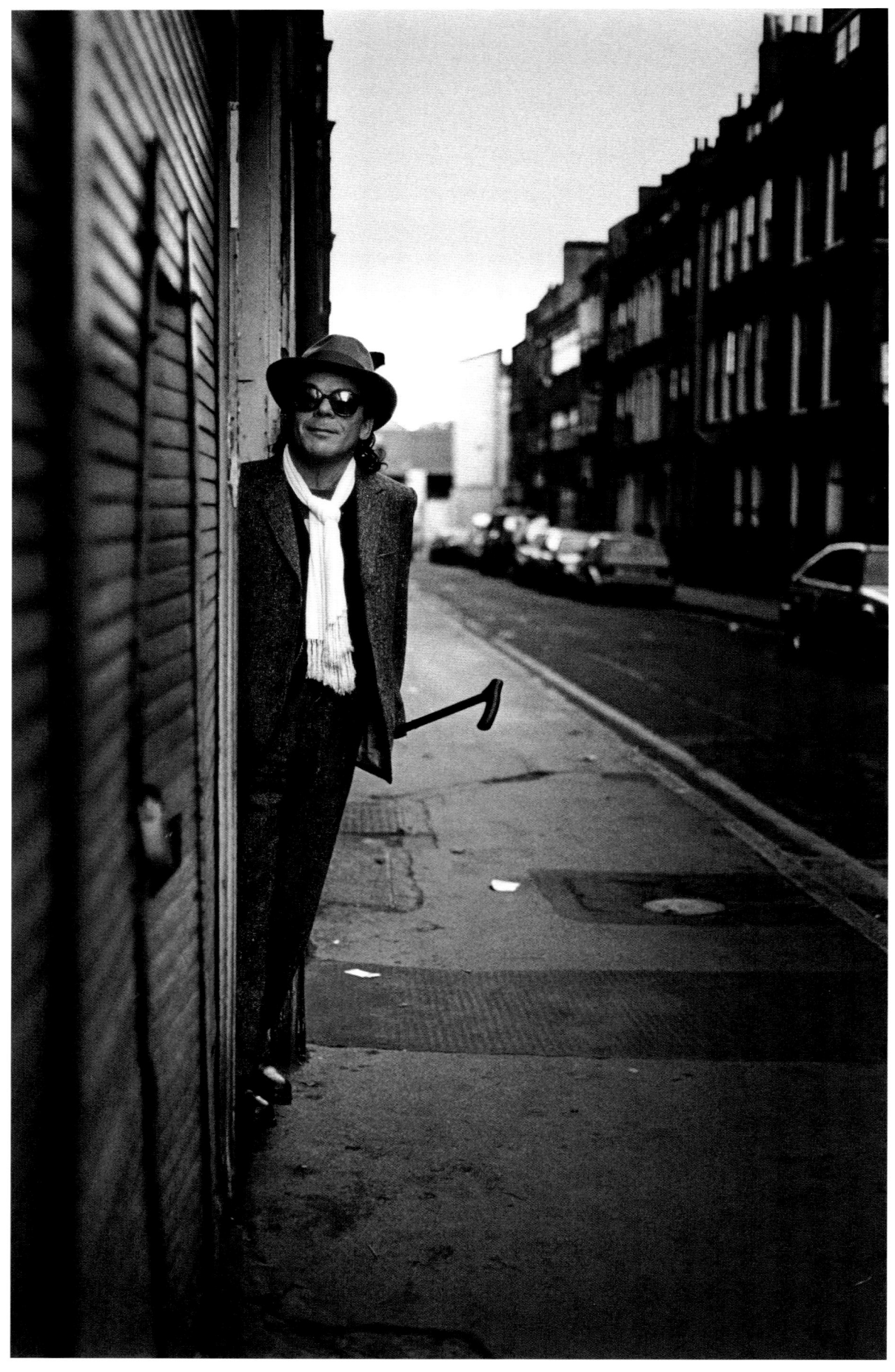

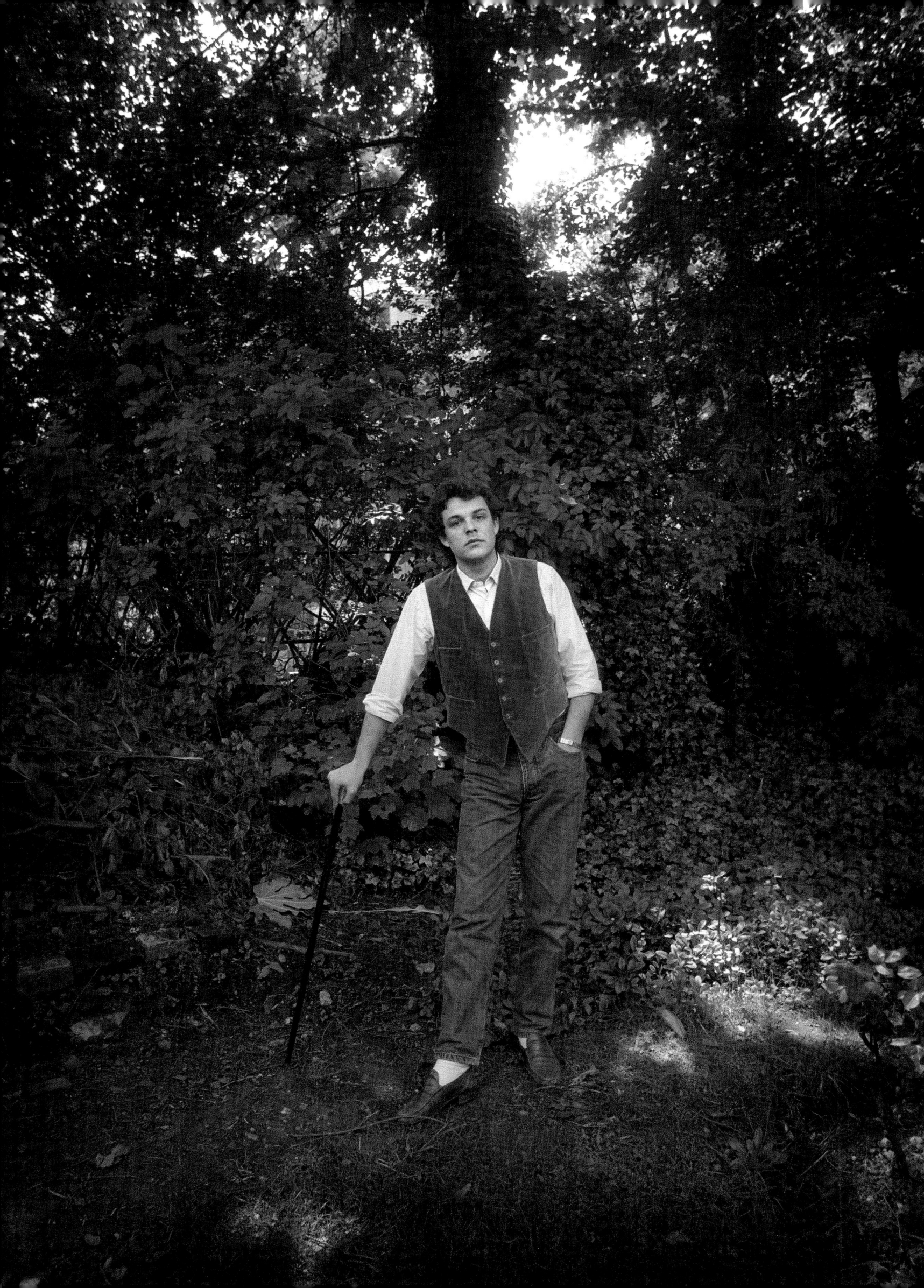

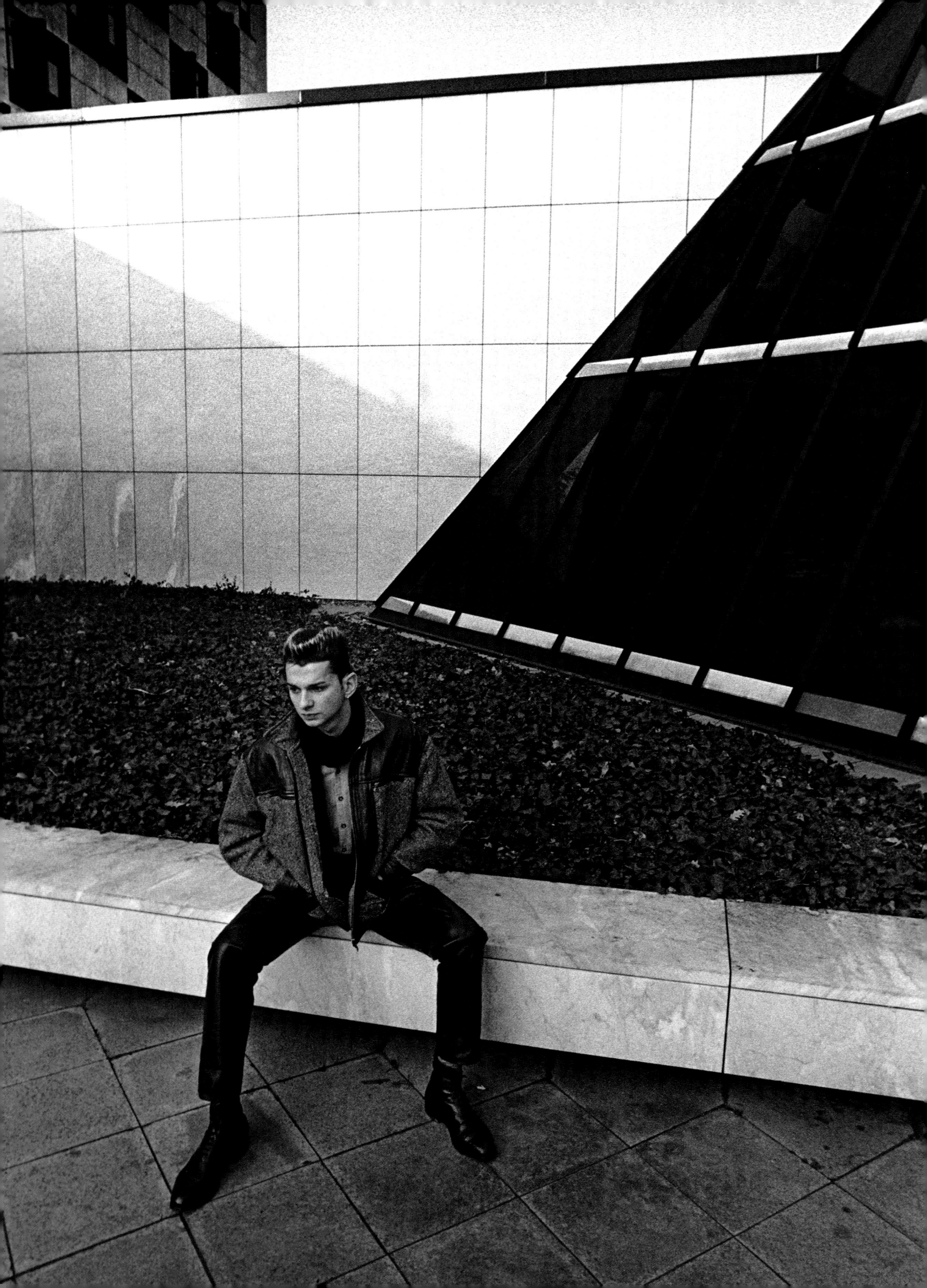

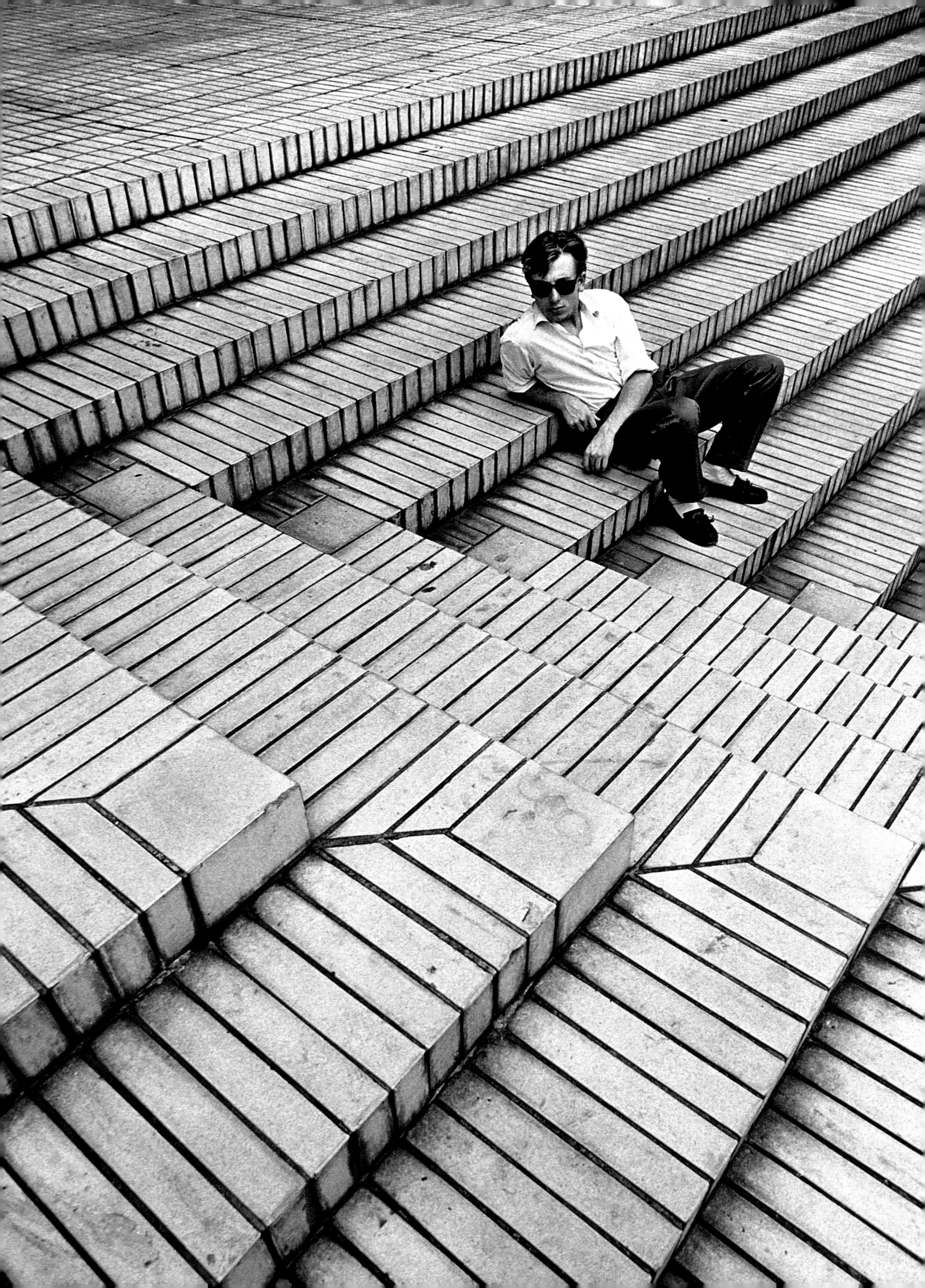

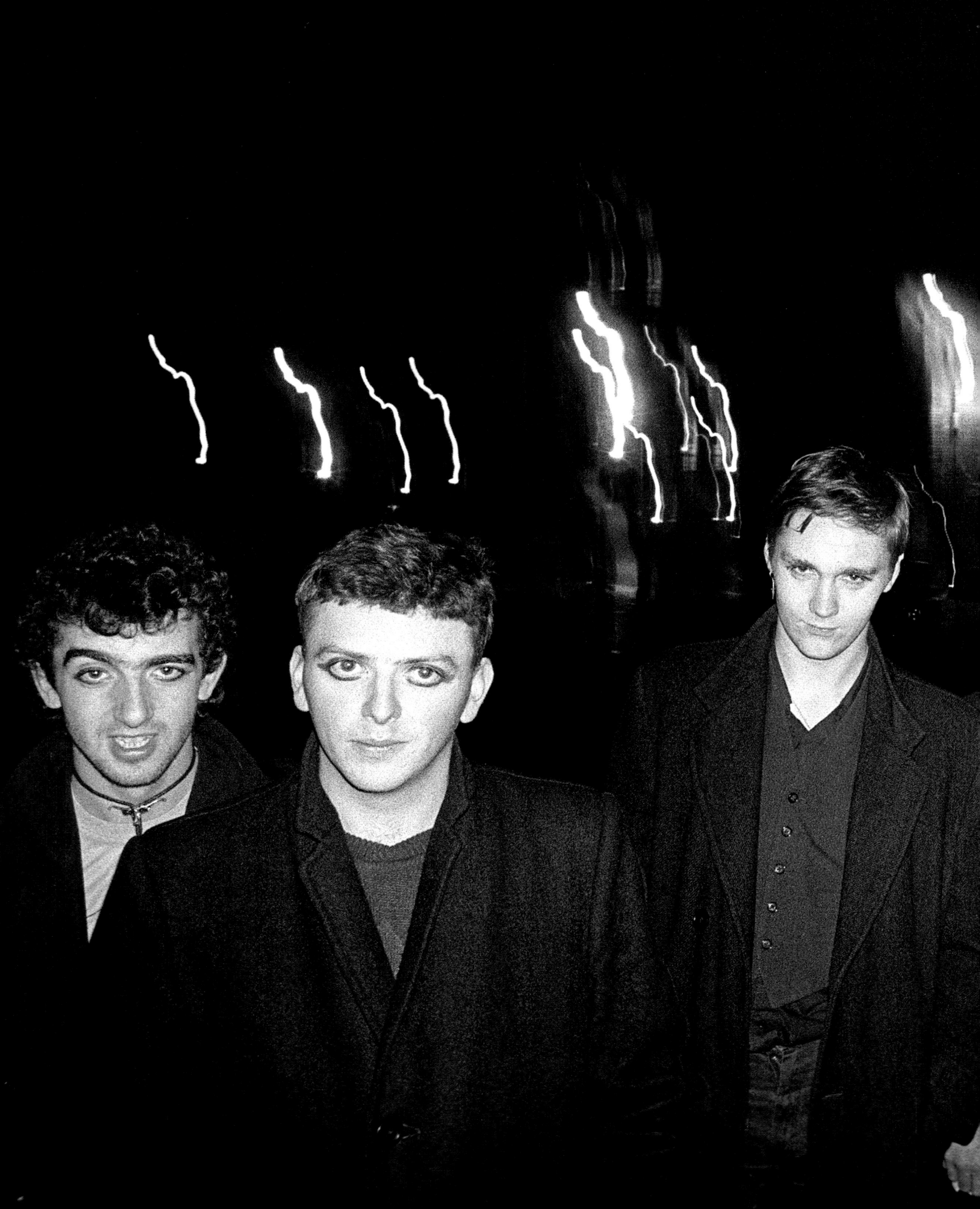

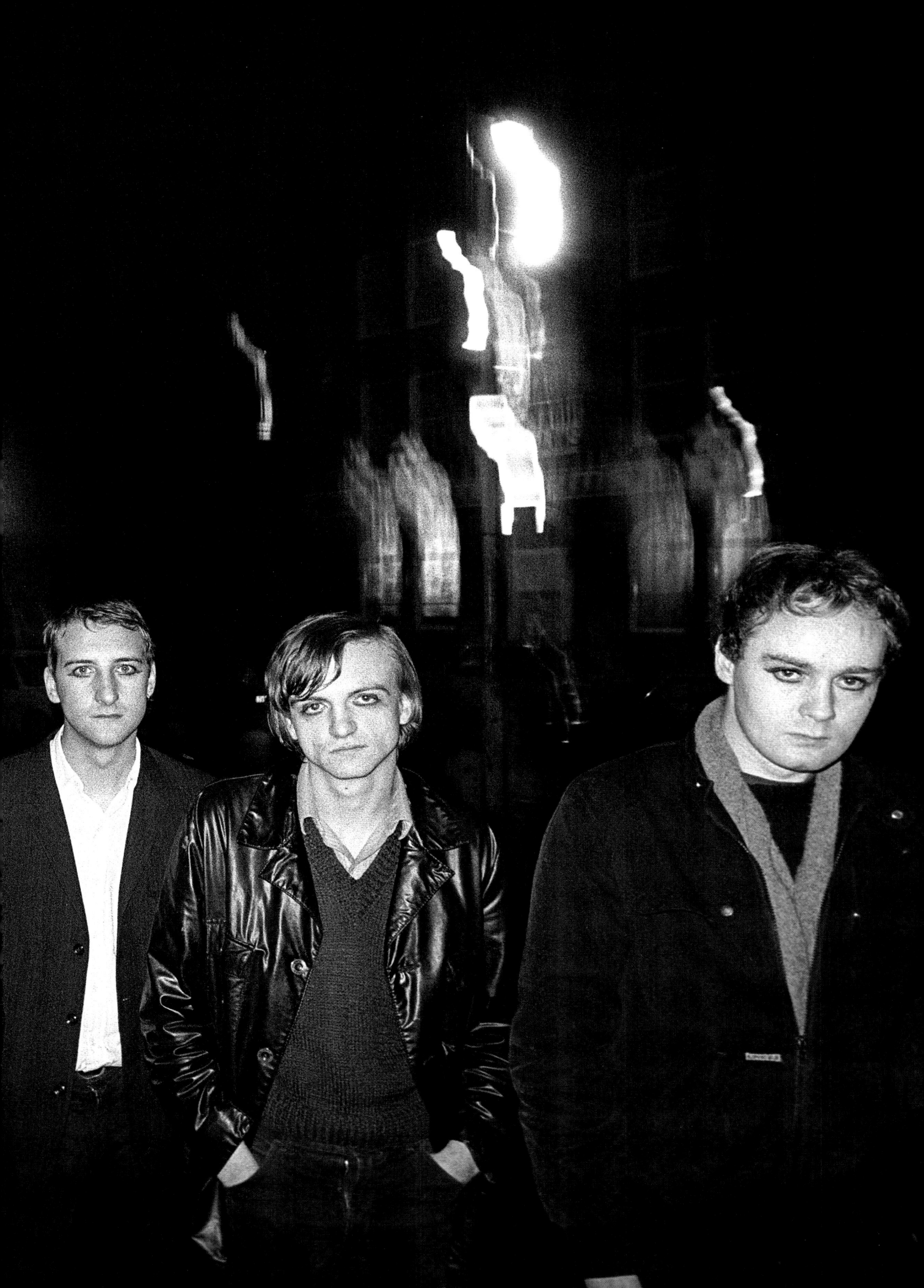

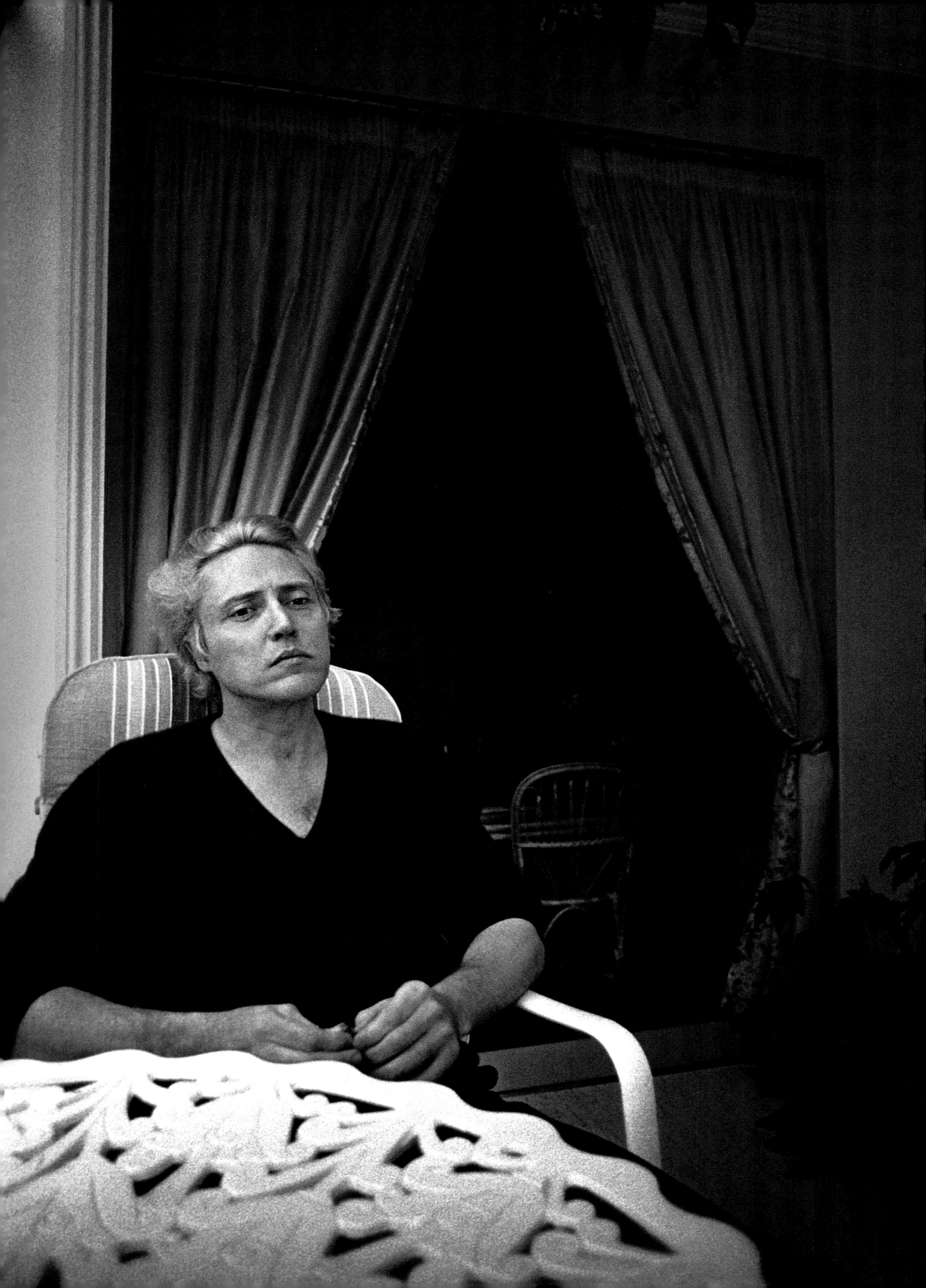

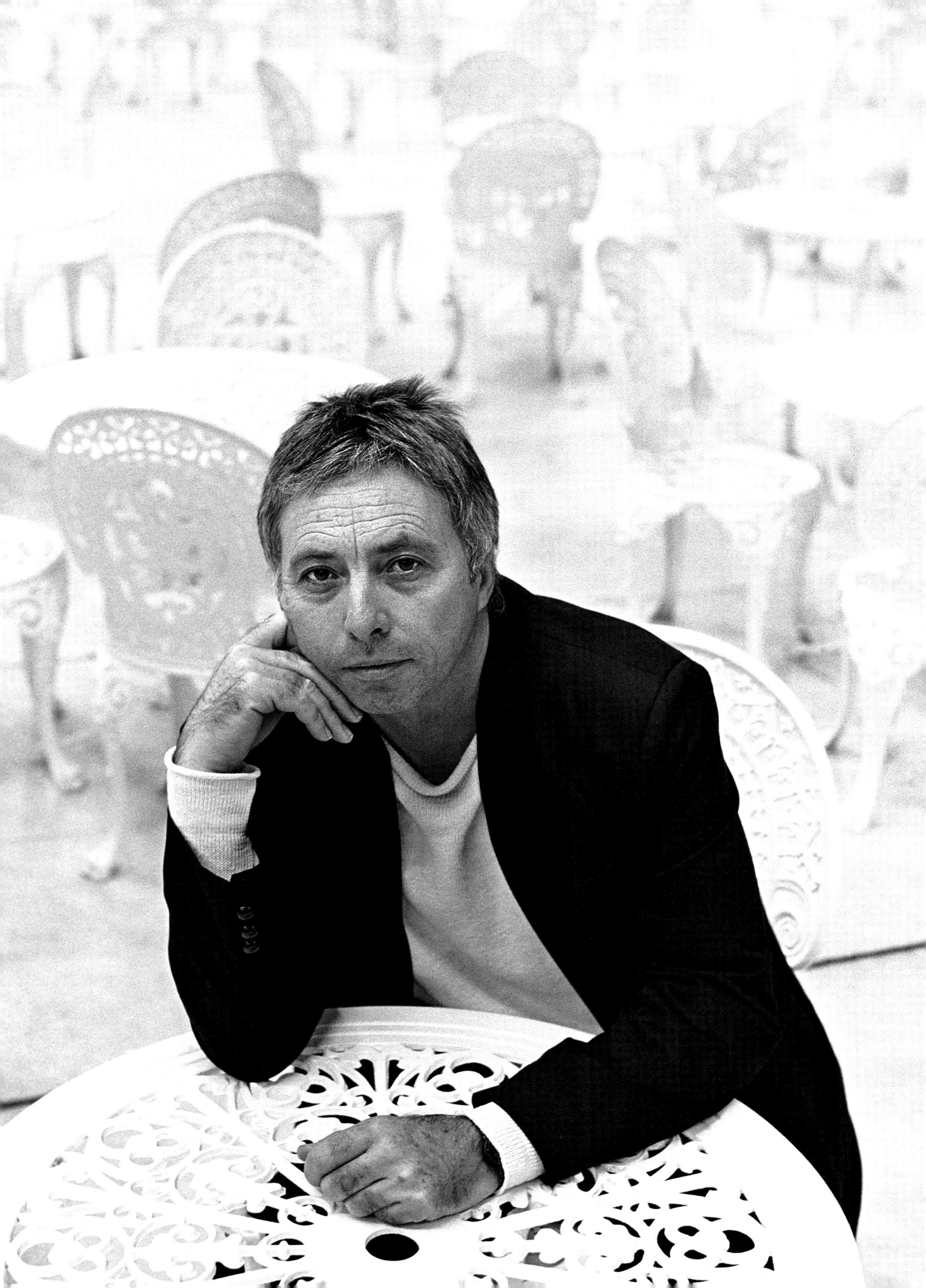

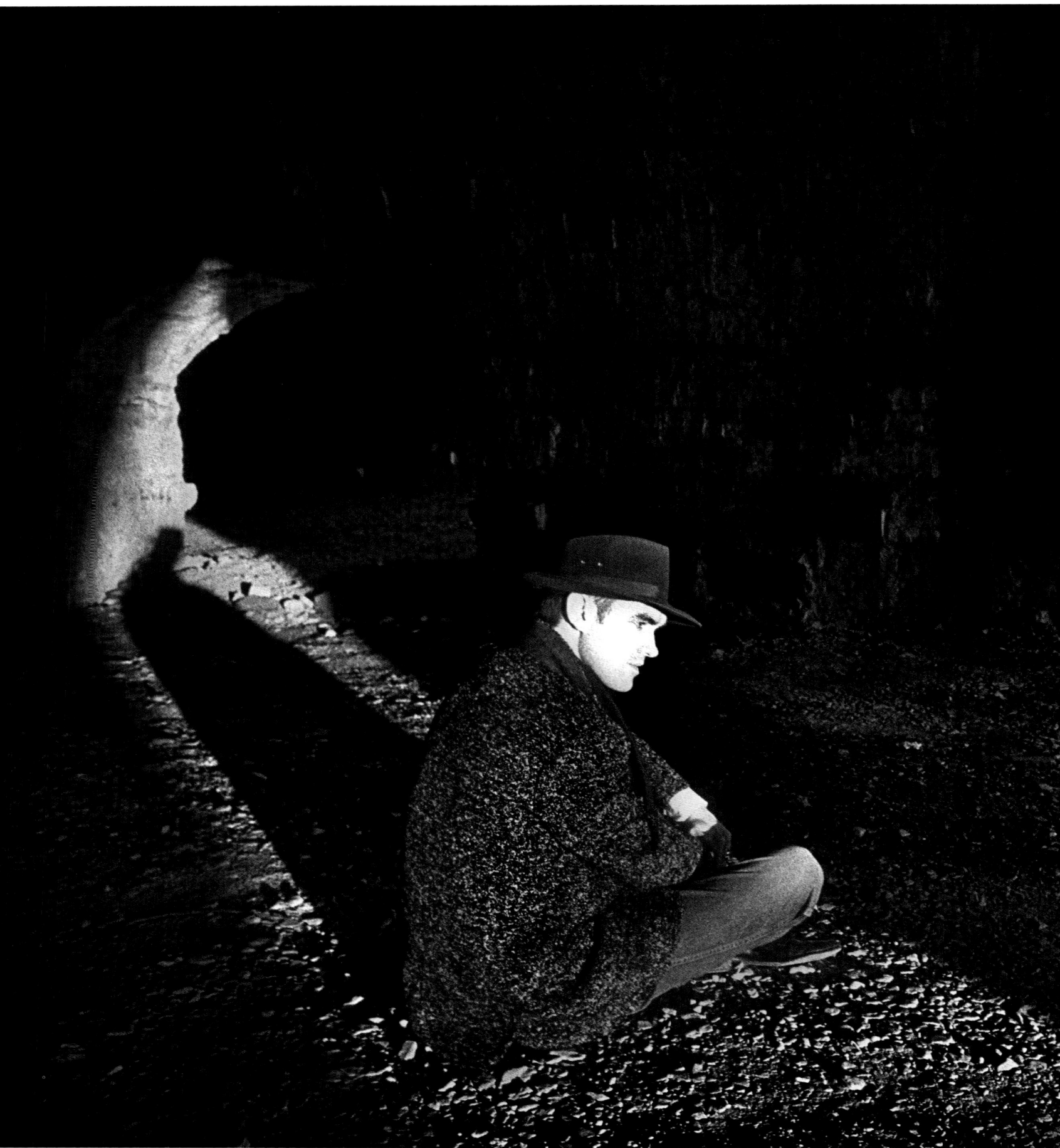

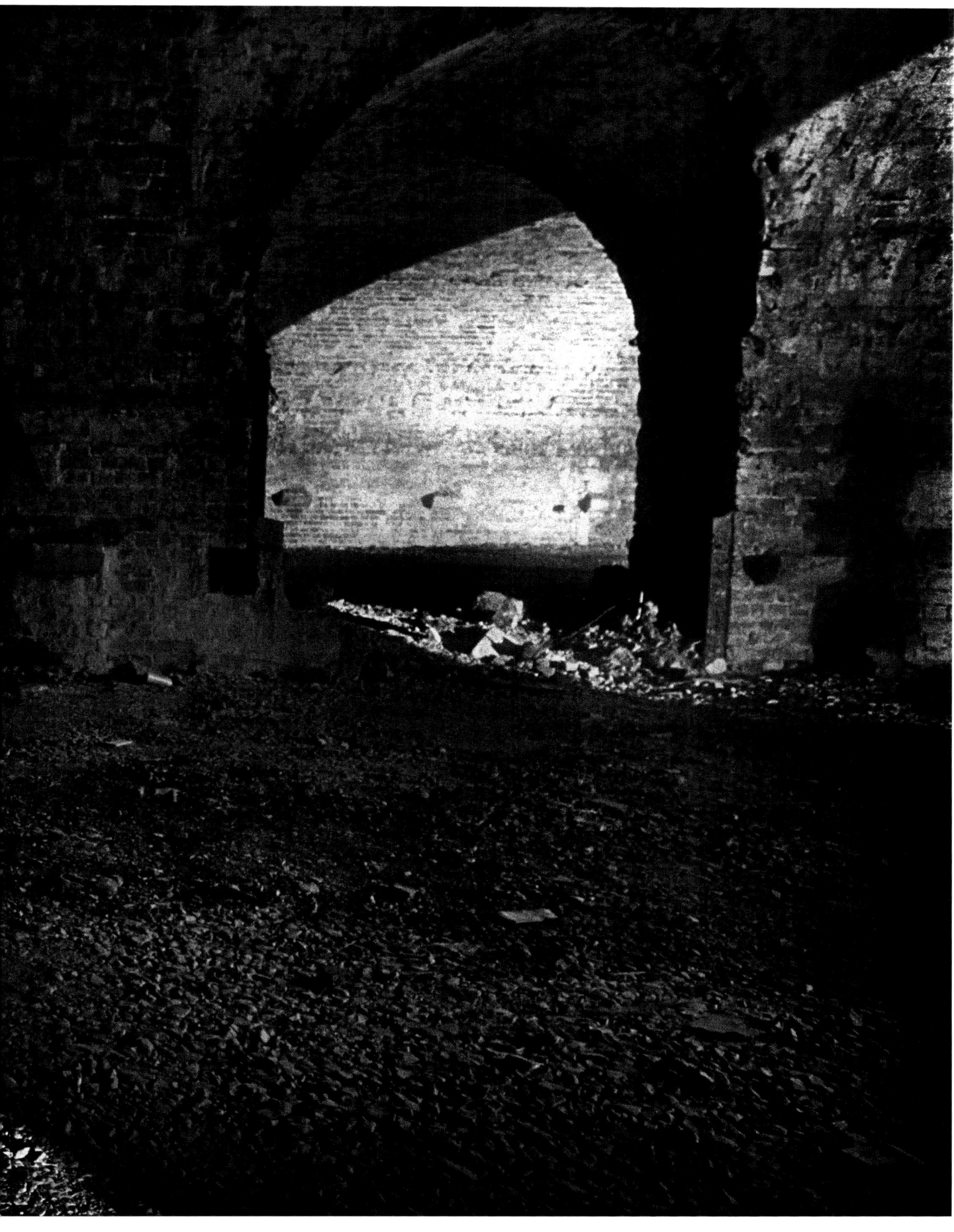

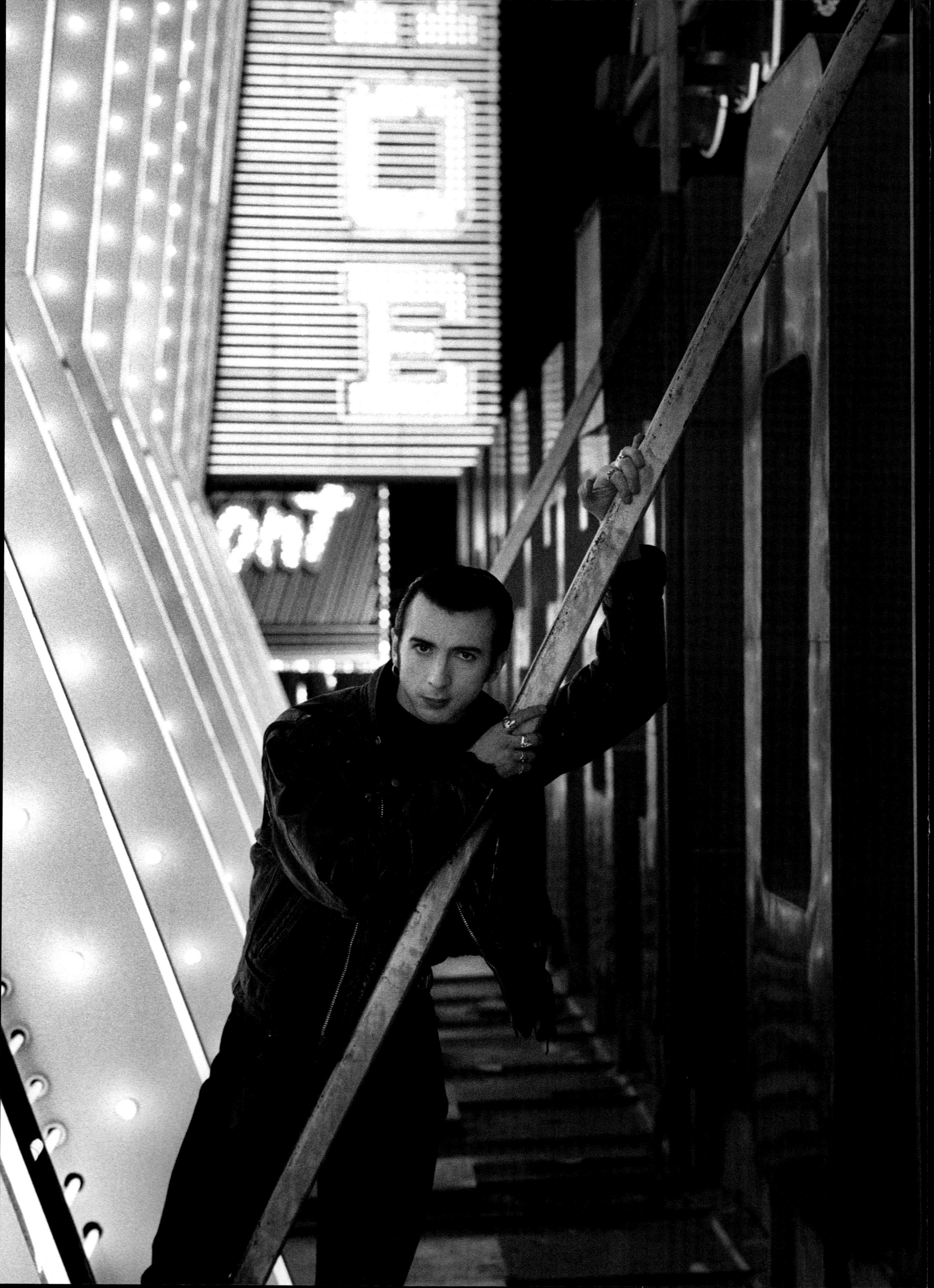

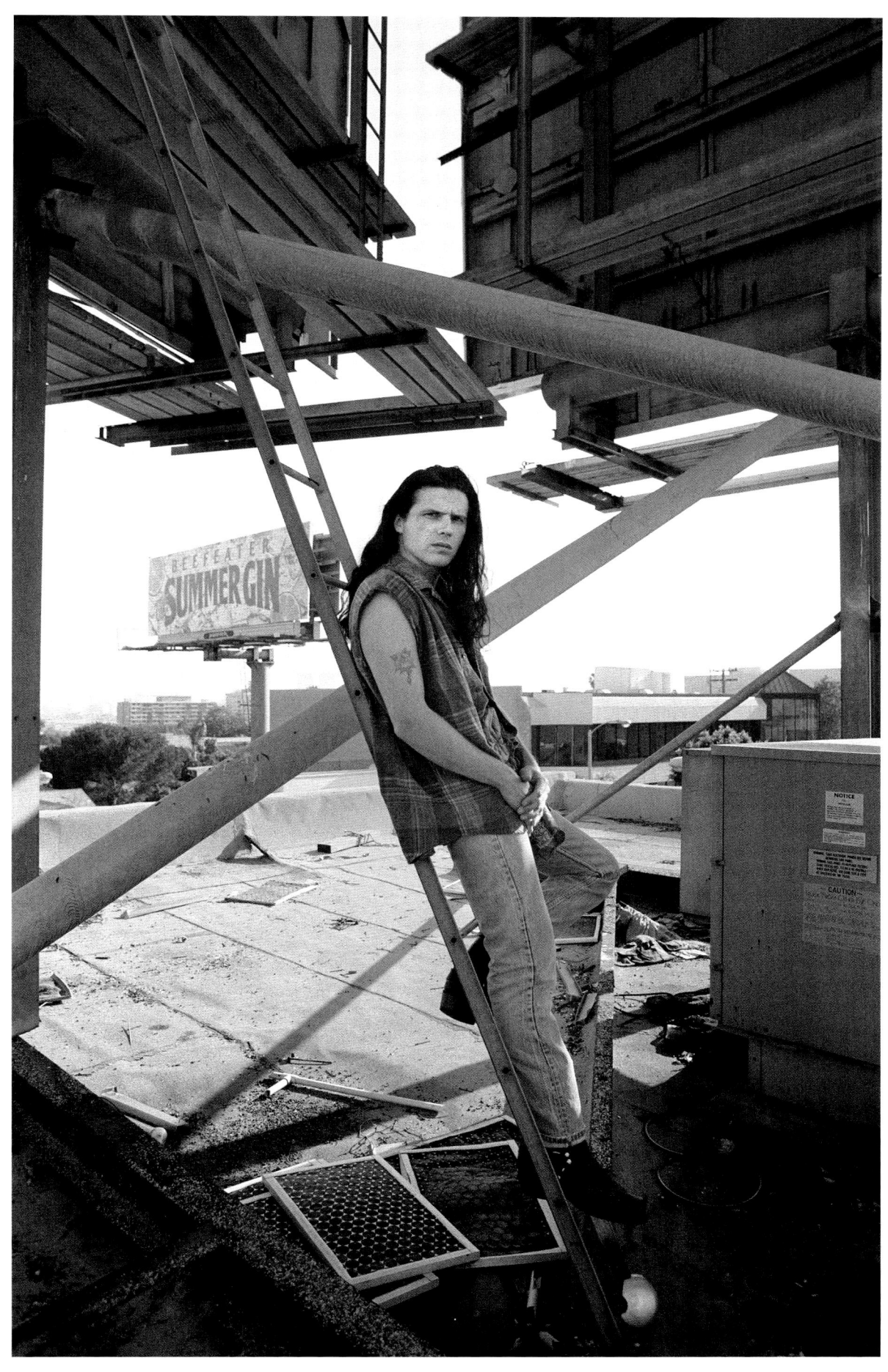

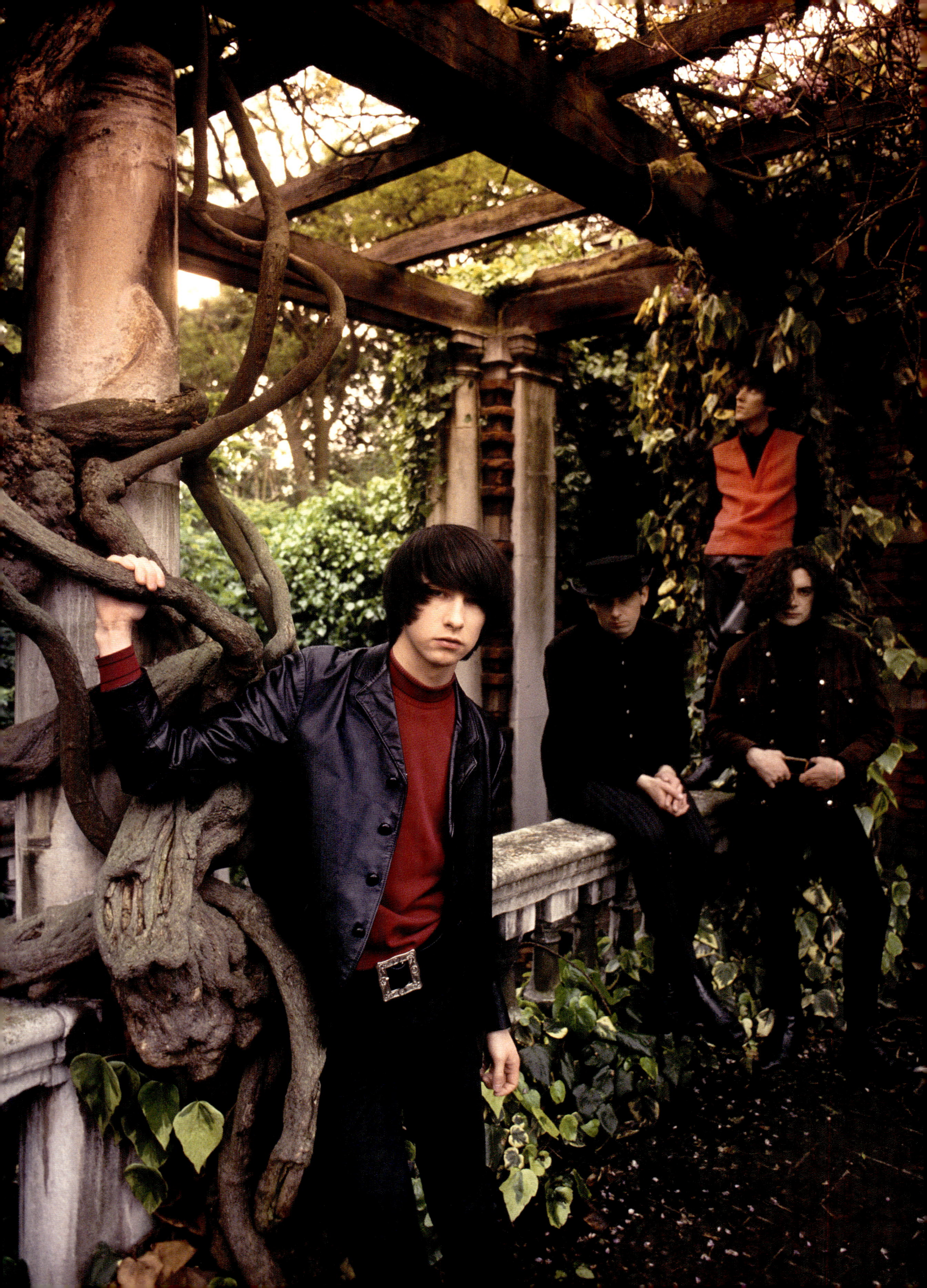

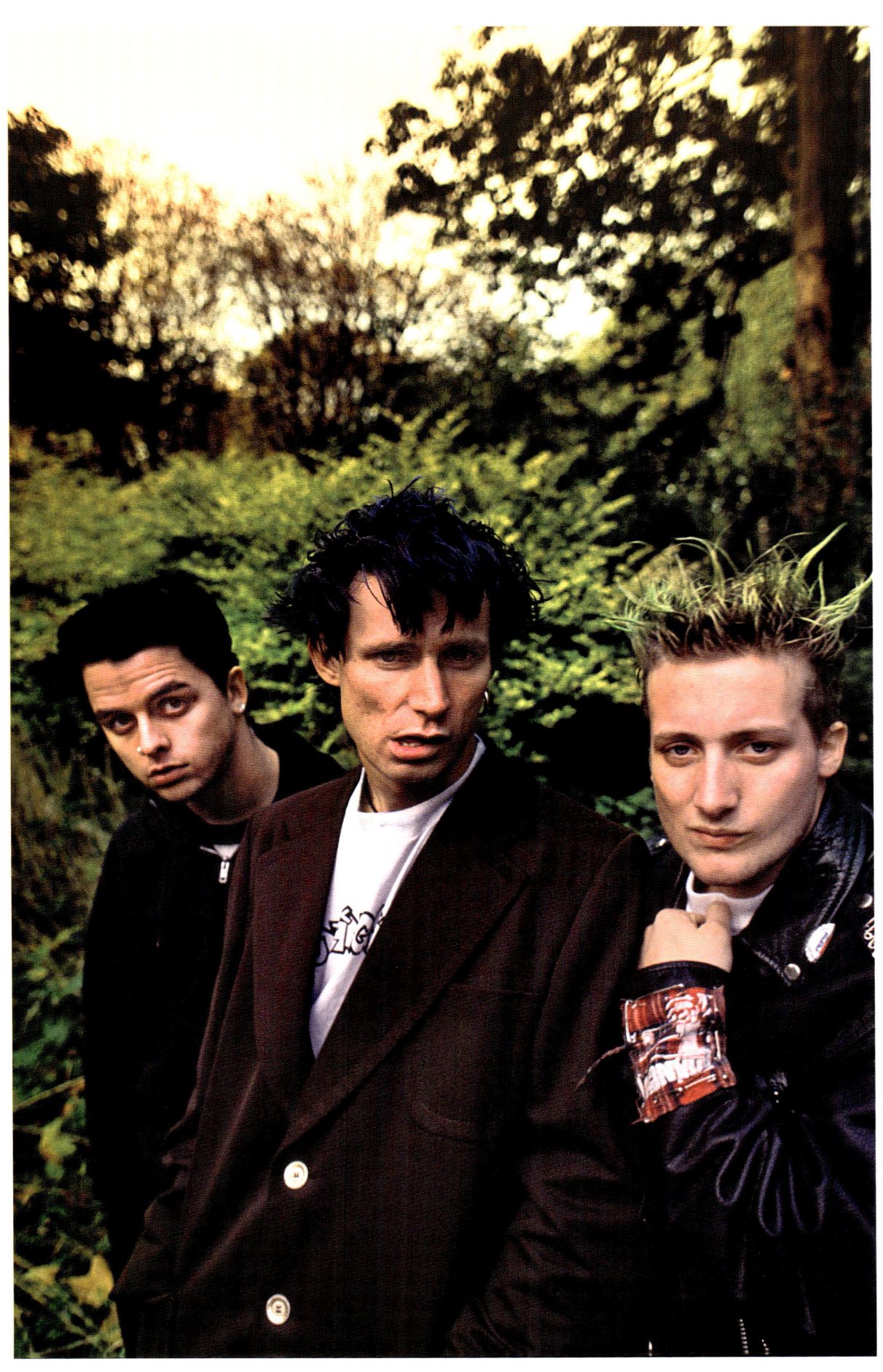

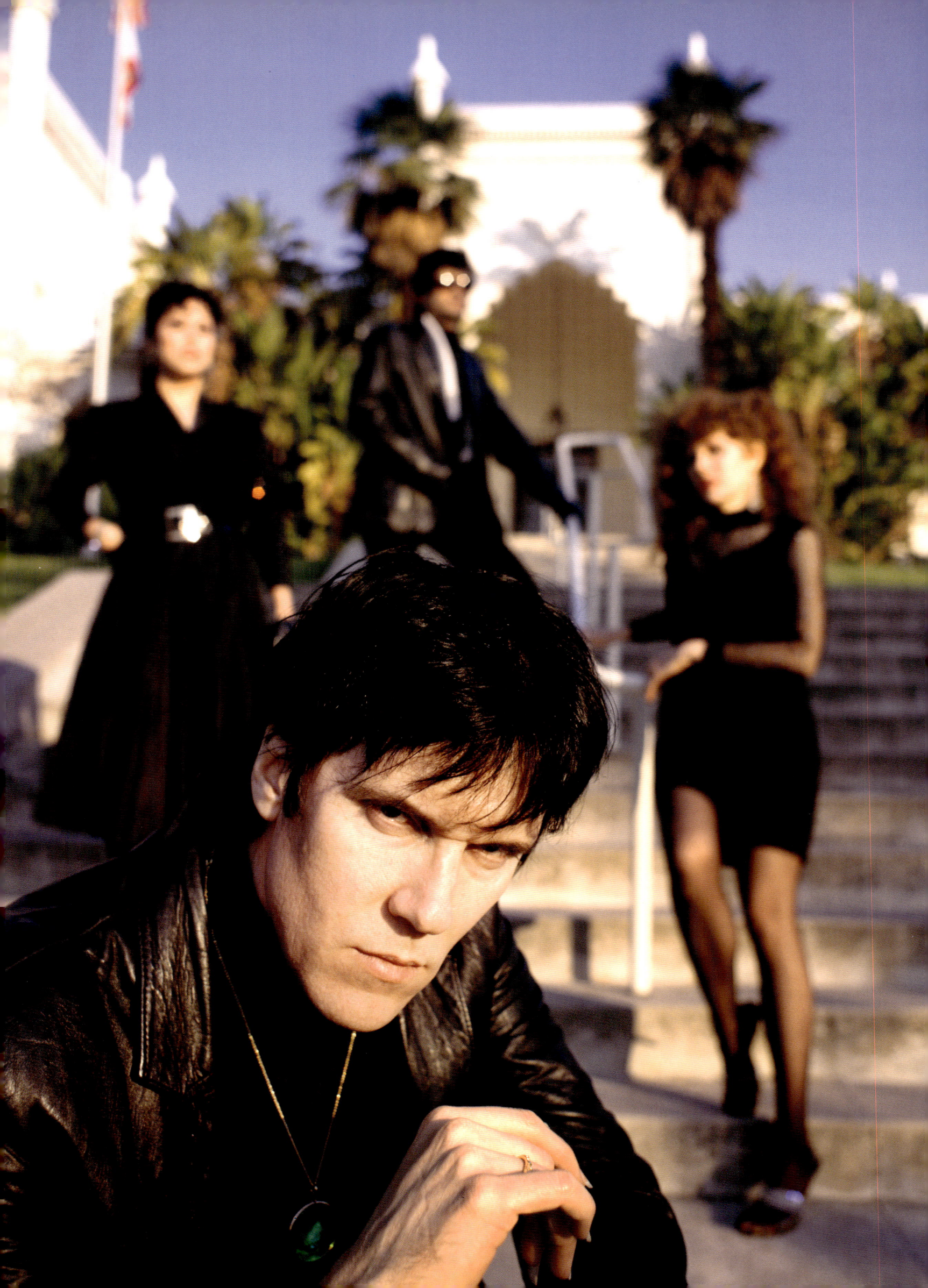

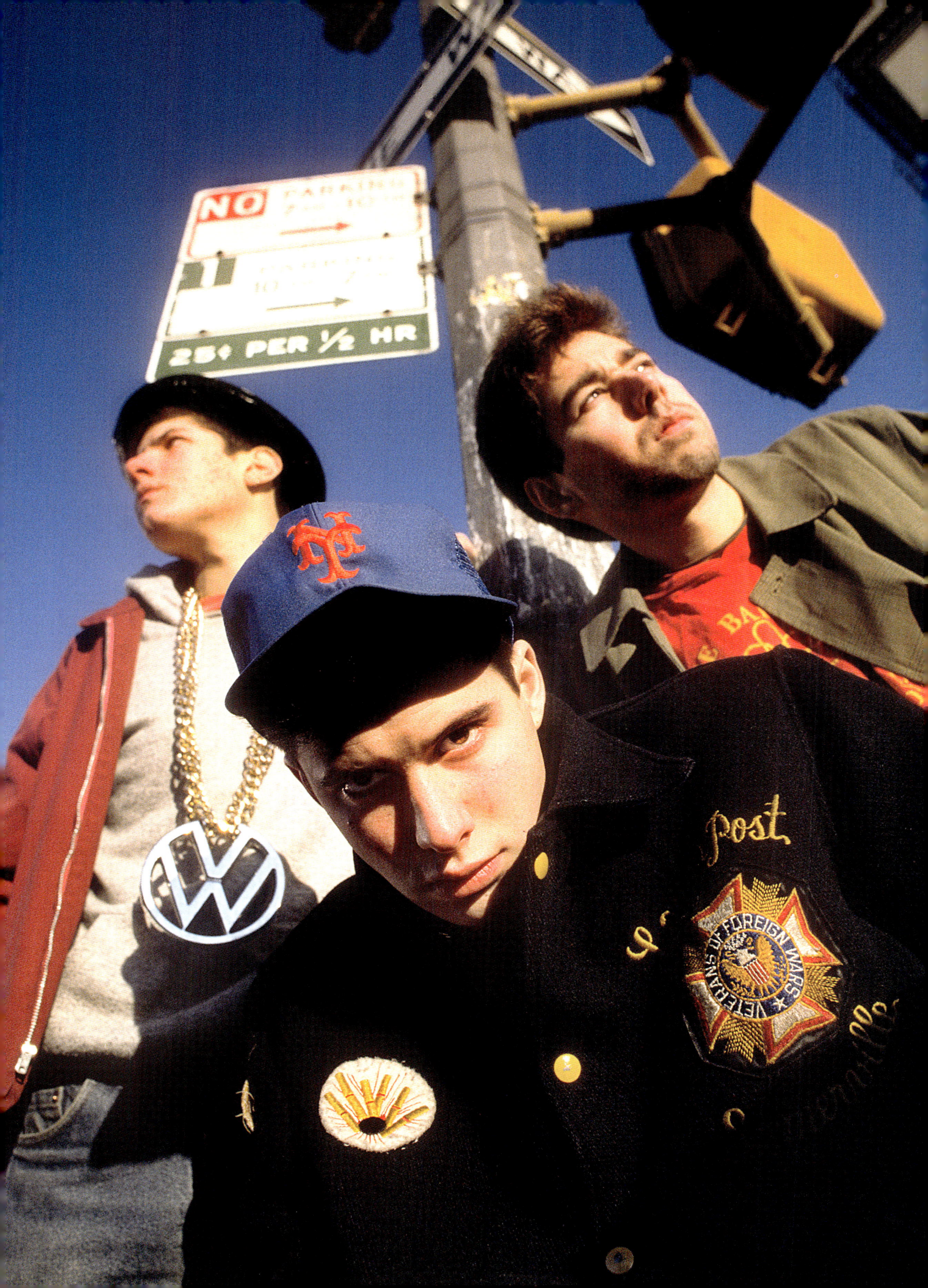

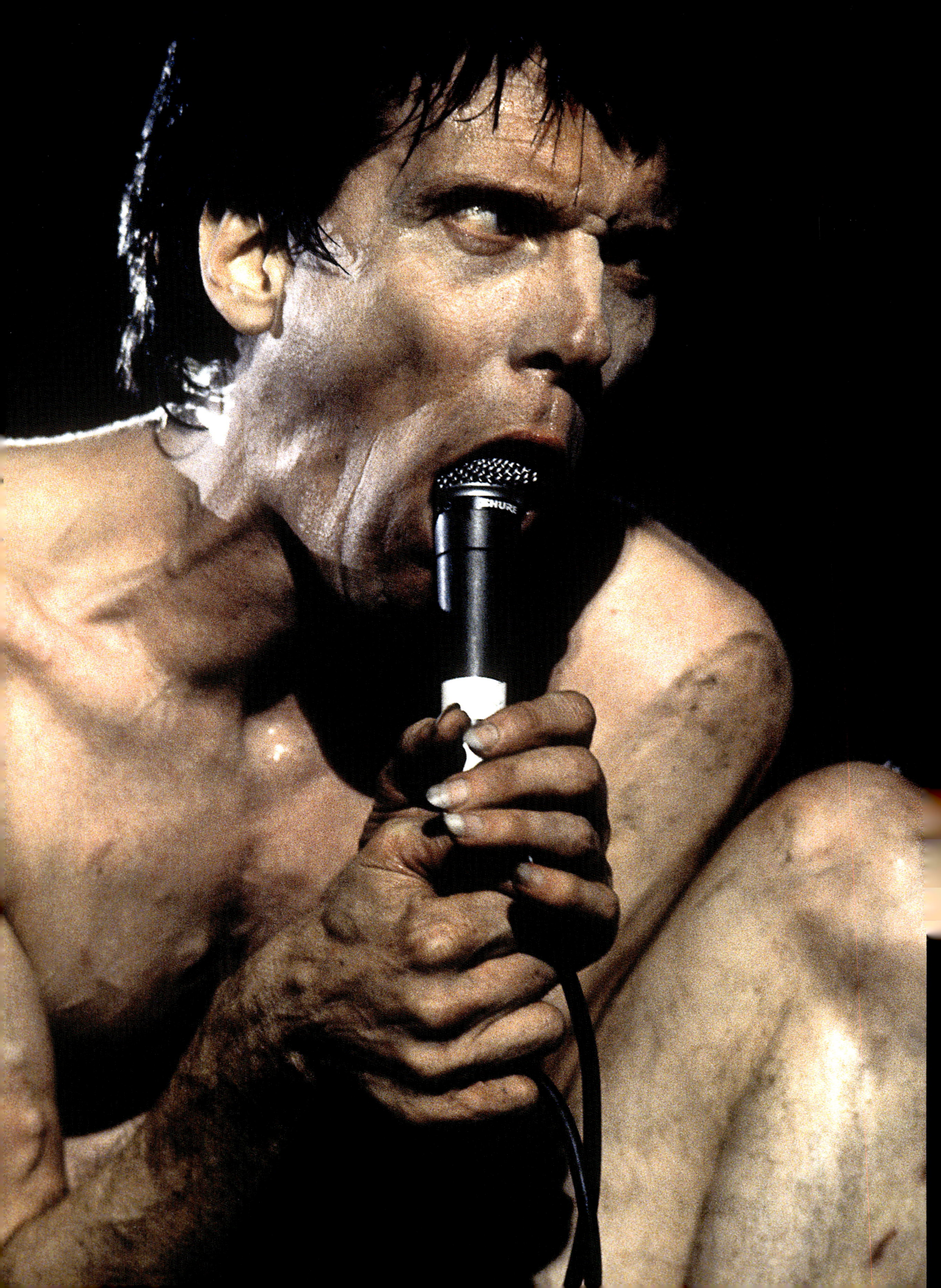

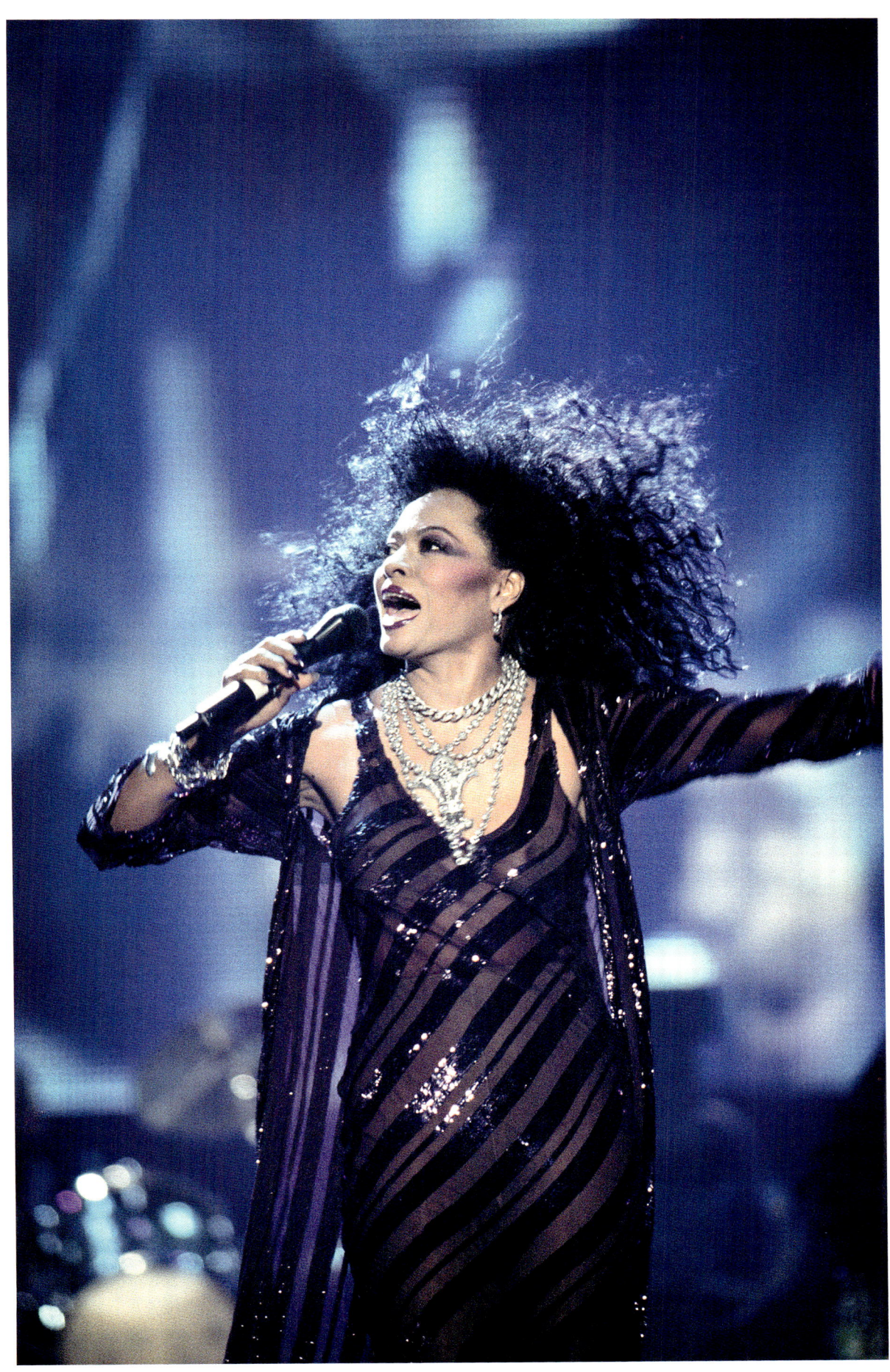

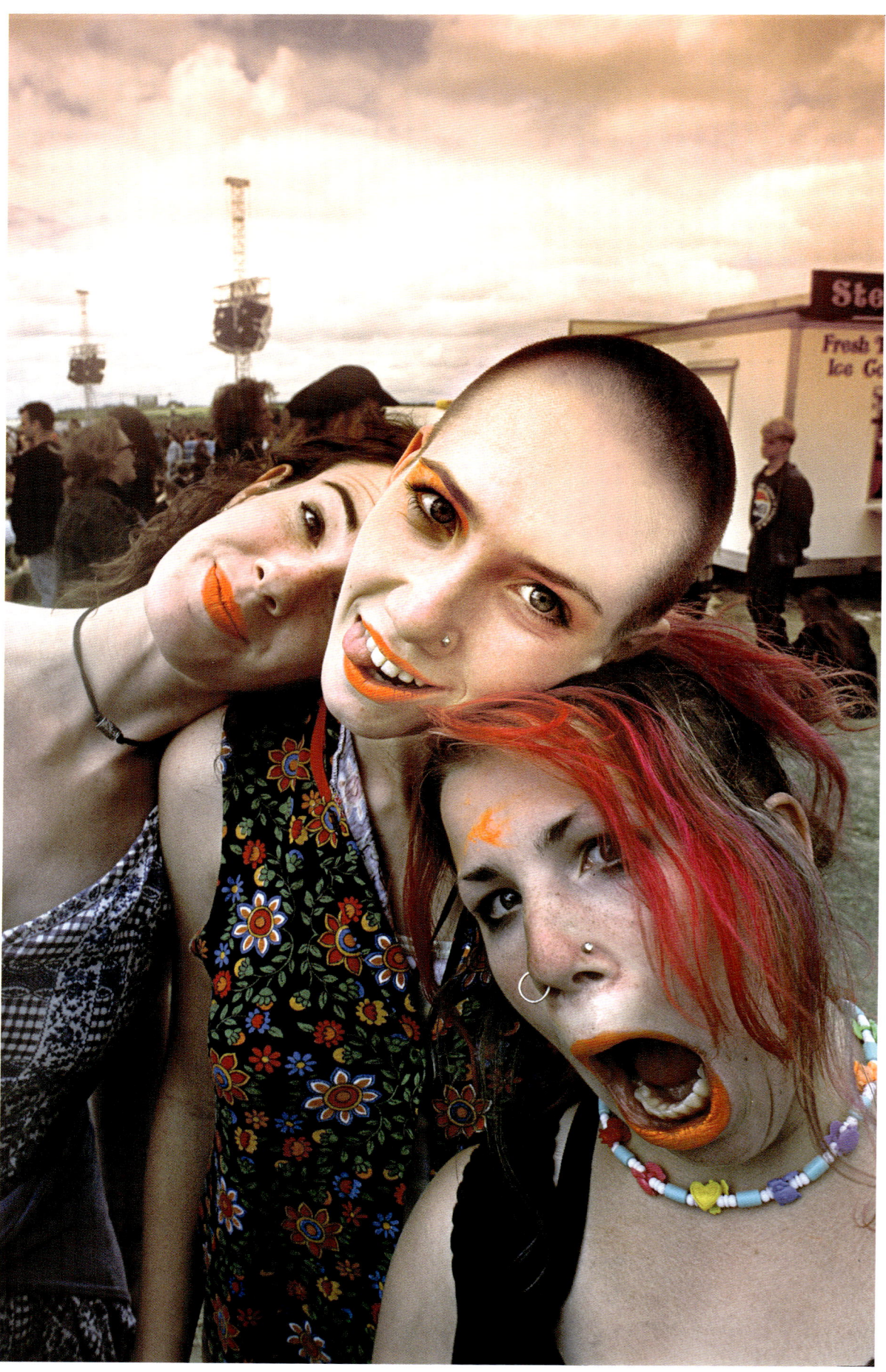

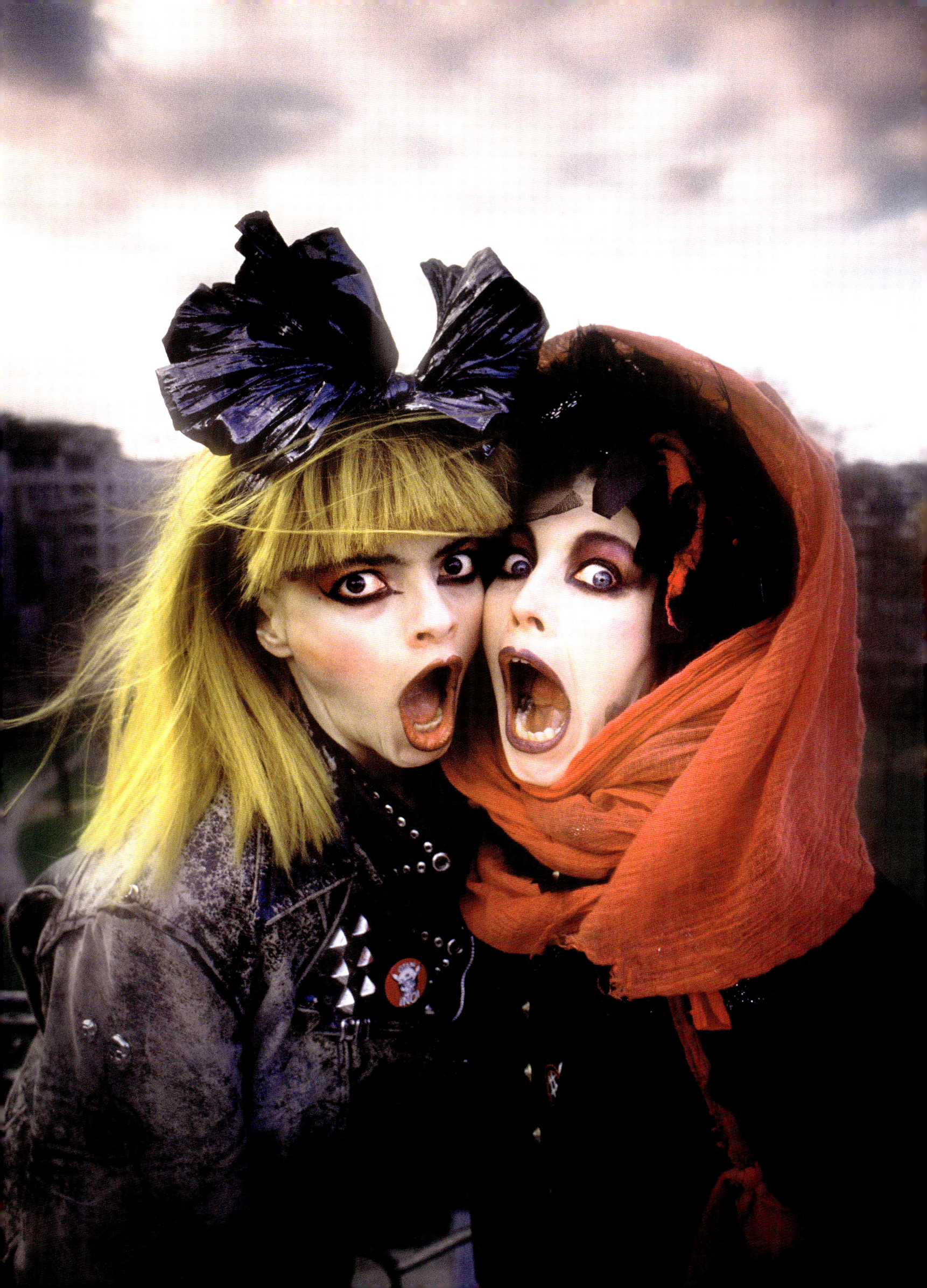

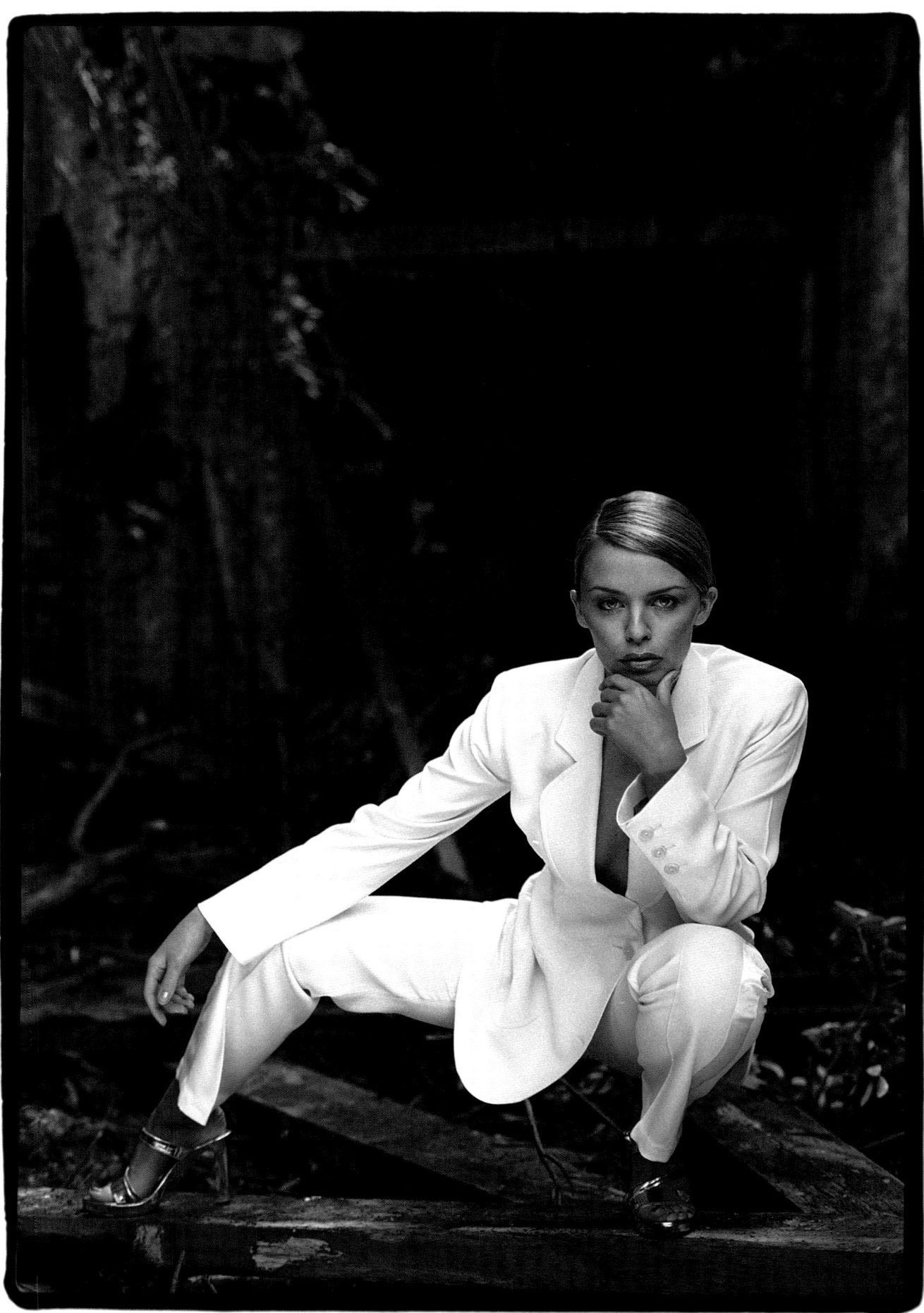

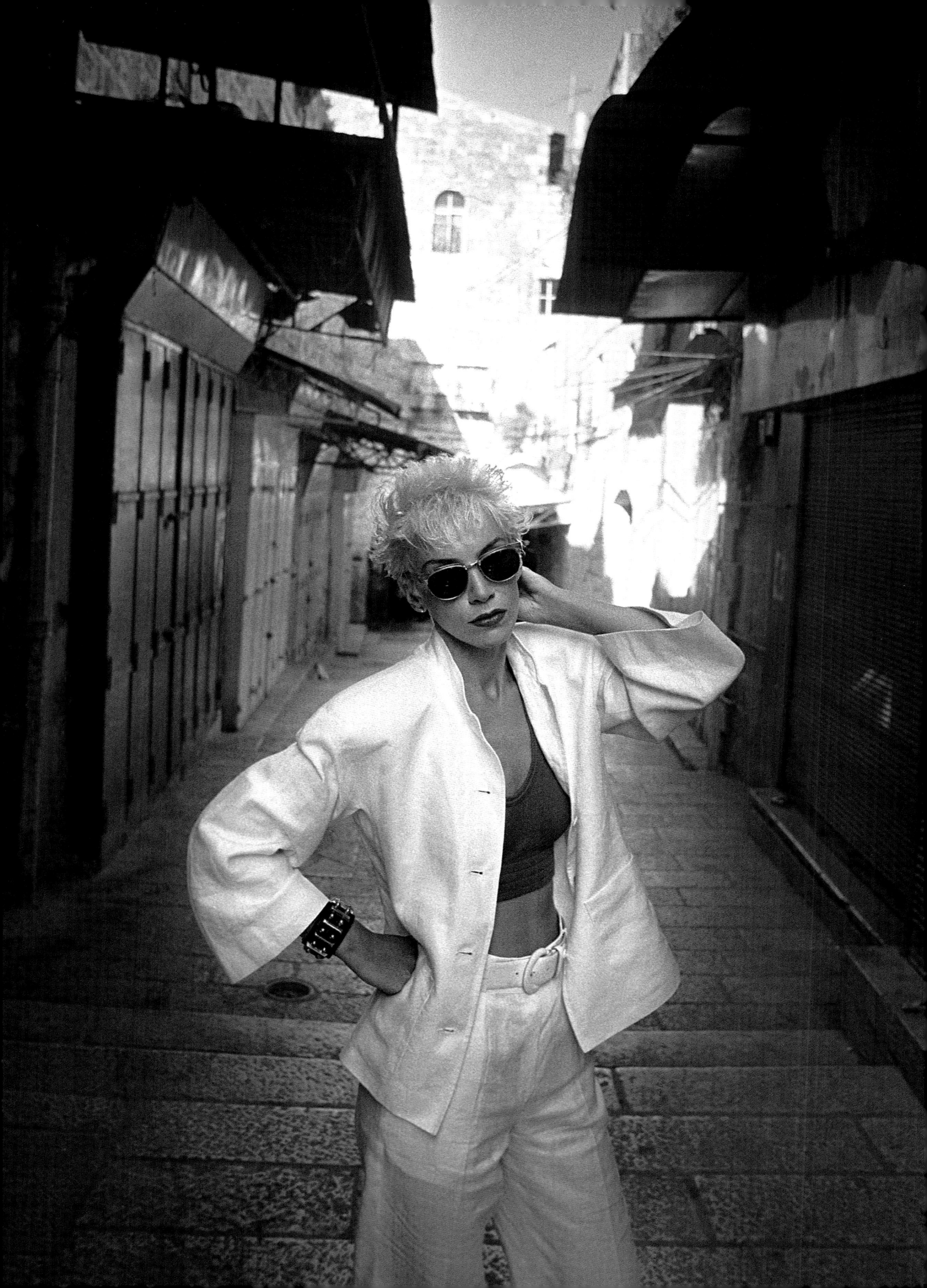

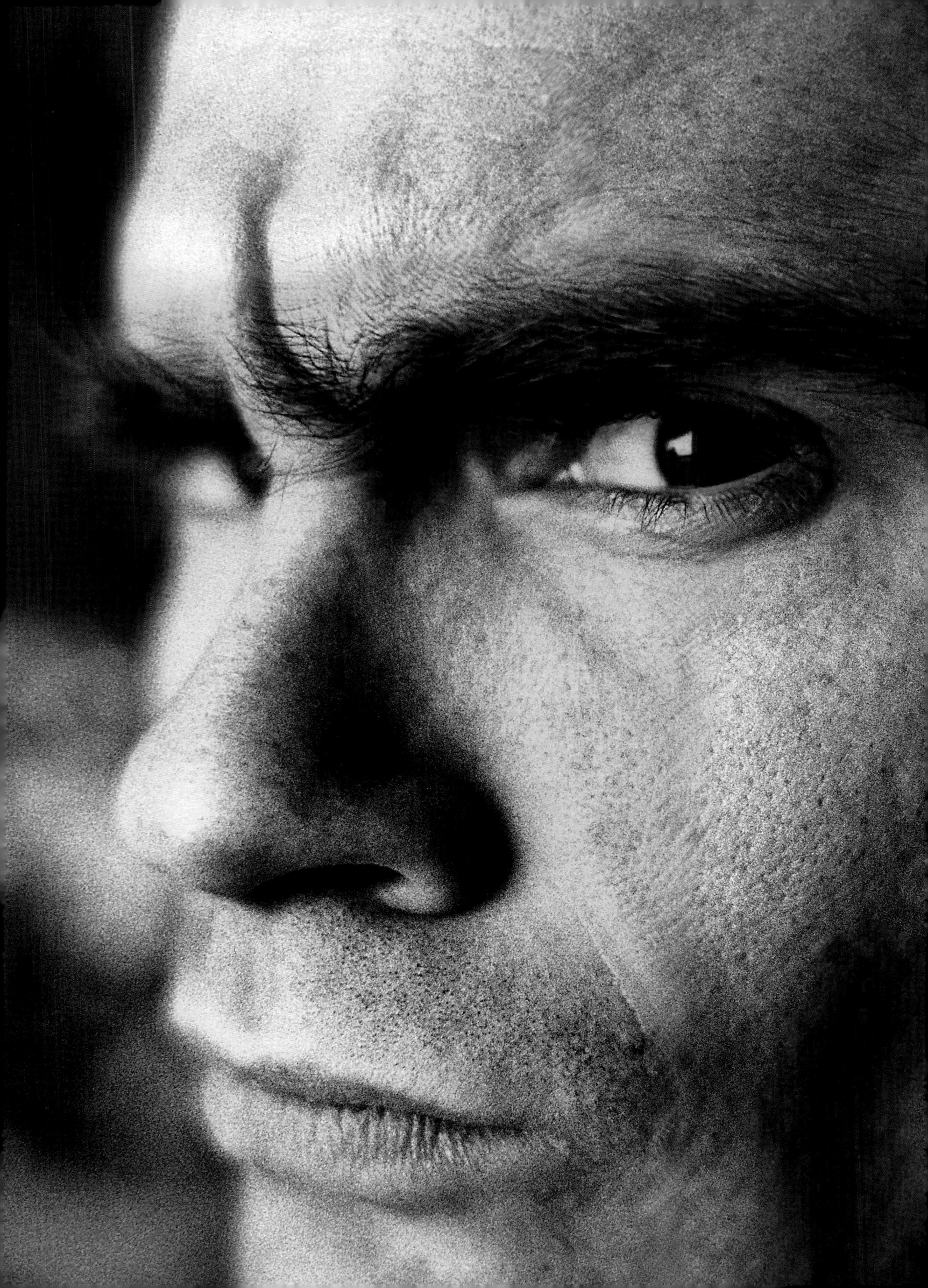

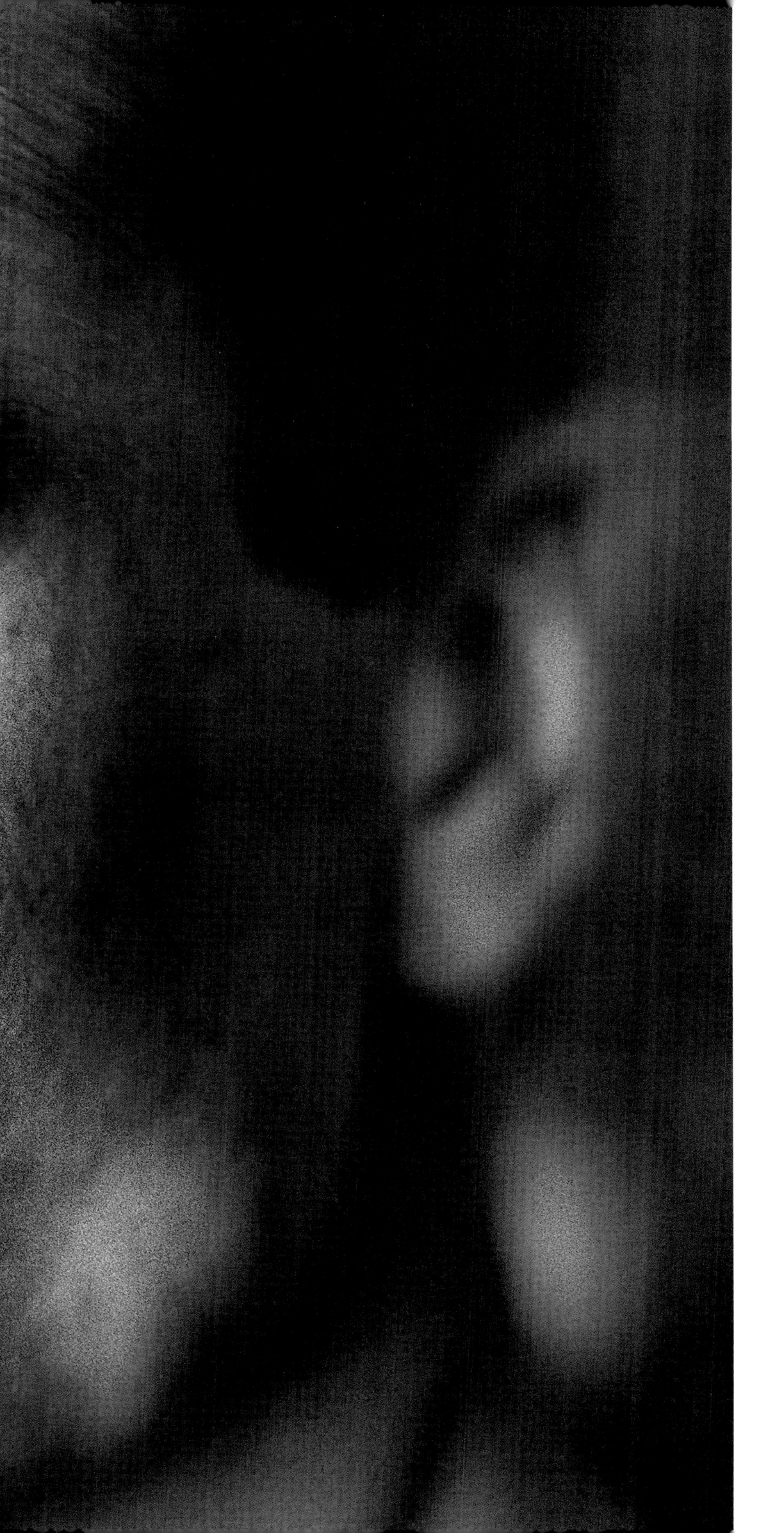

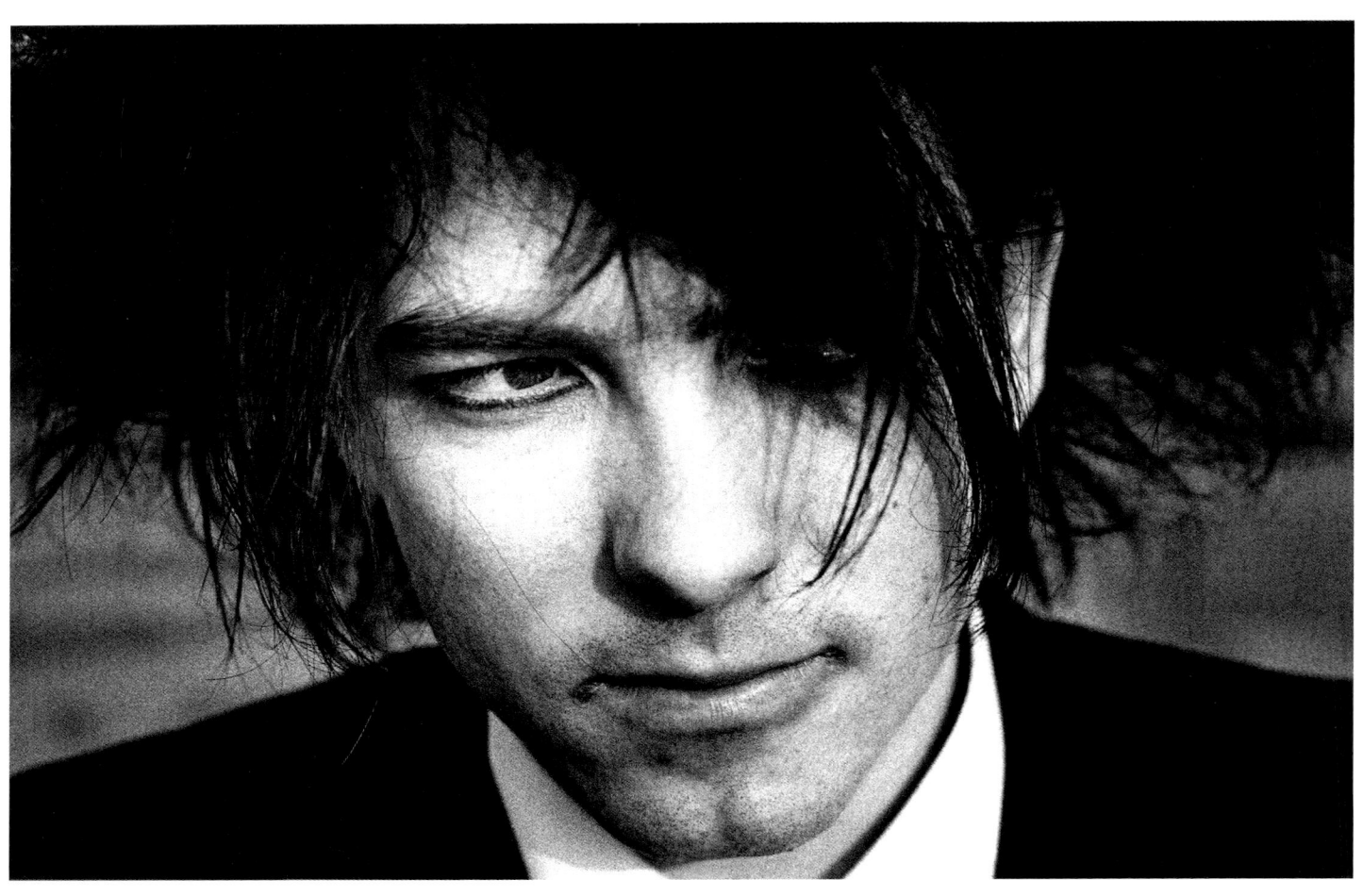

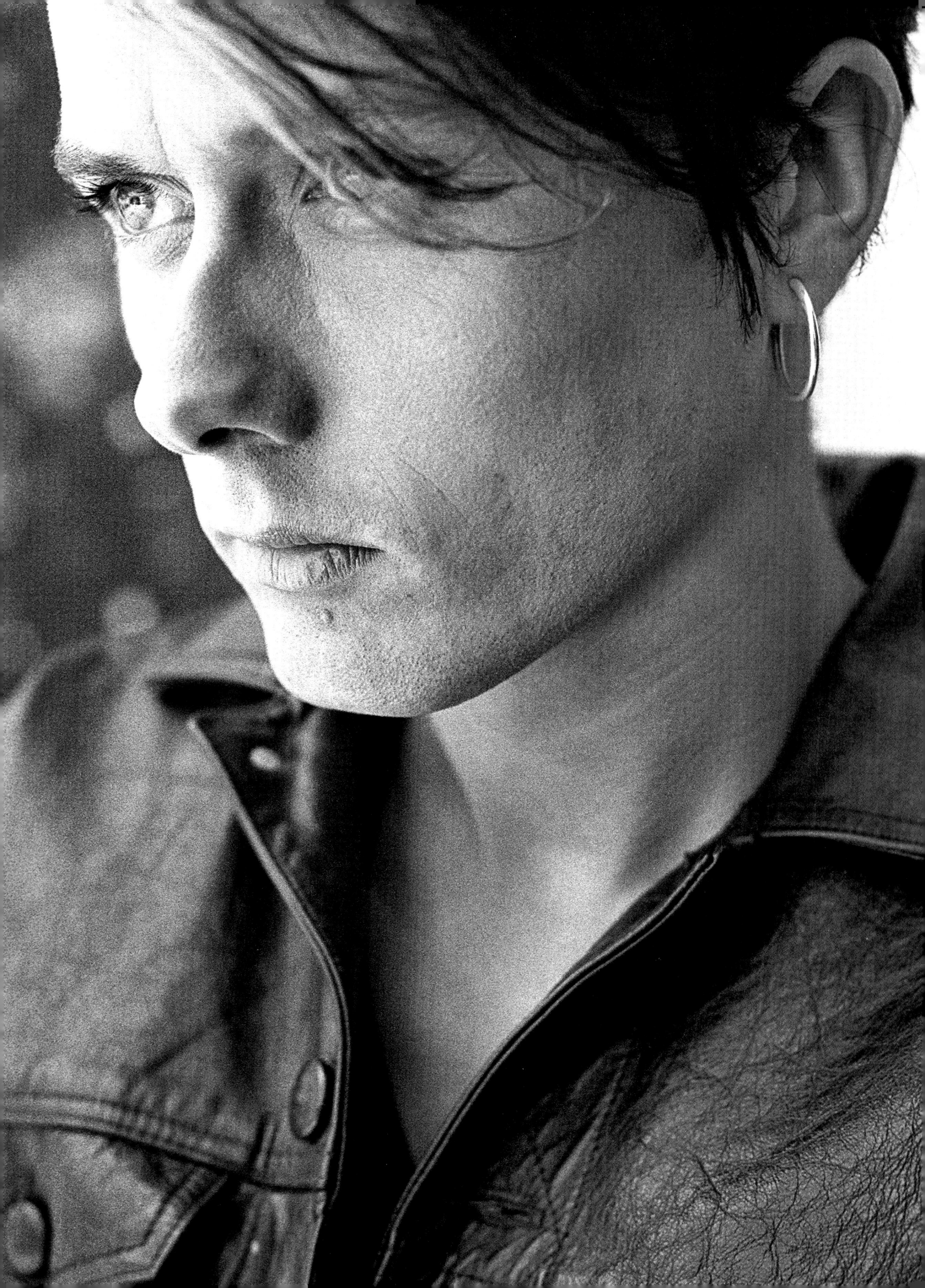

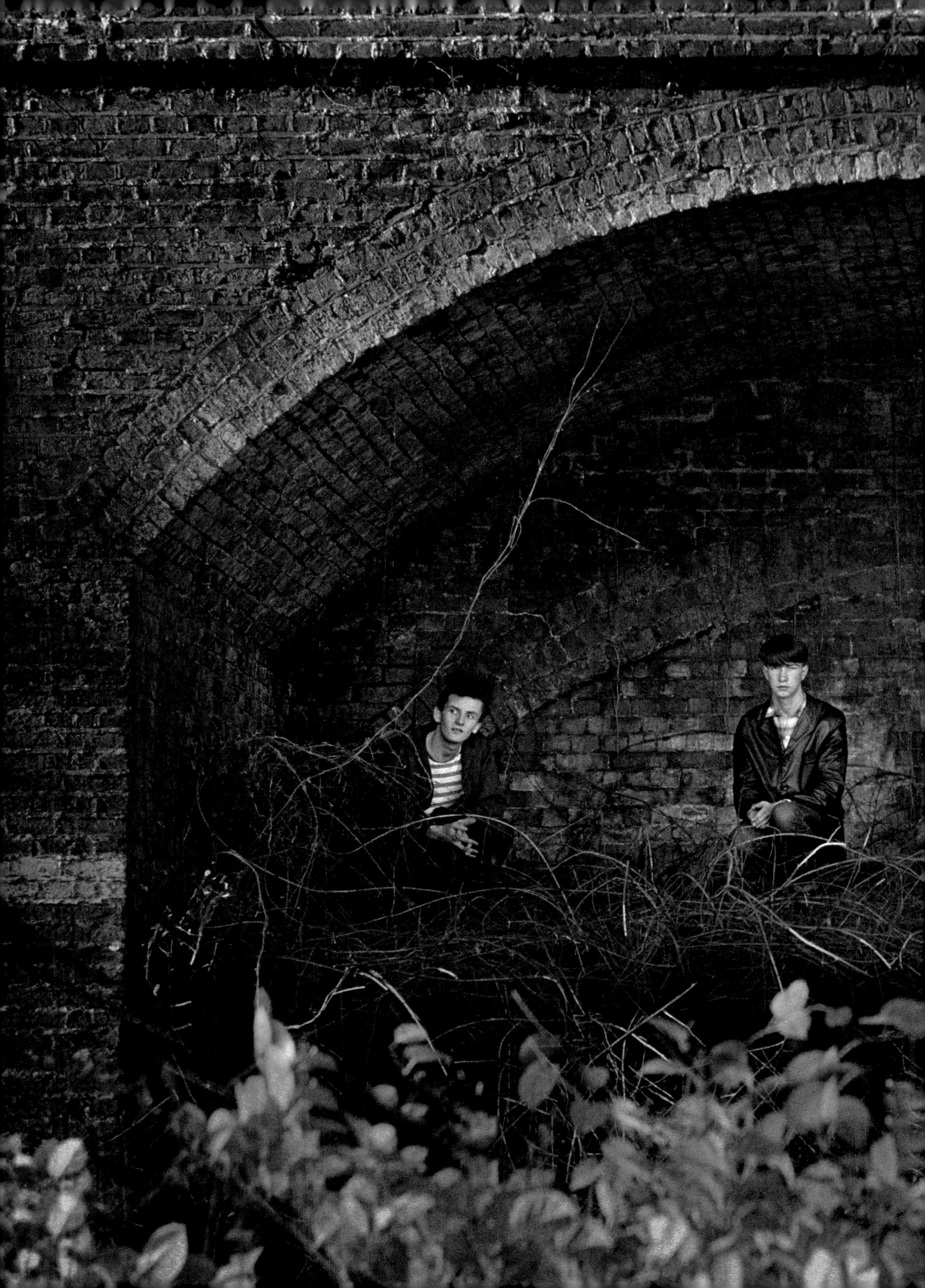

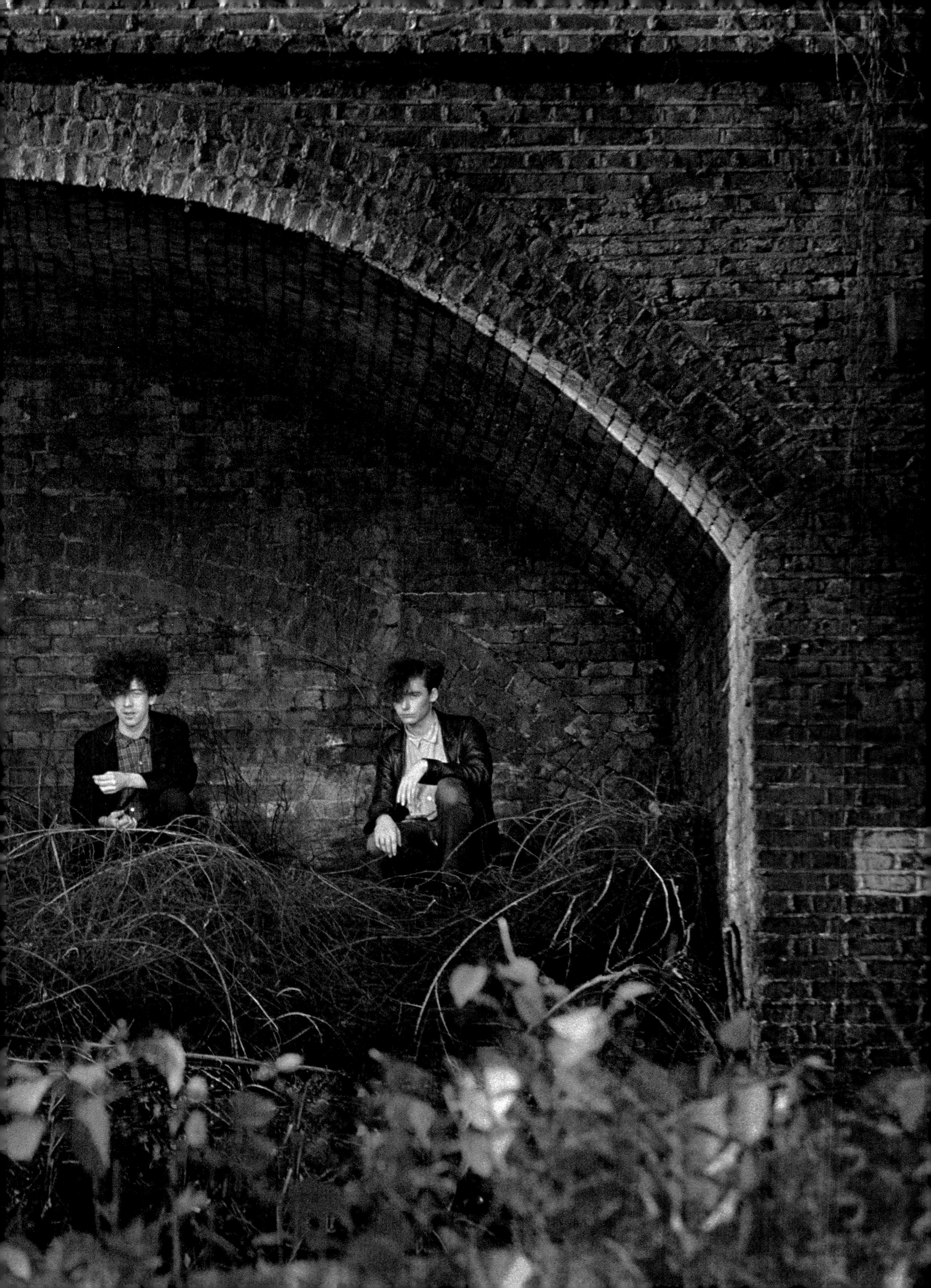

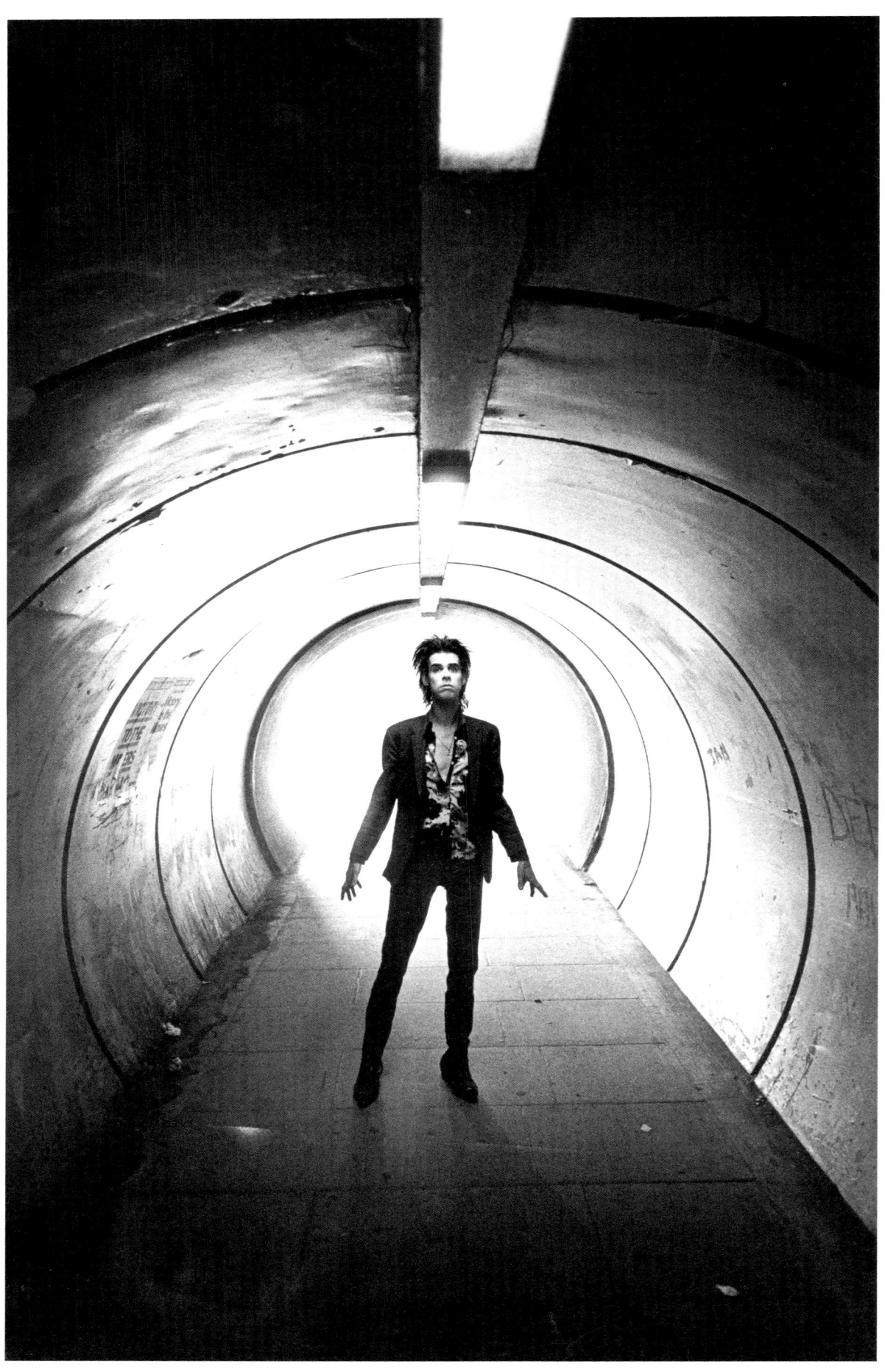

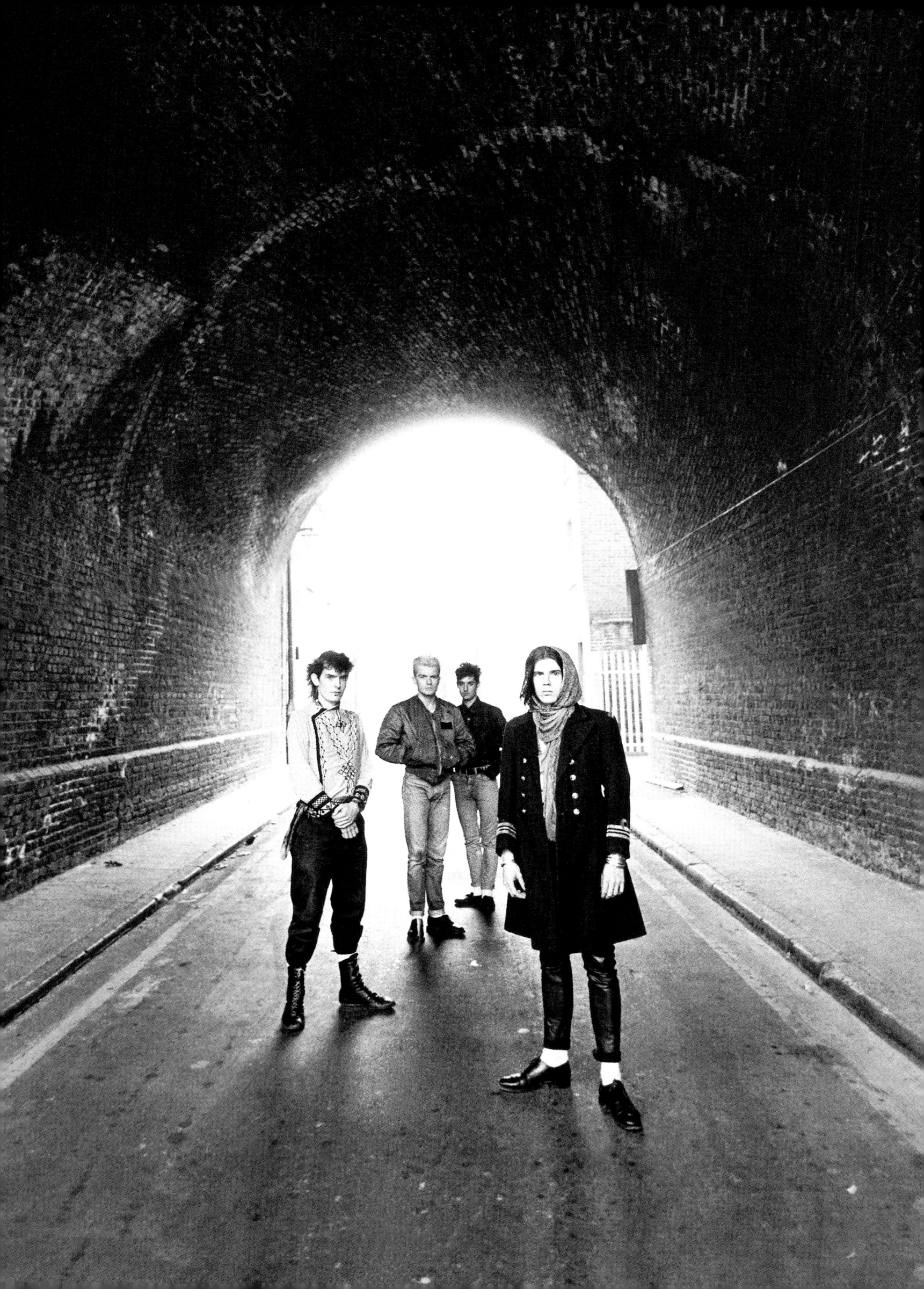

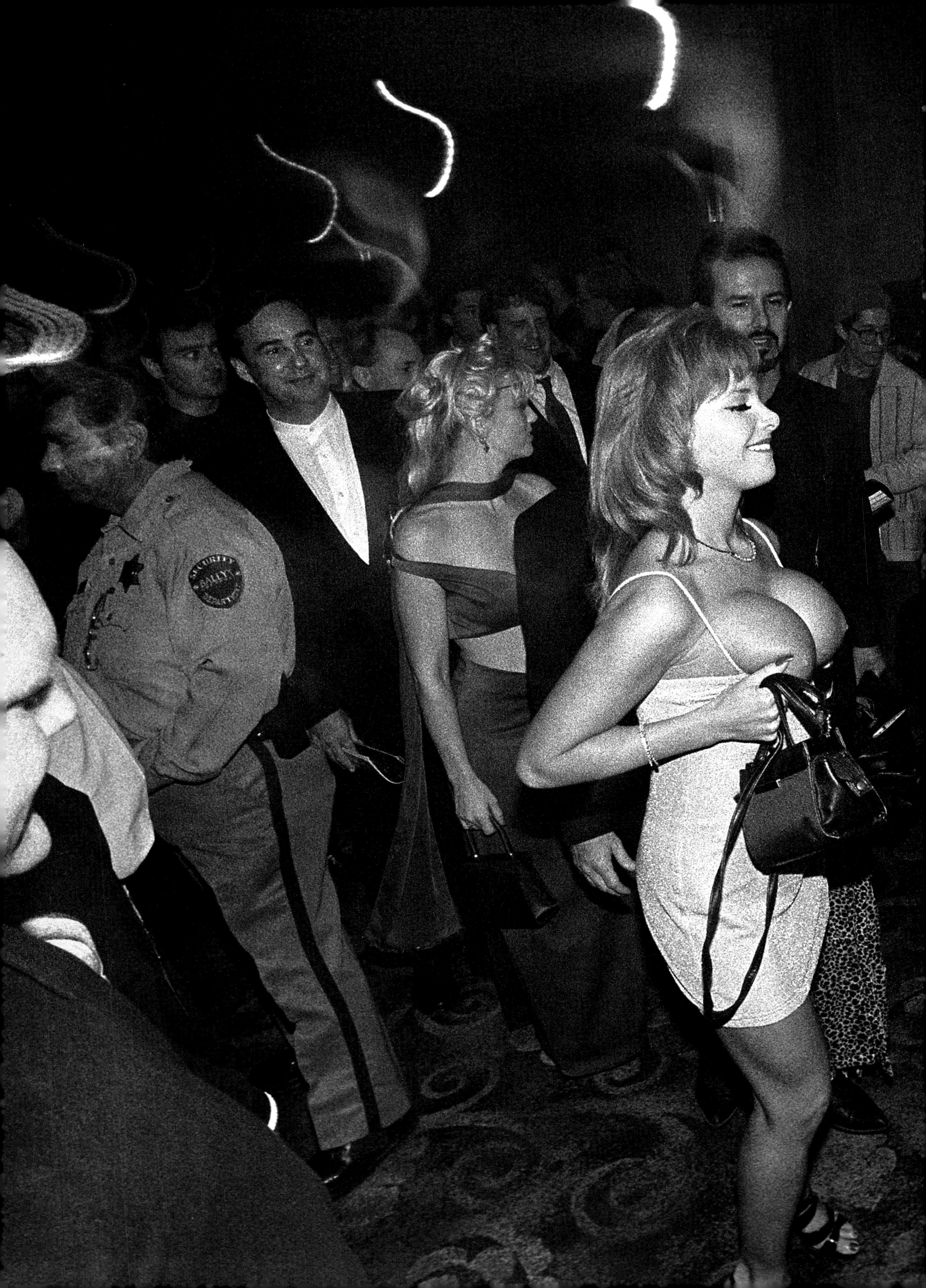

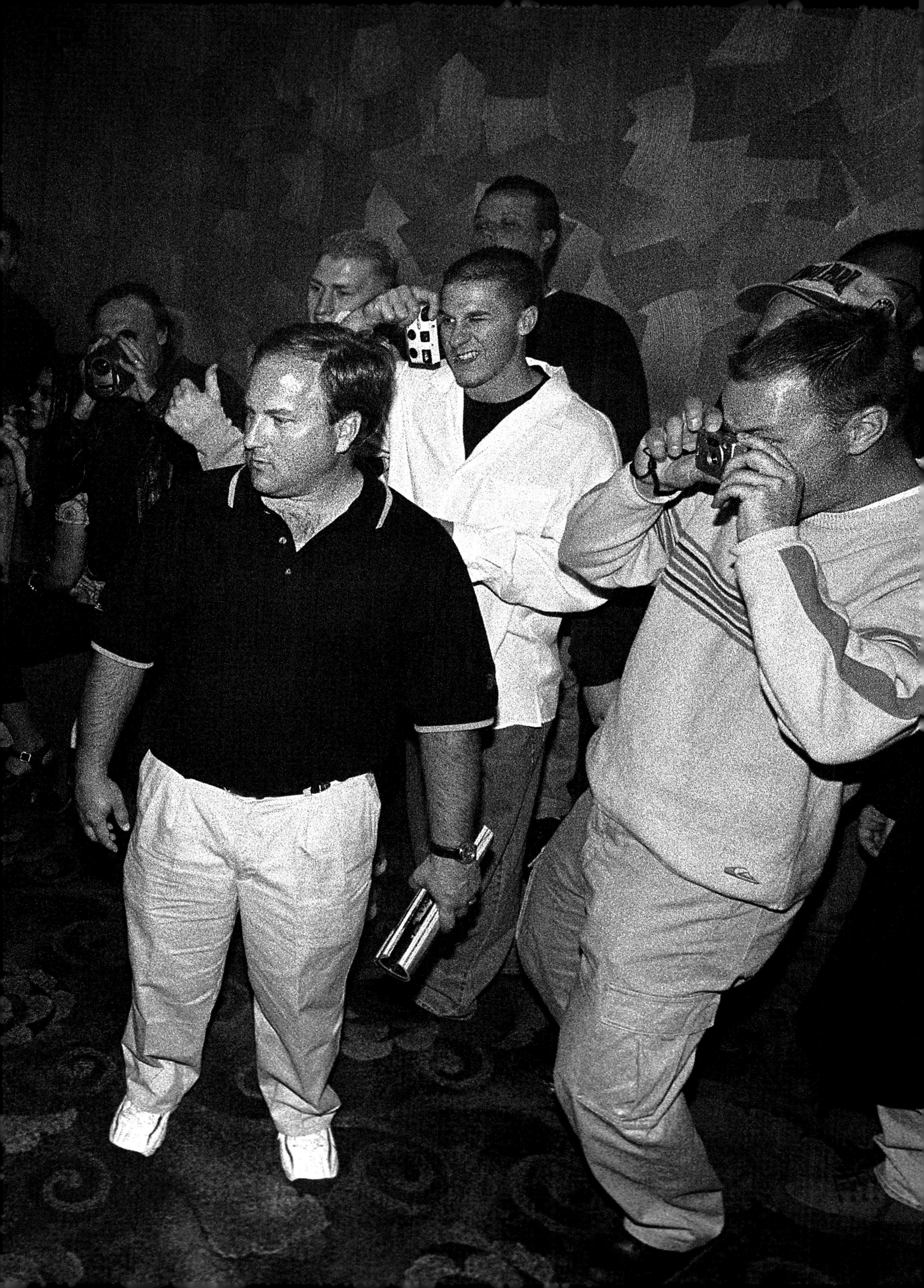

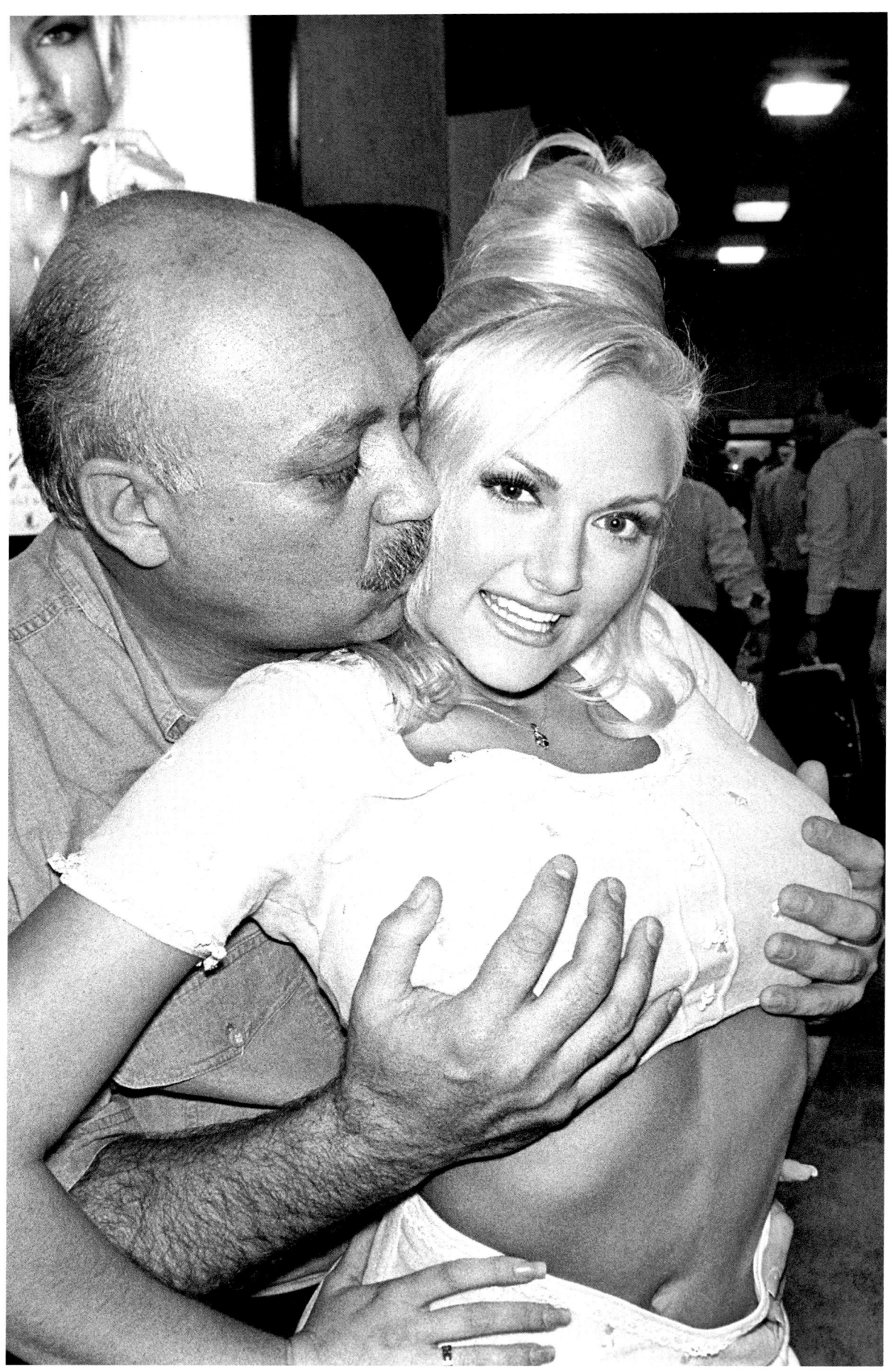

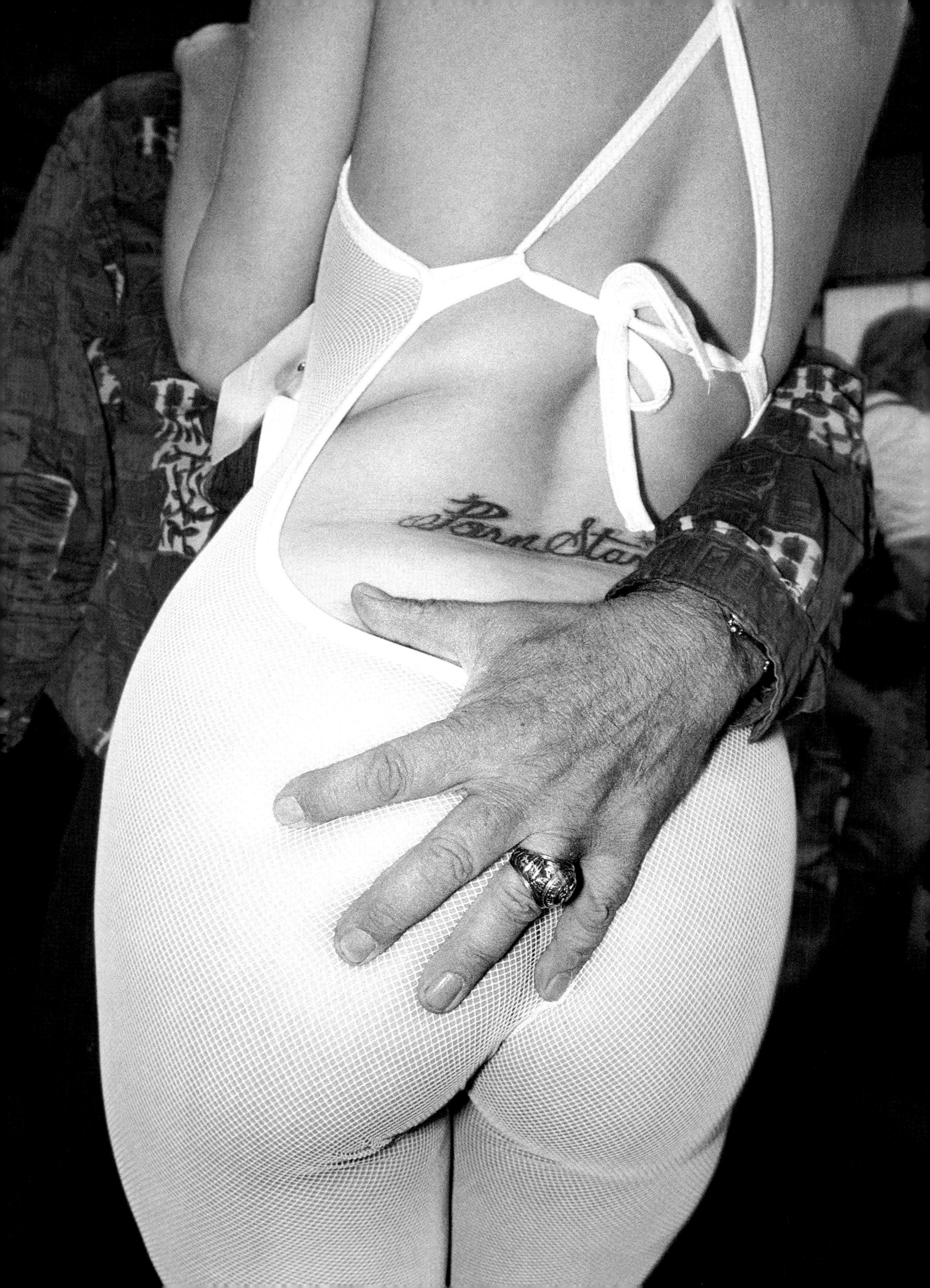

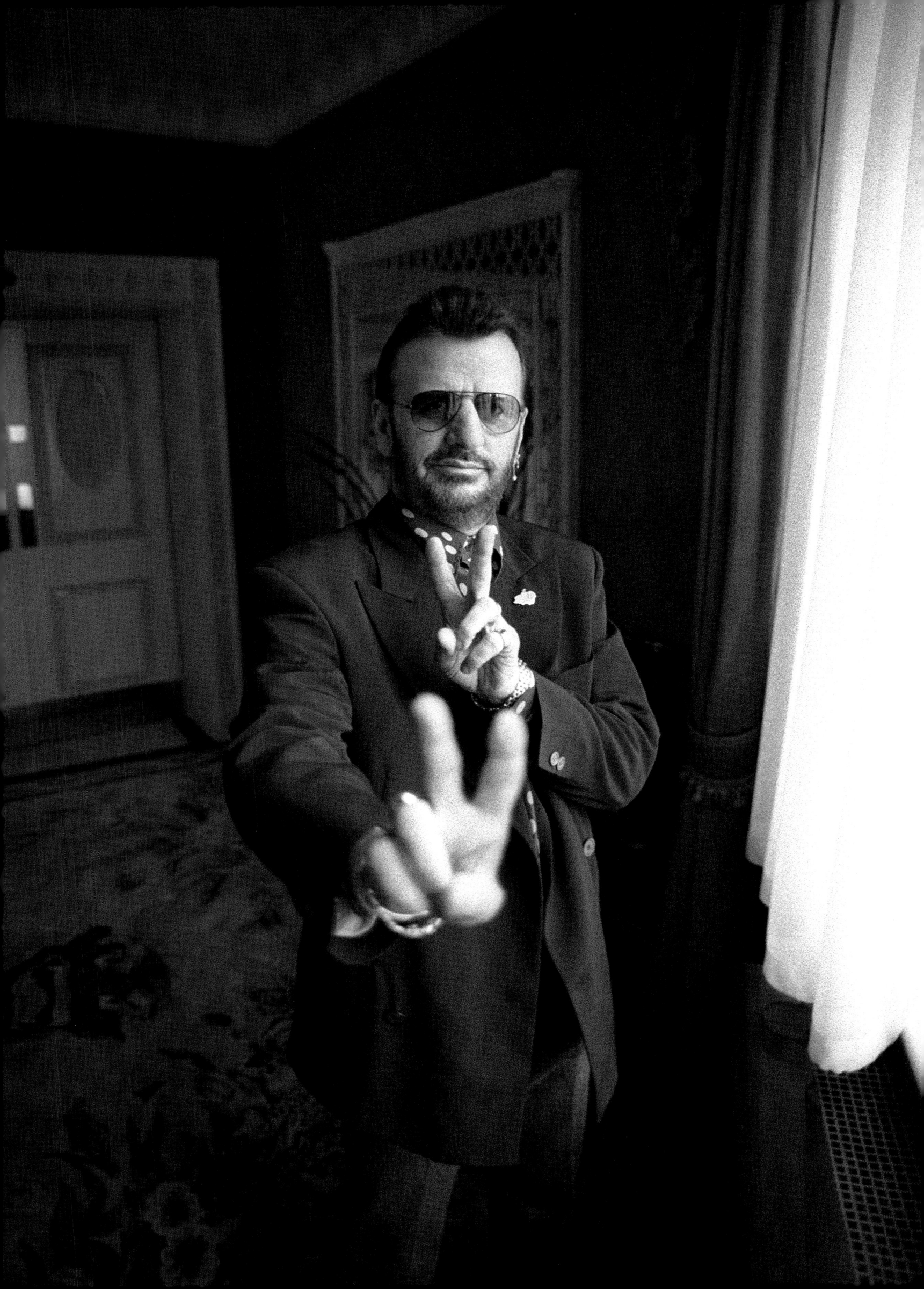

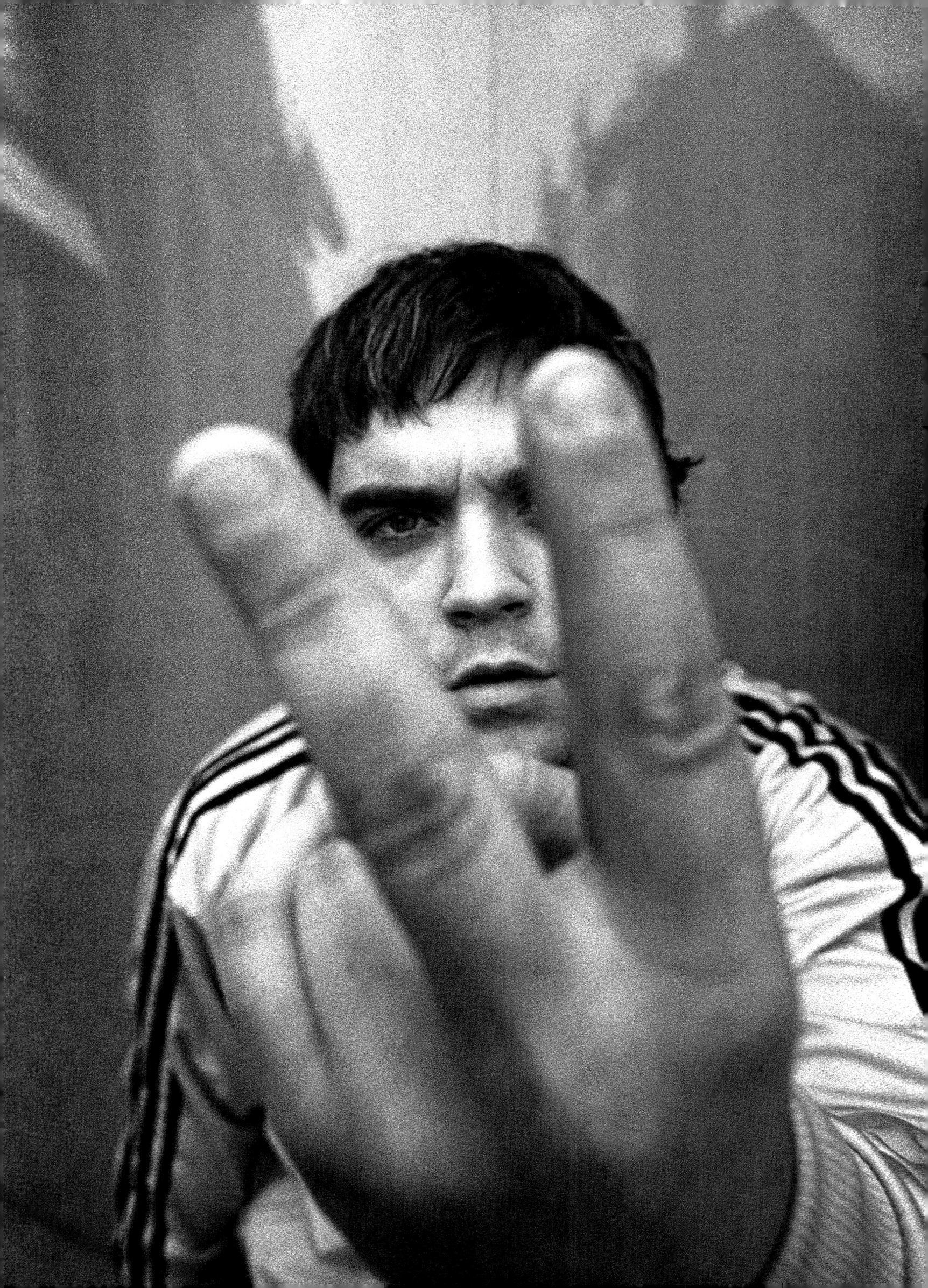

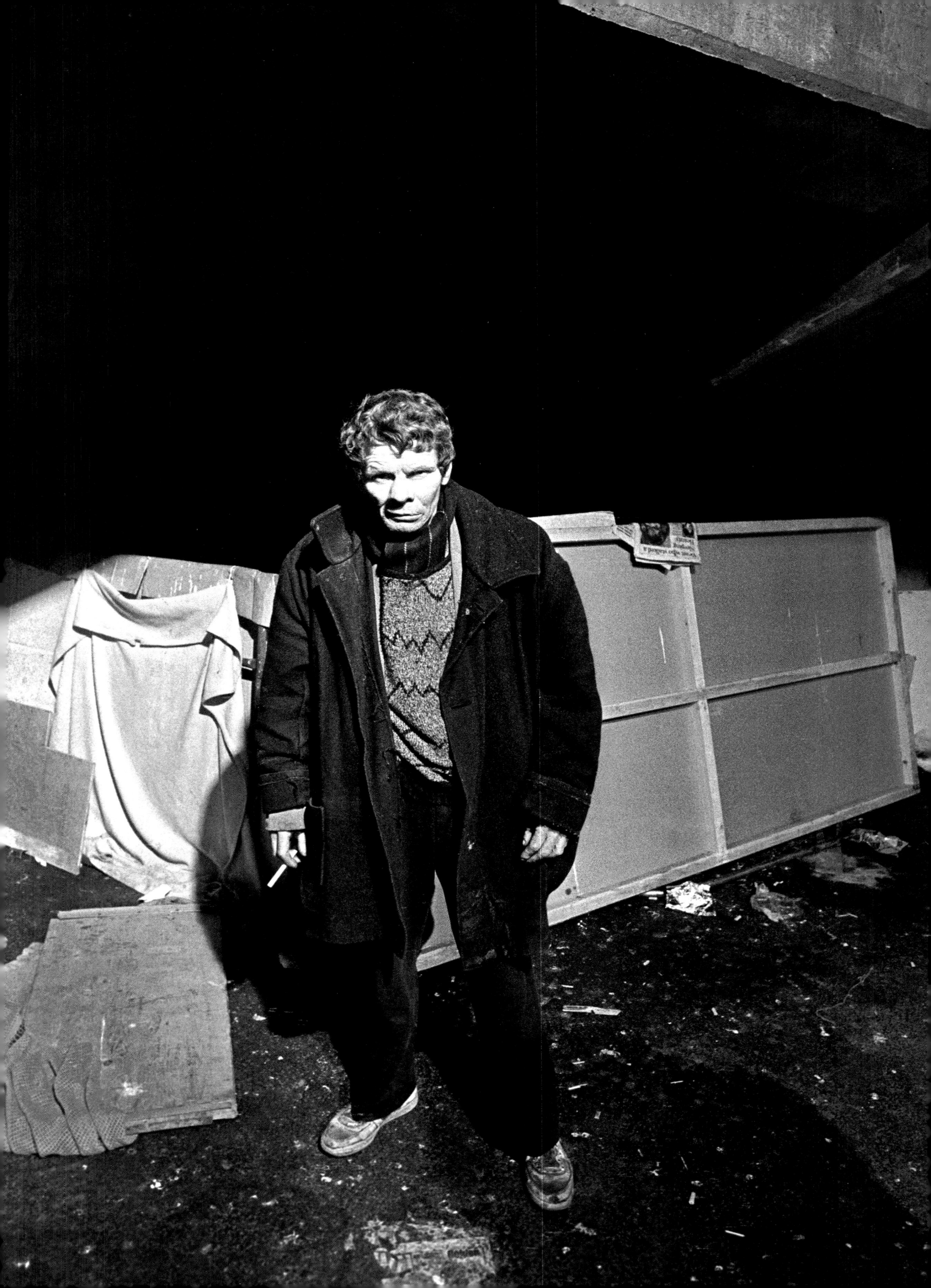

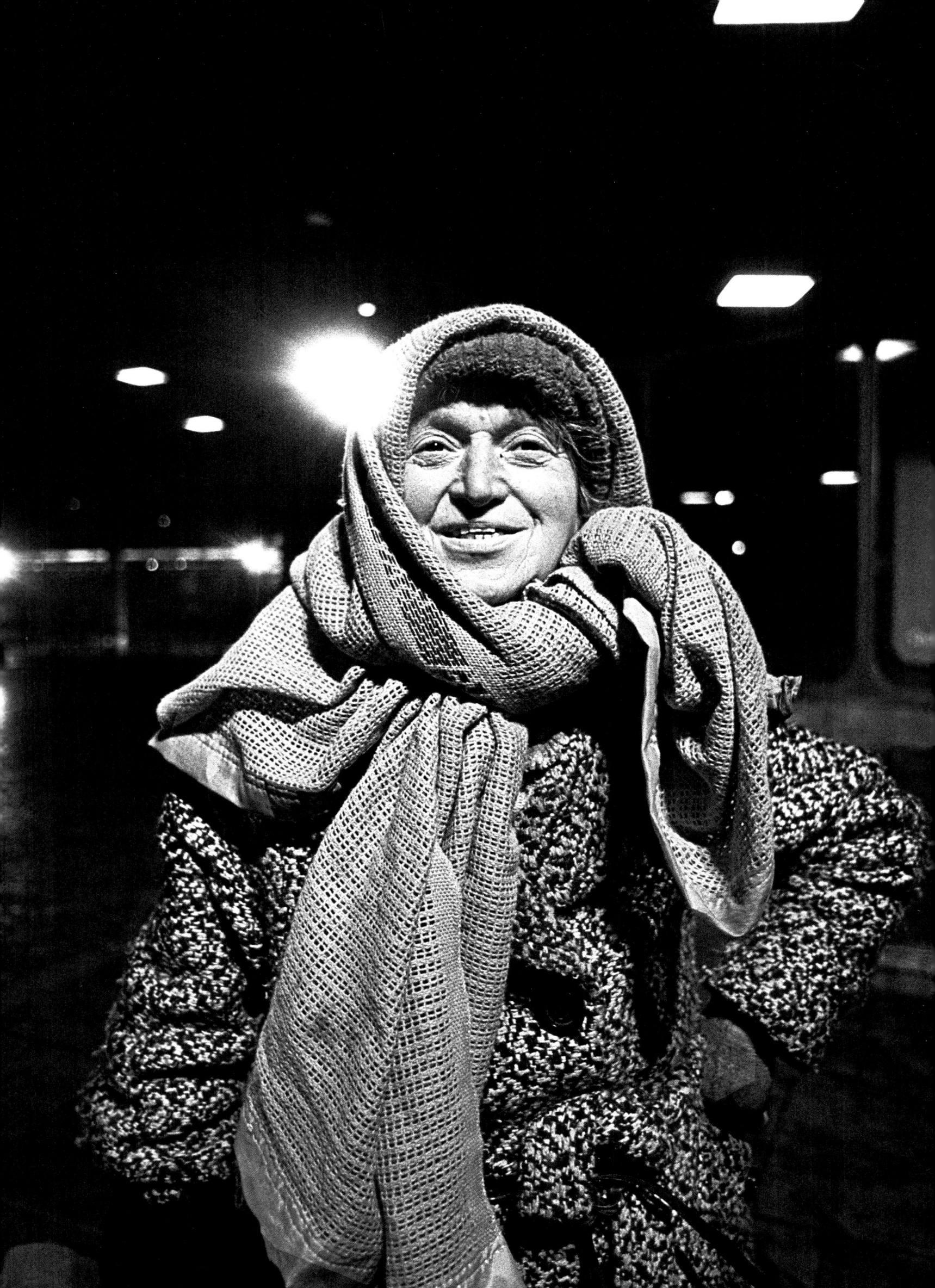

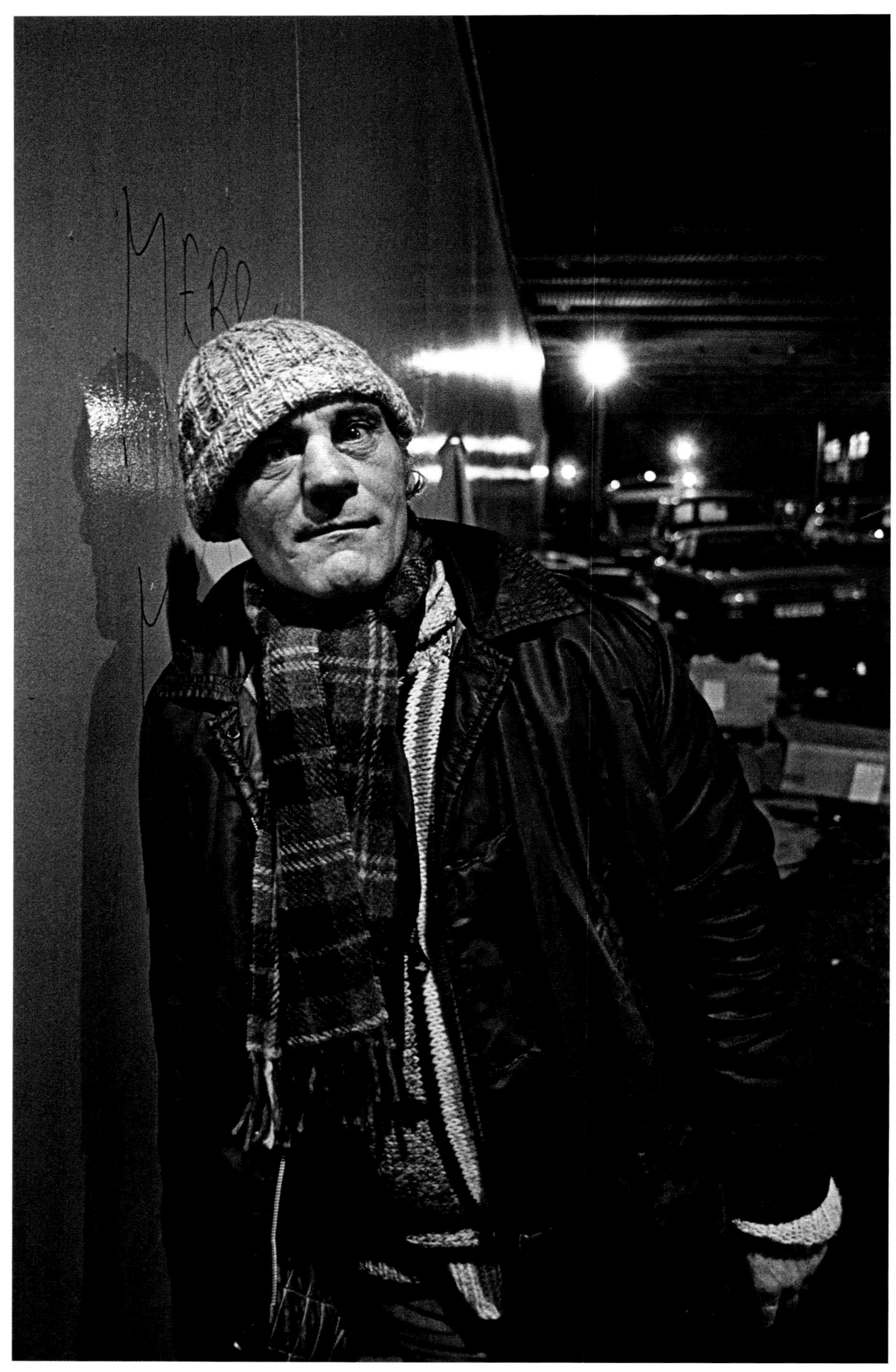

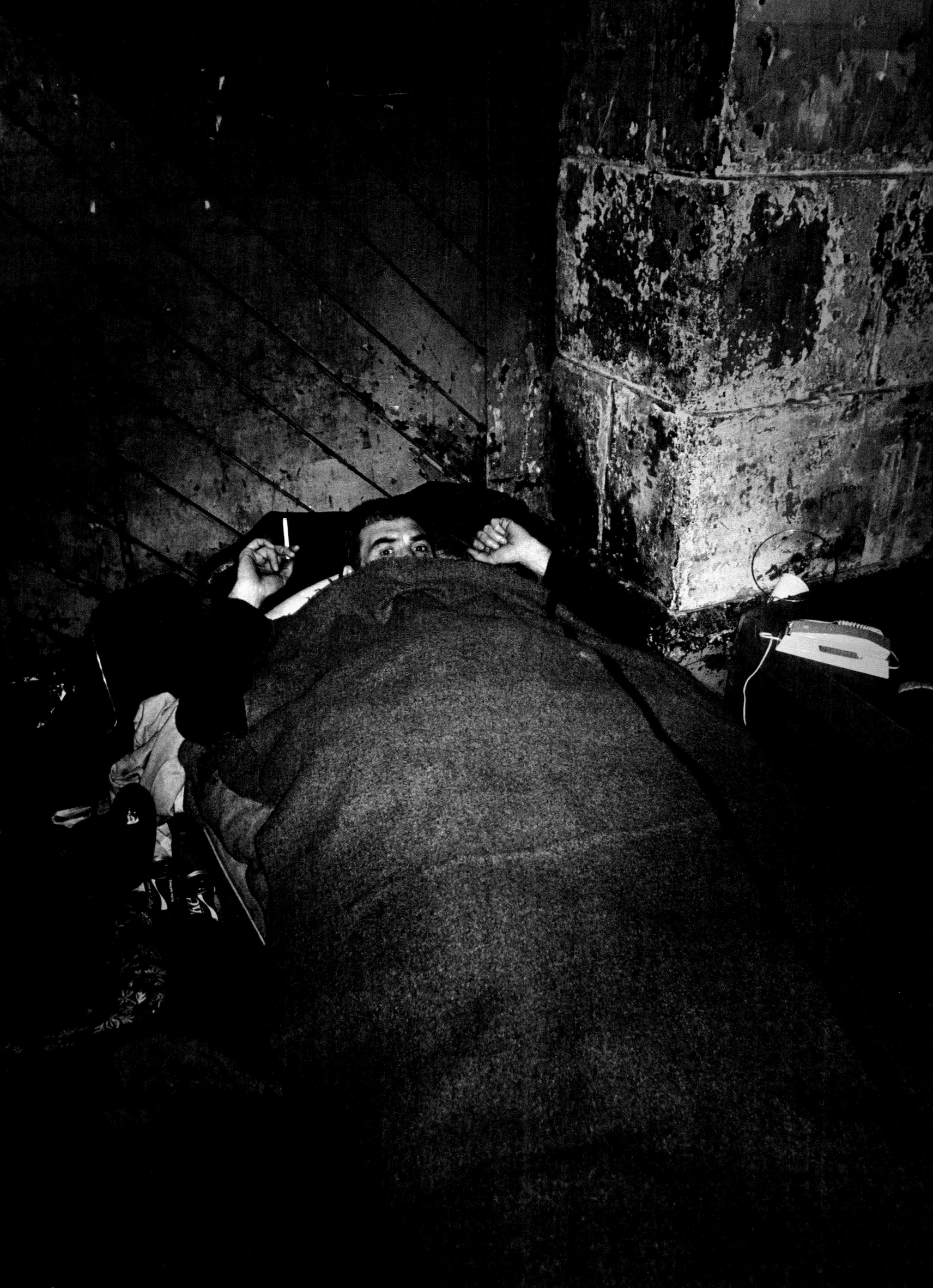

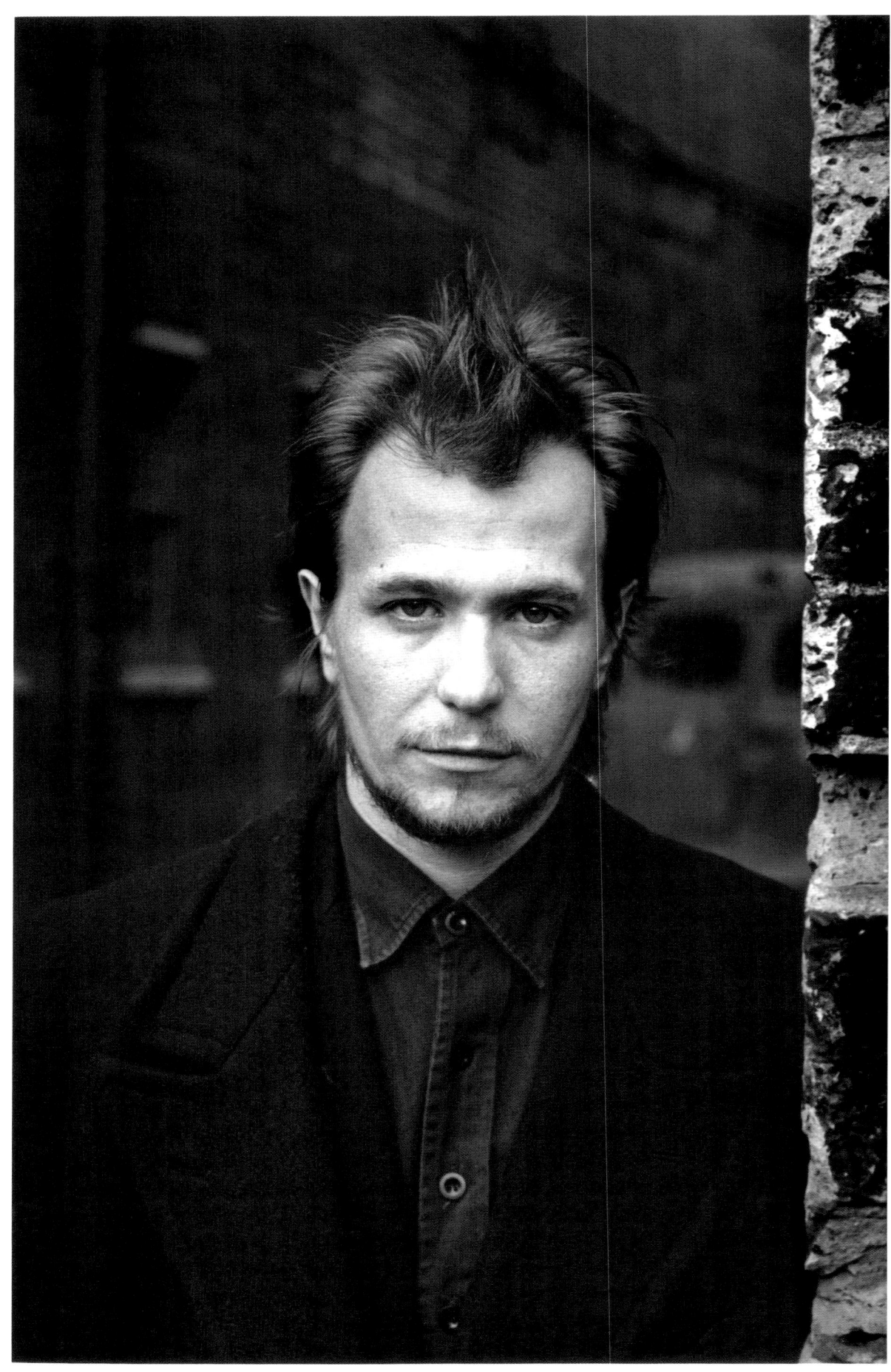

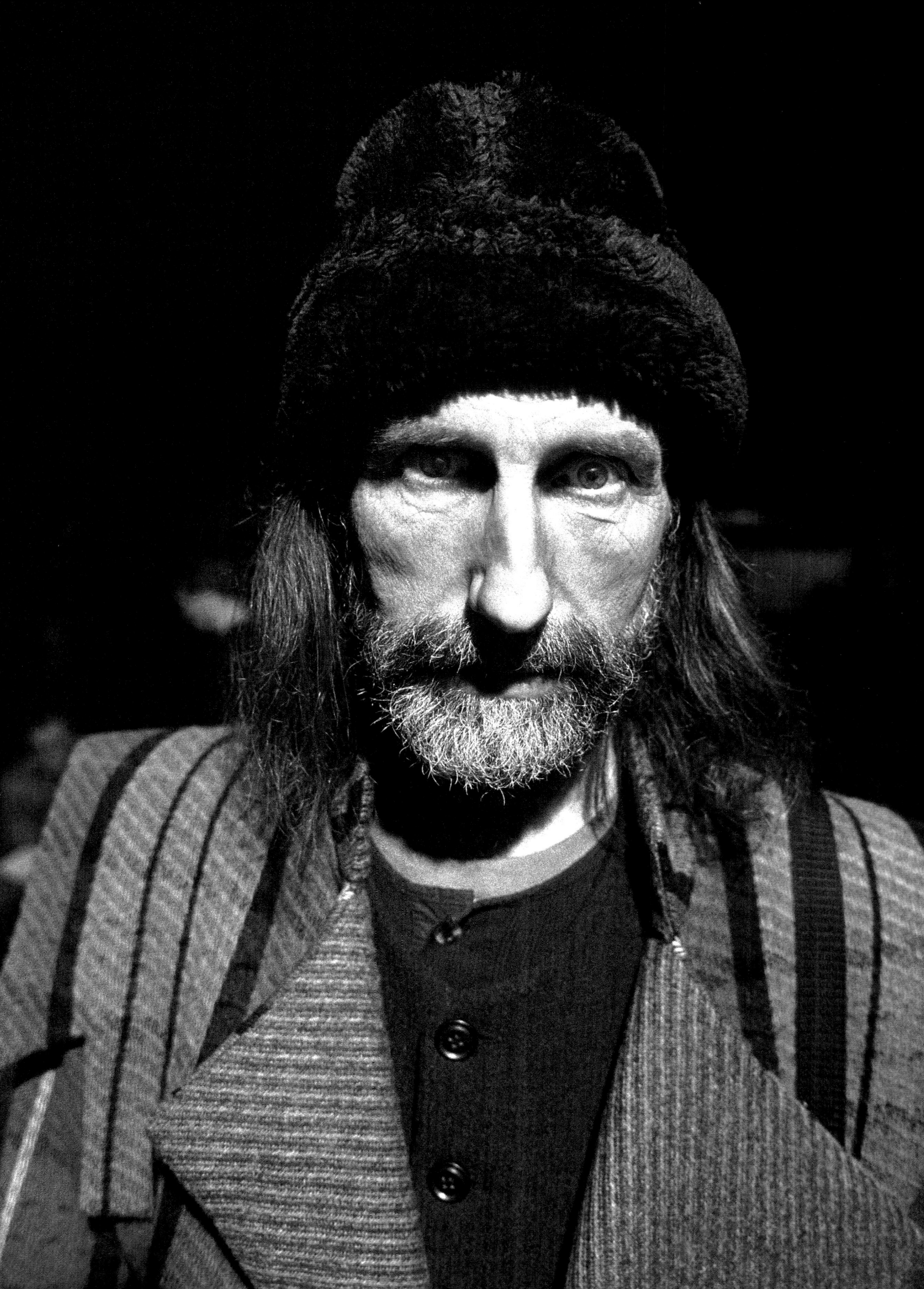

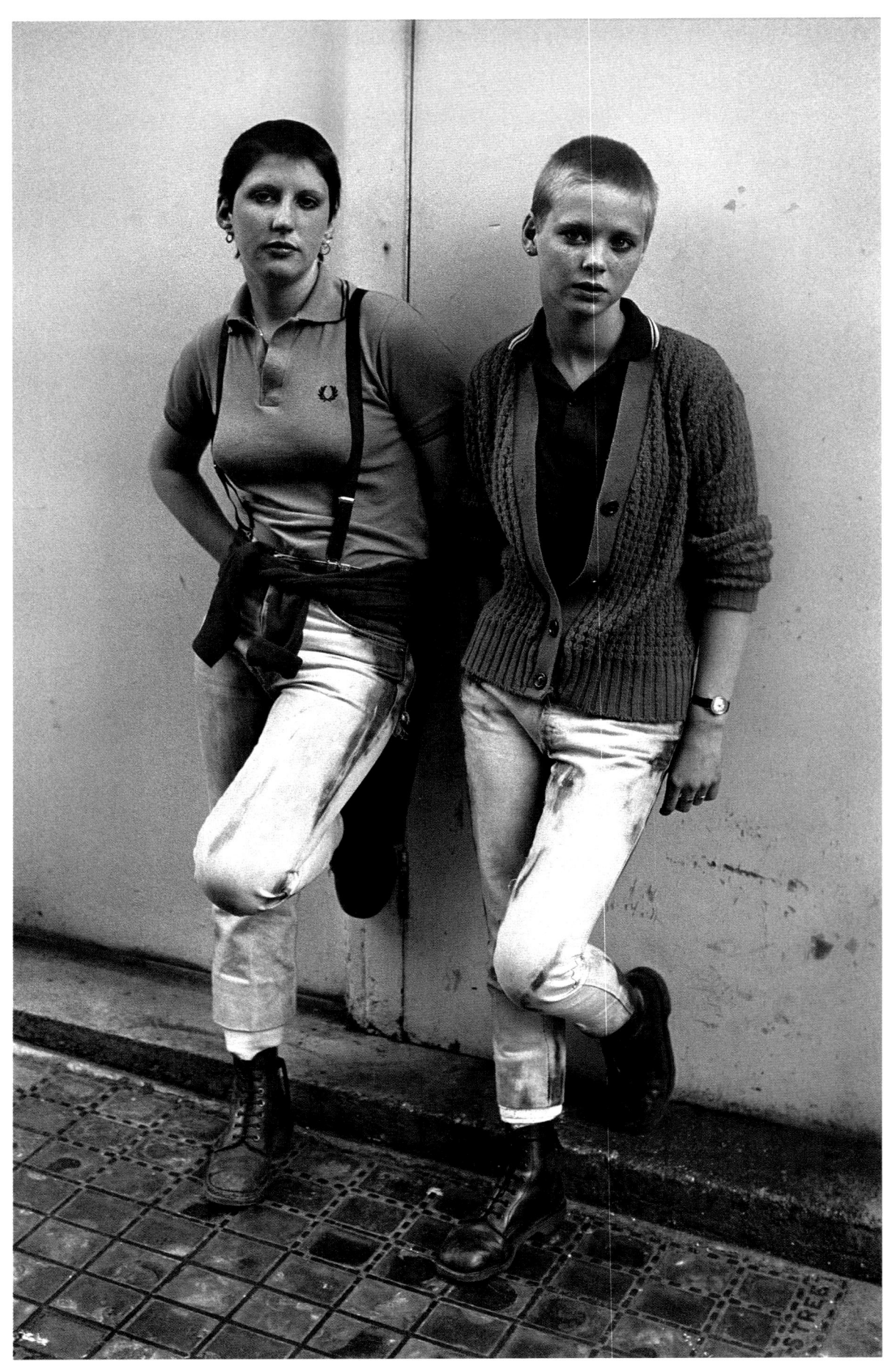

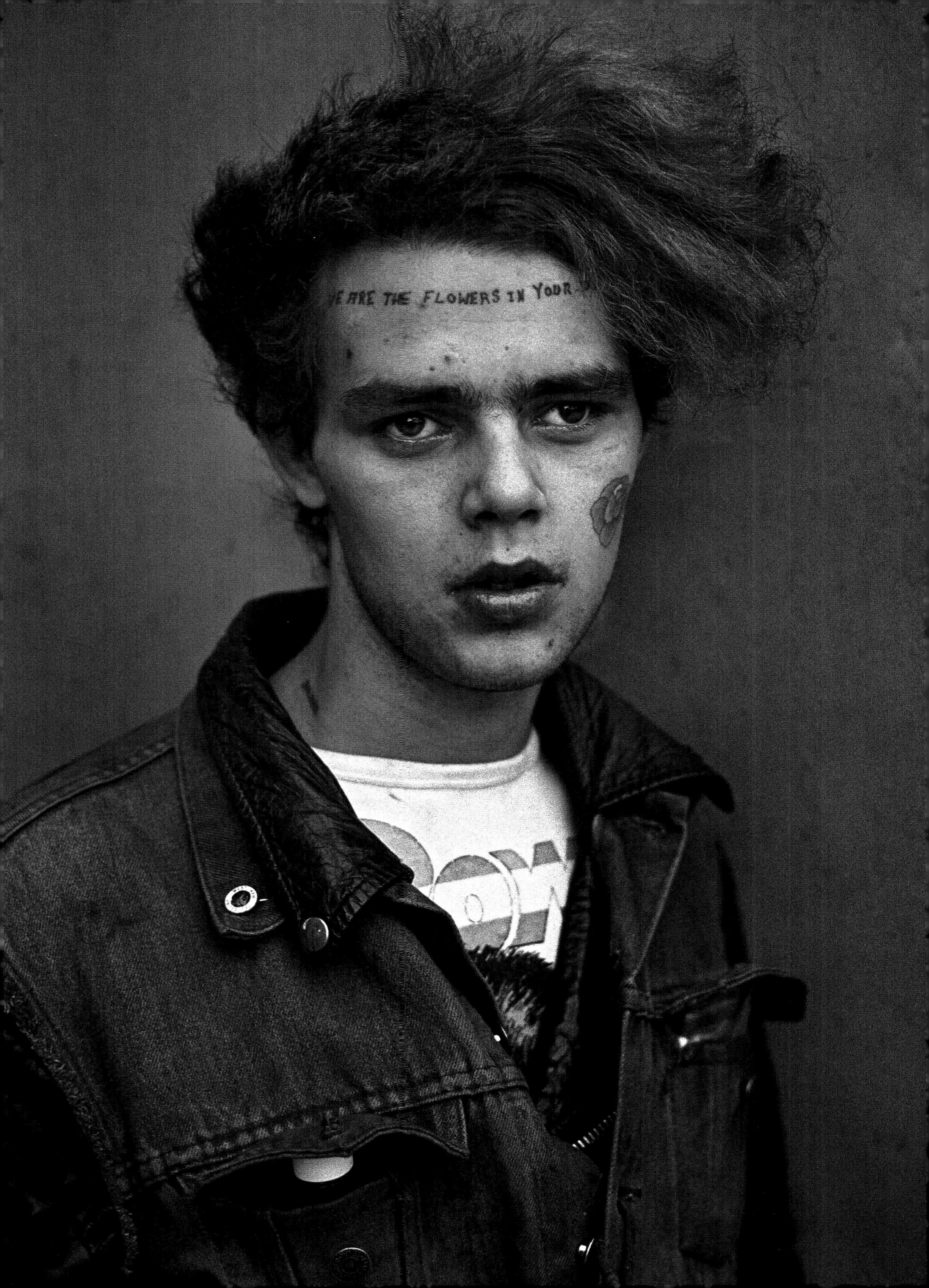
ARE THE FLOWERS IN YOUR

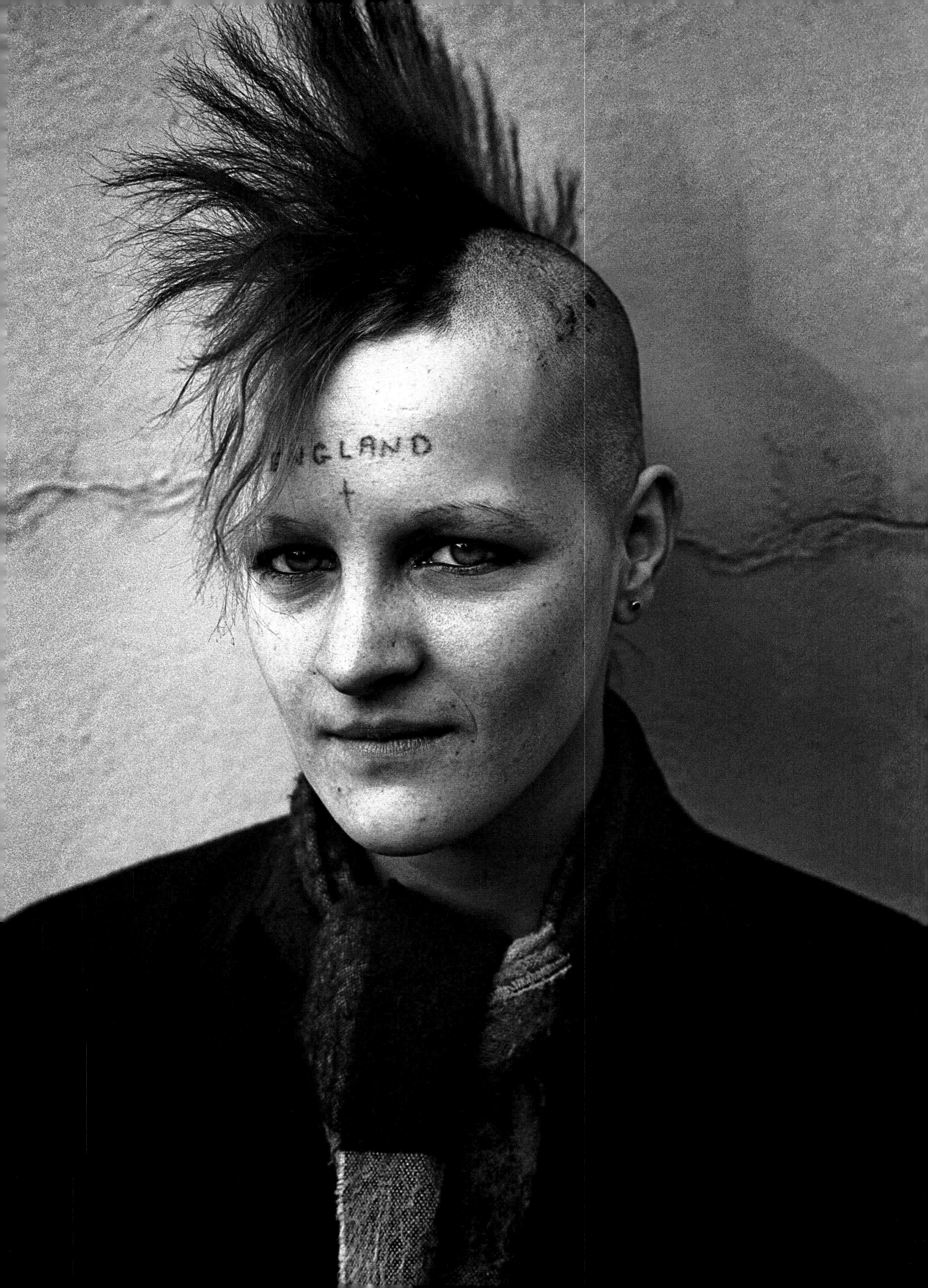

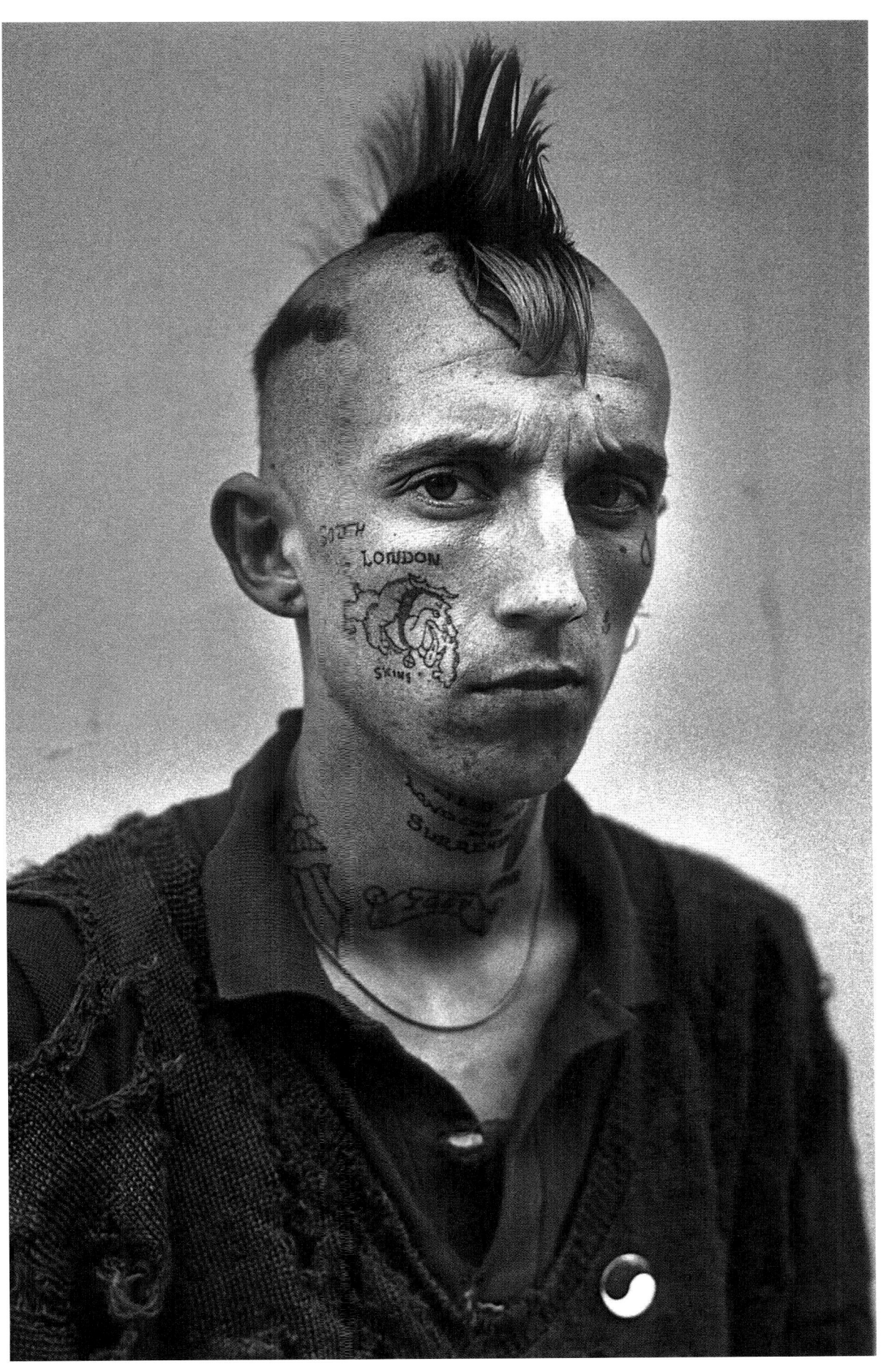

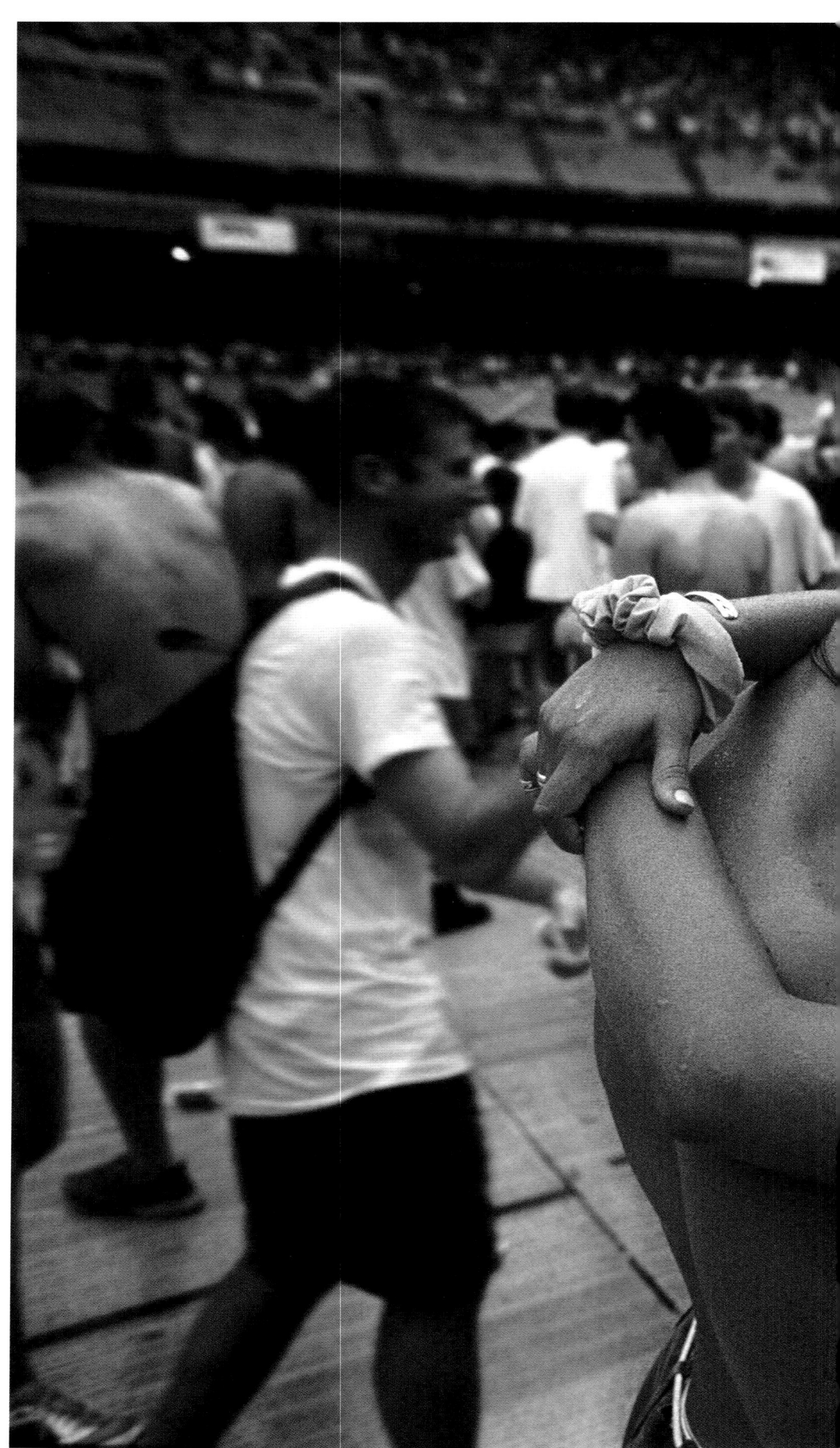

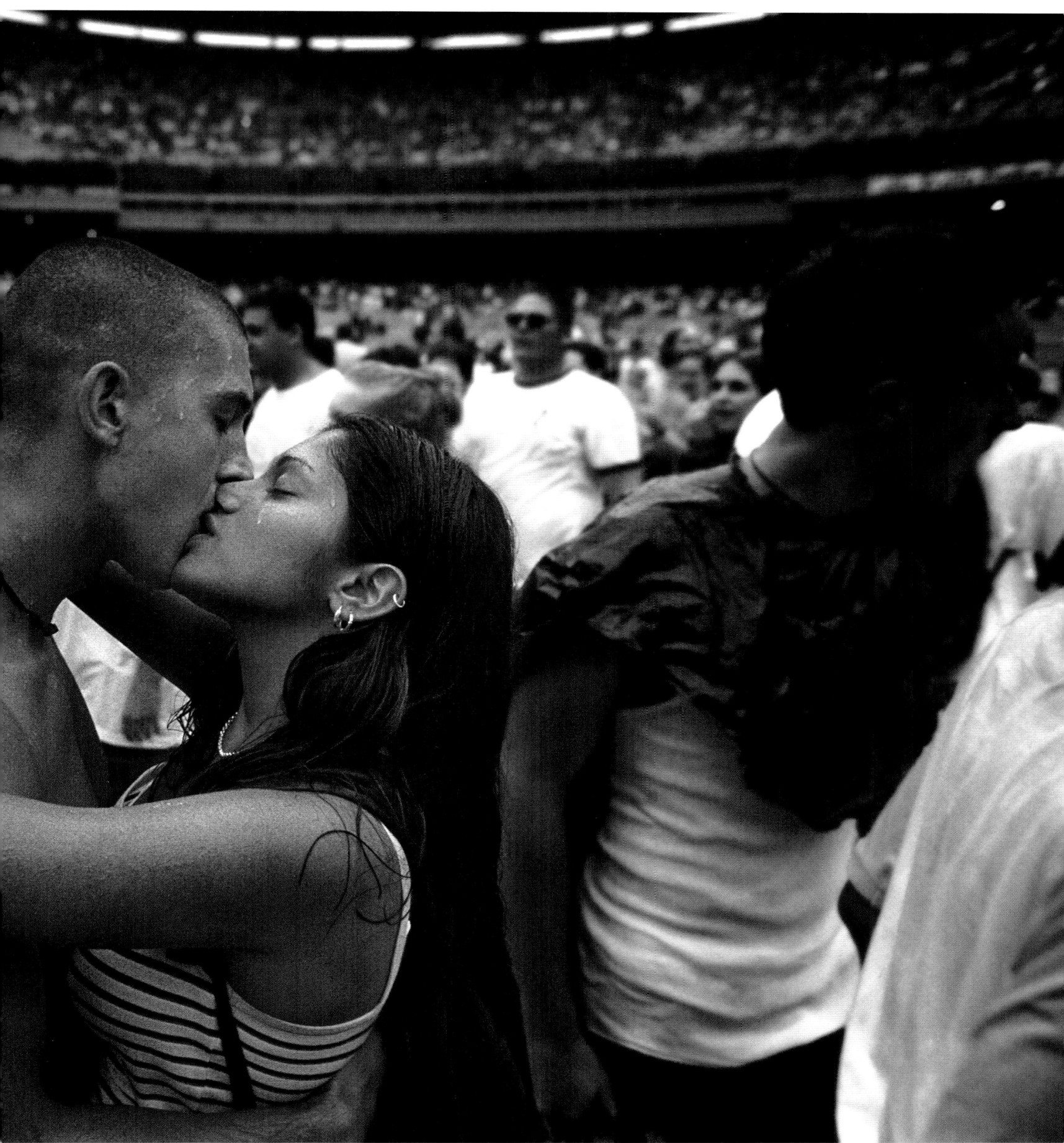

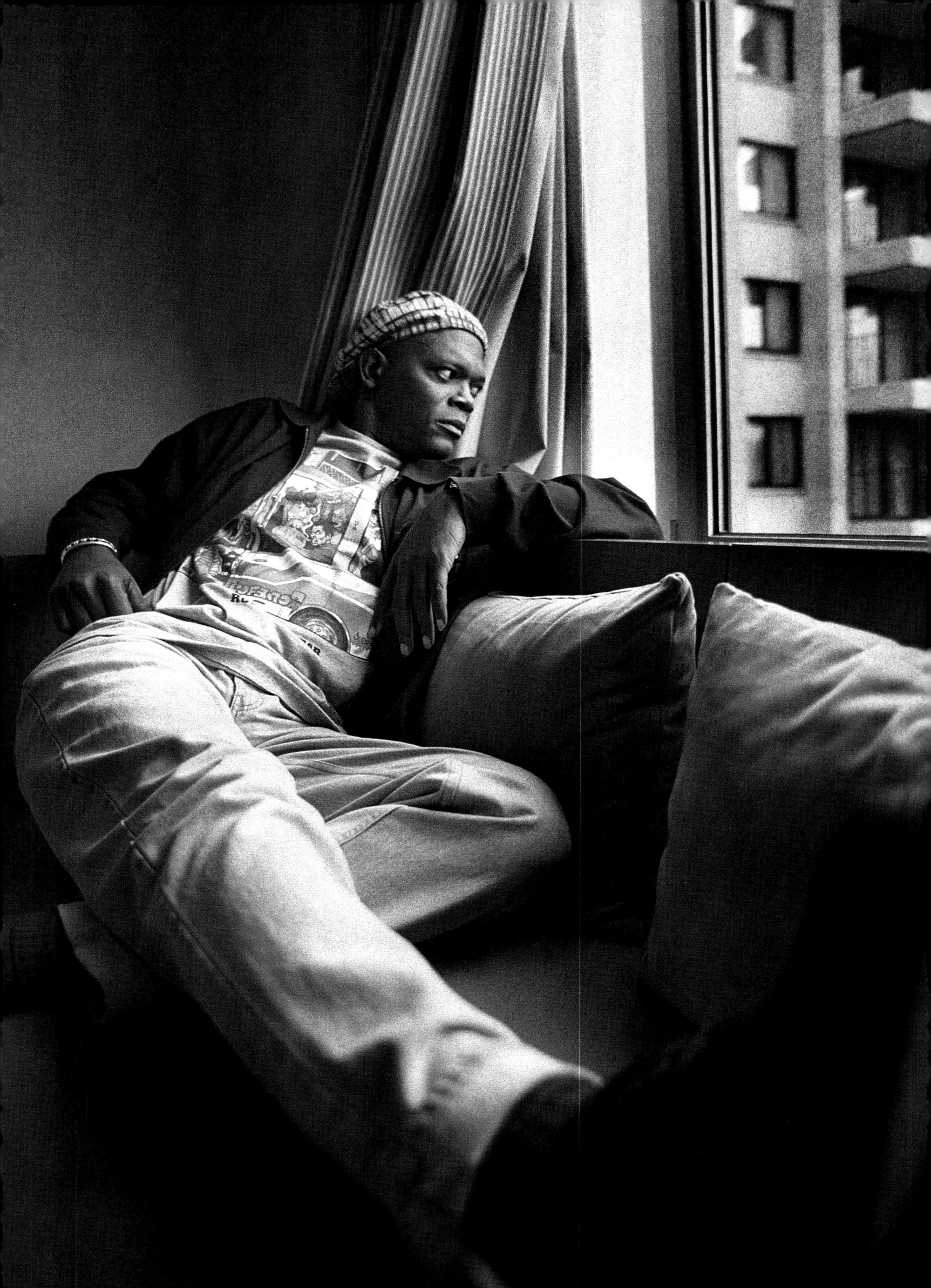

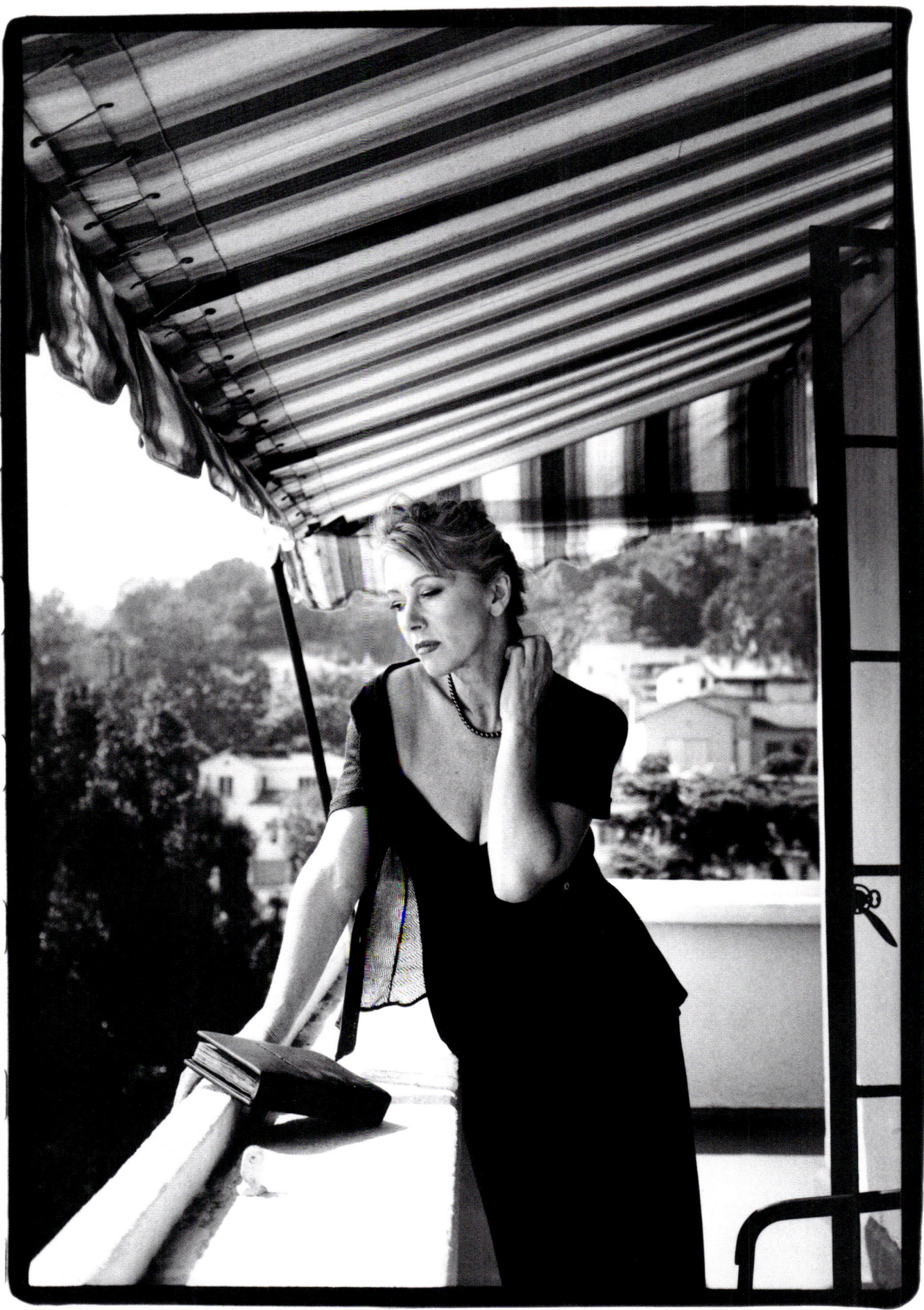

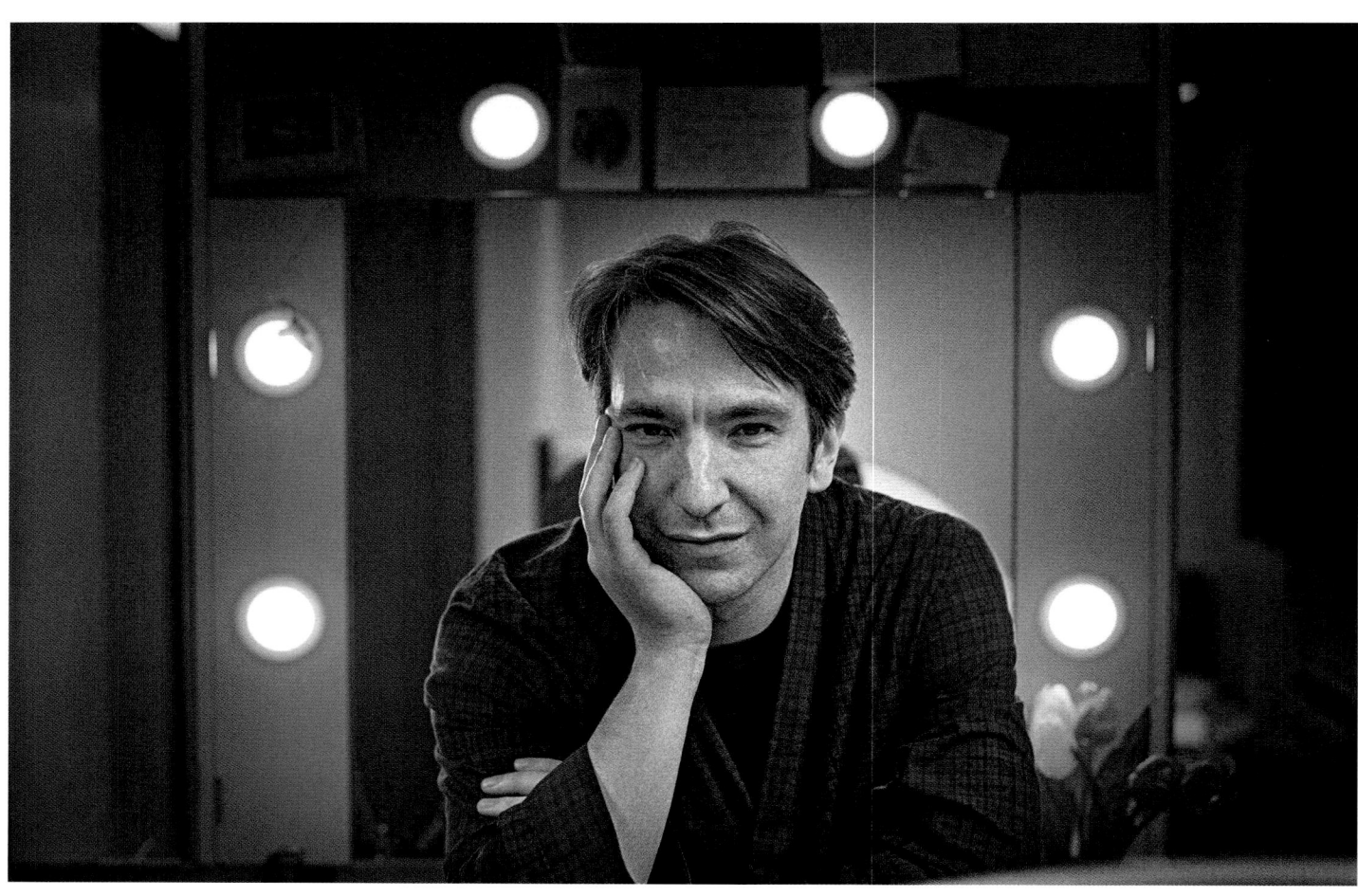

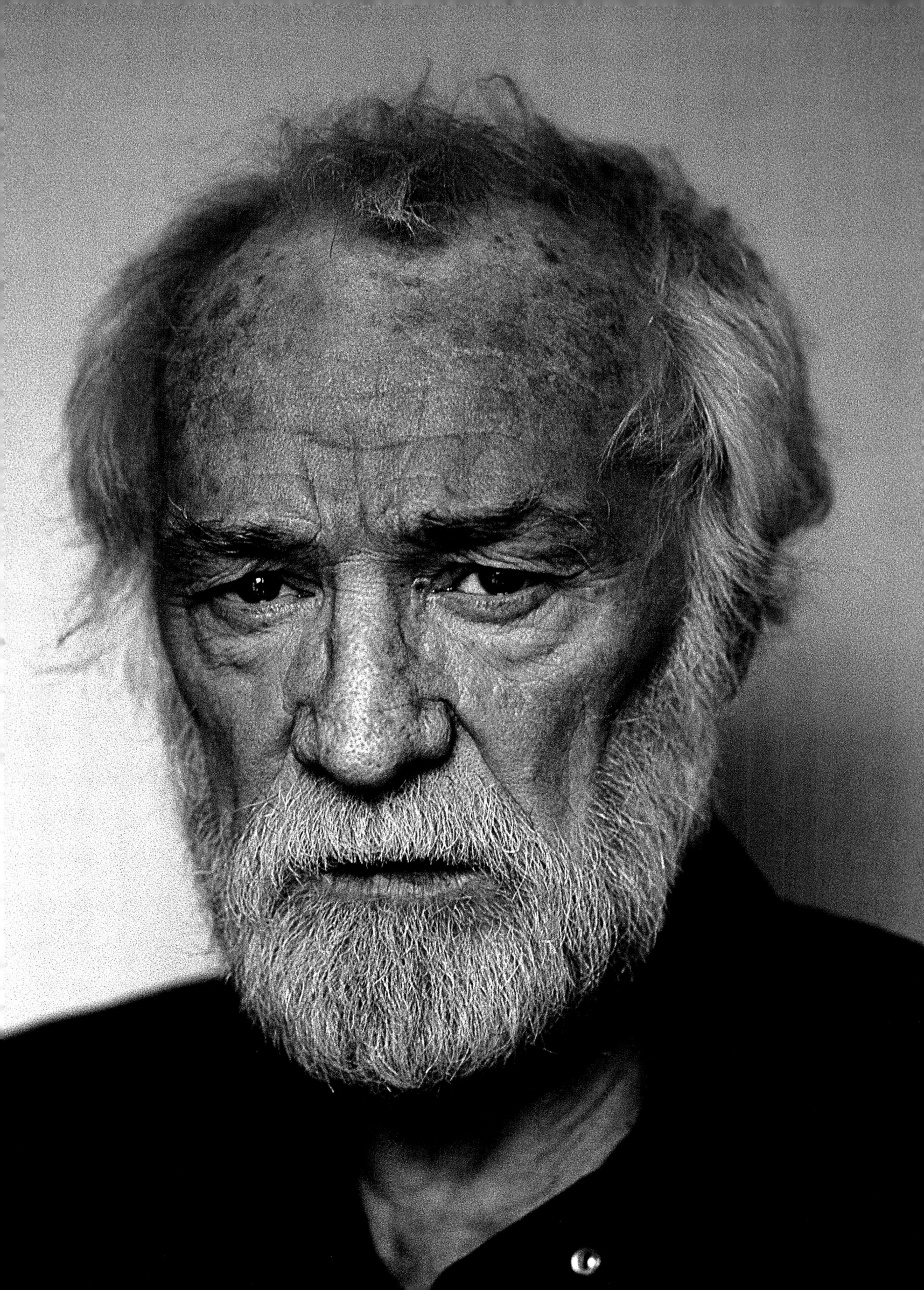

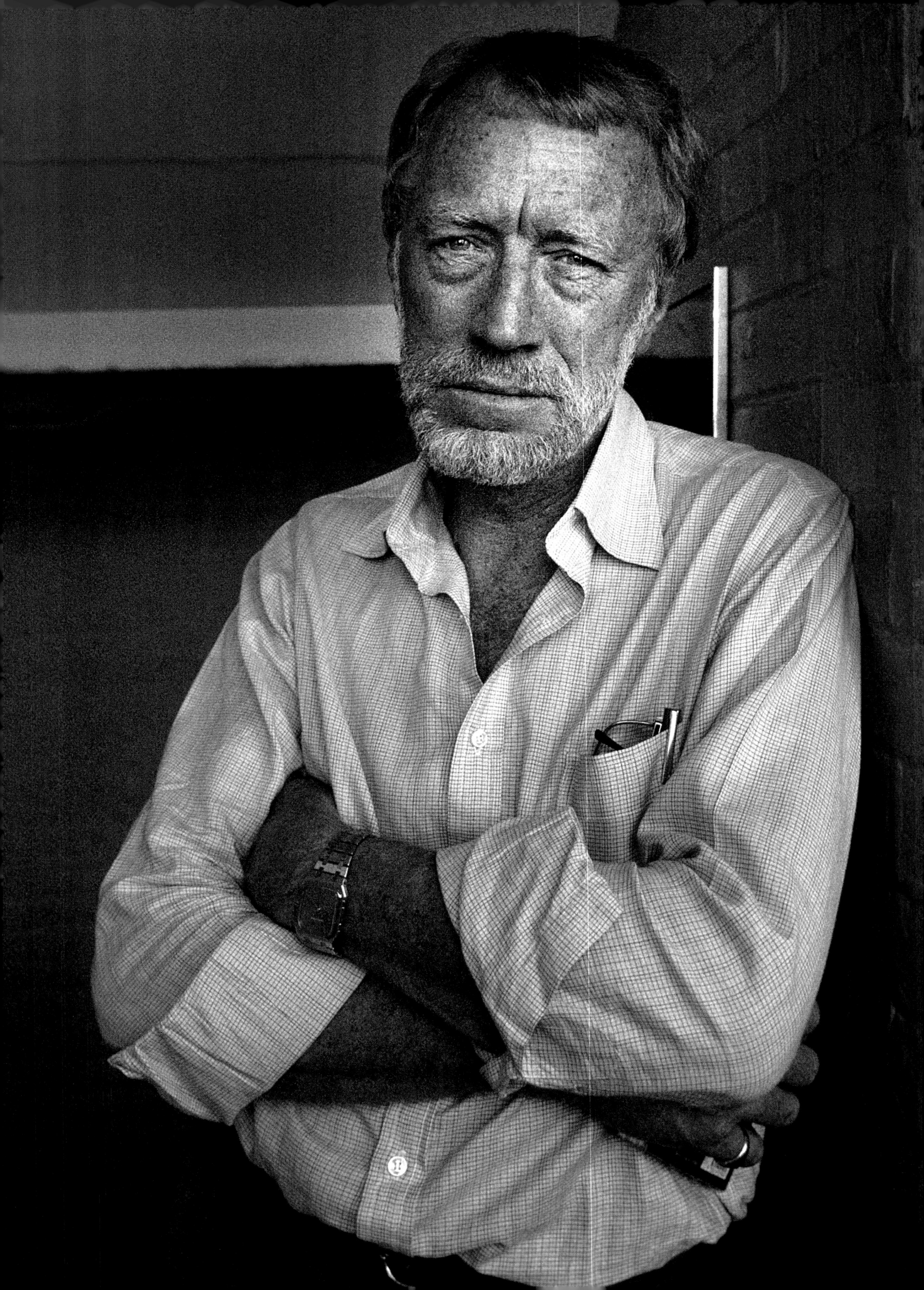

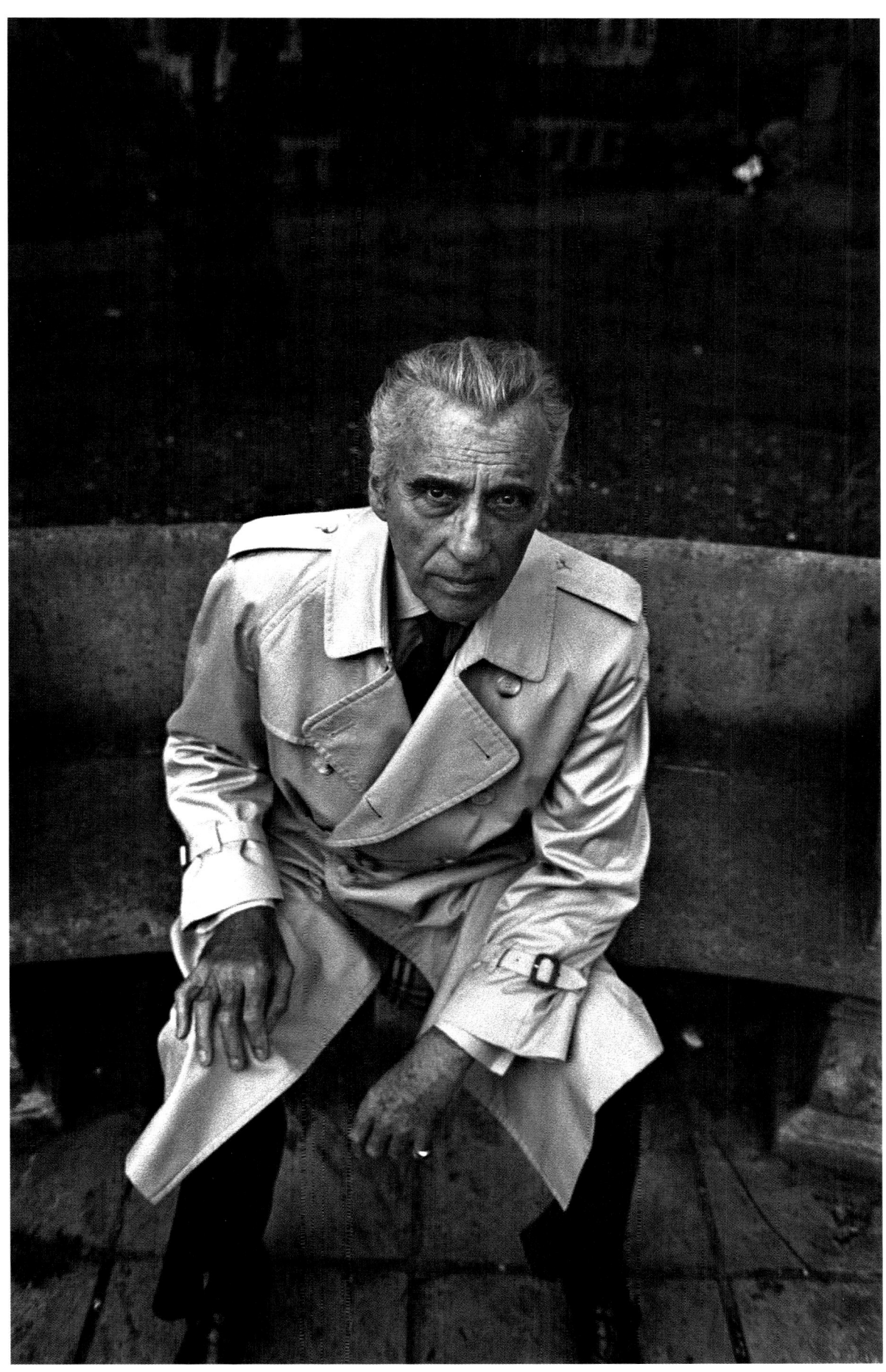

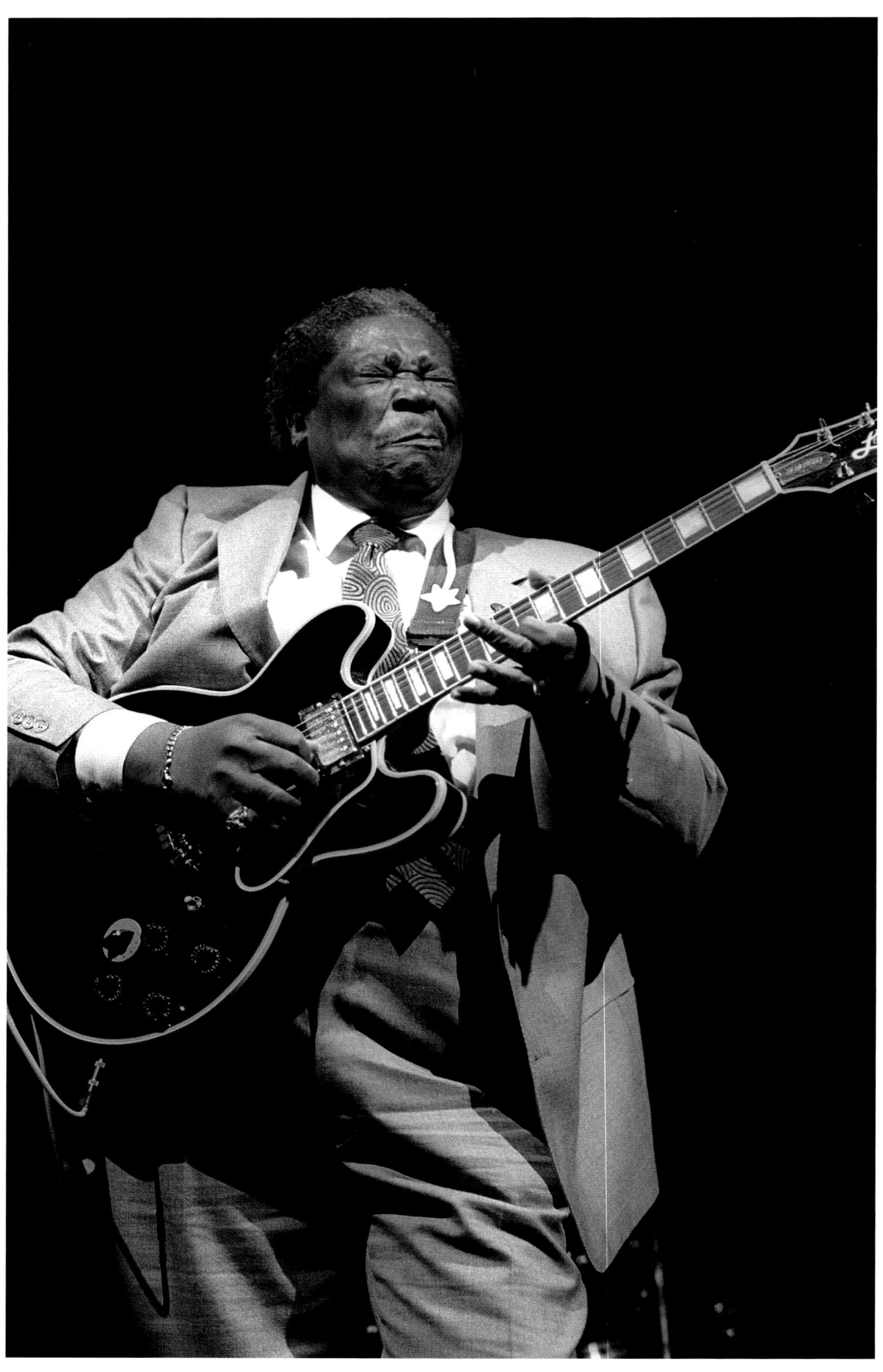

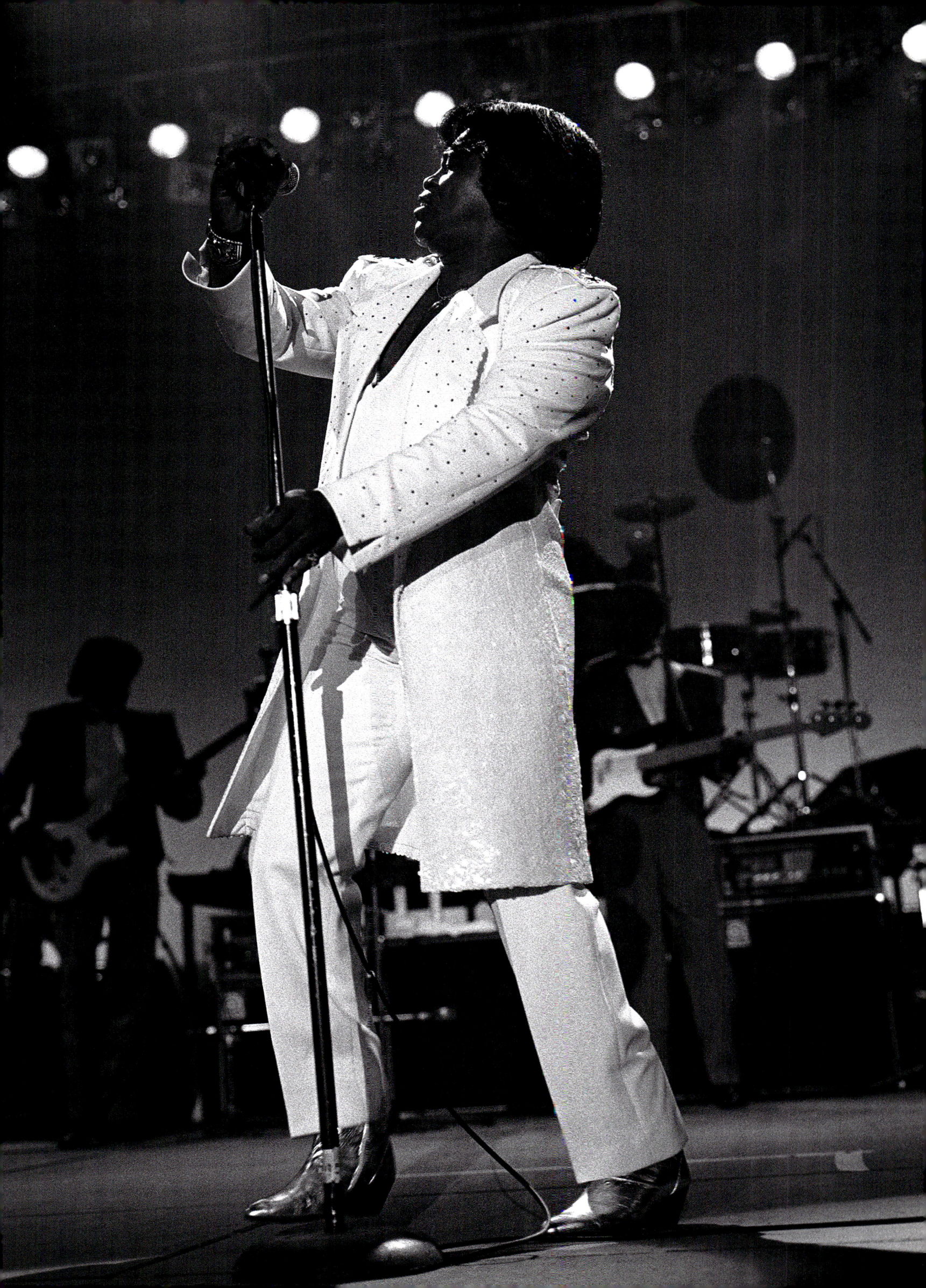

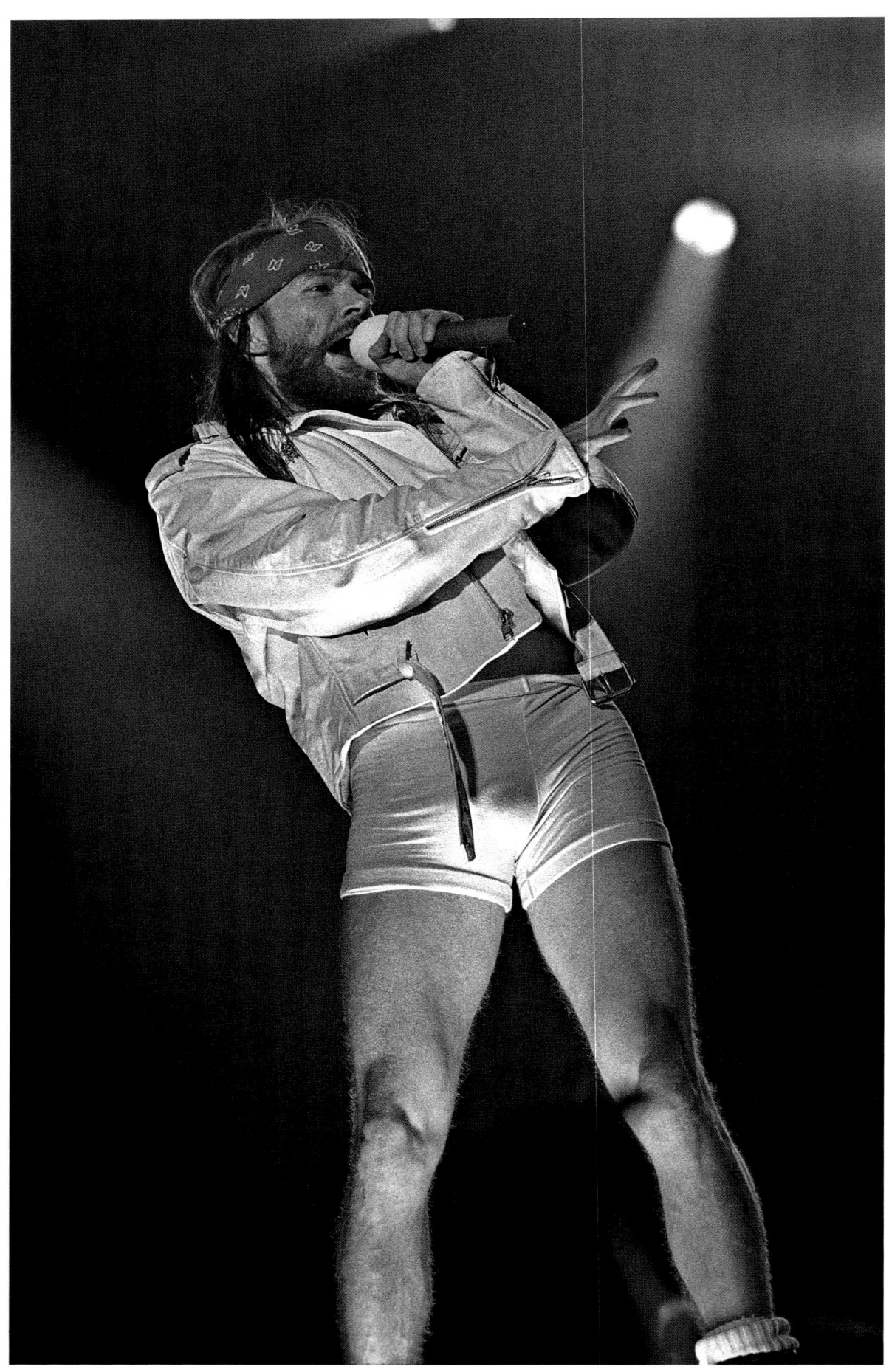

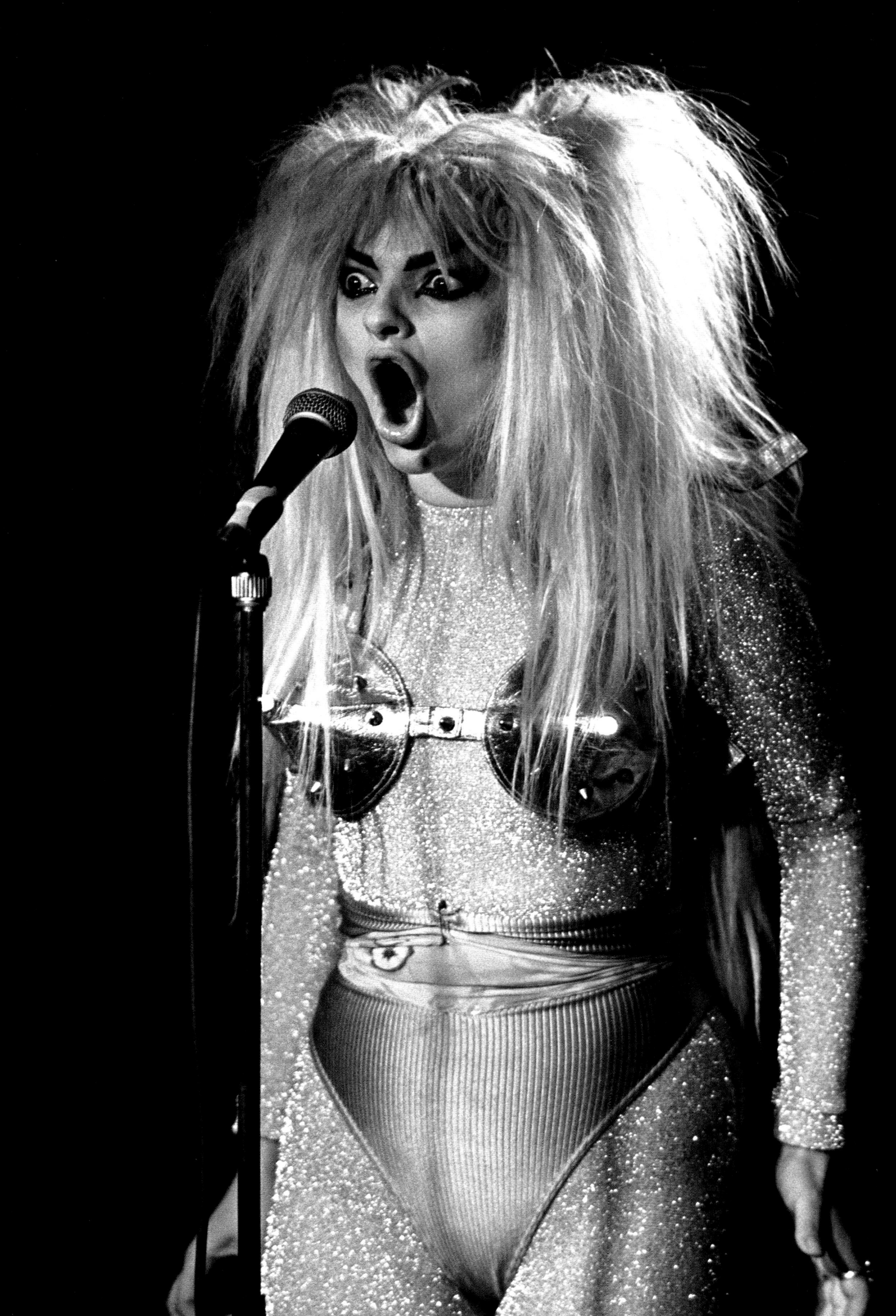

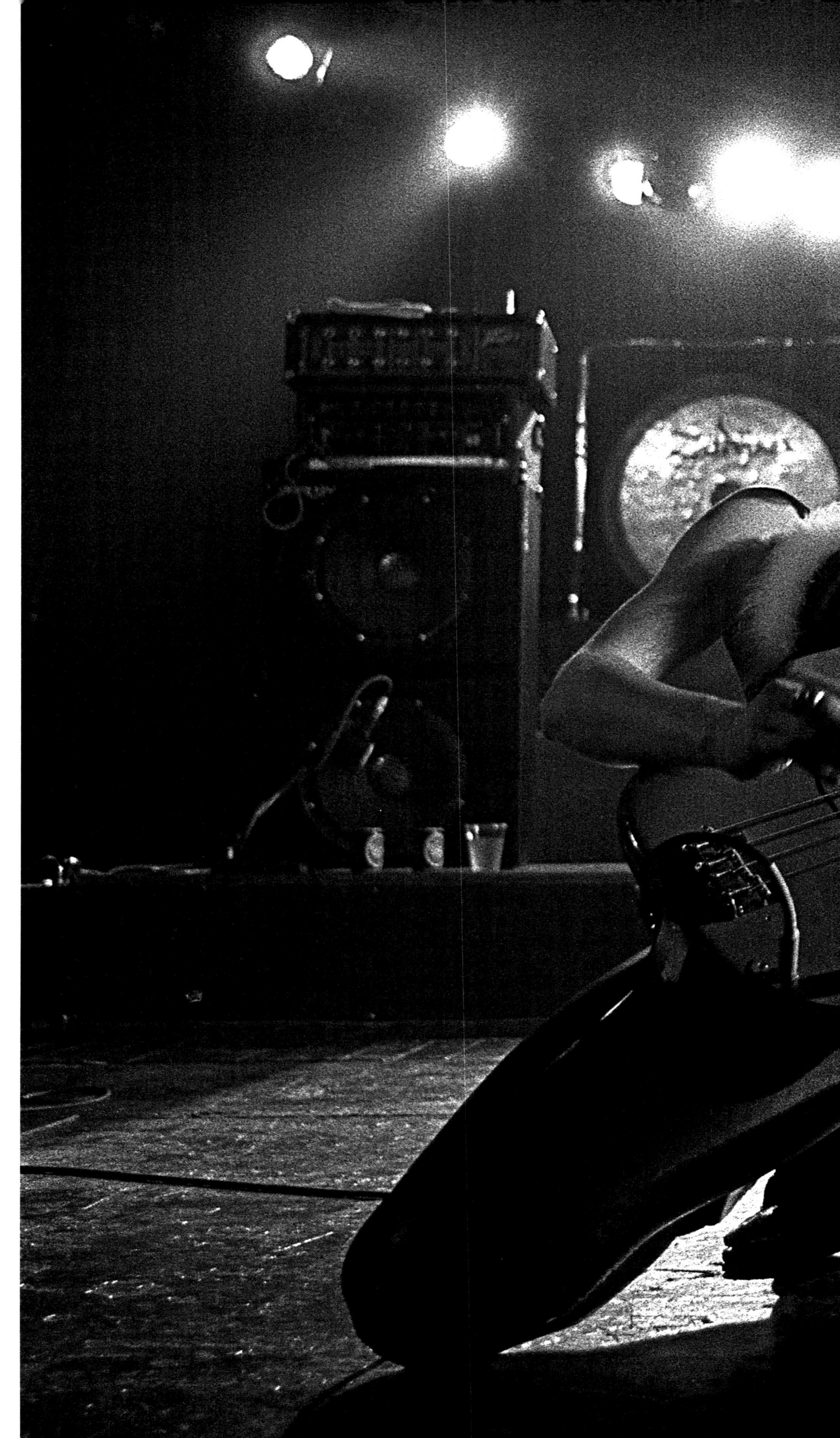

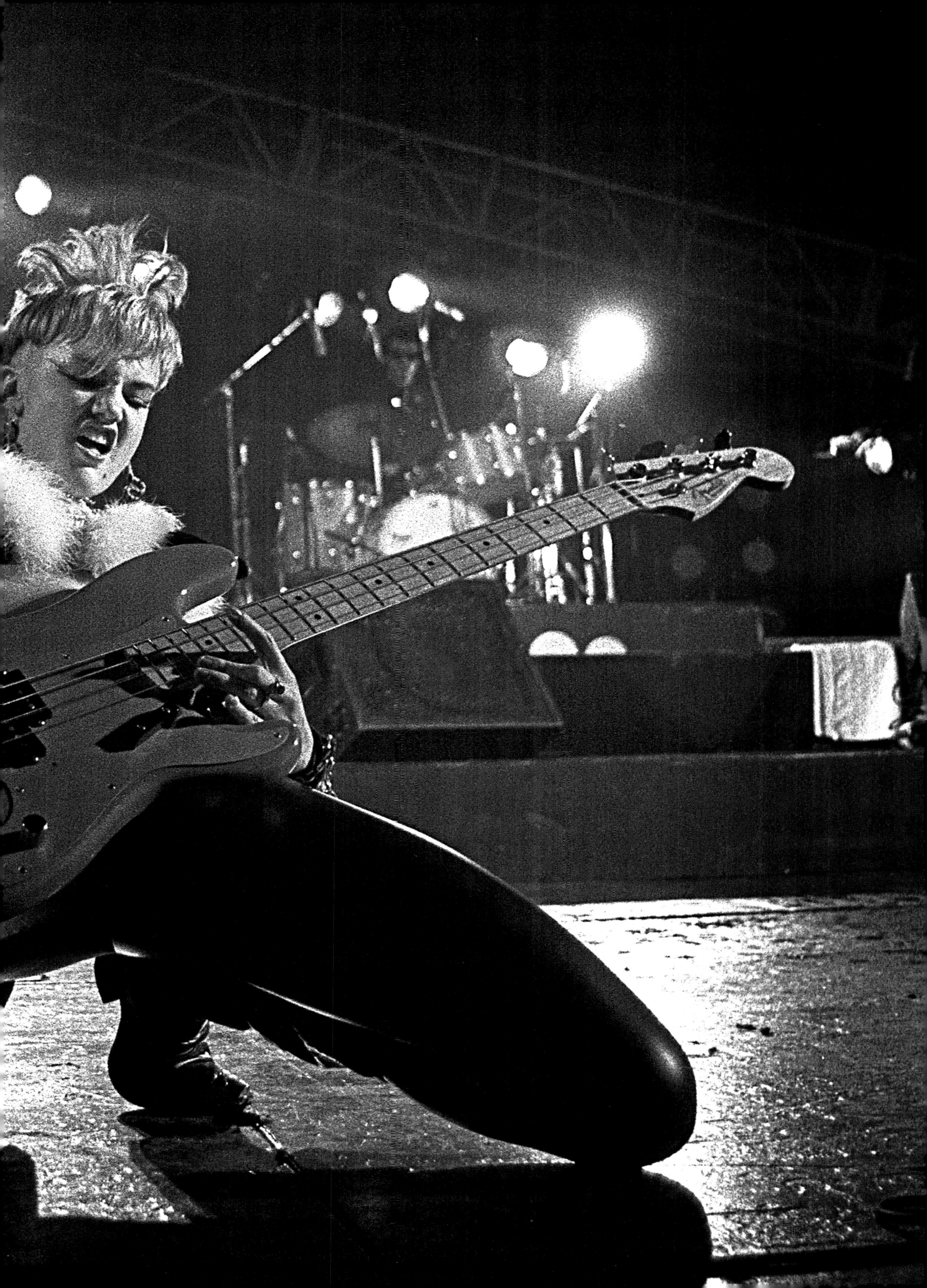

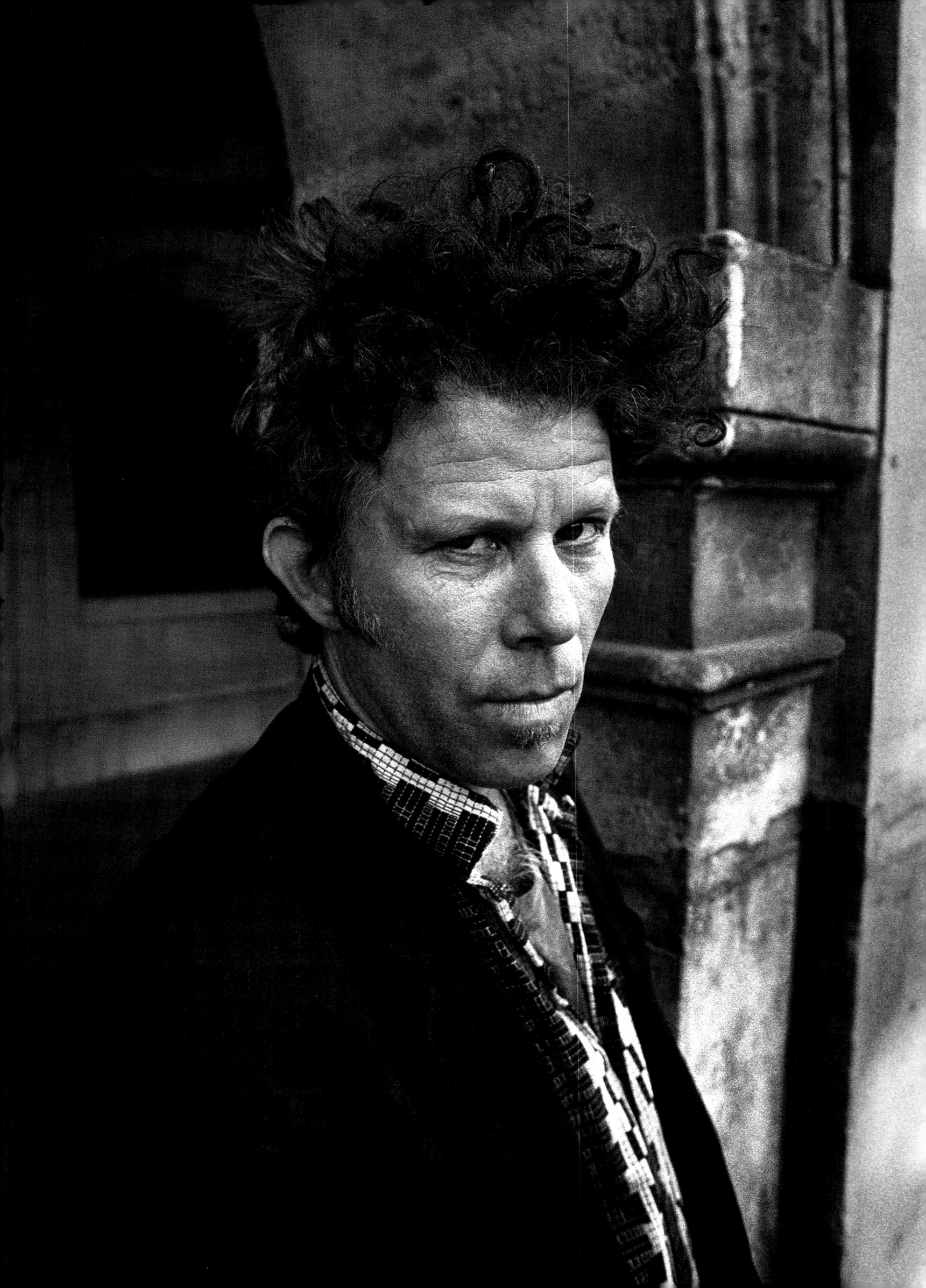

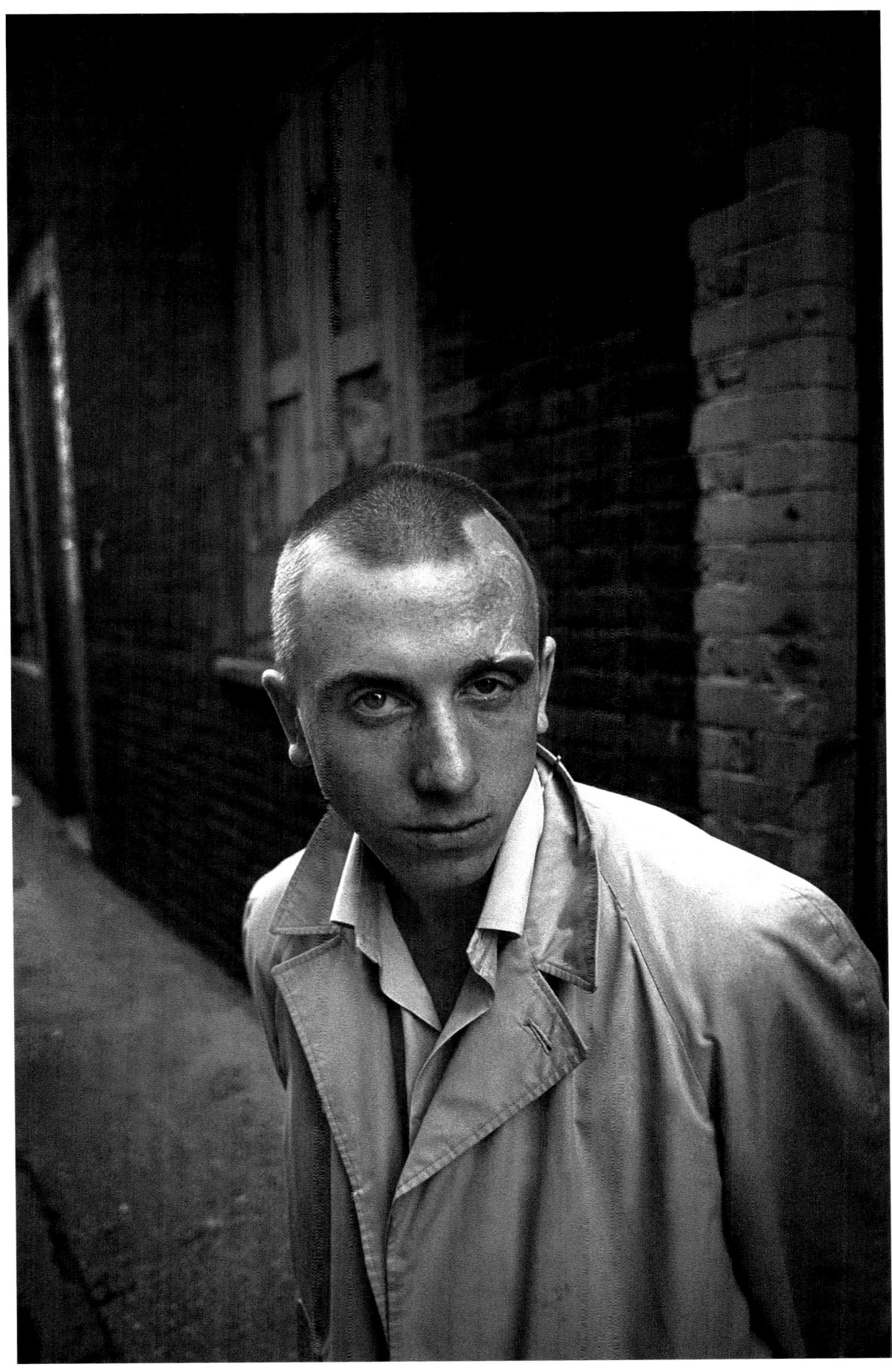

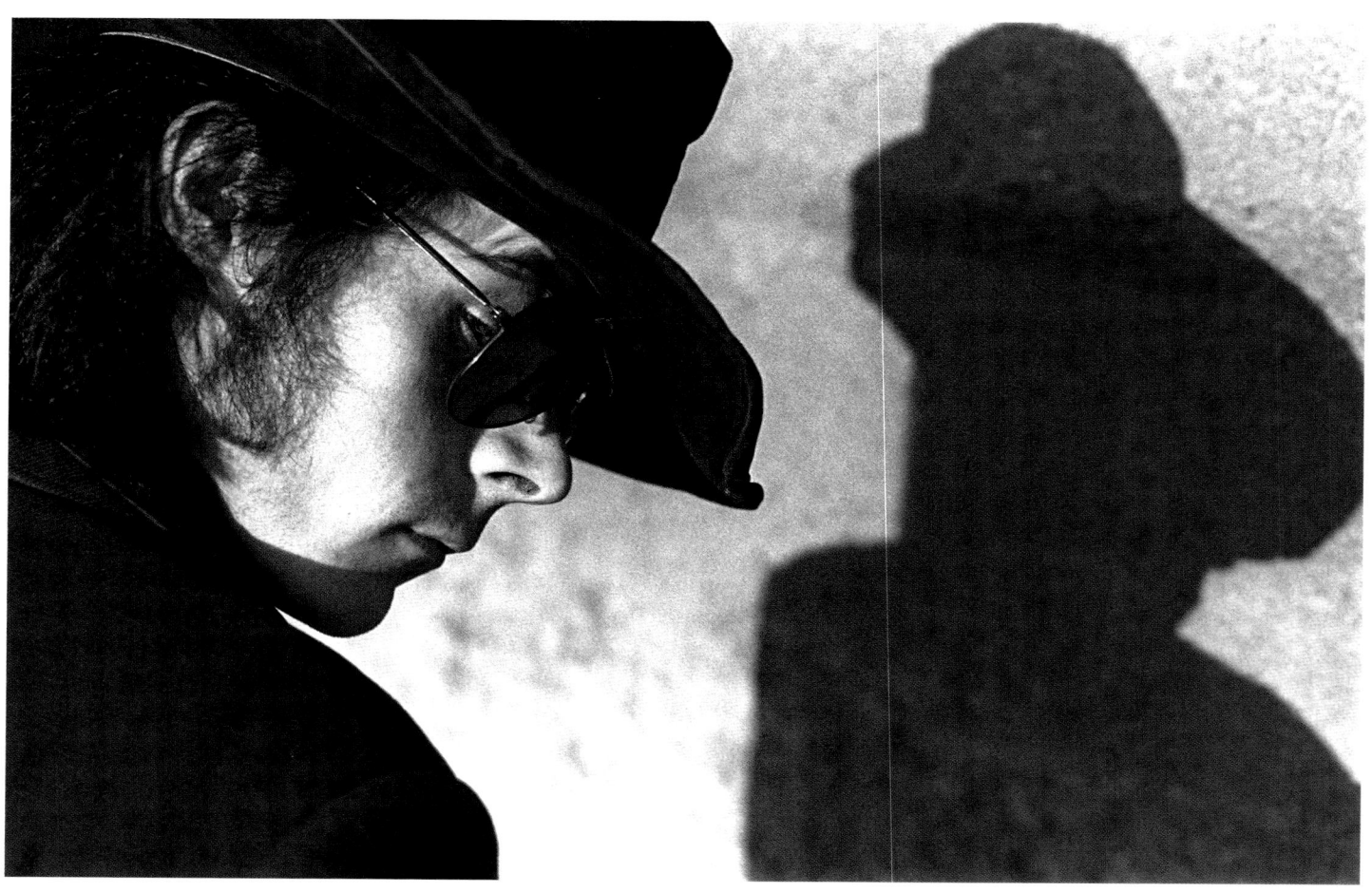

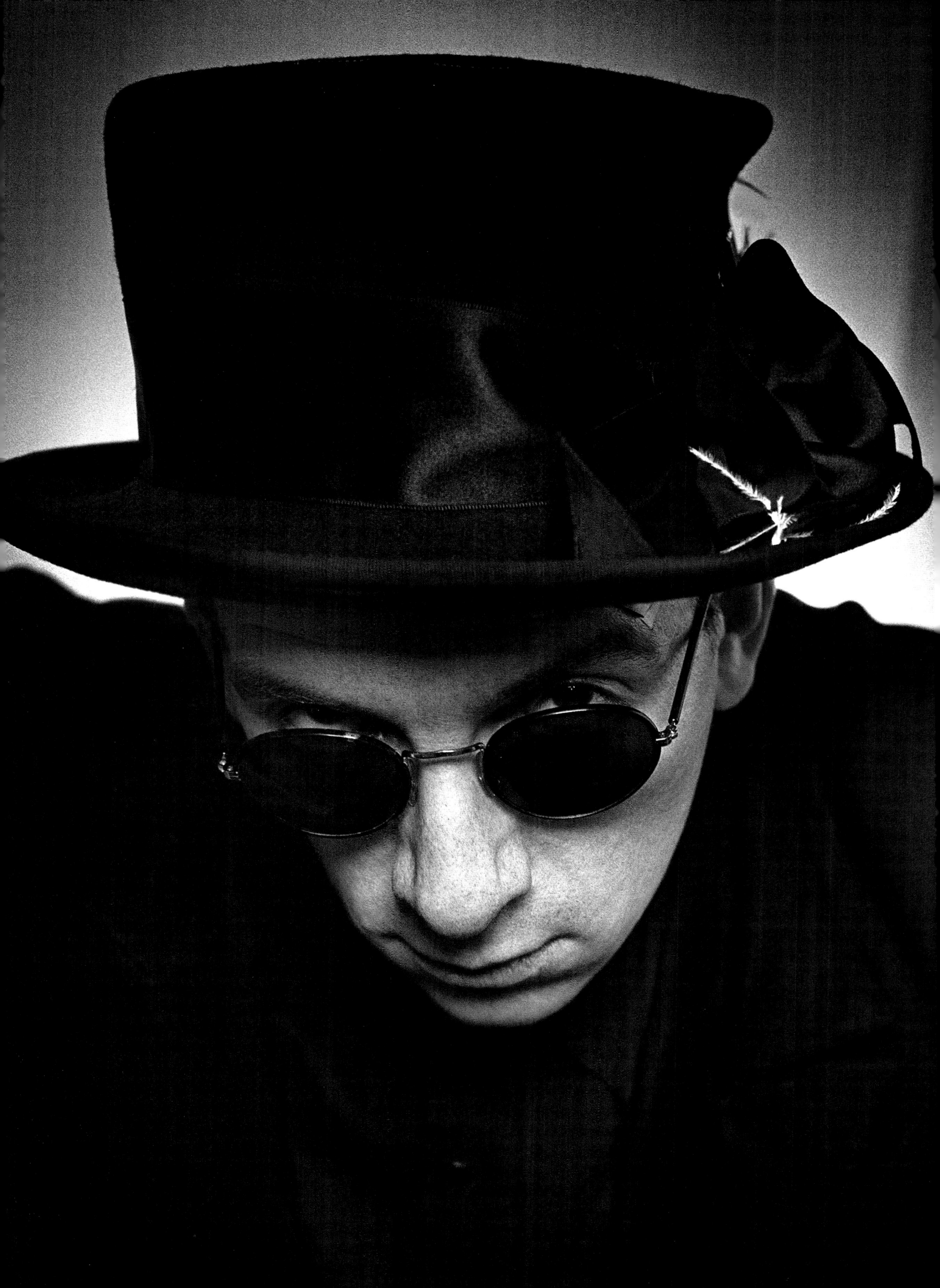

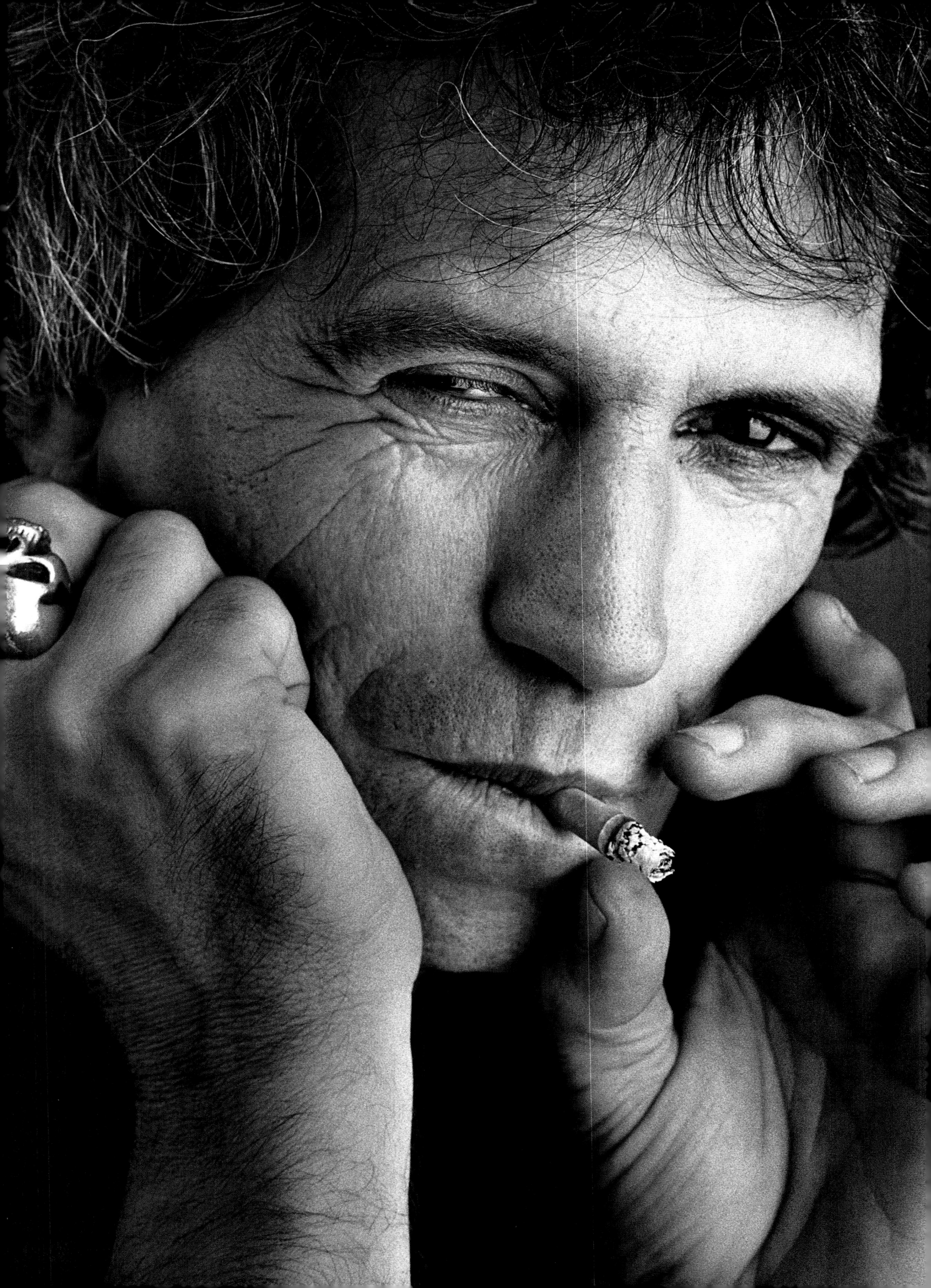

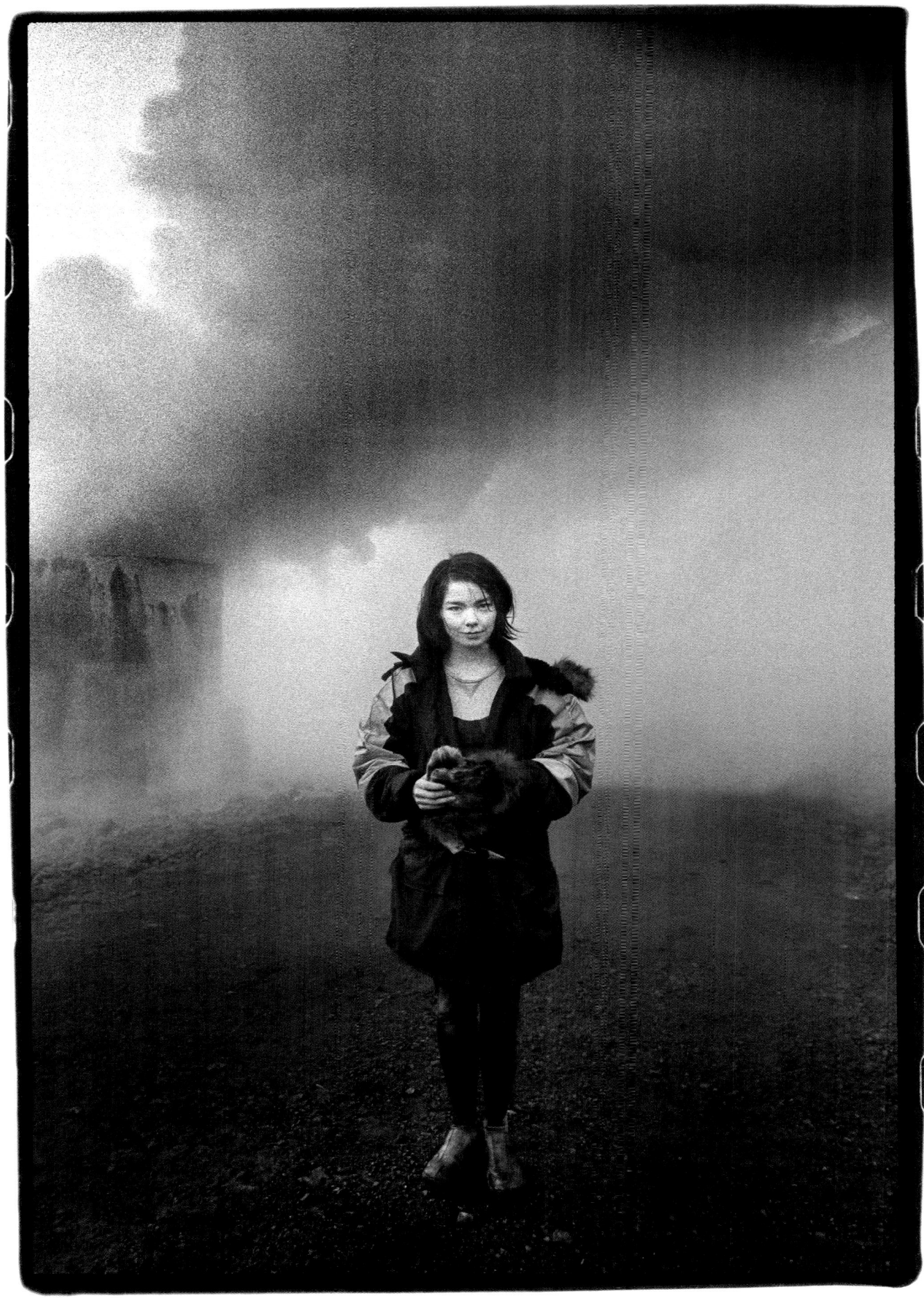

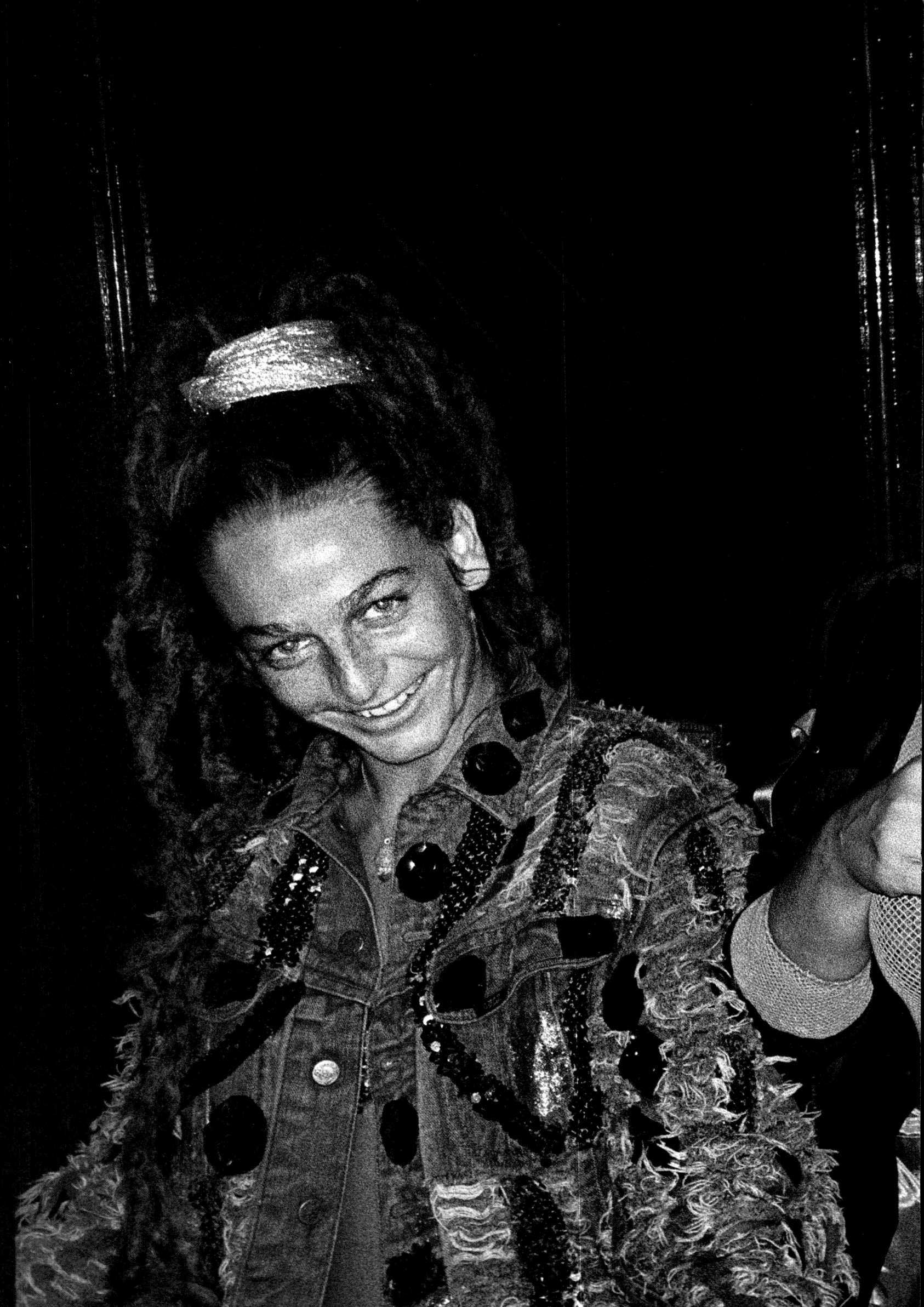

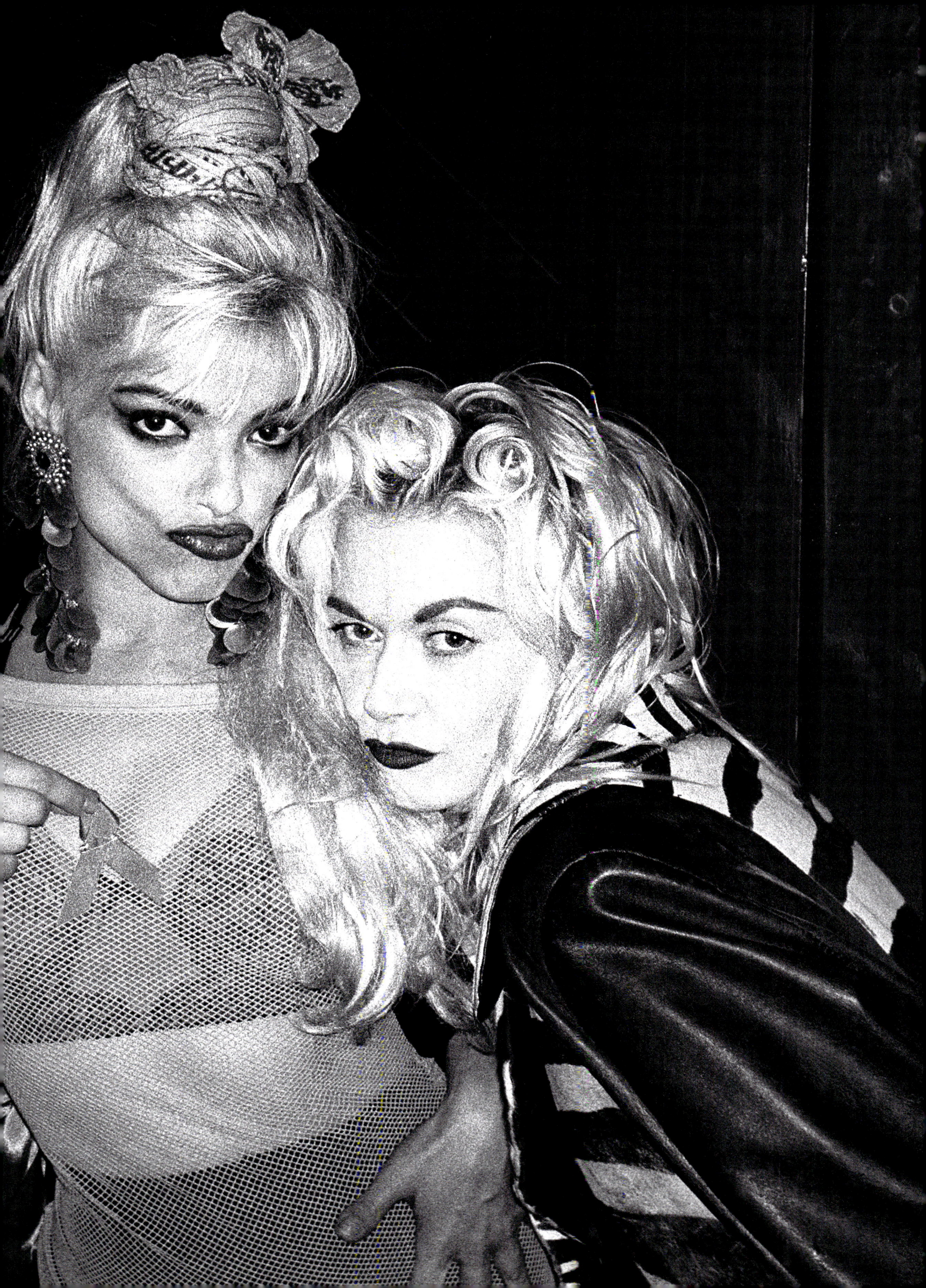

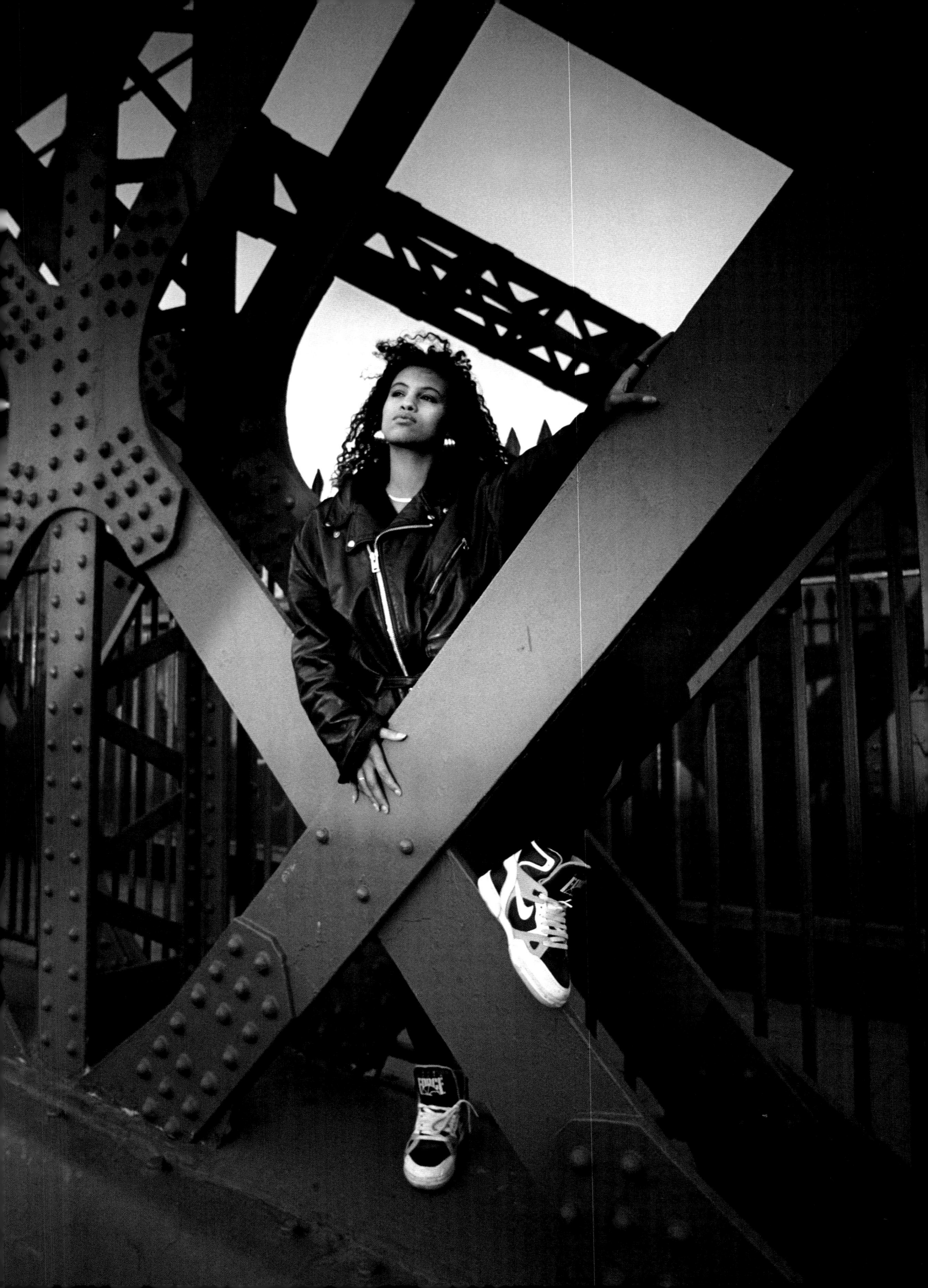

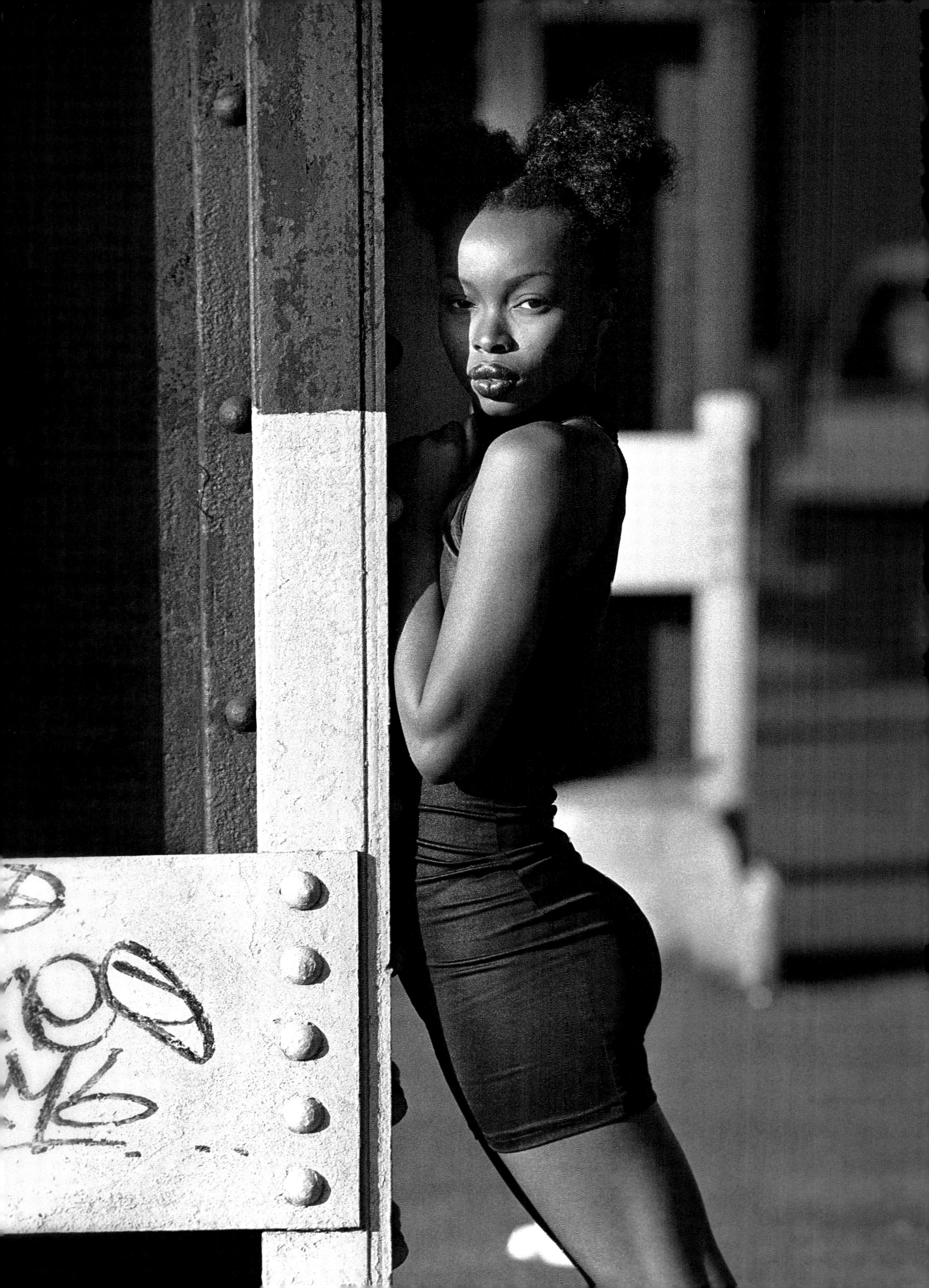

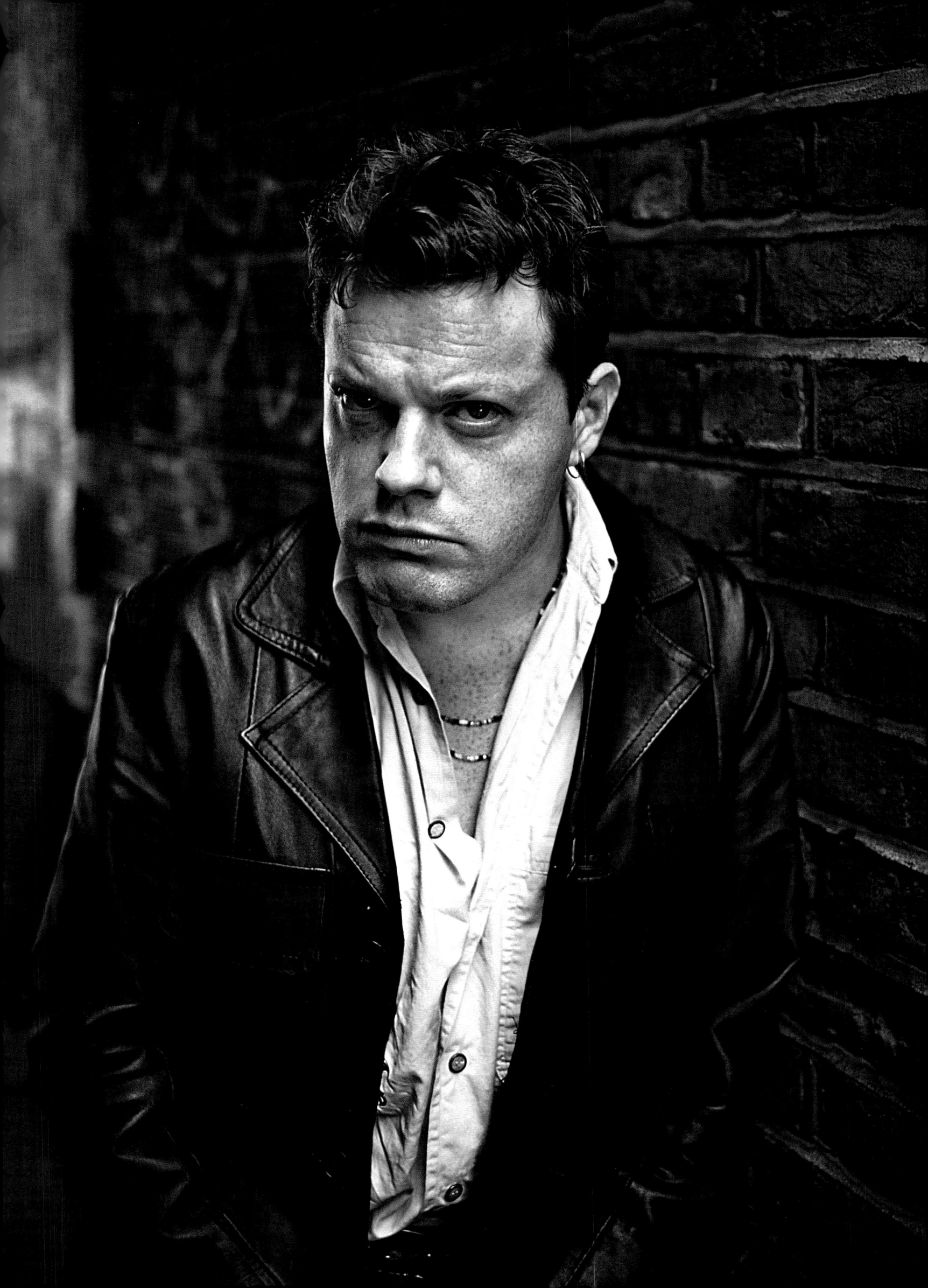

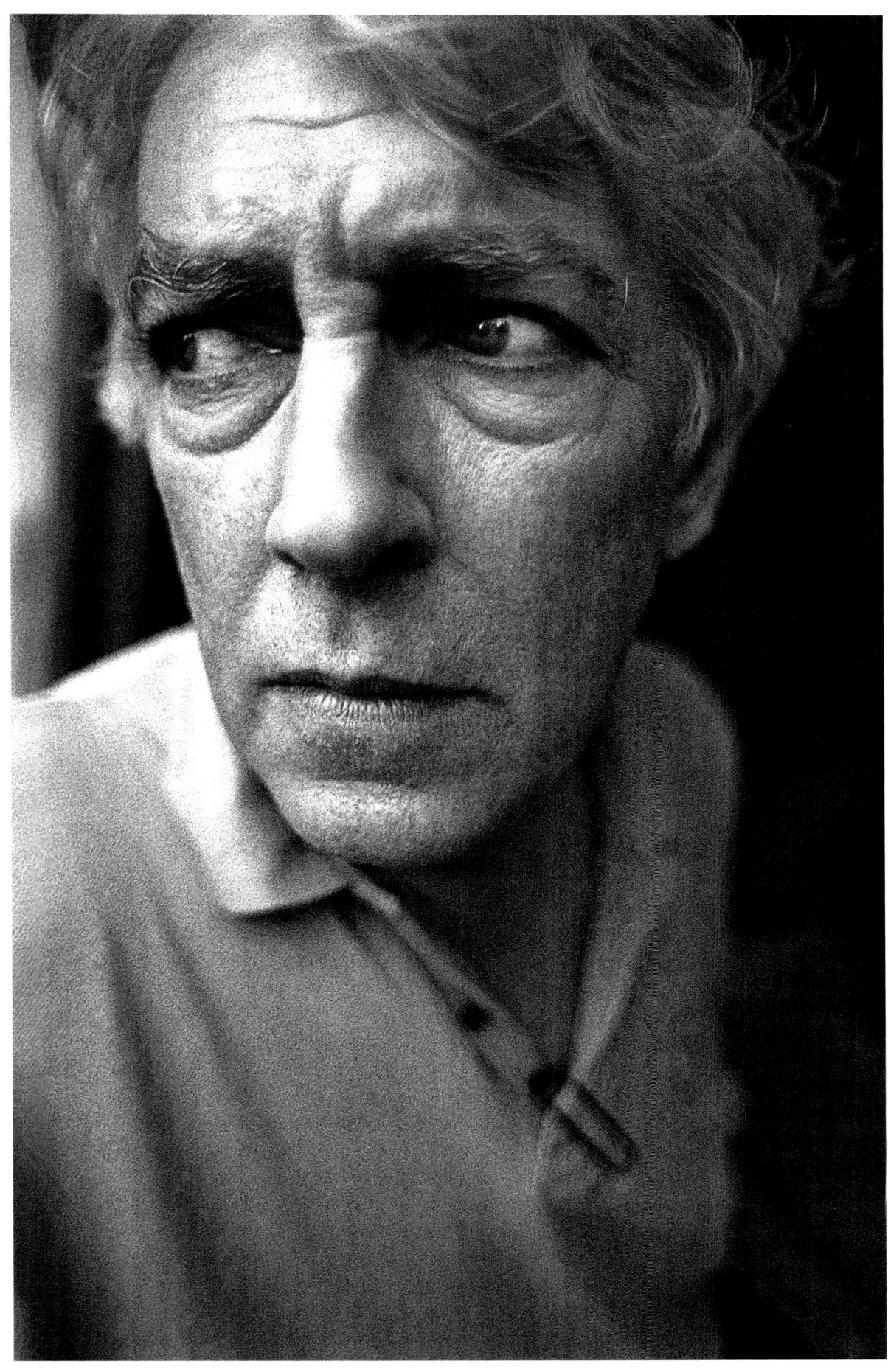

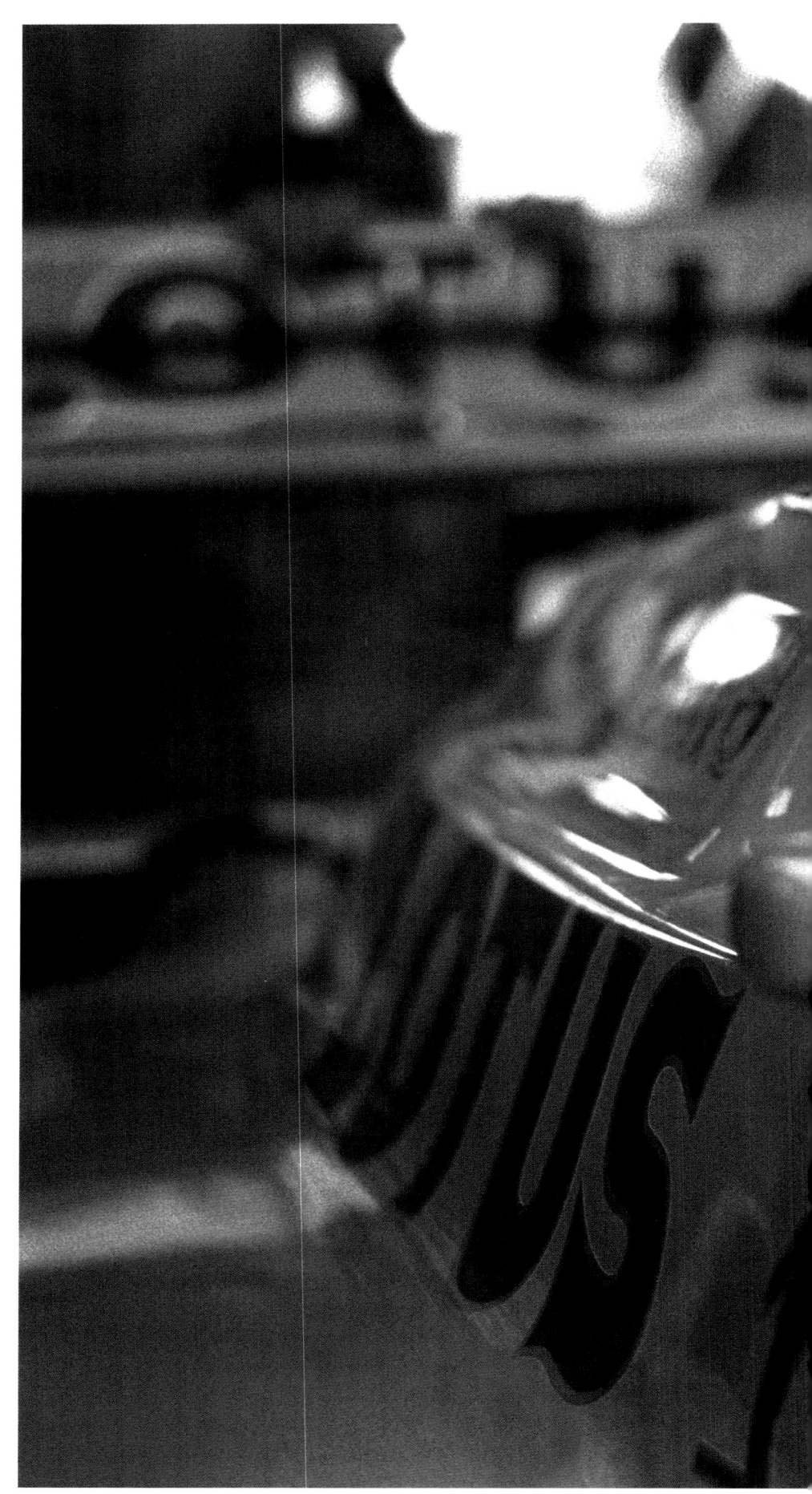

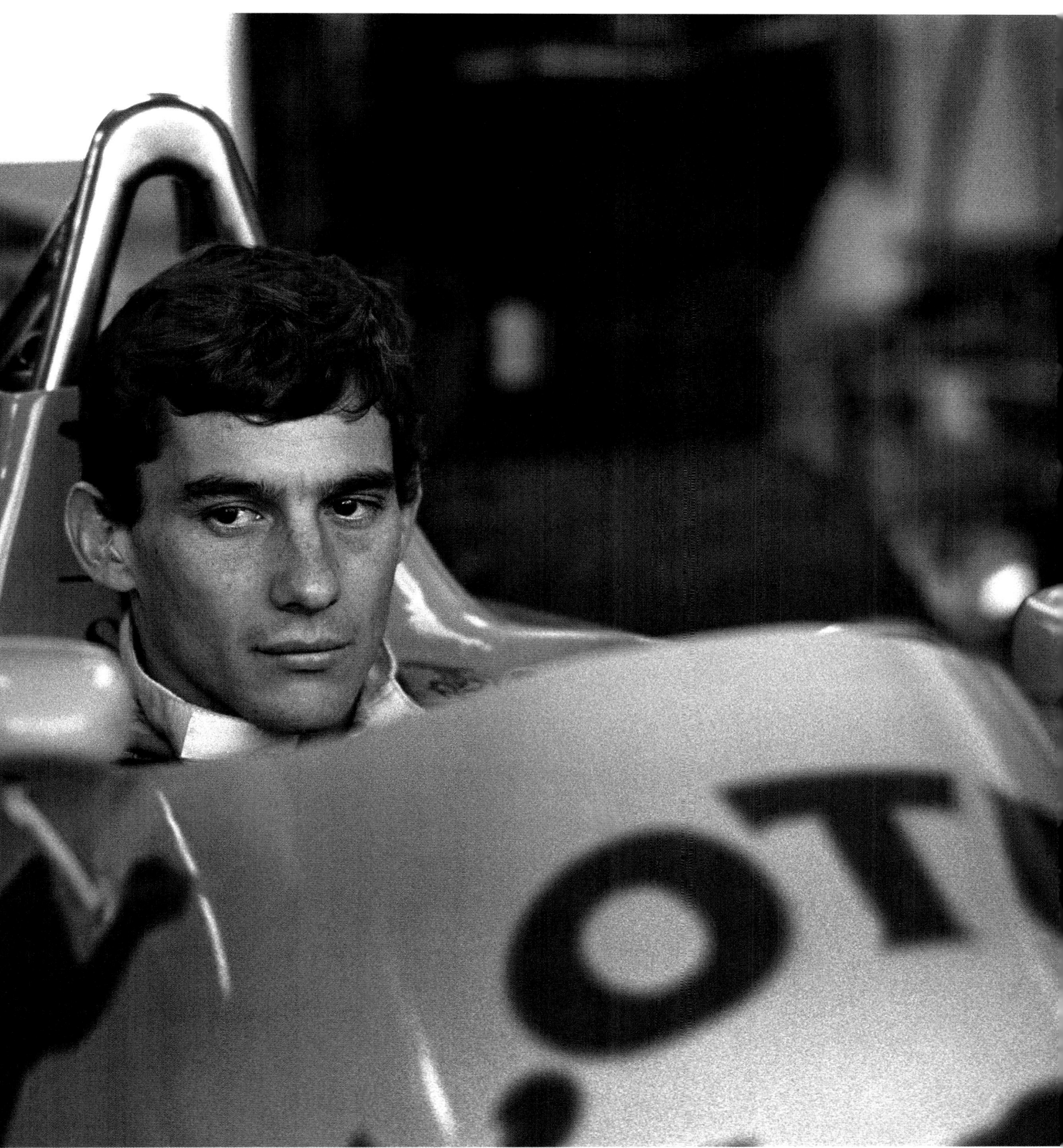

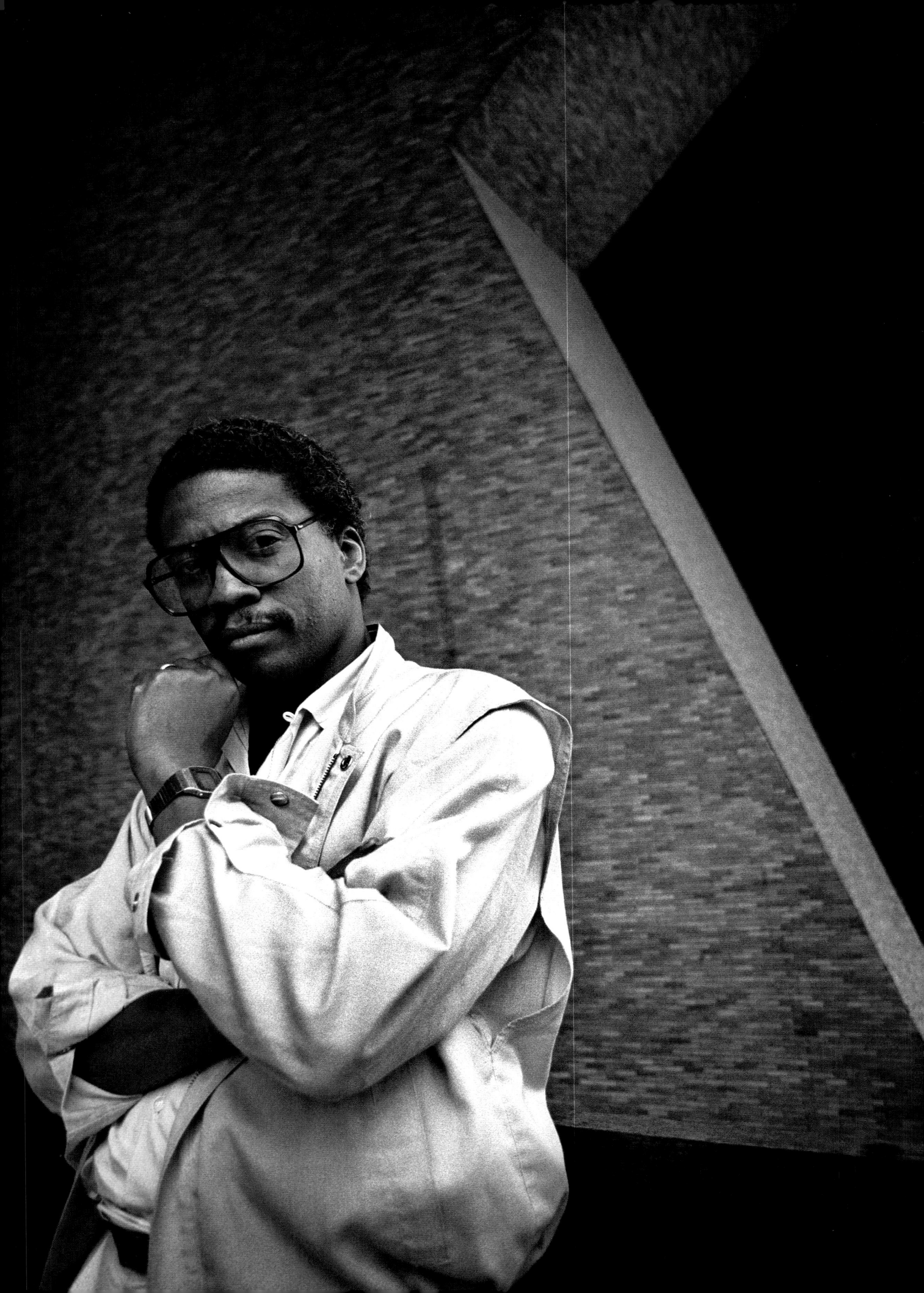

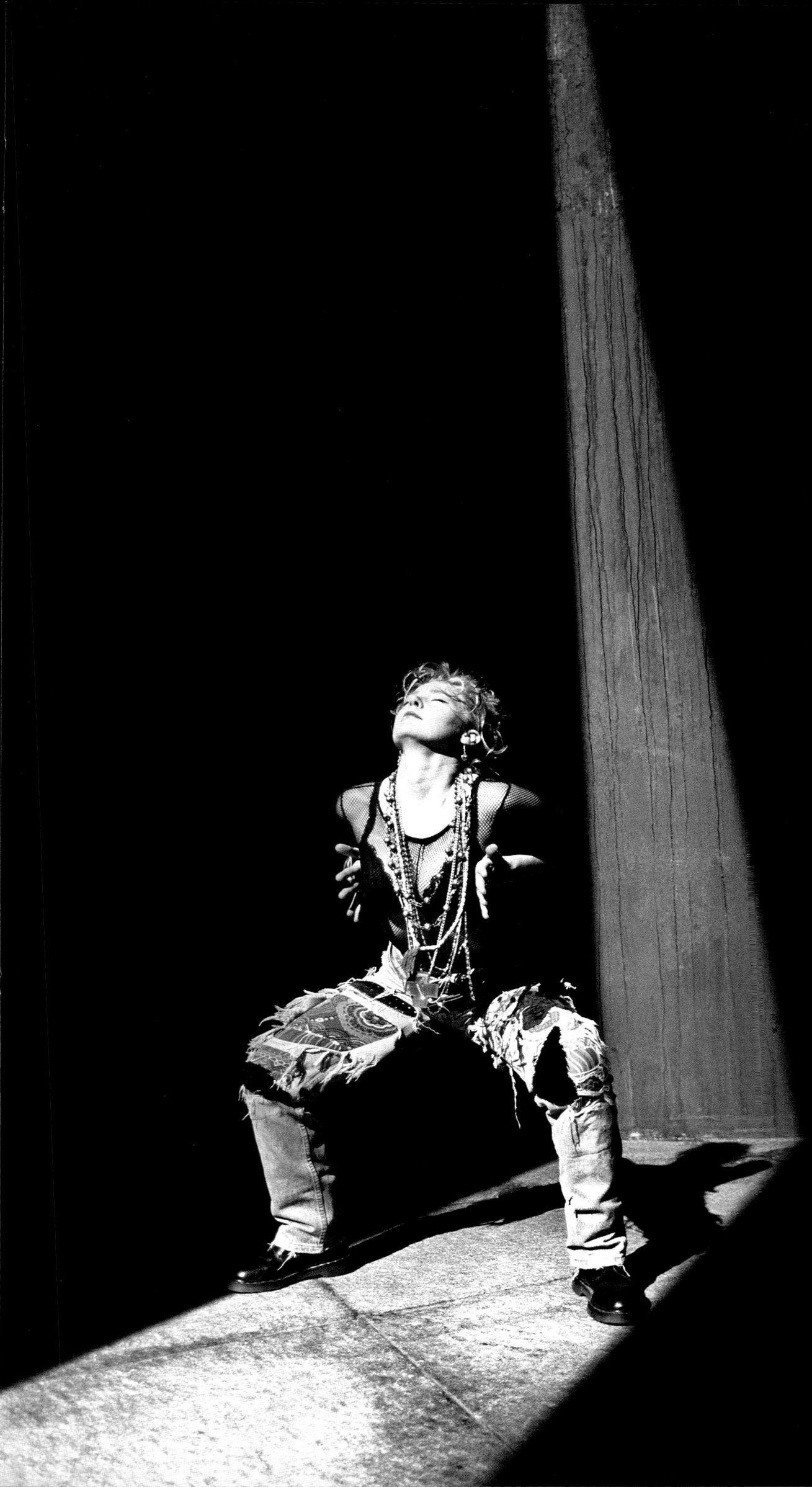

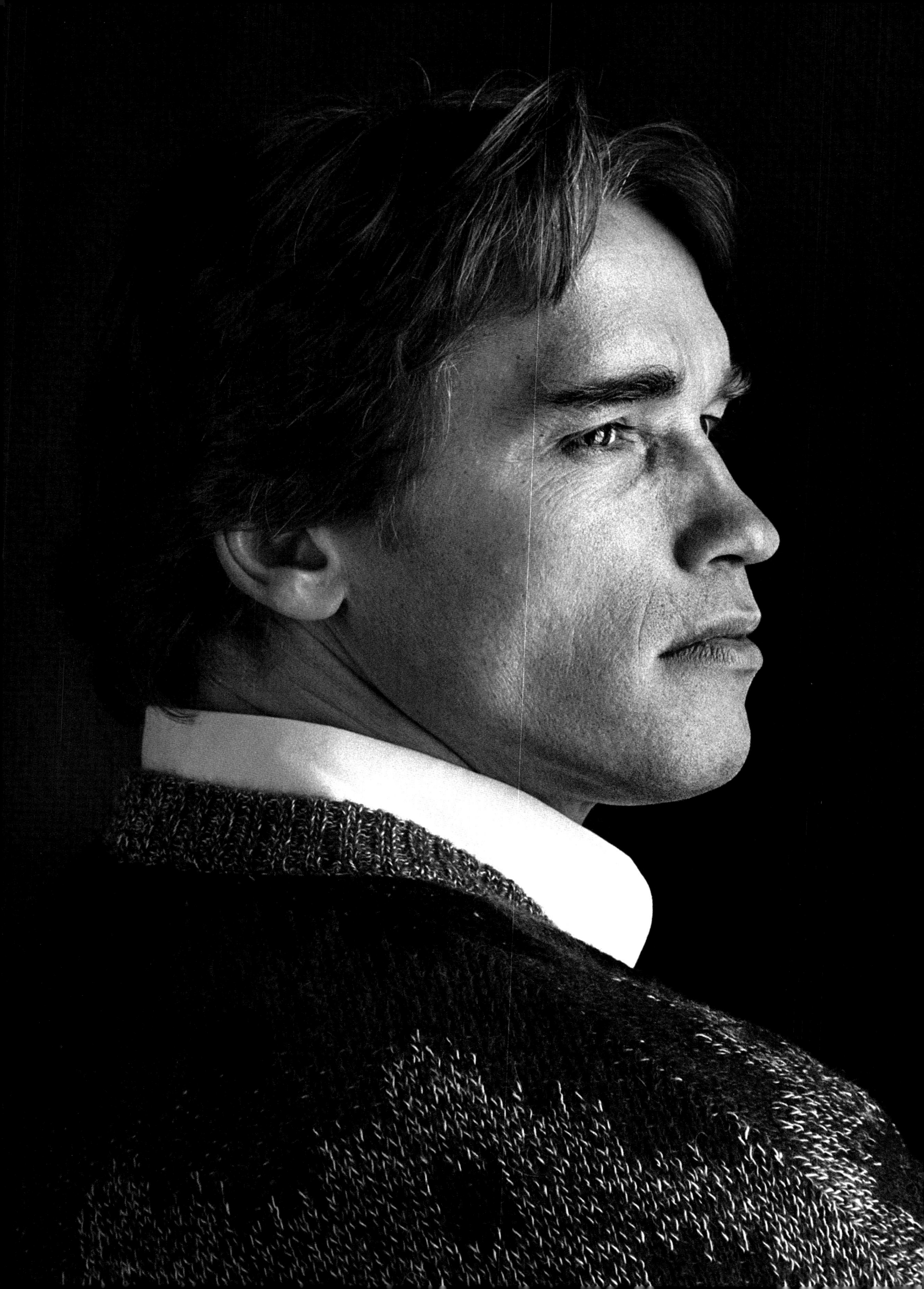

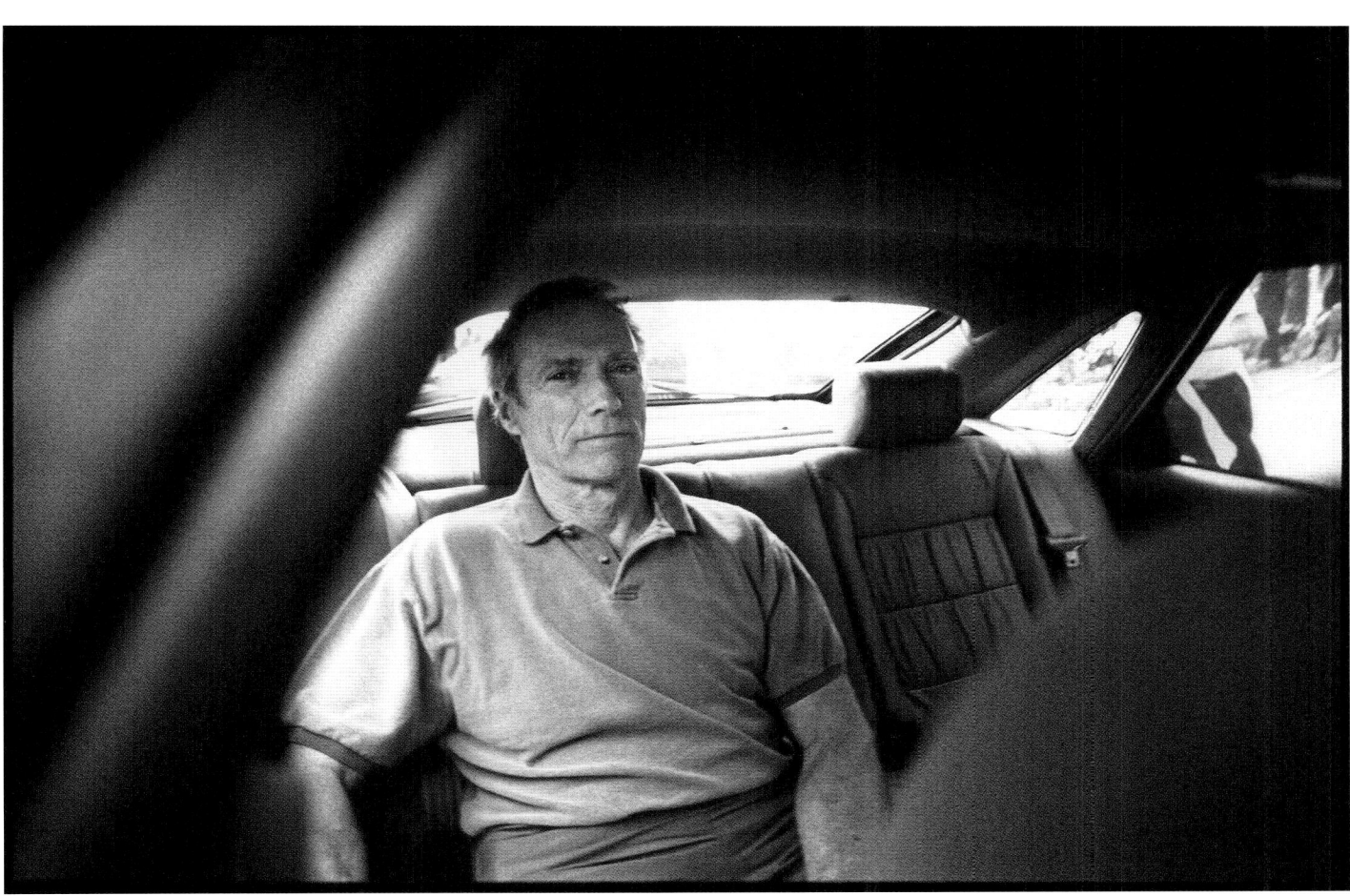

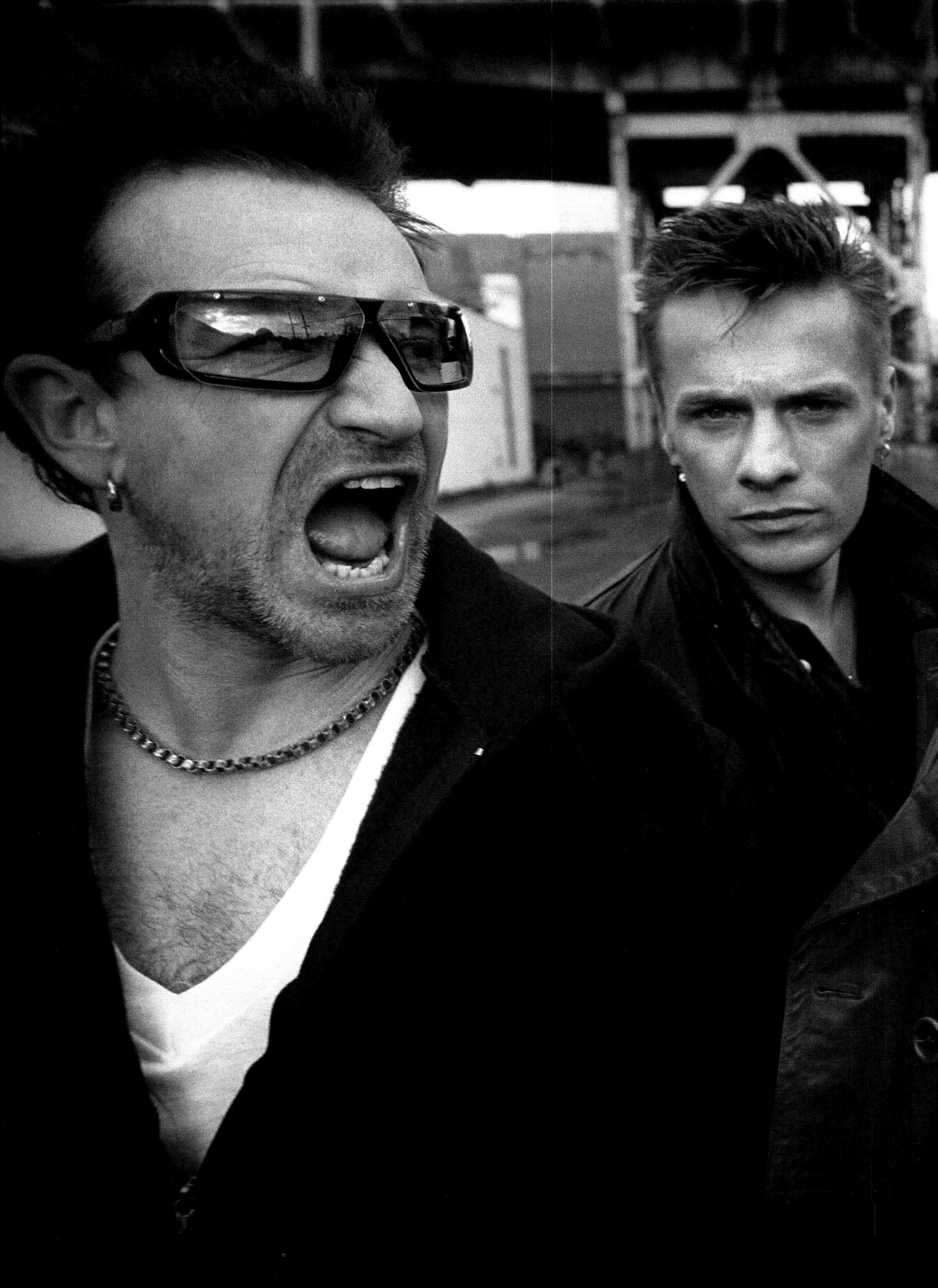

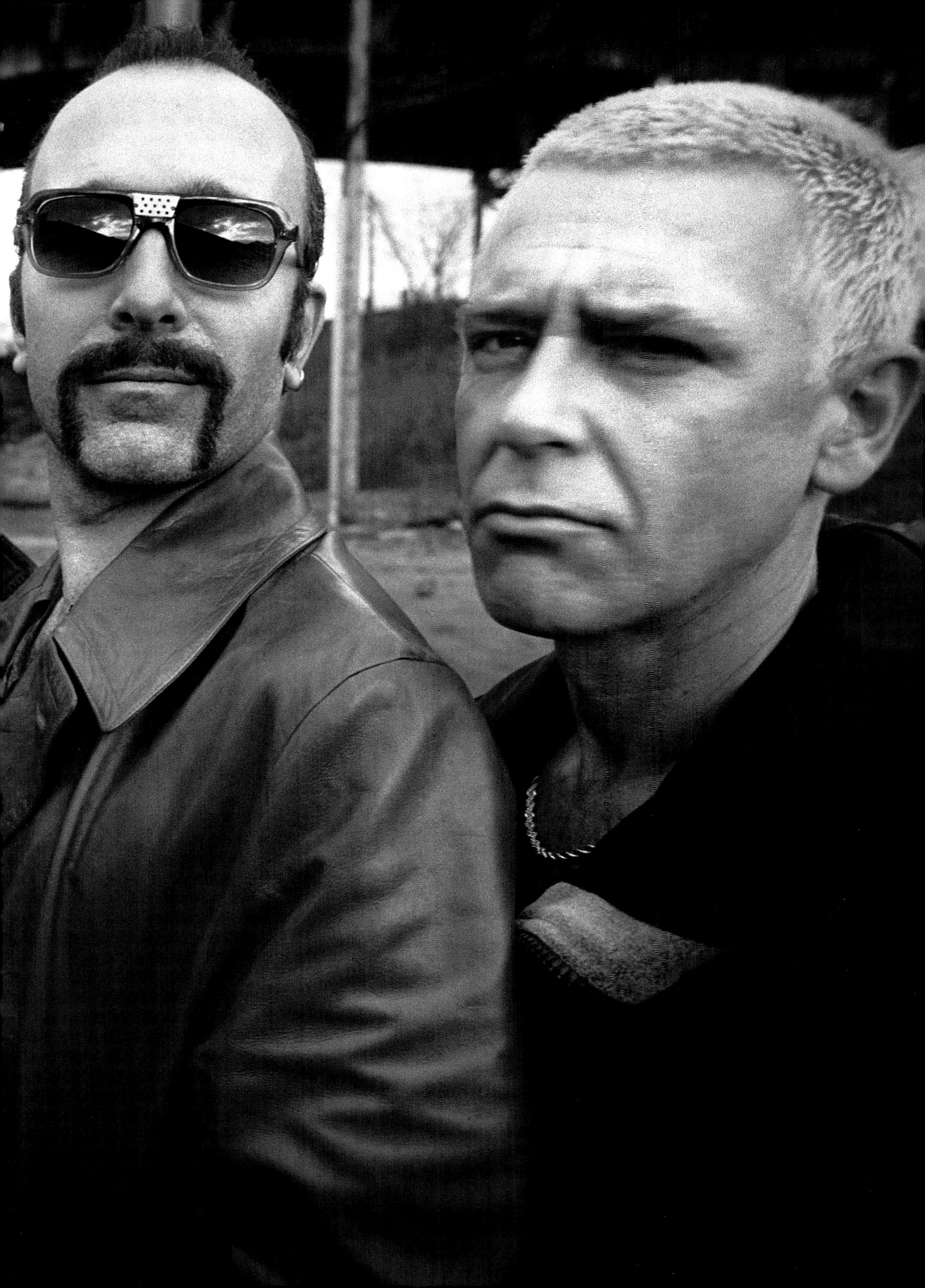

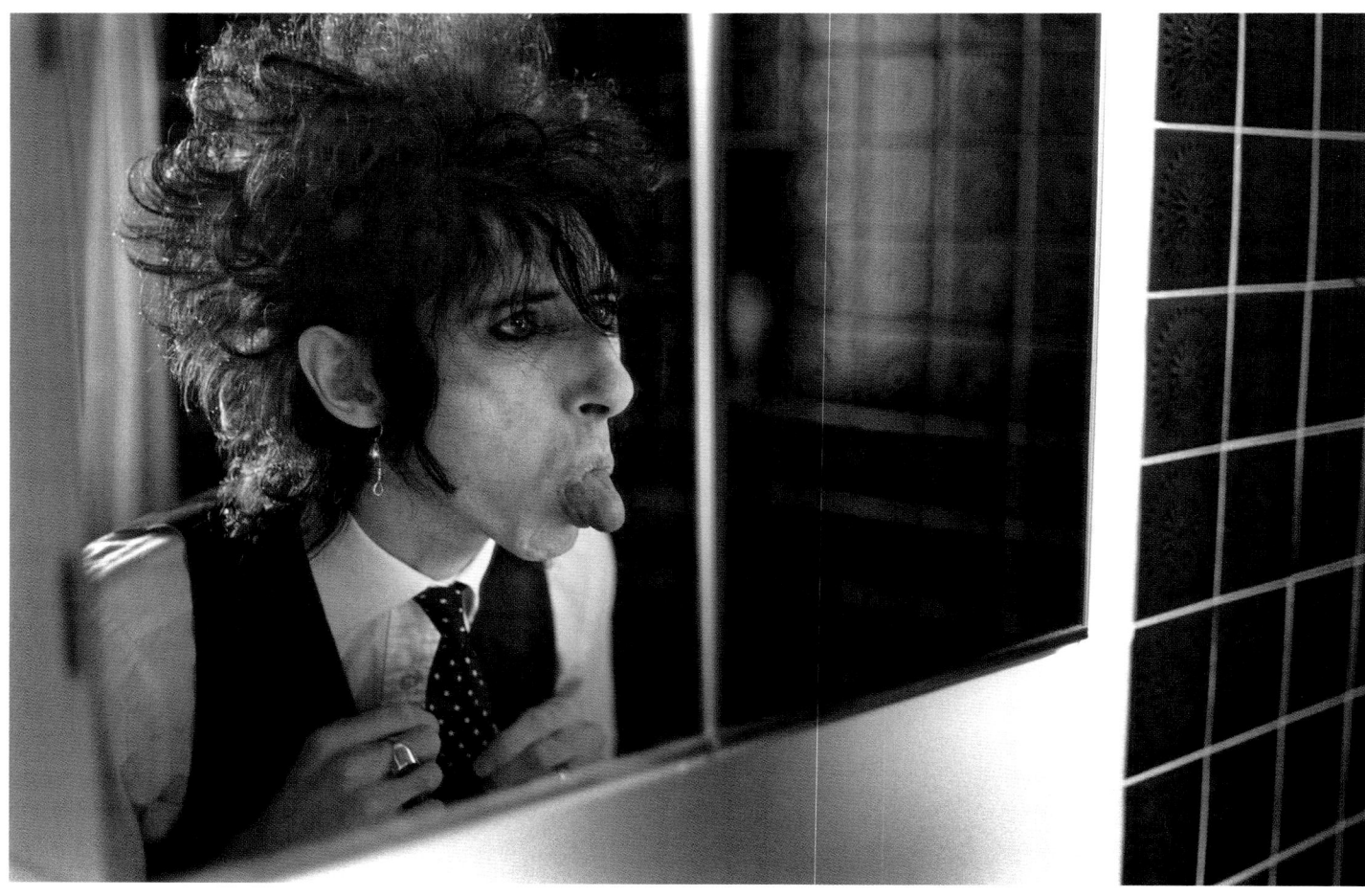

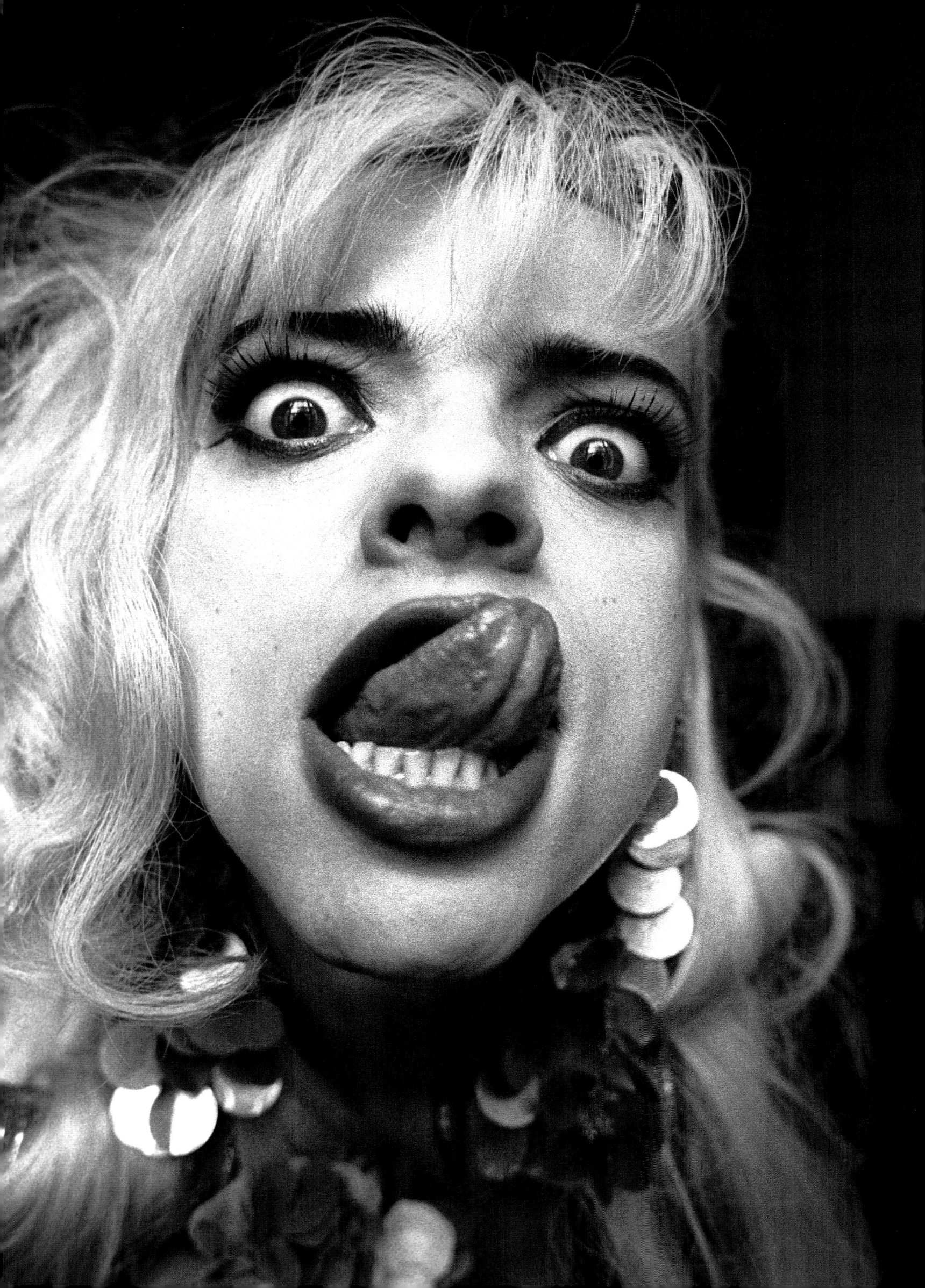

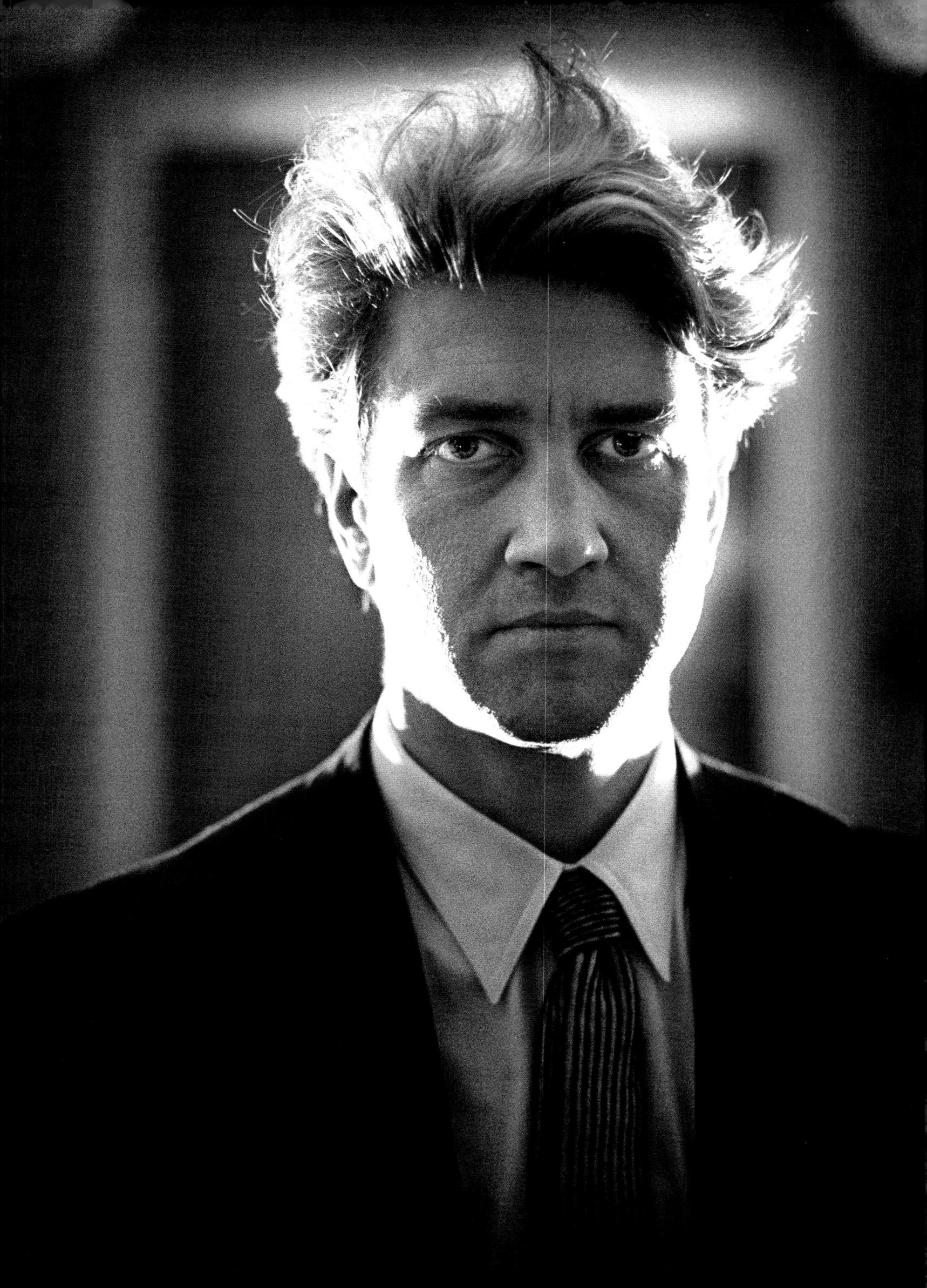

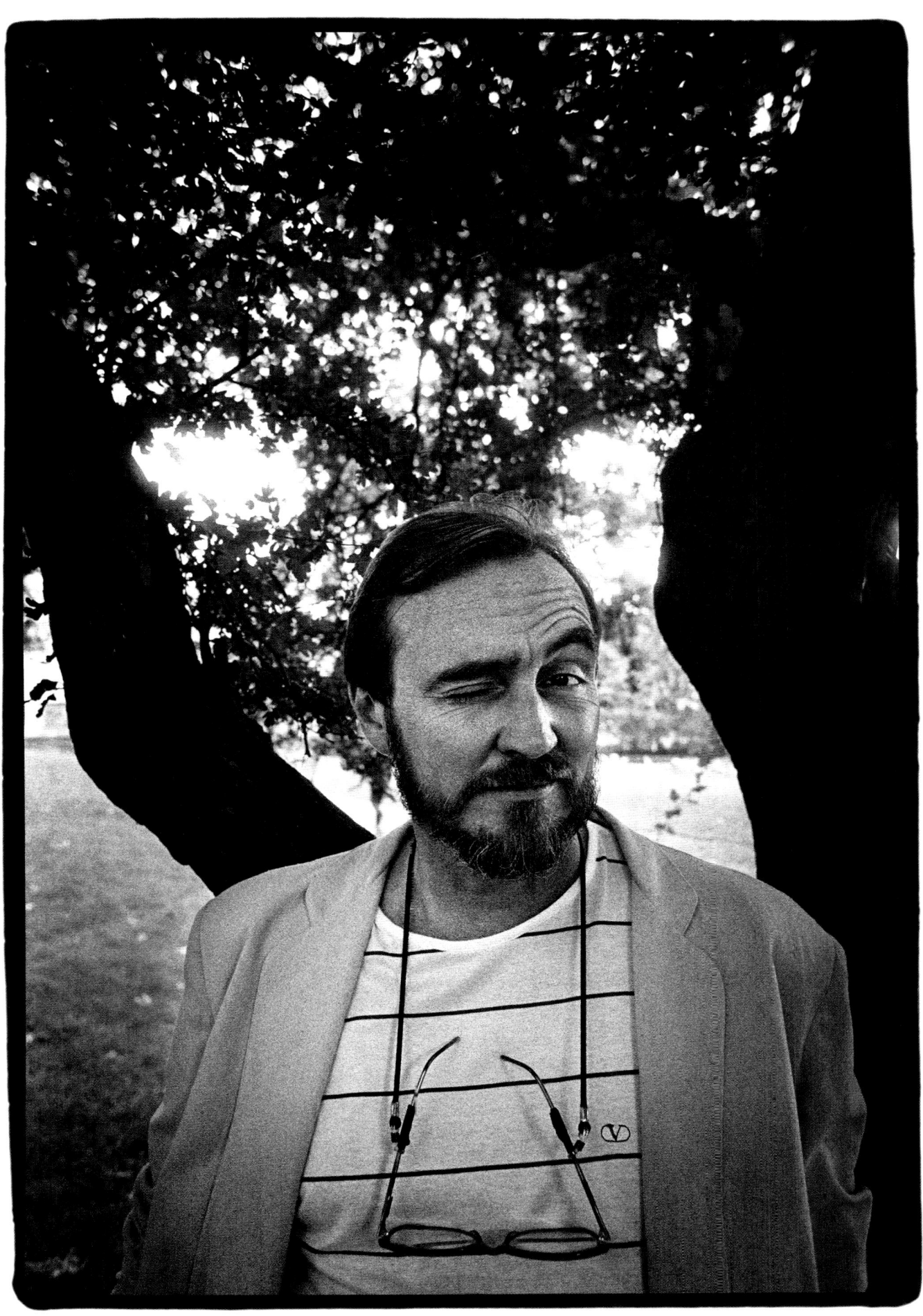

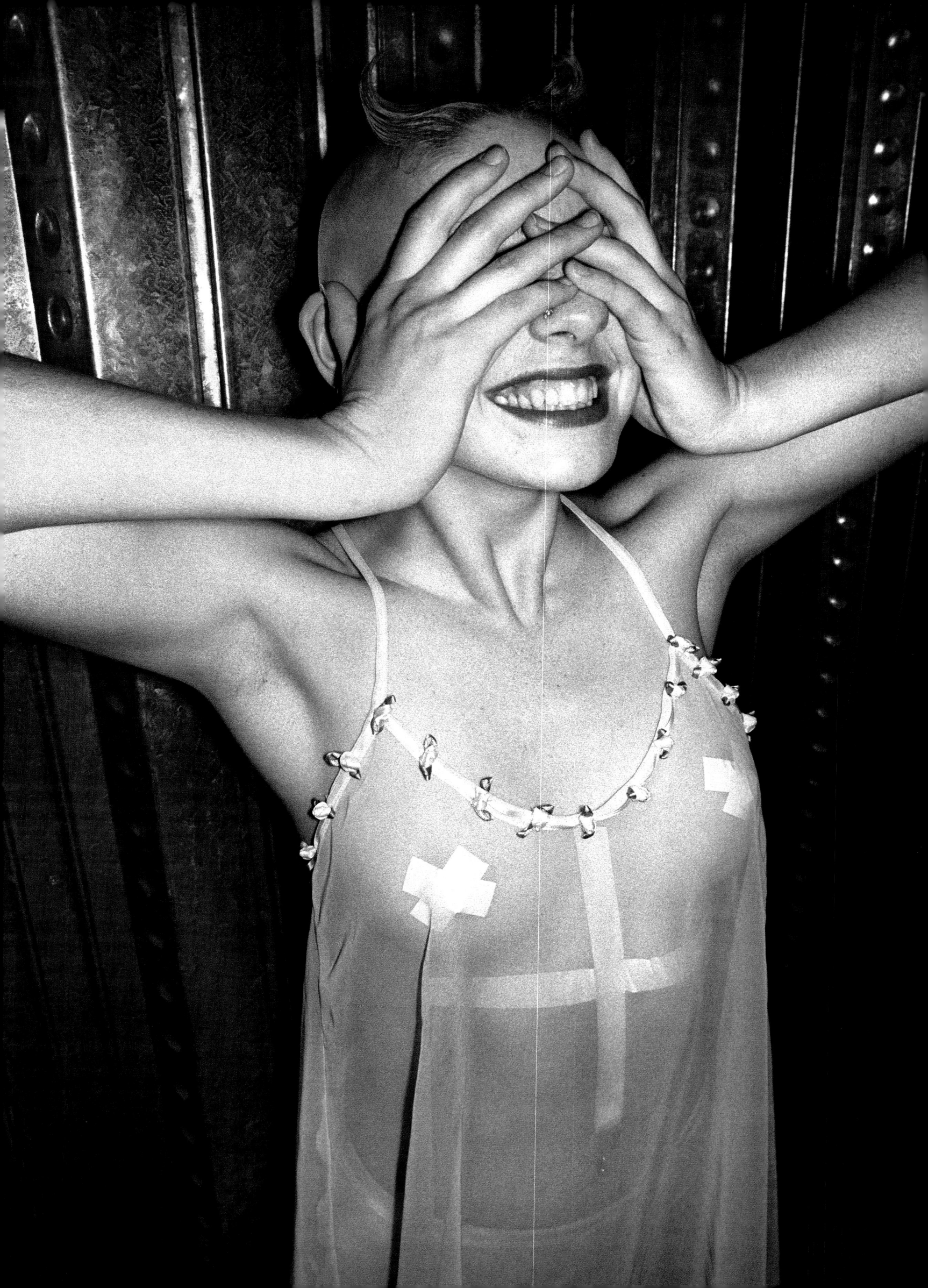

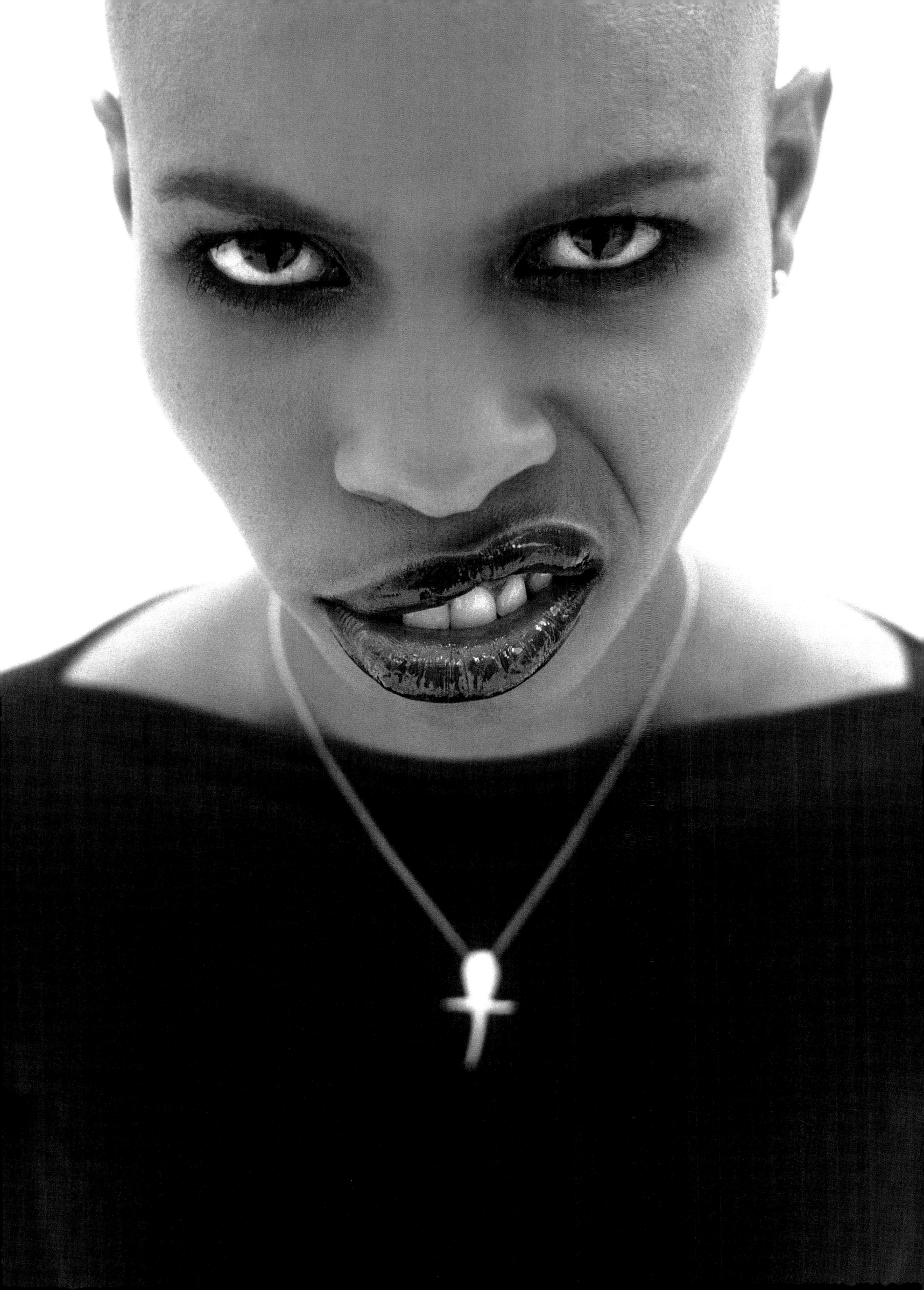

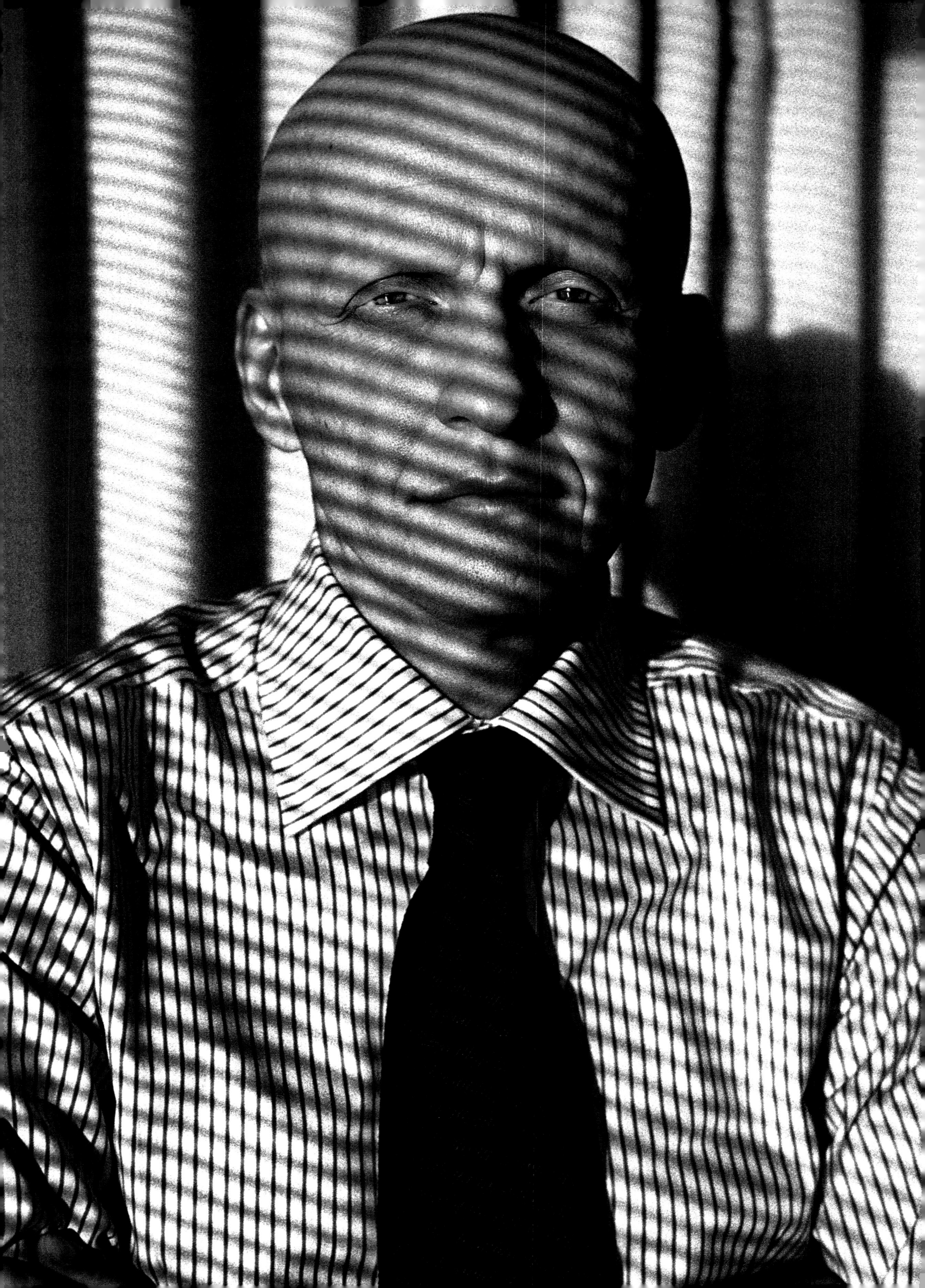

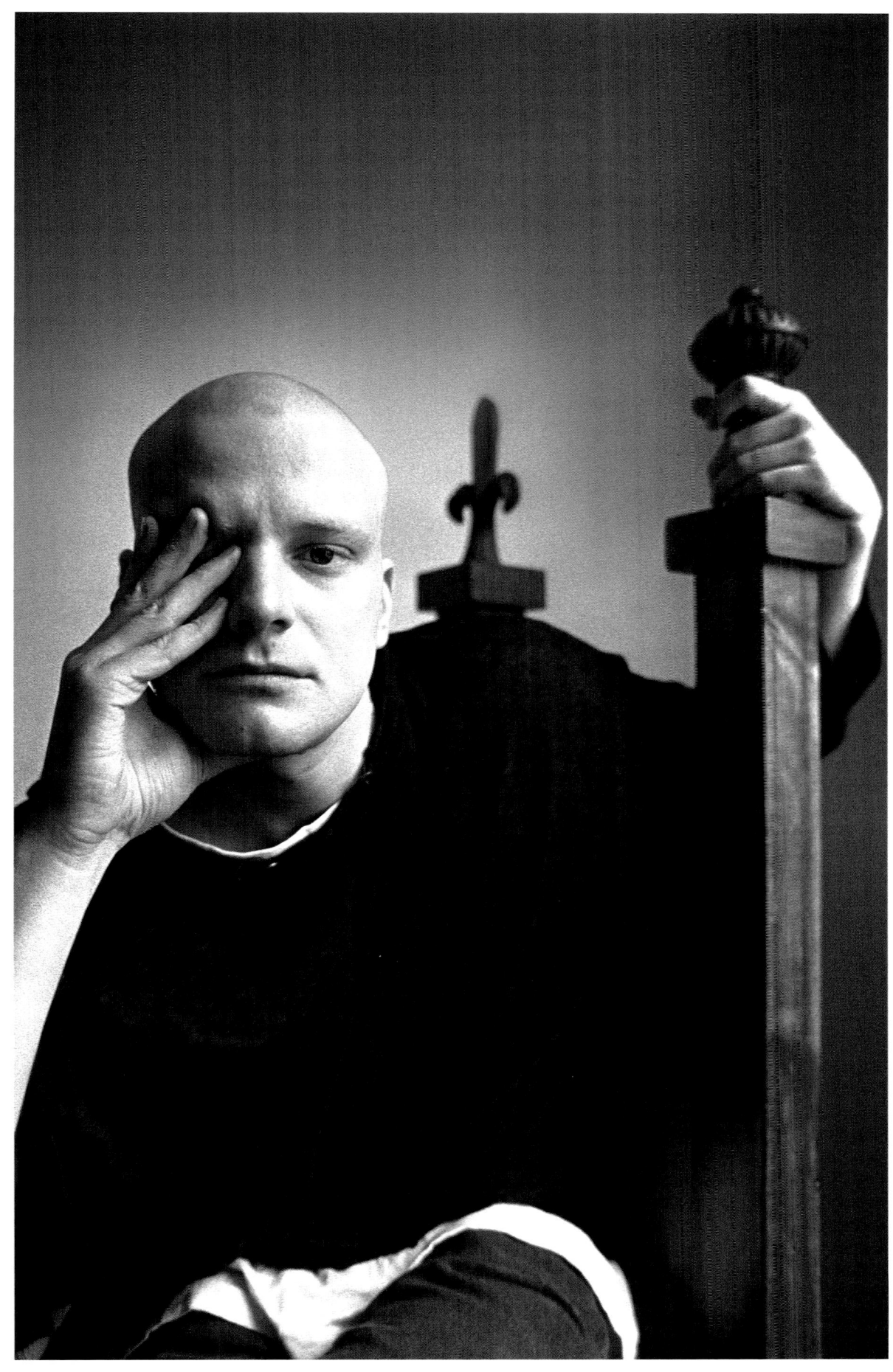

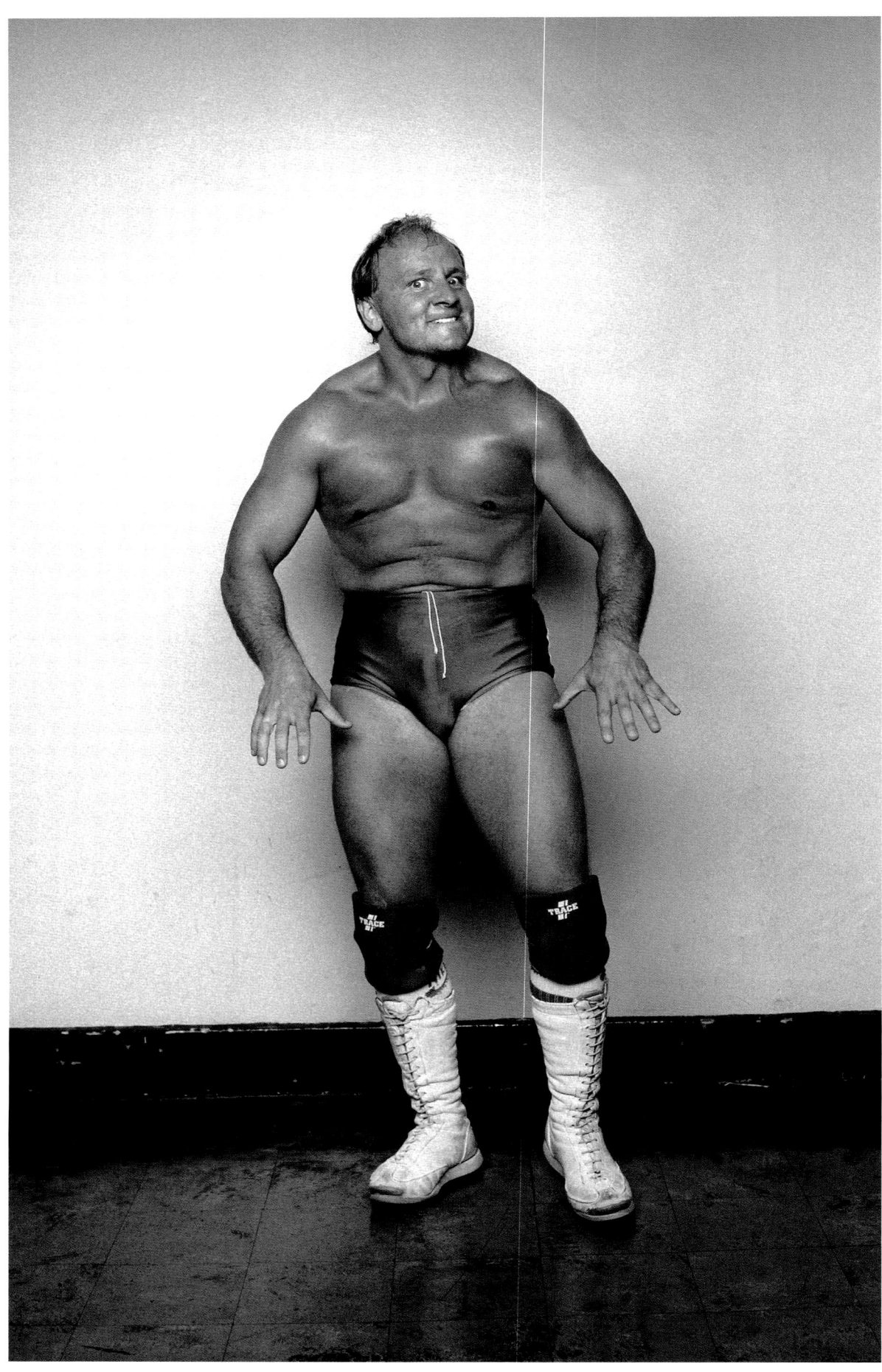

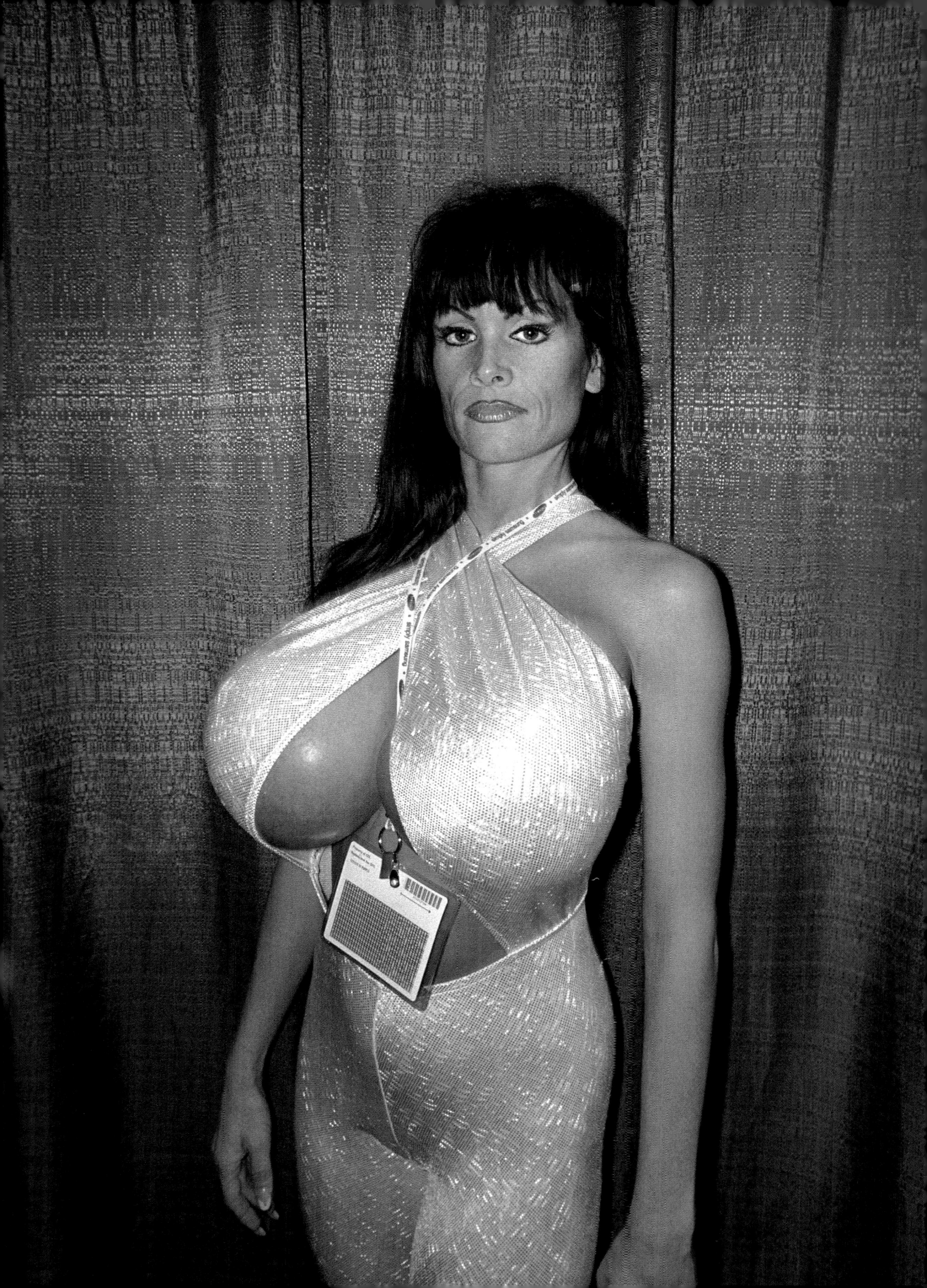

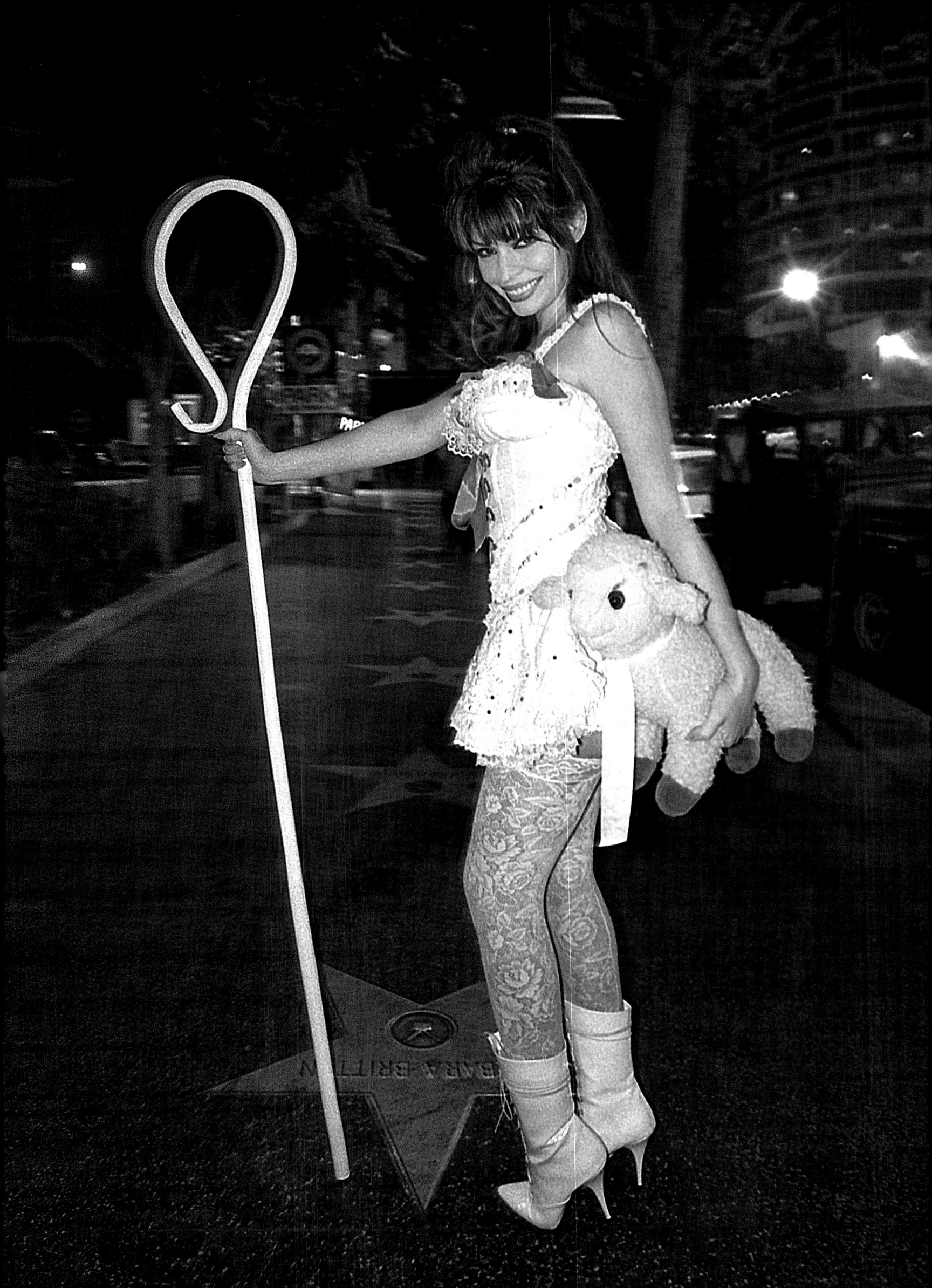

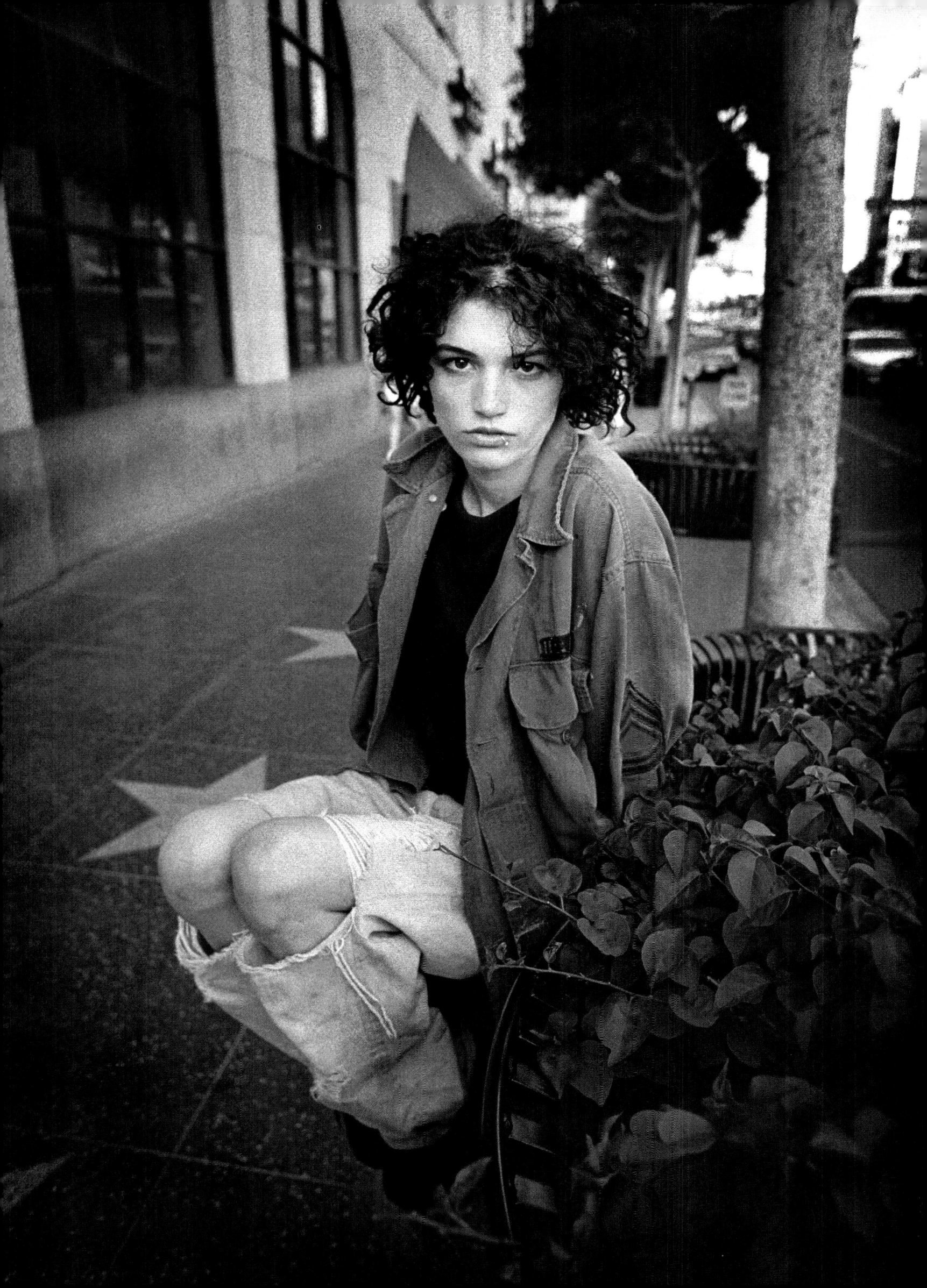

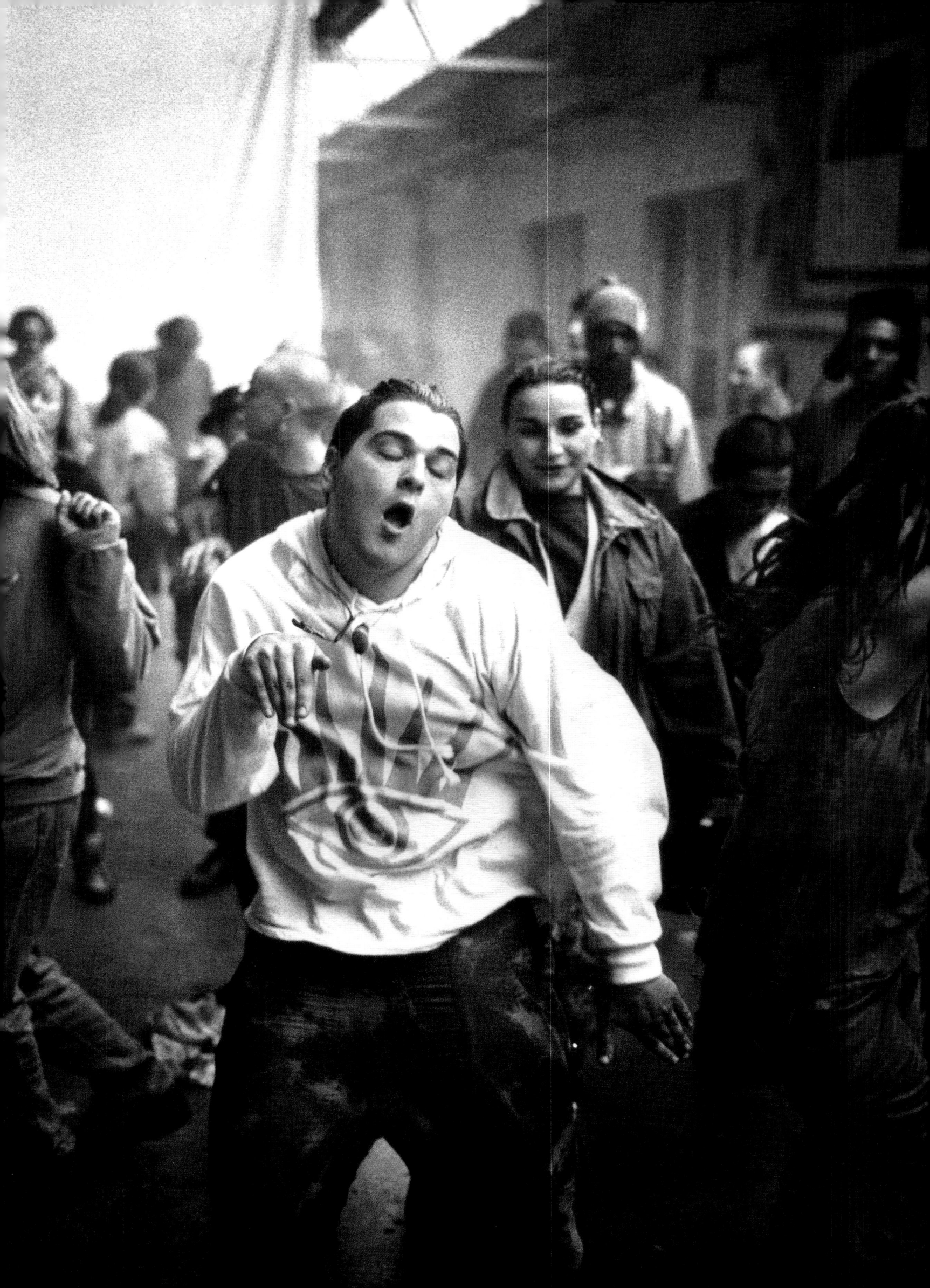

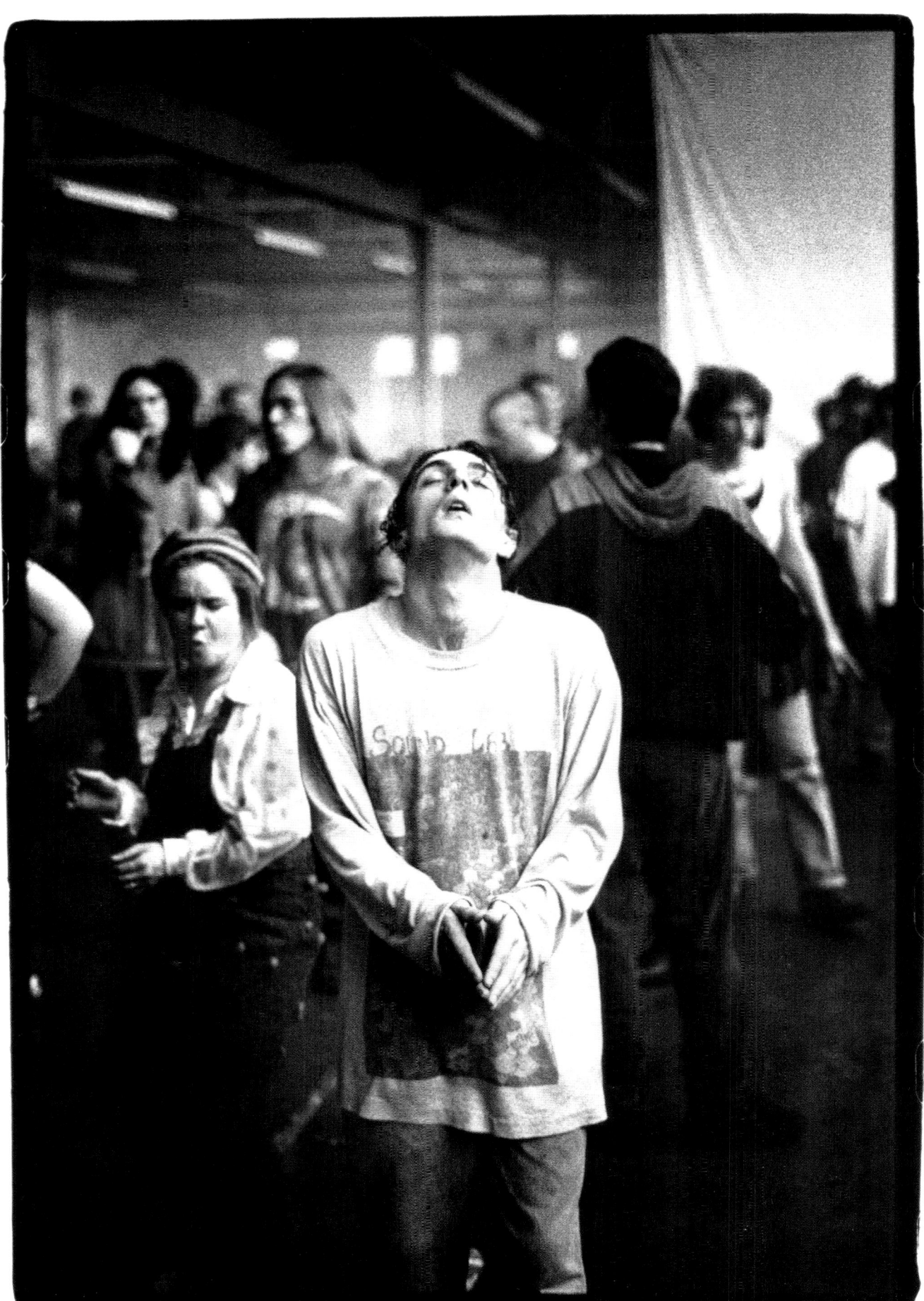

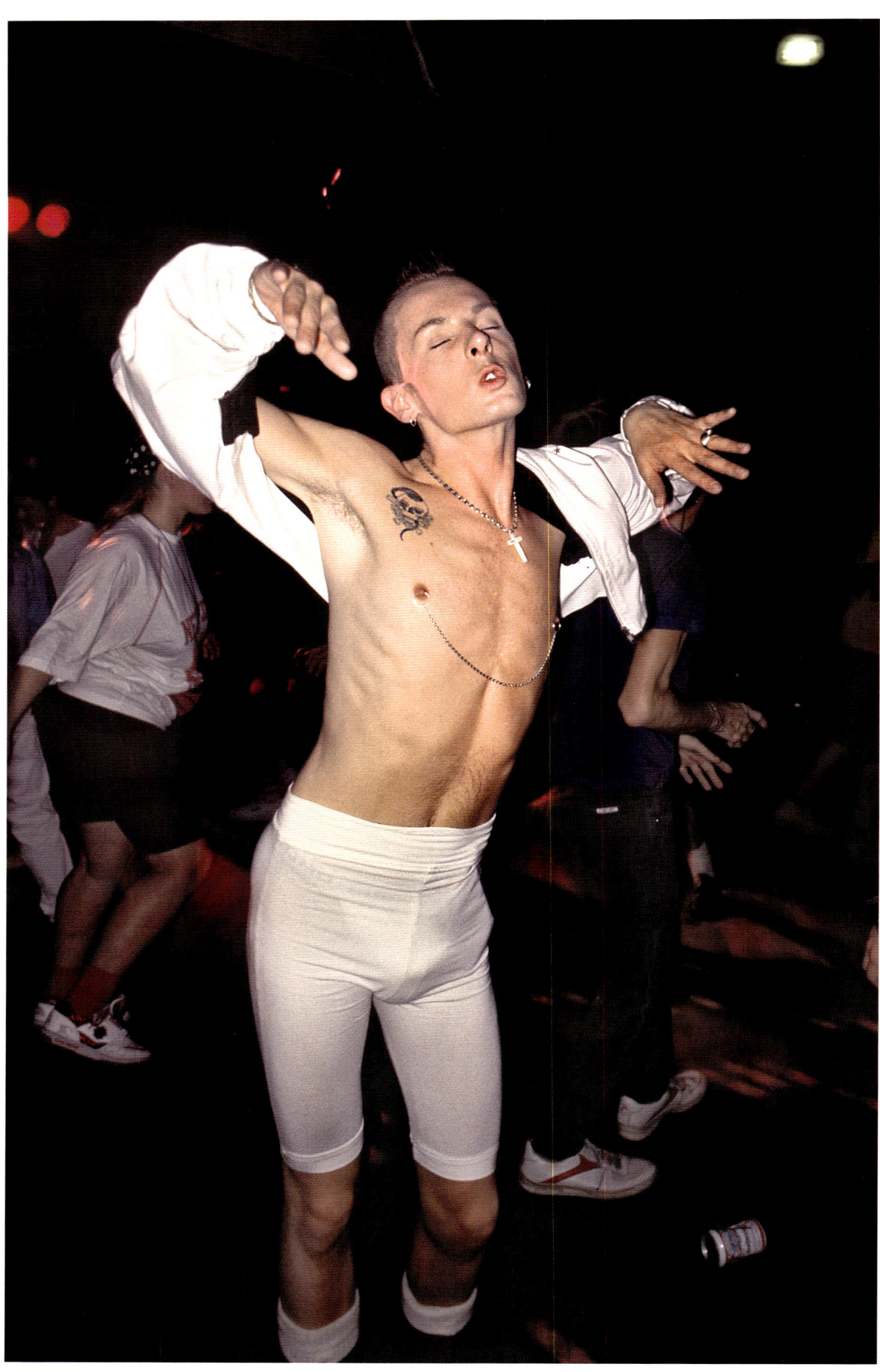

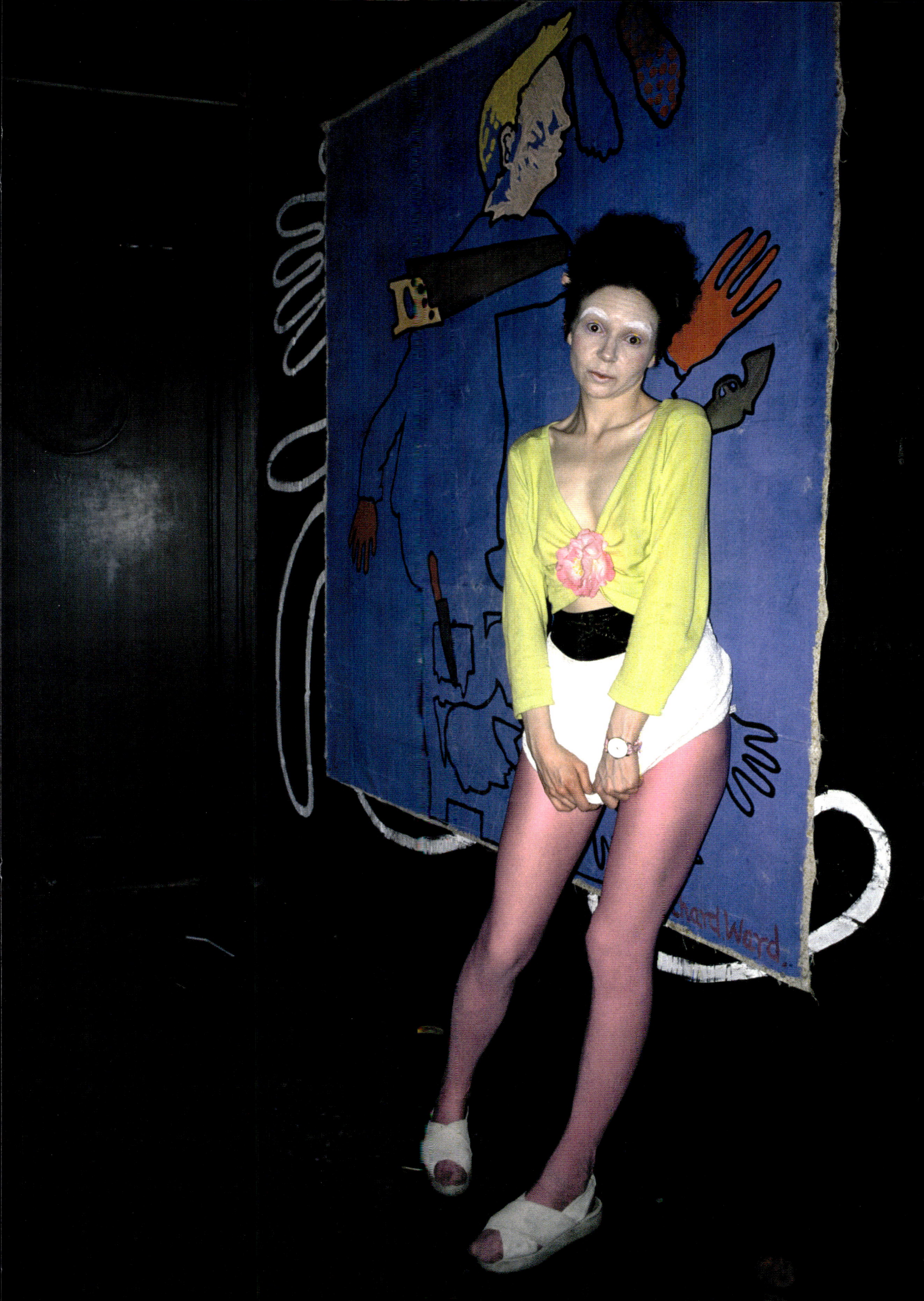

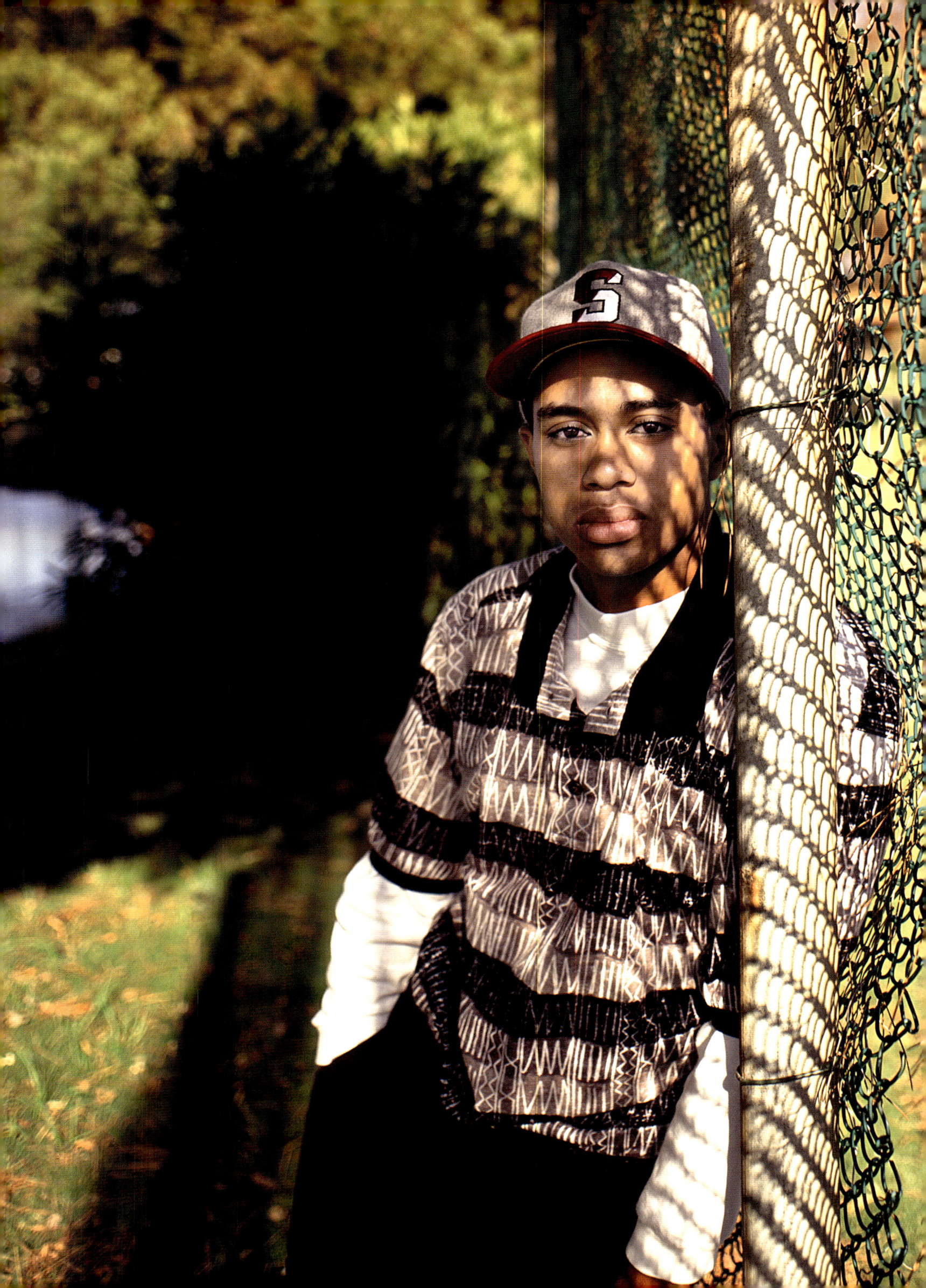

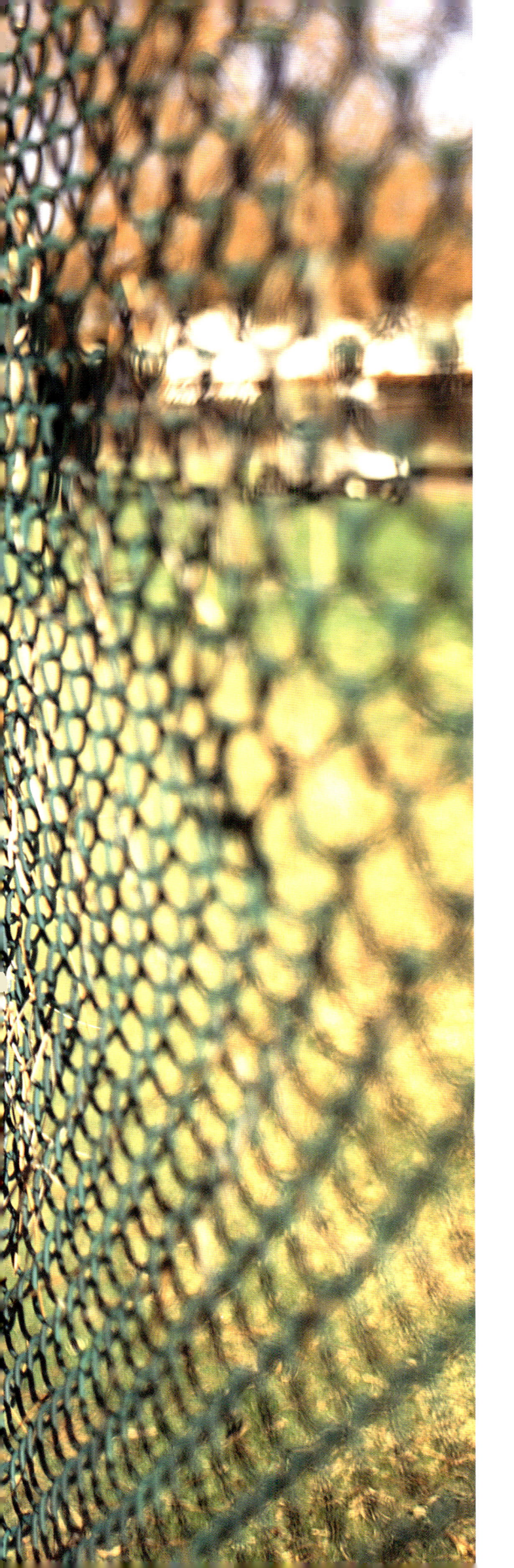

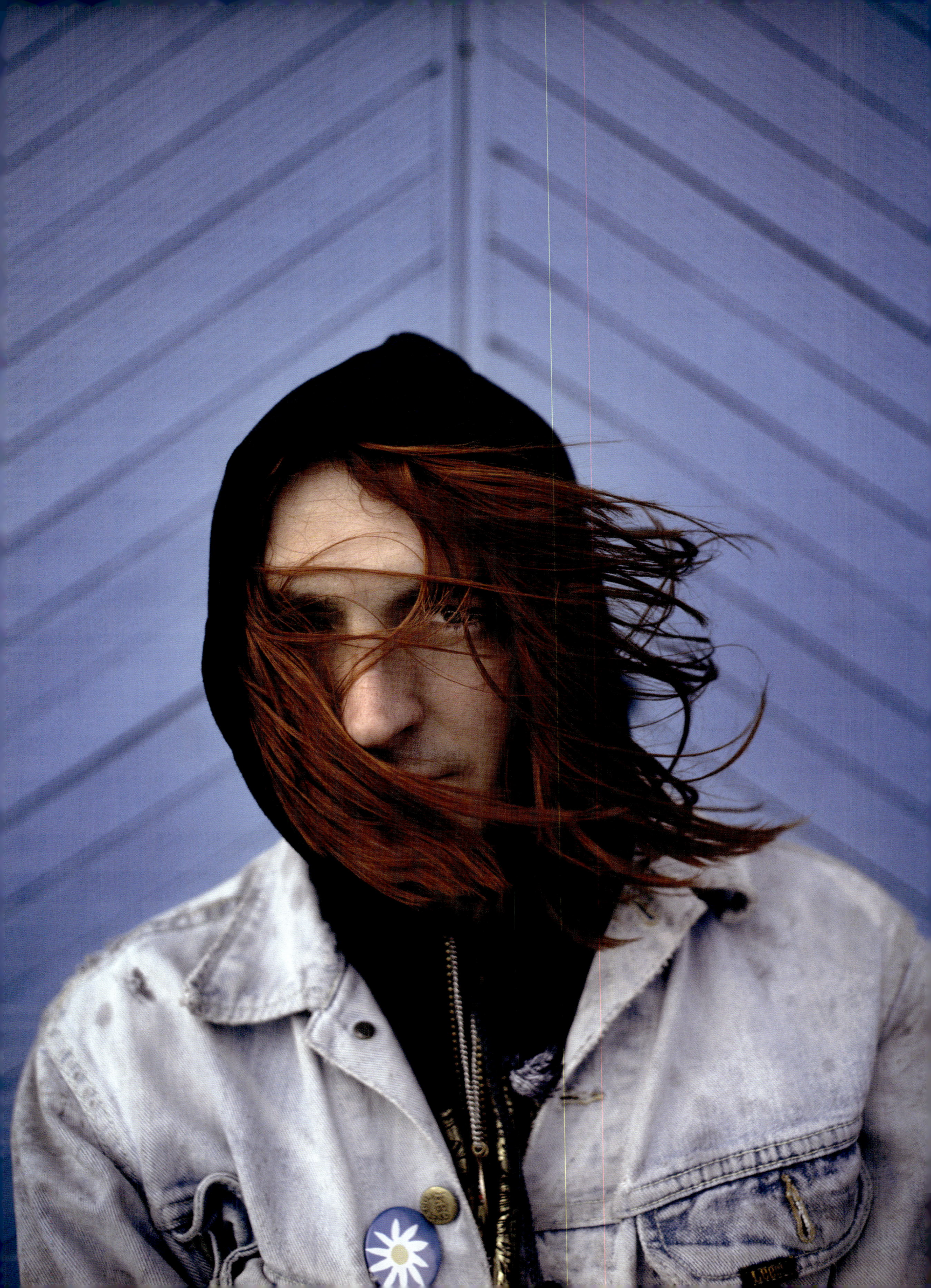

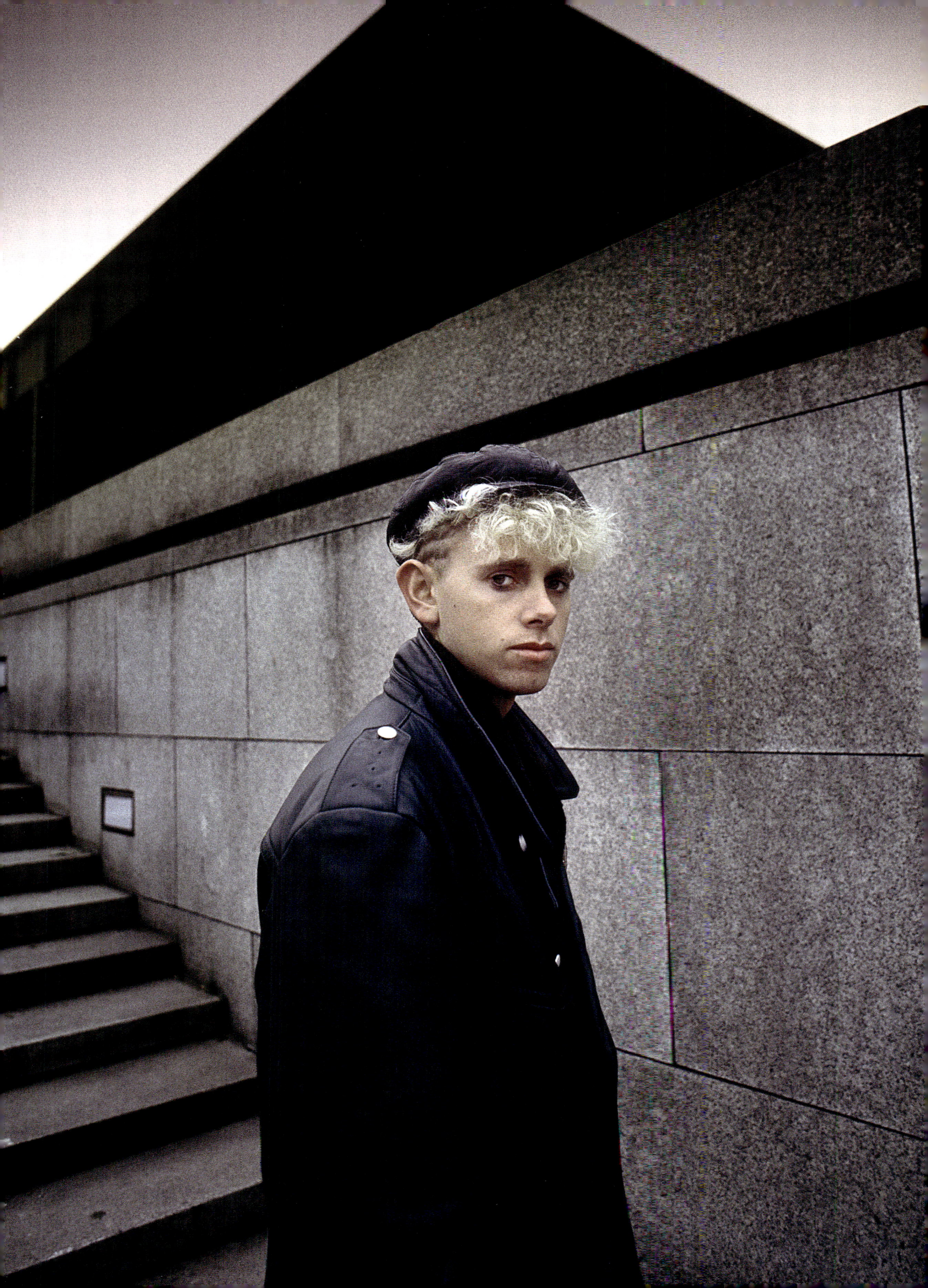

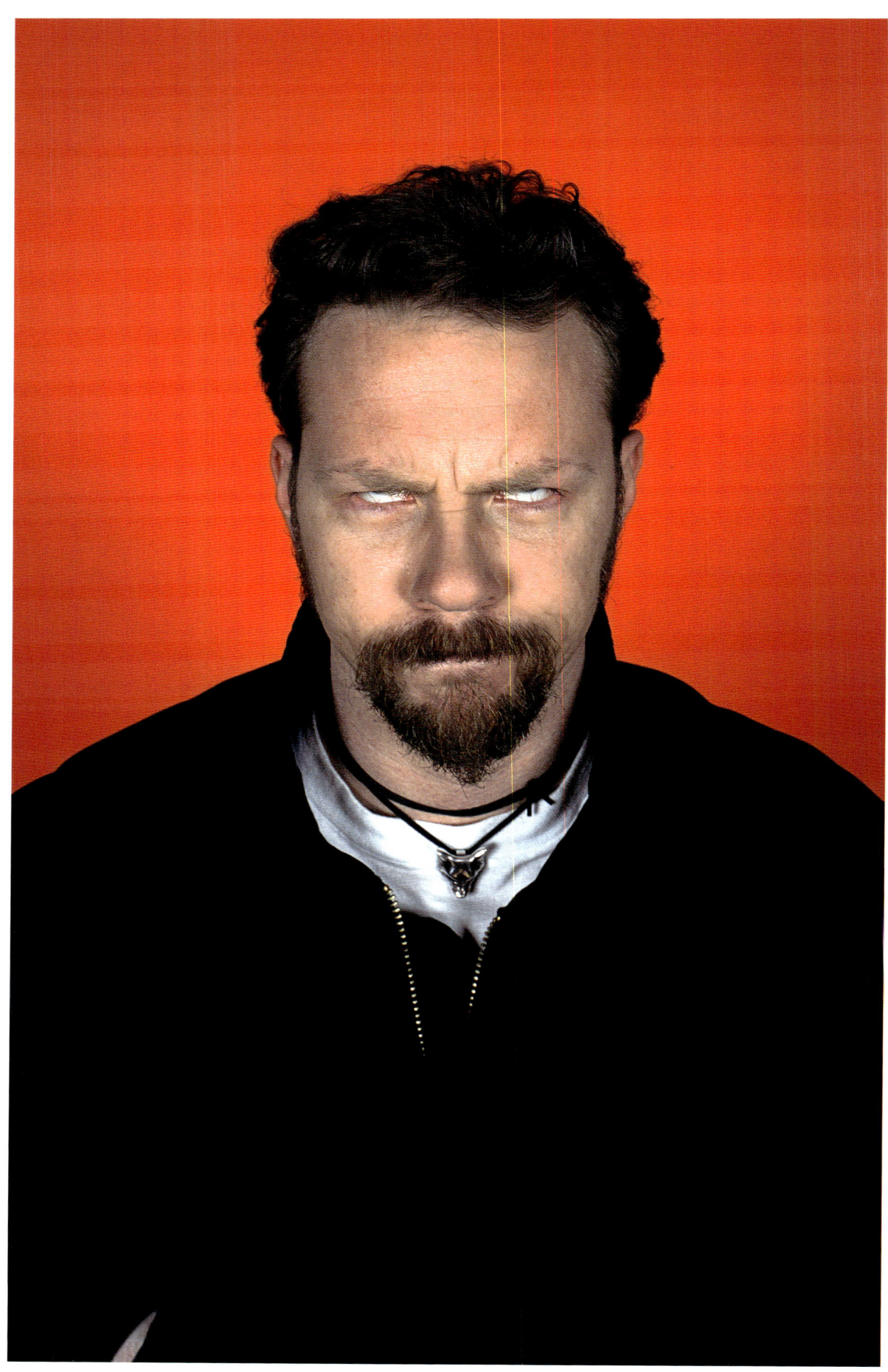

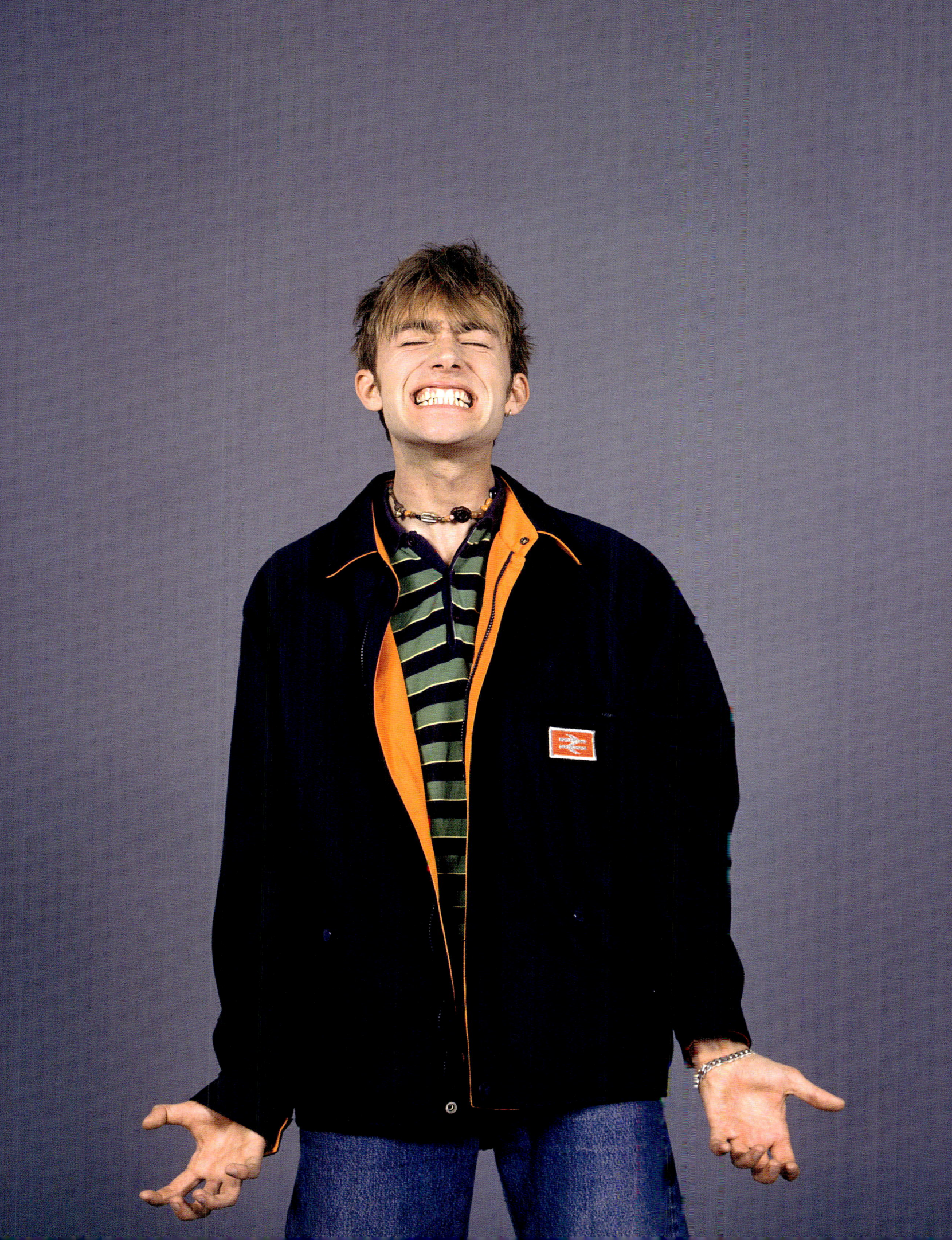

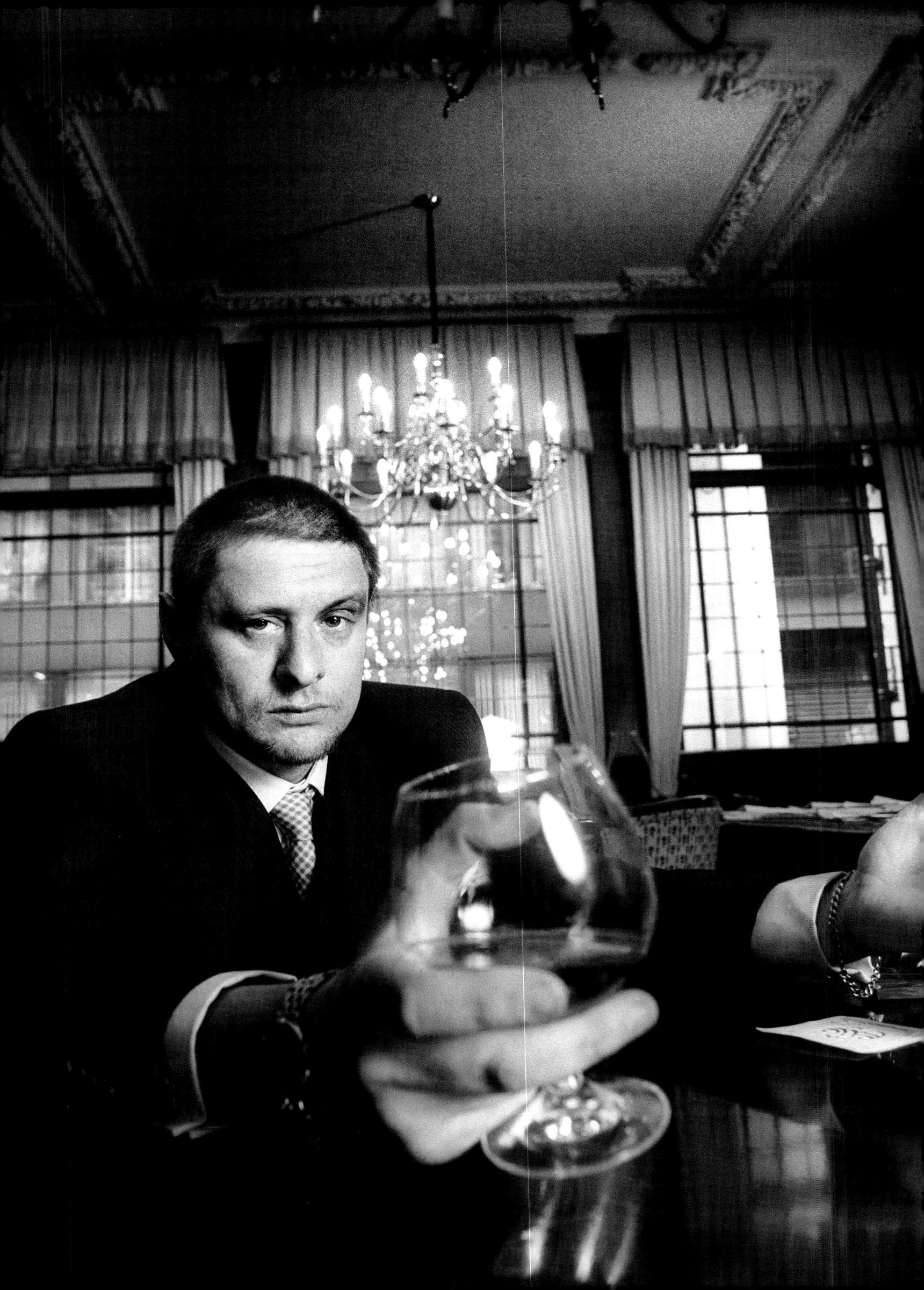

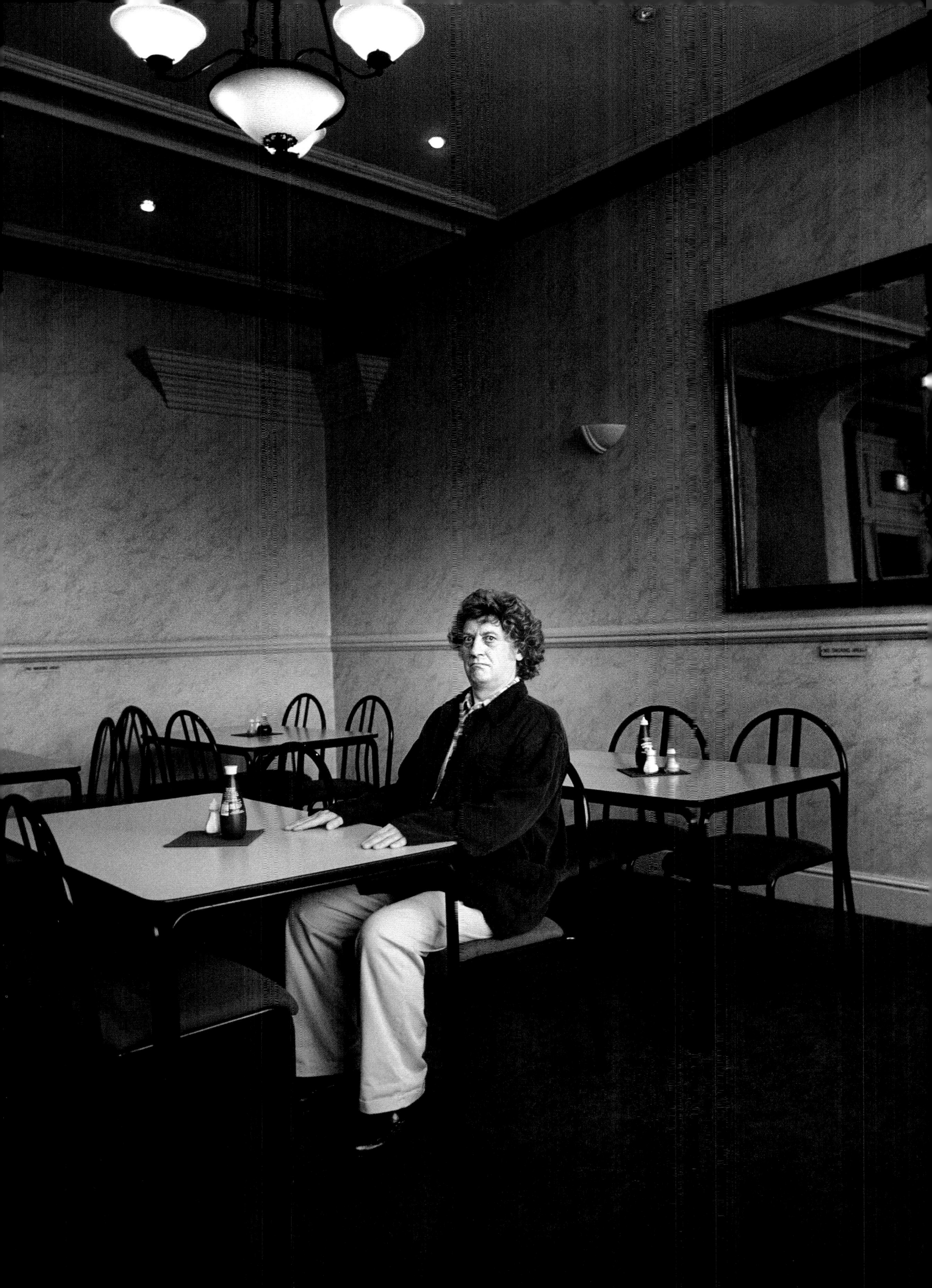

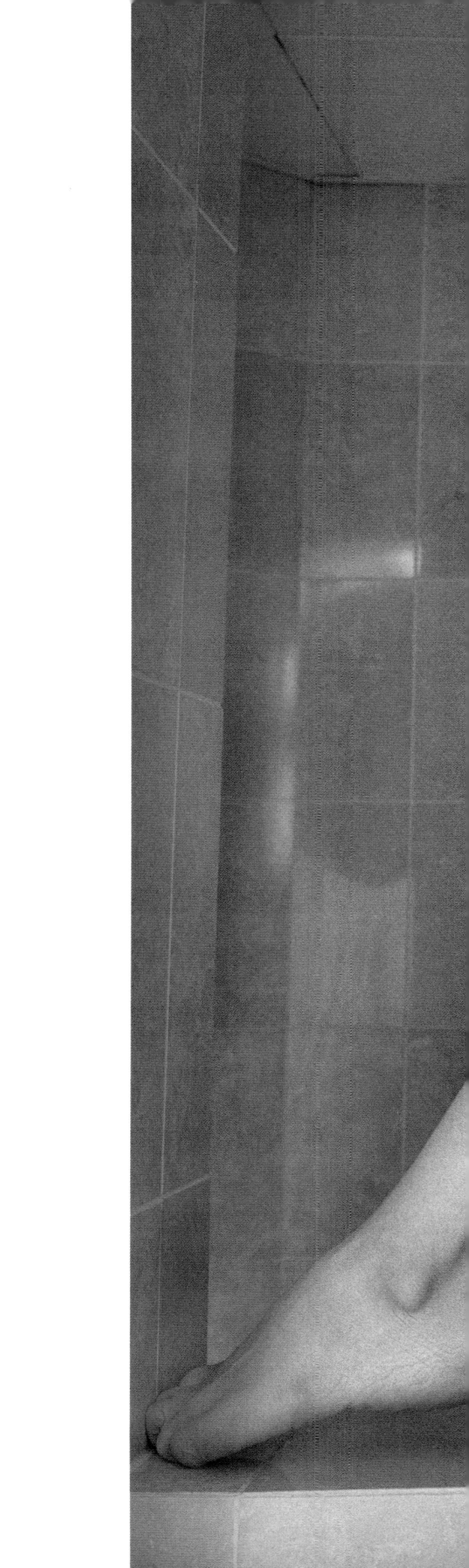

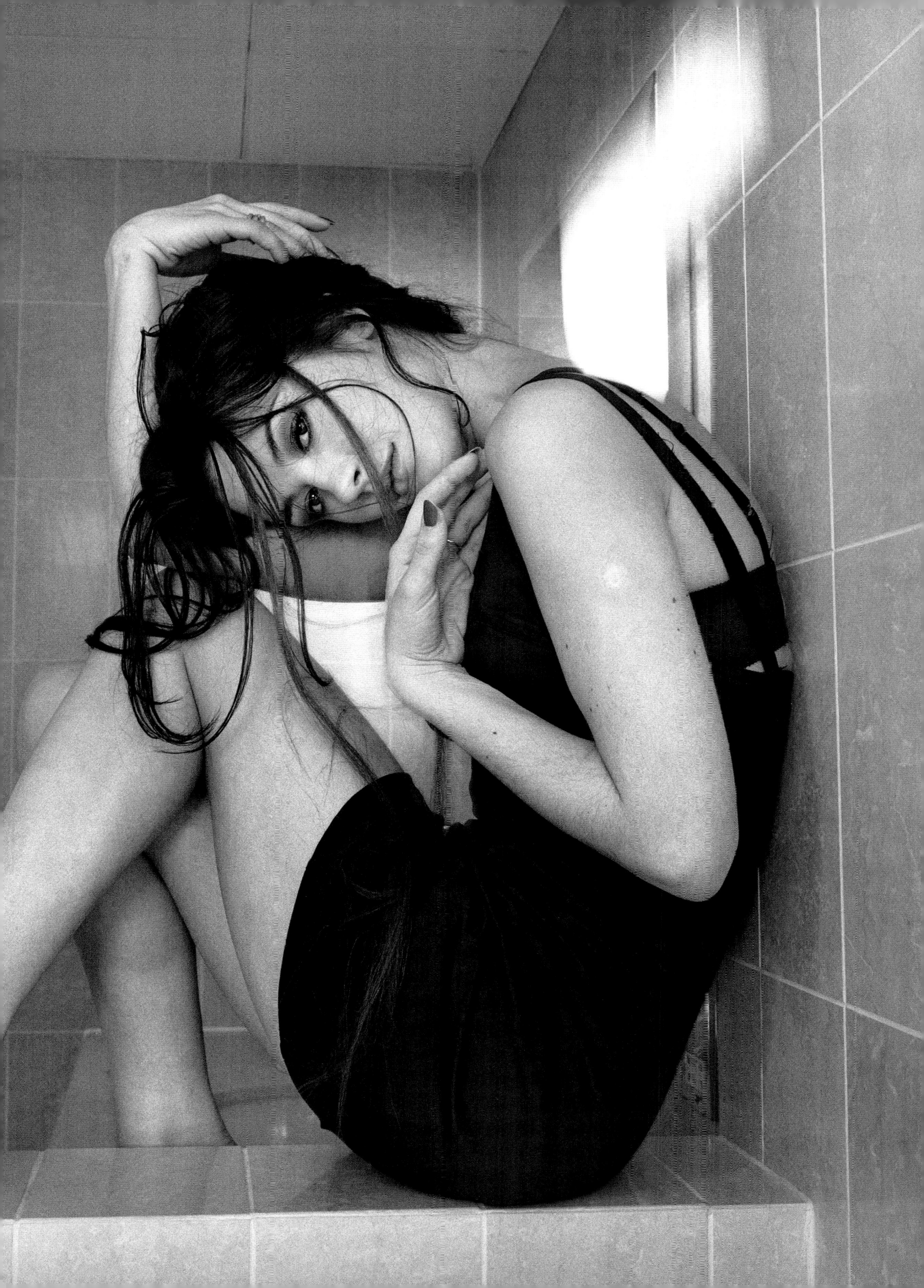

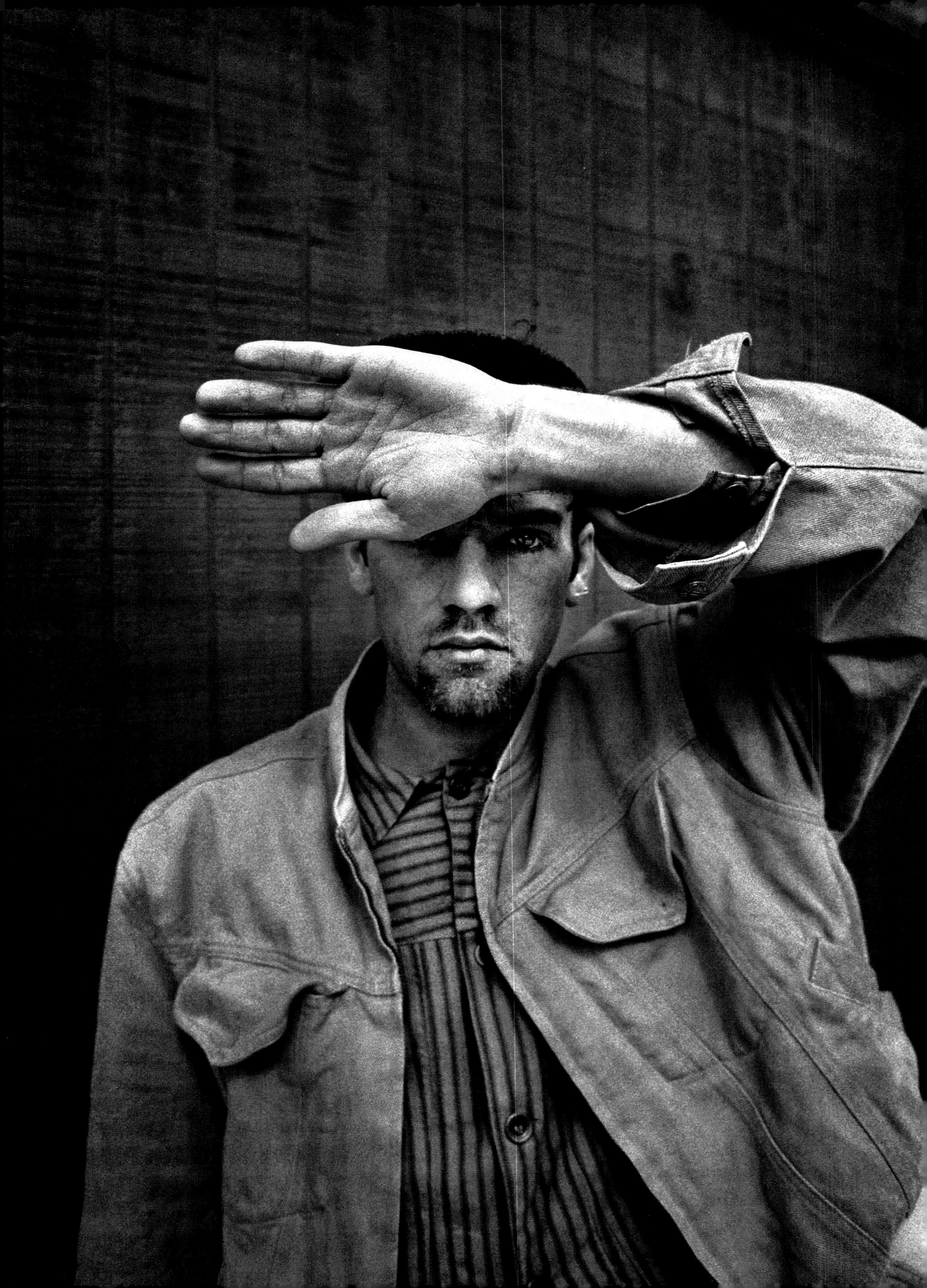

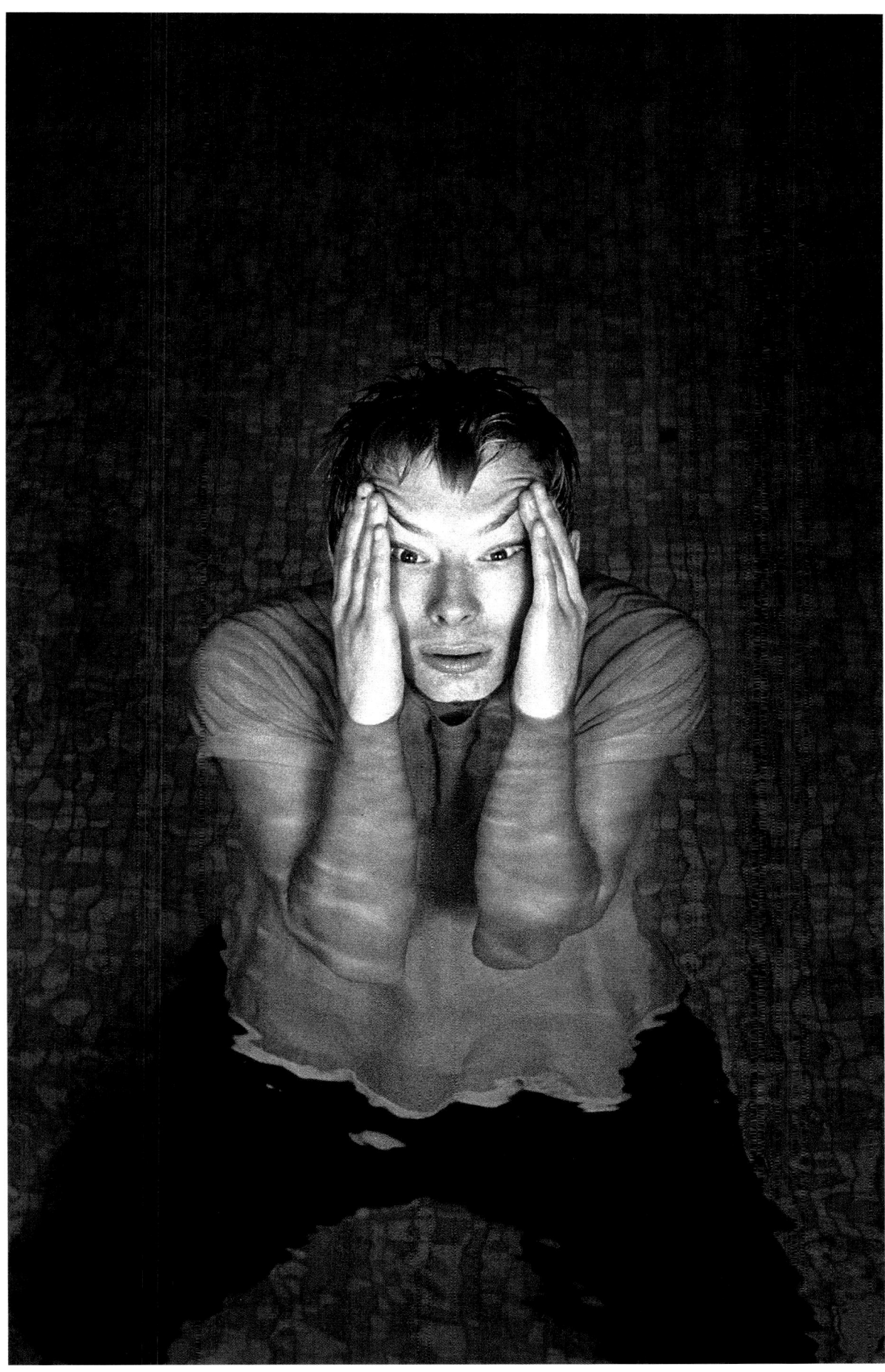

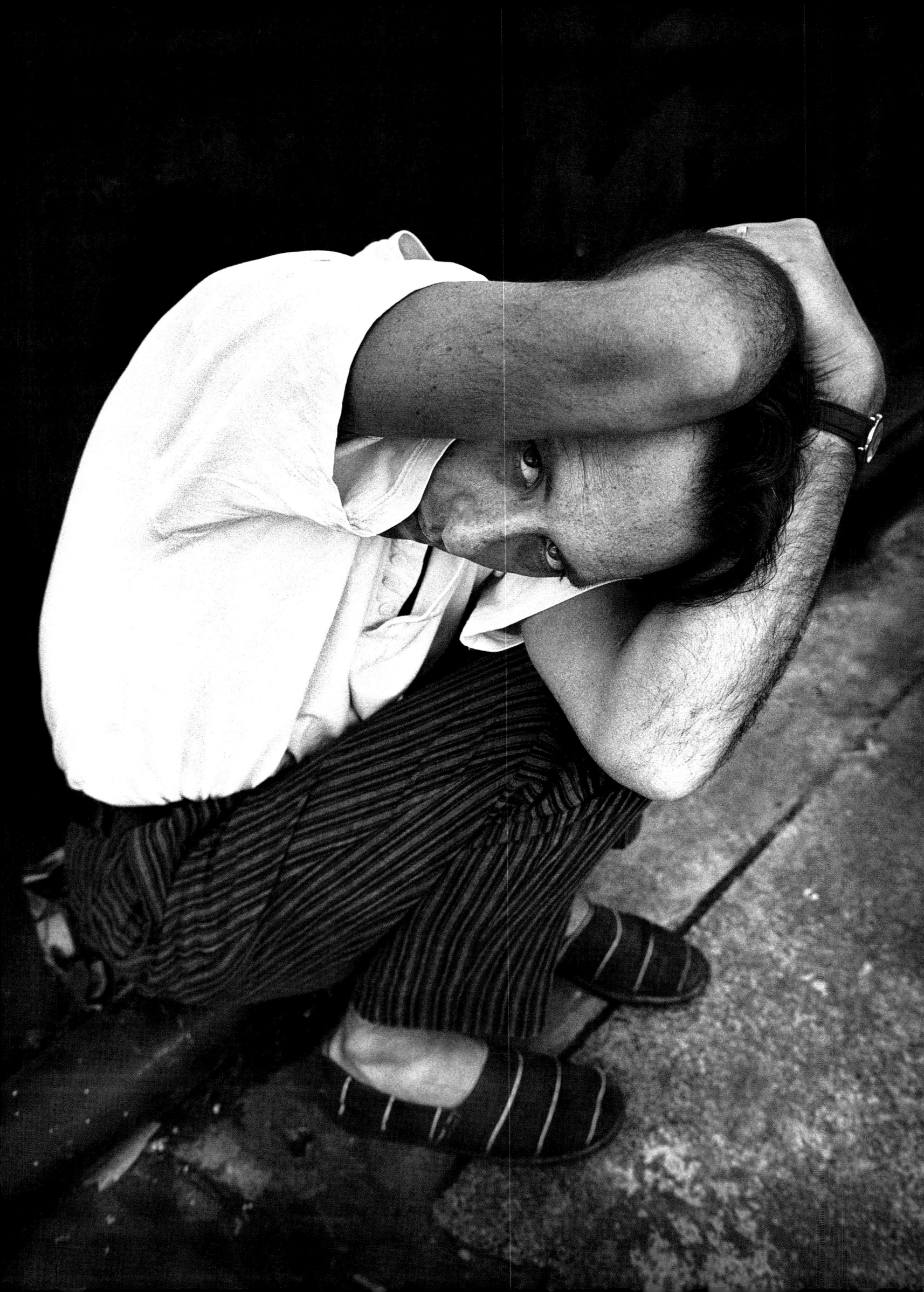

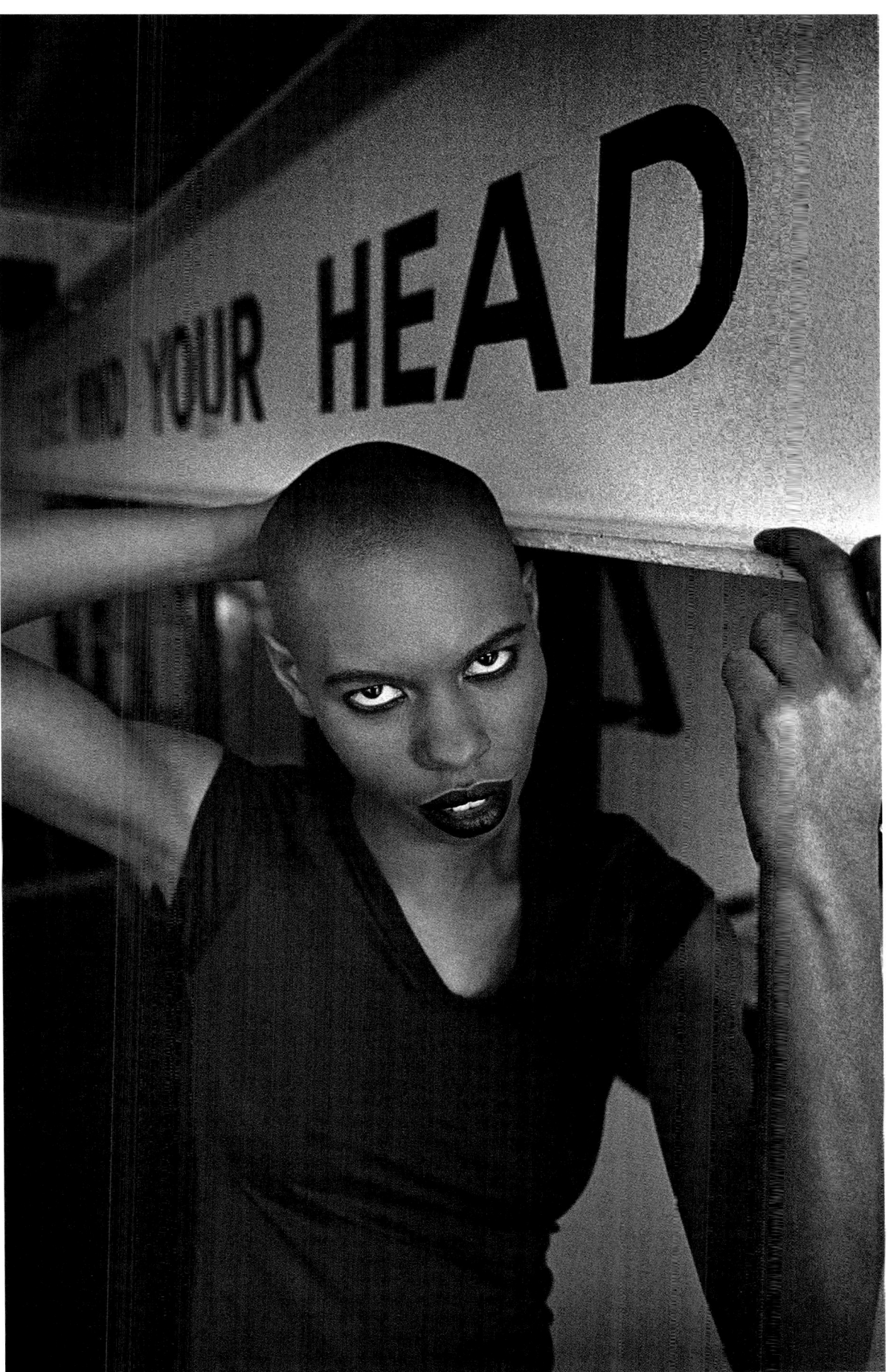

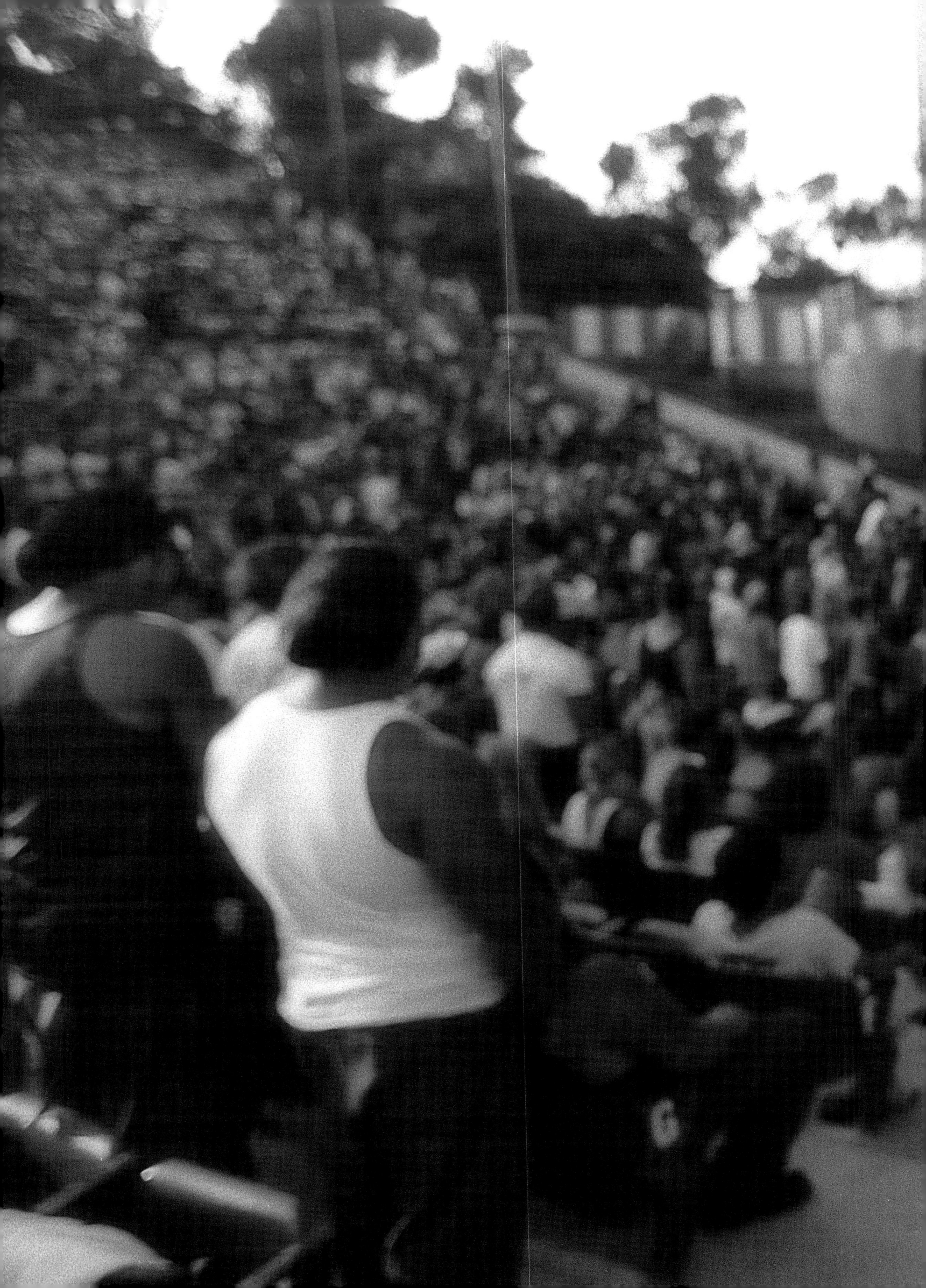

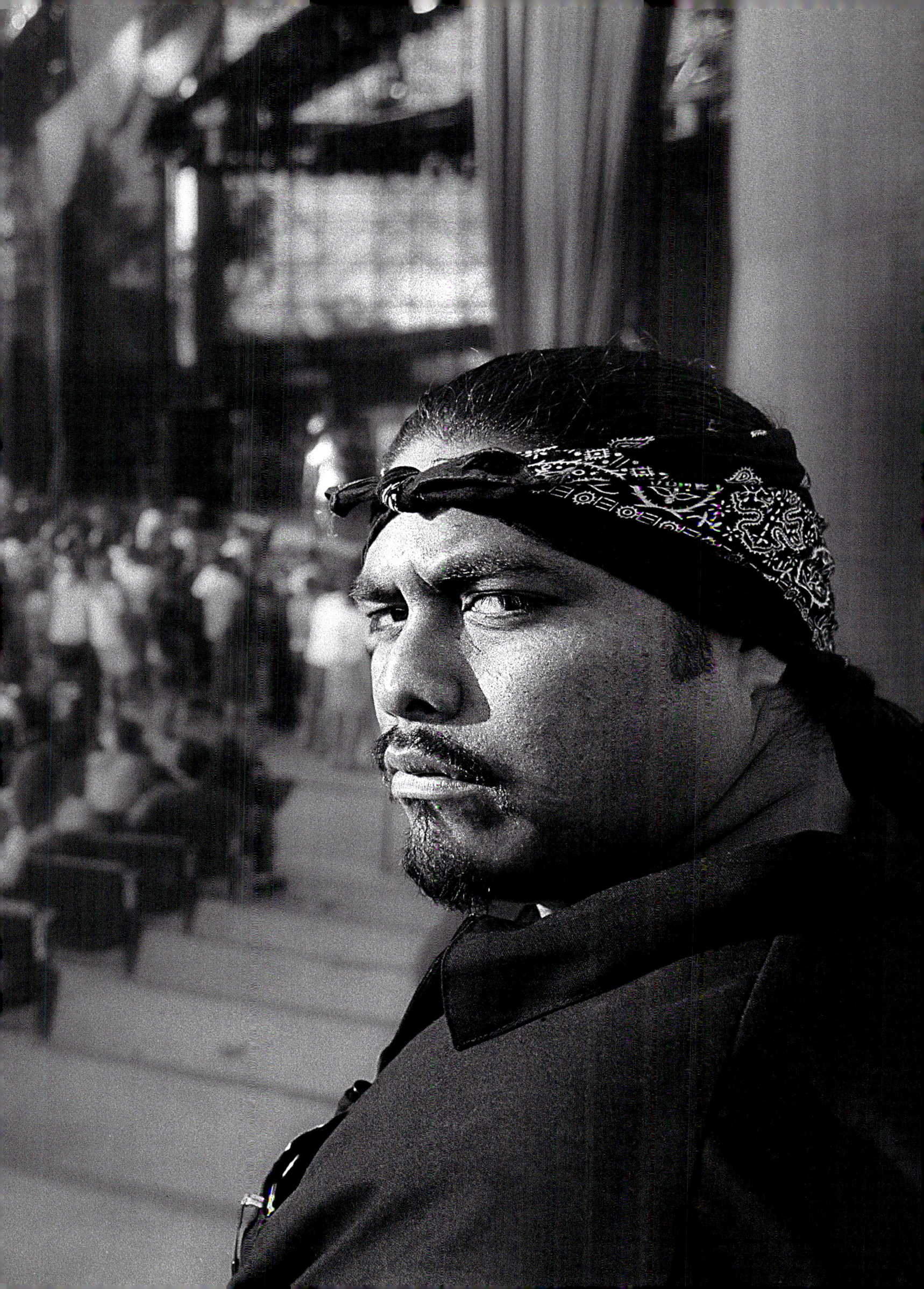

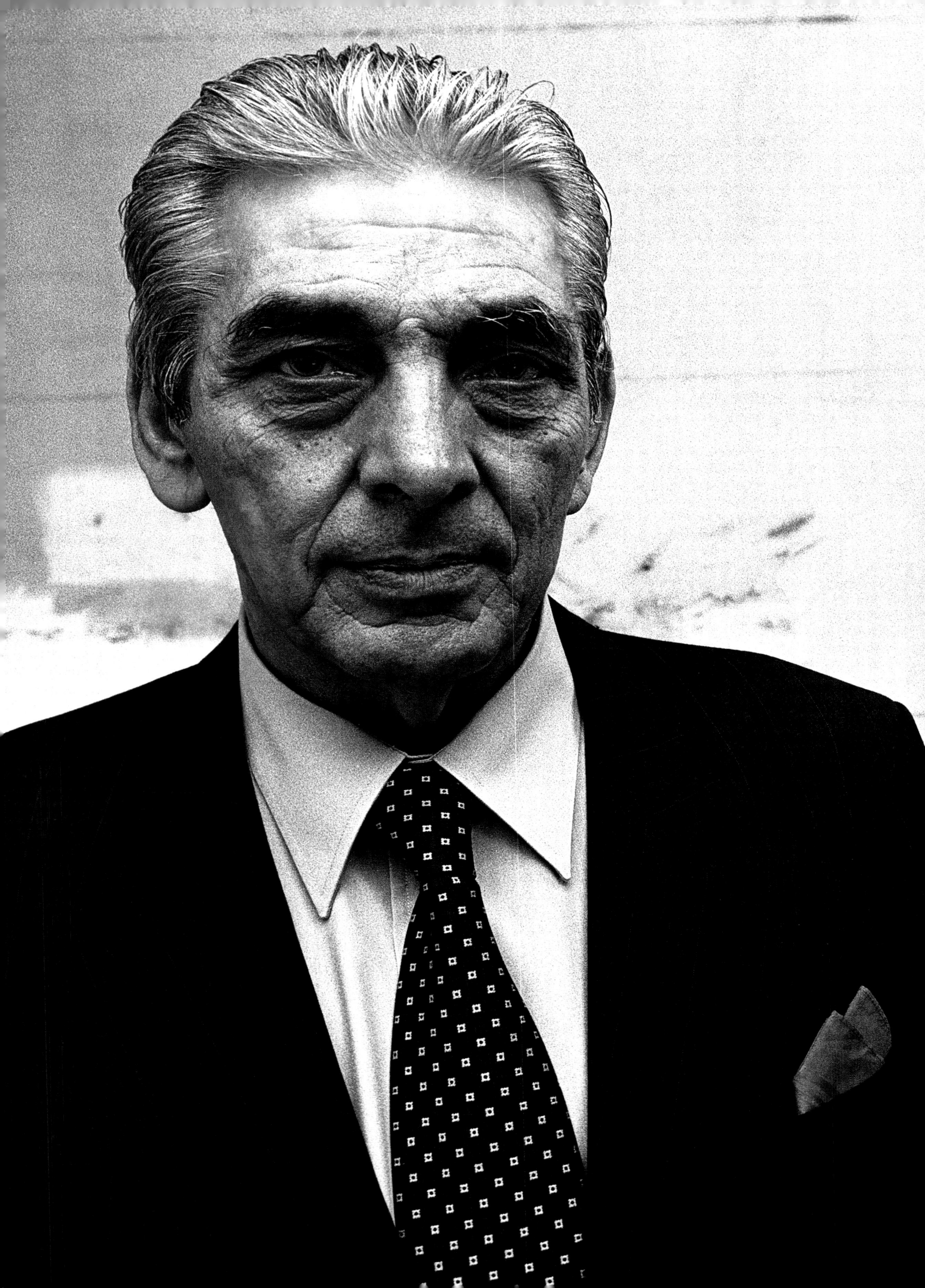

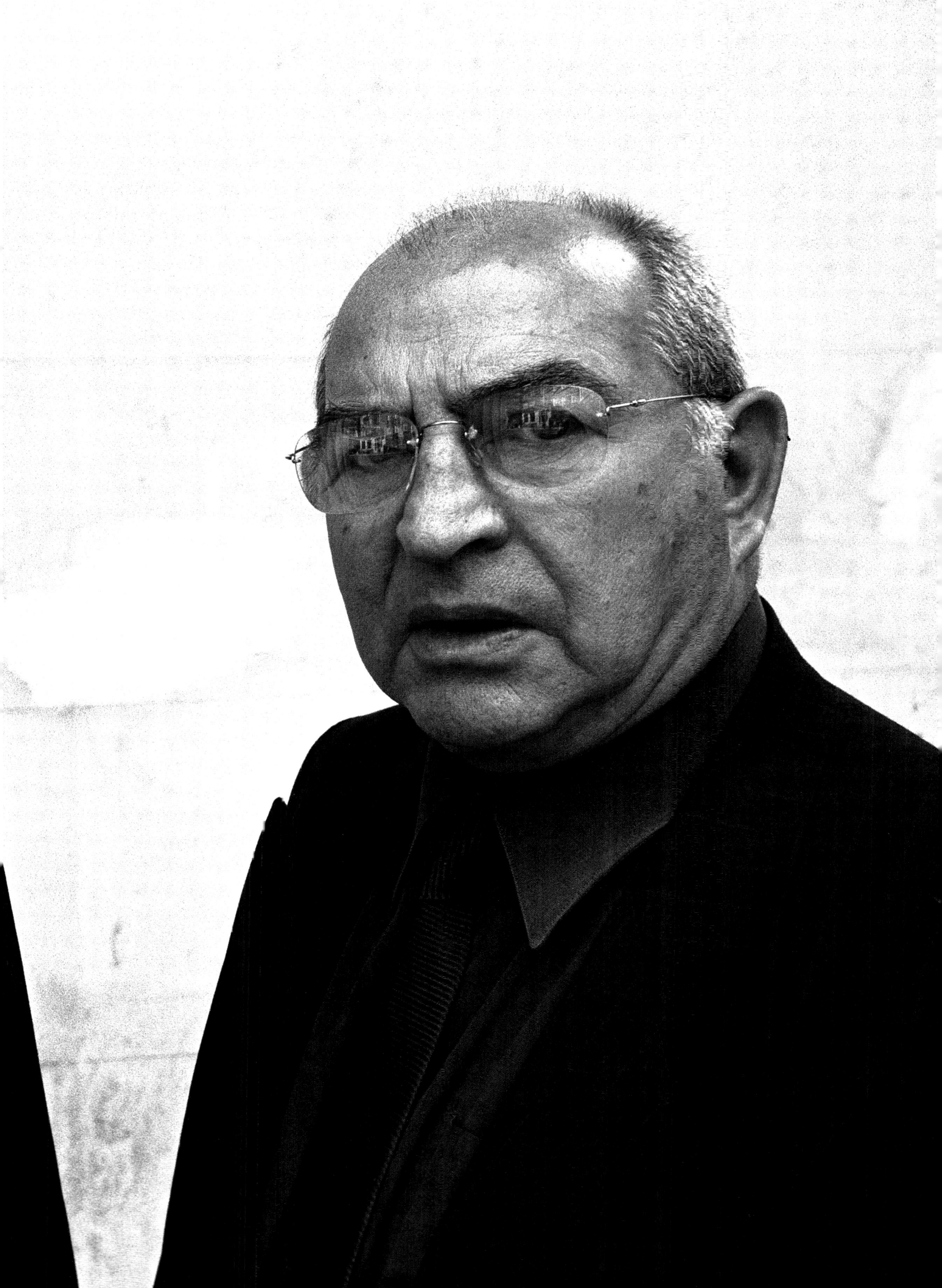

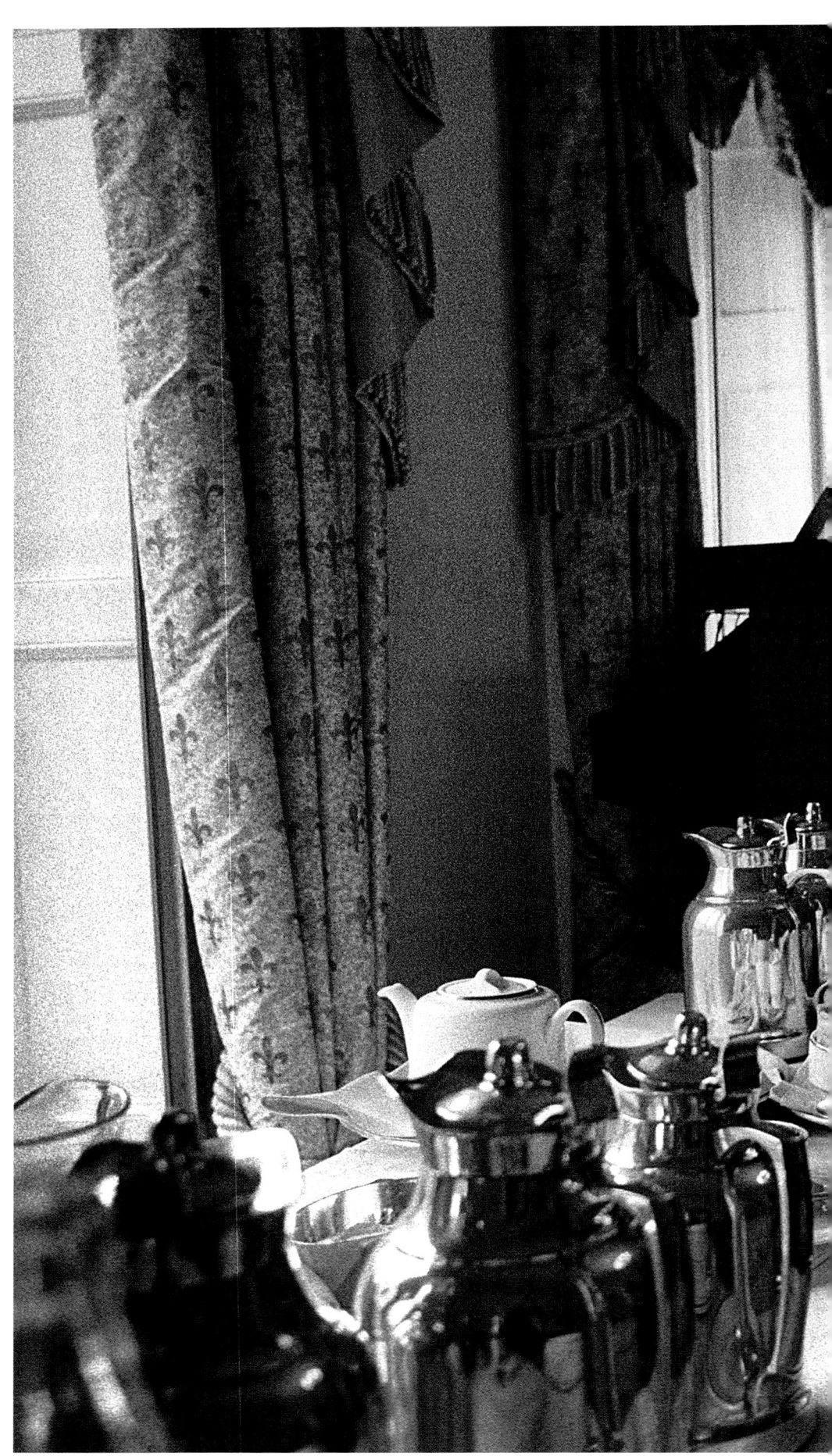

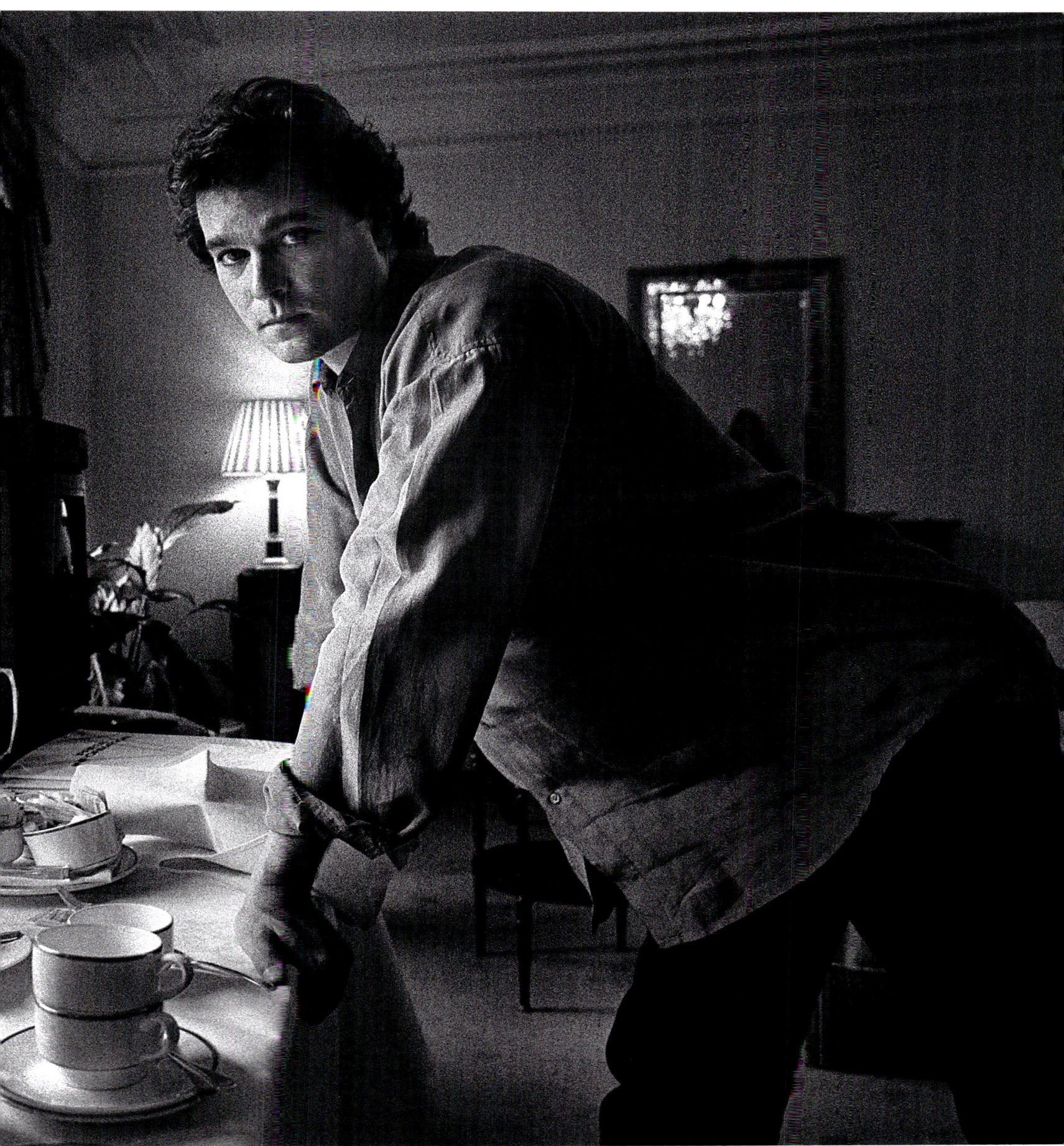

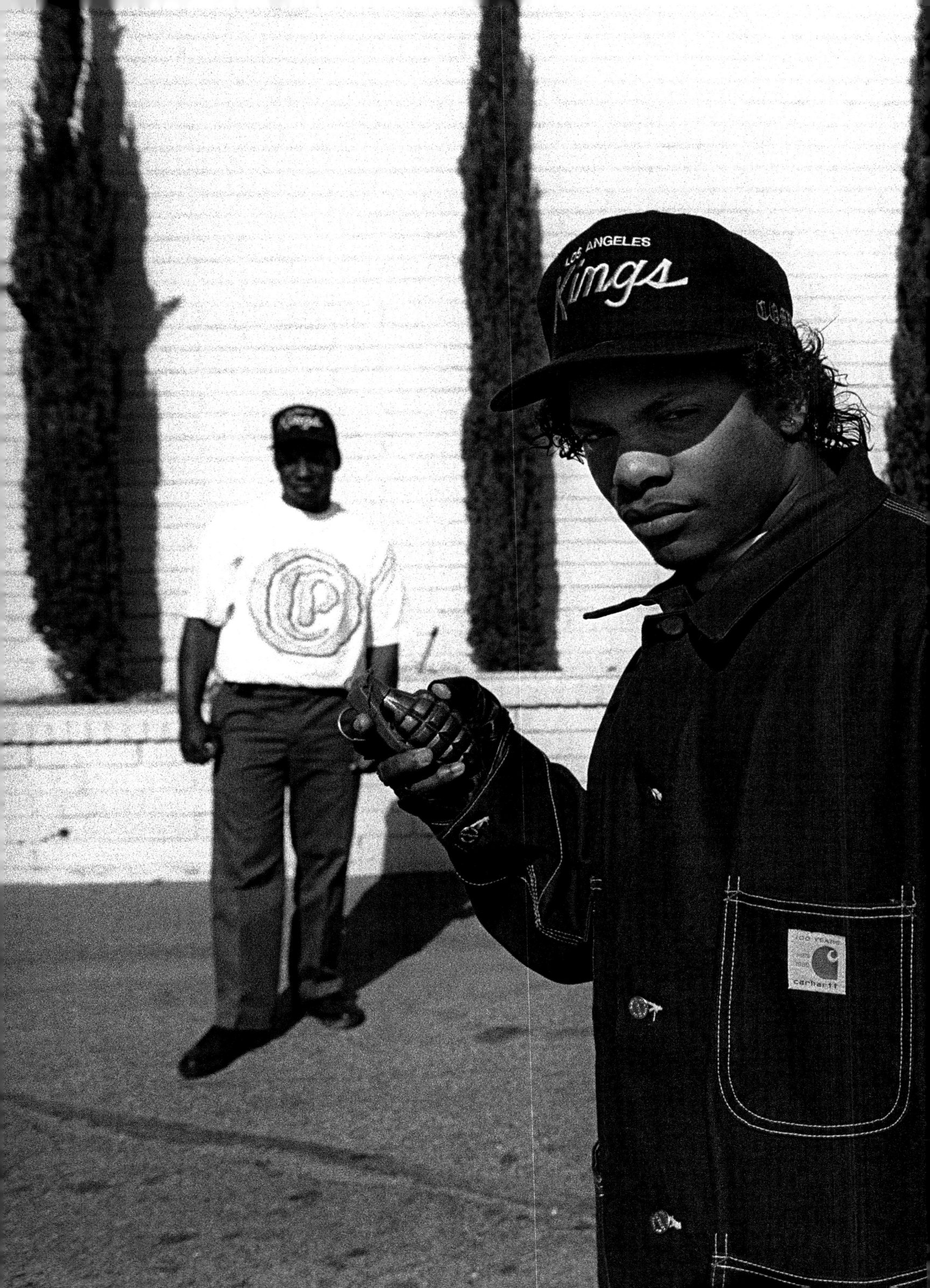

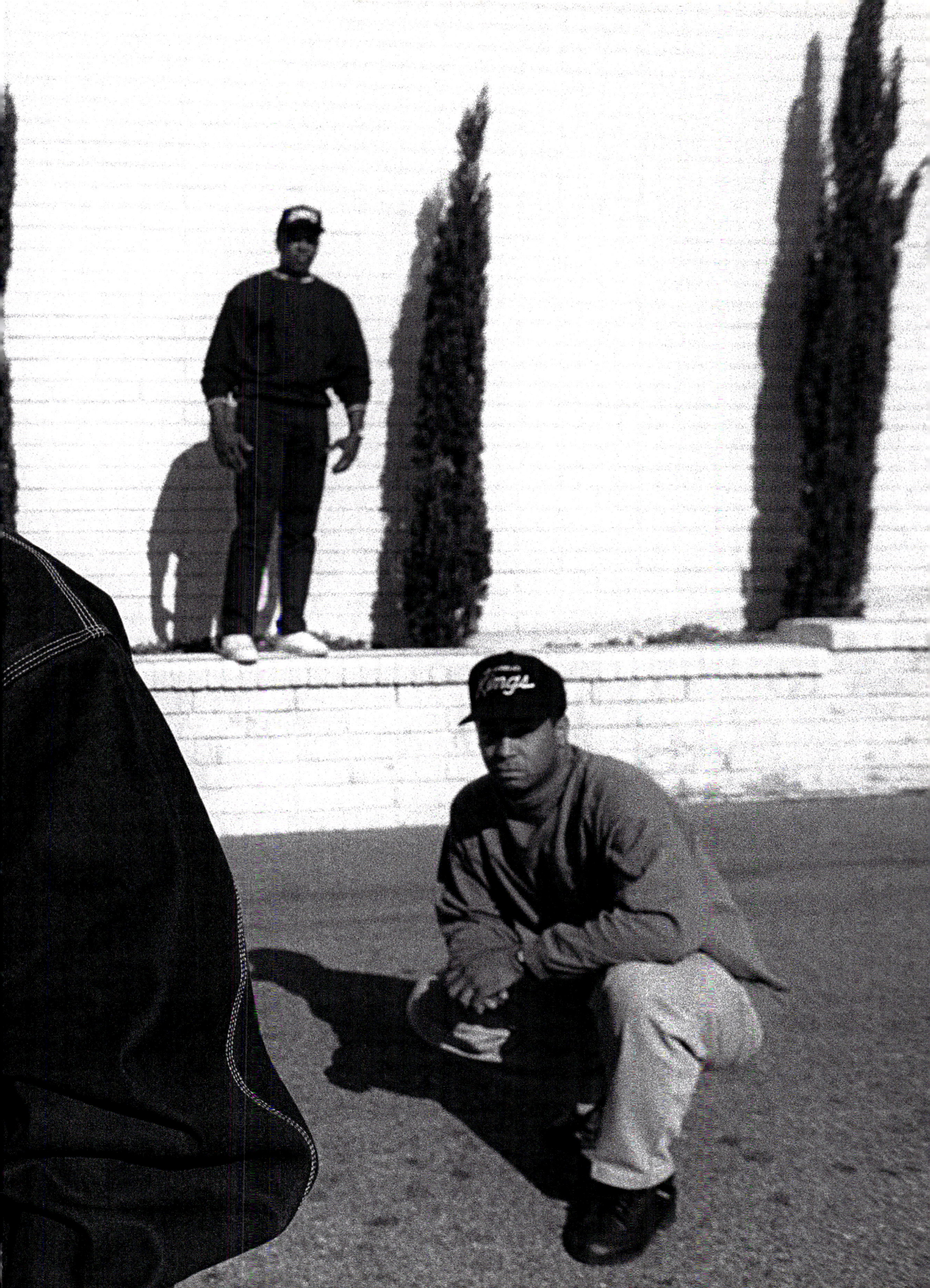

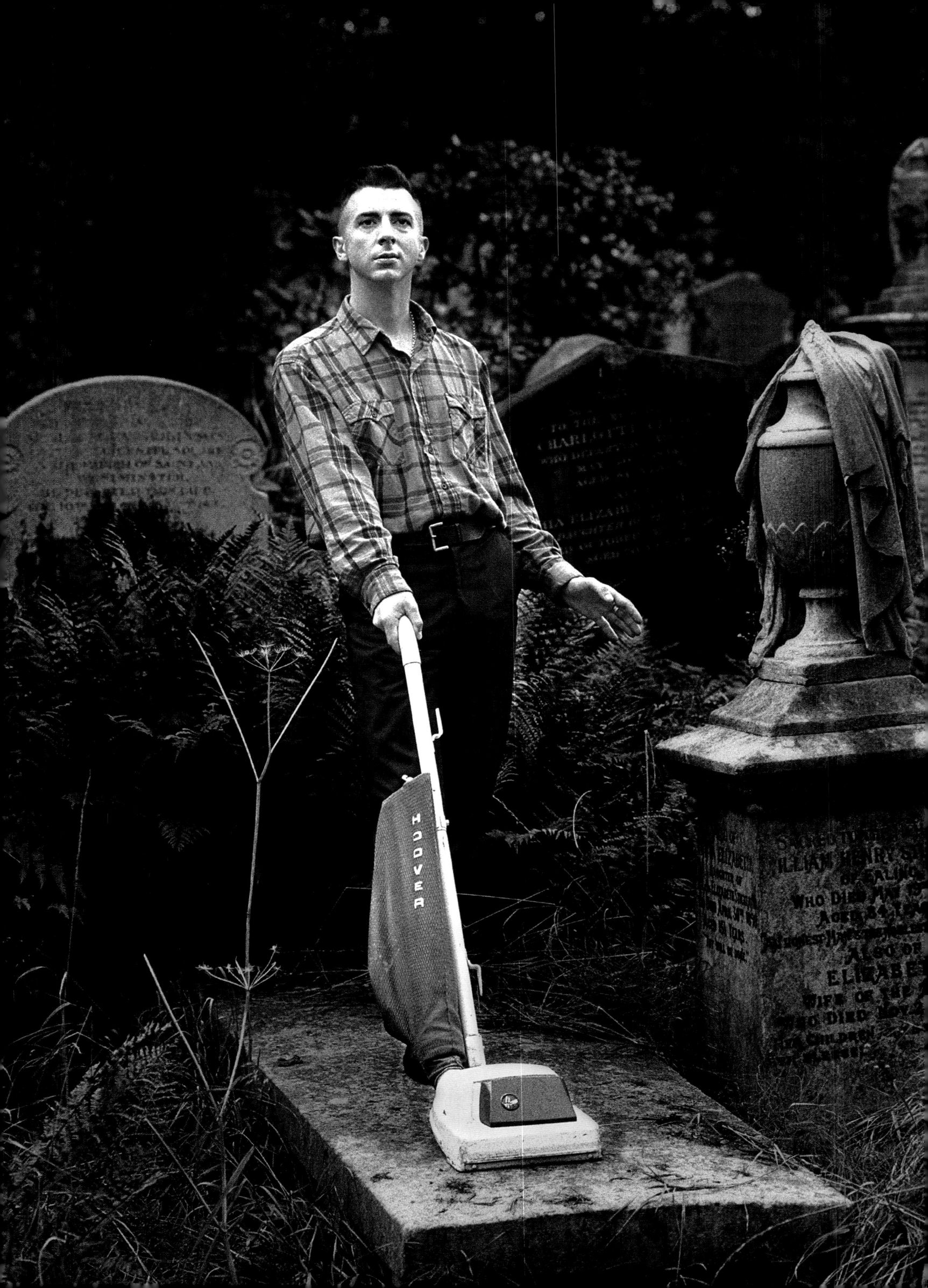

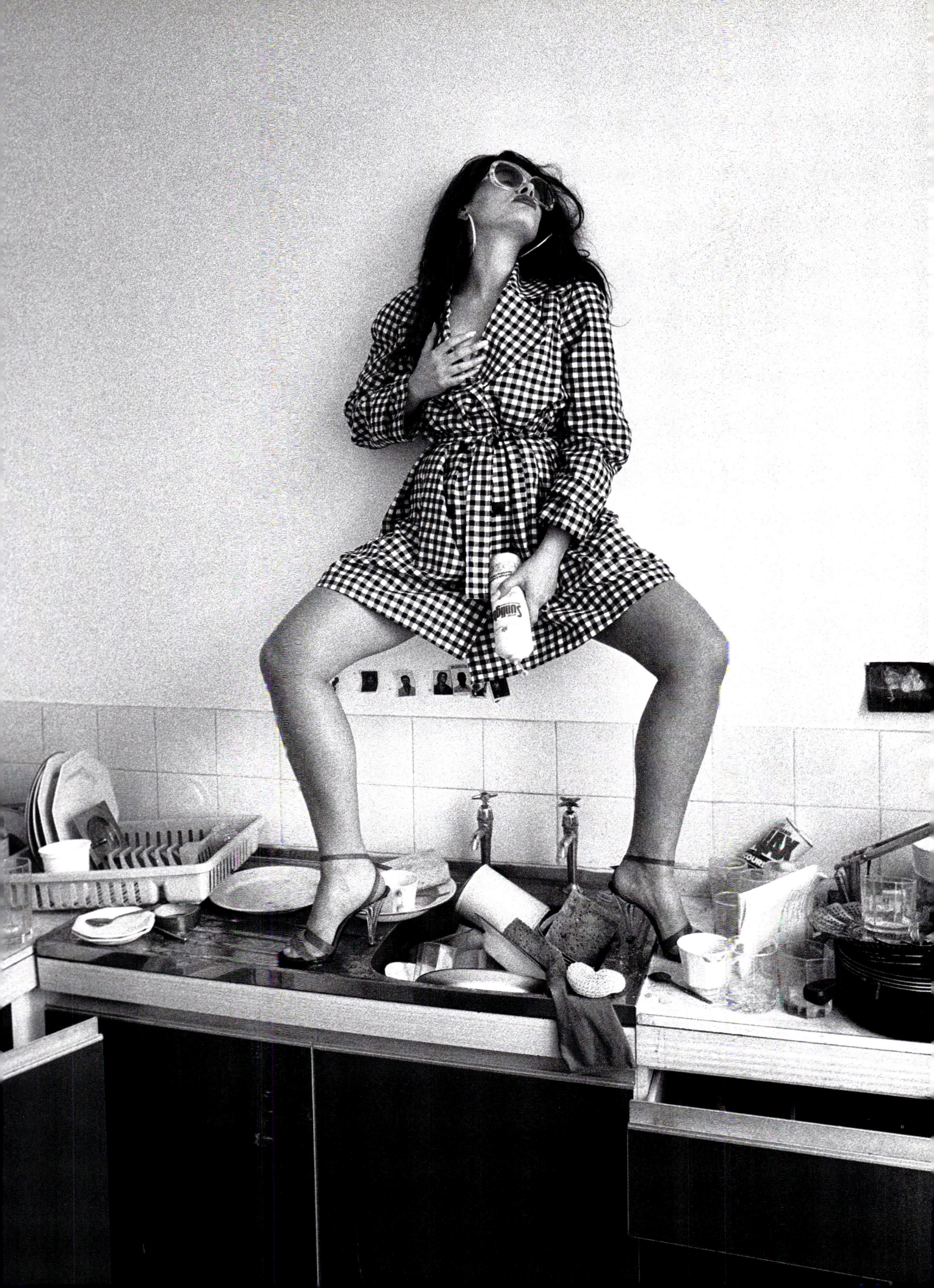

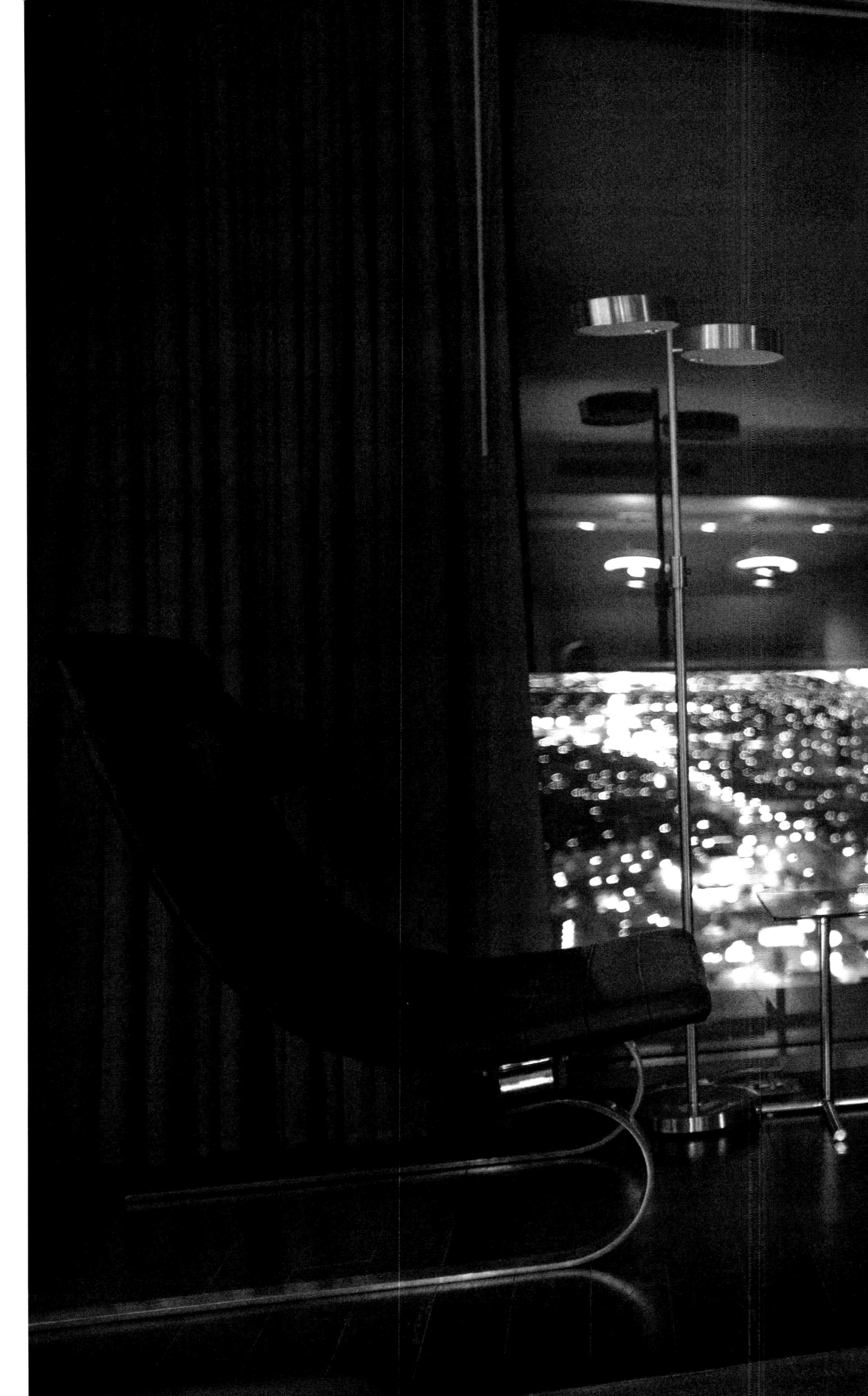

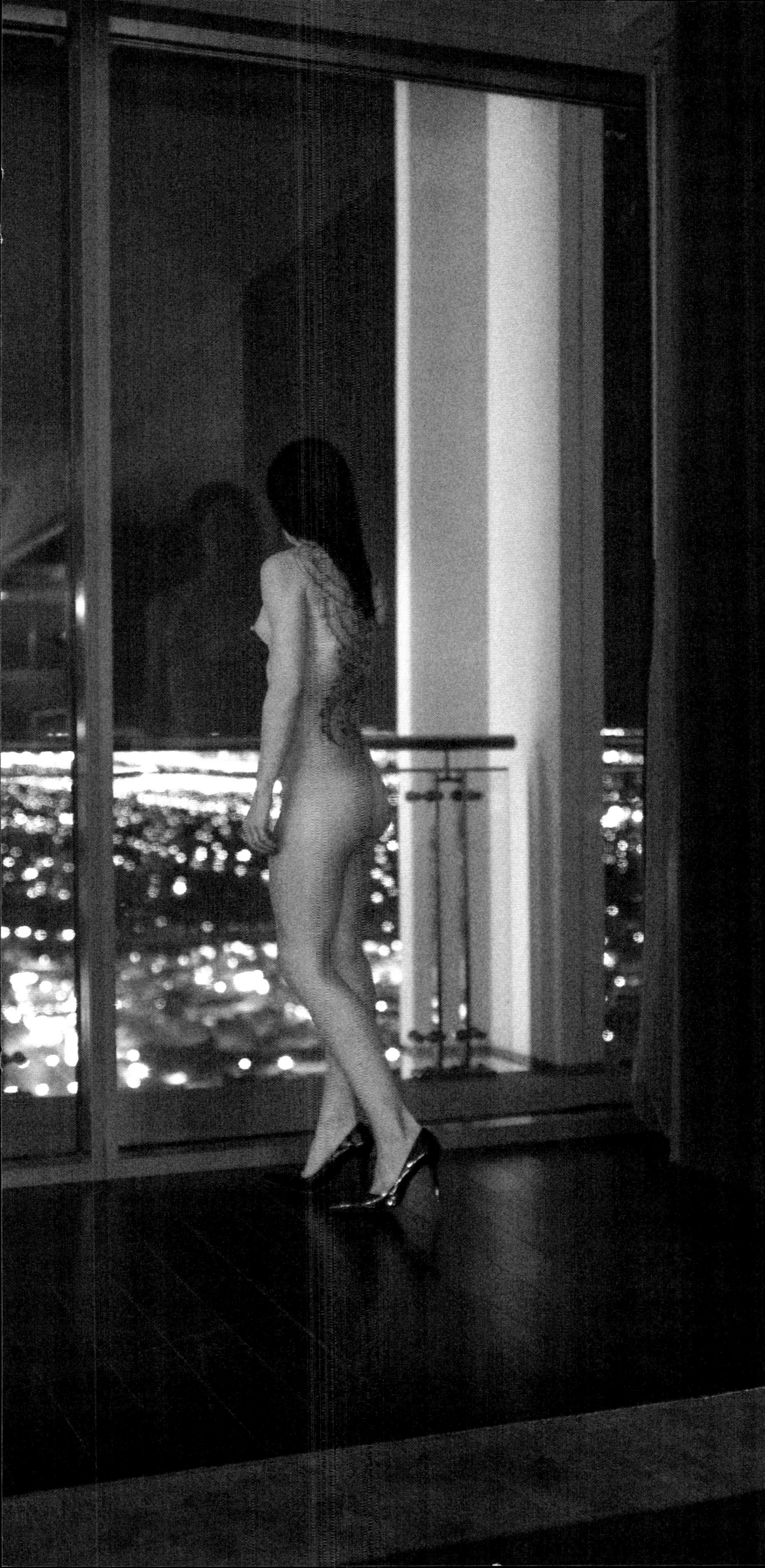

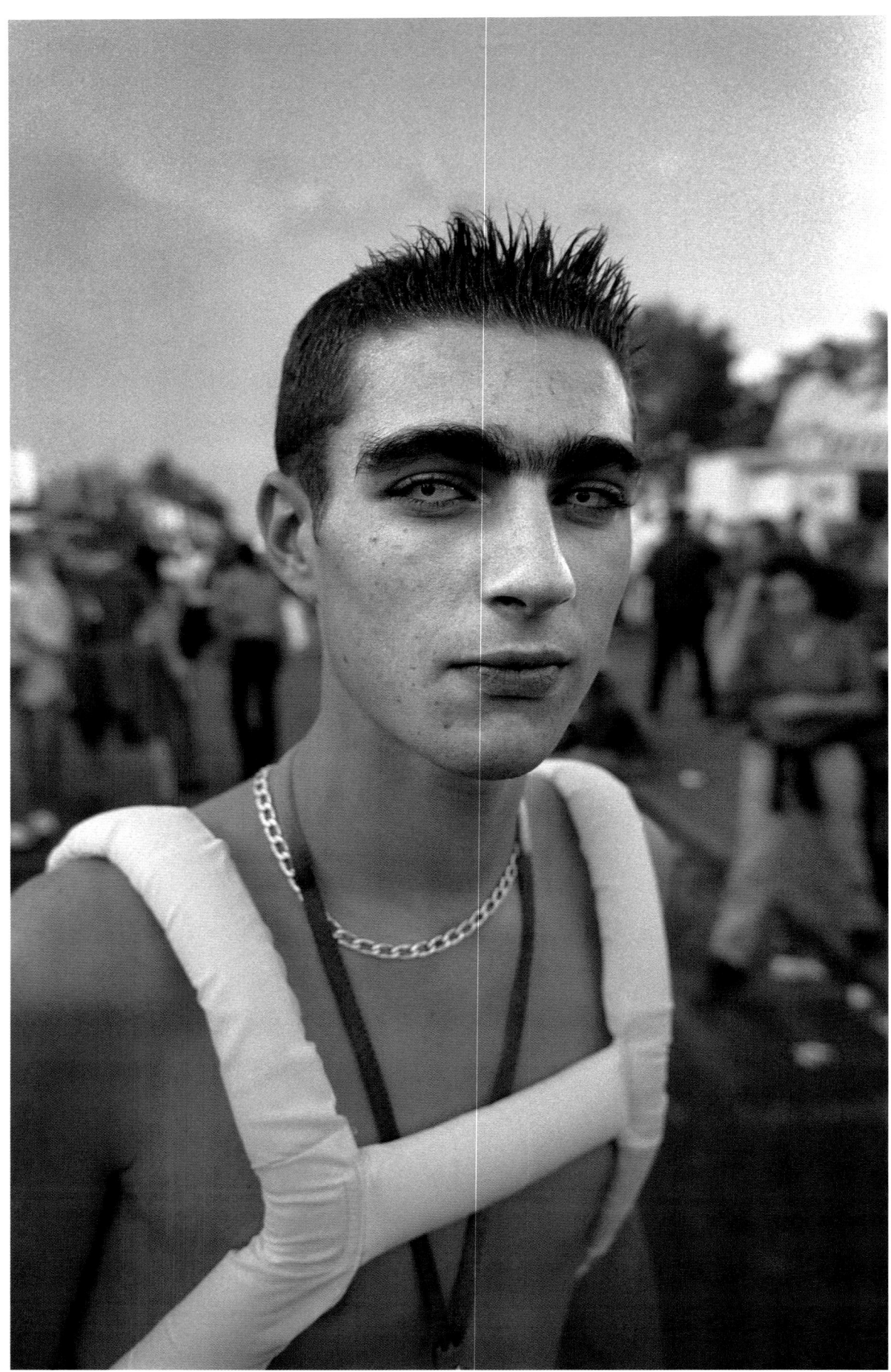

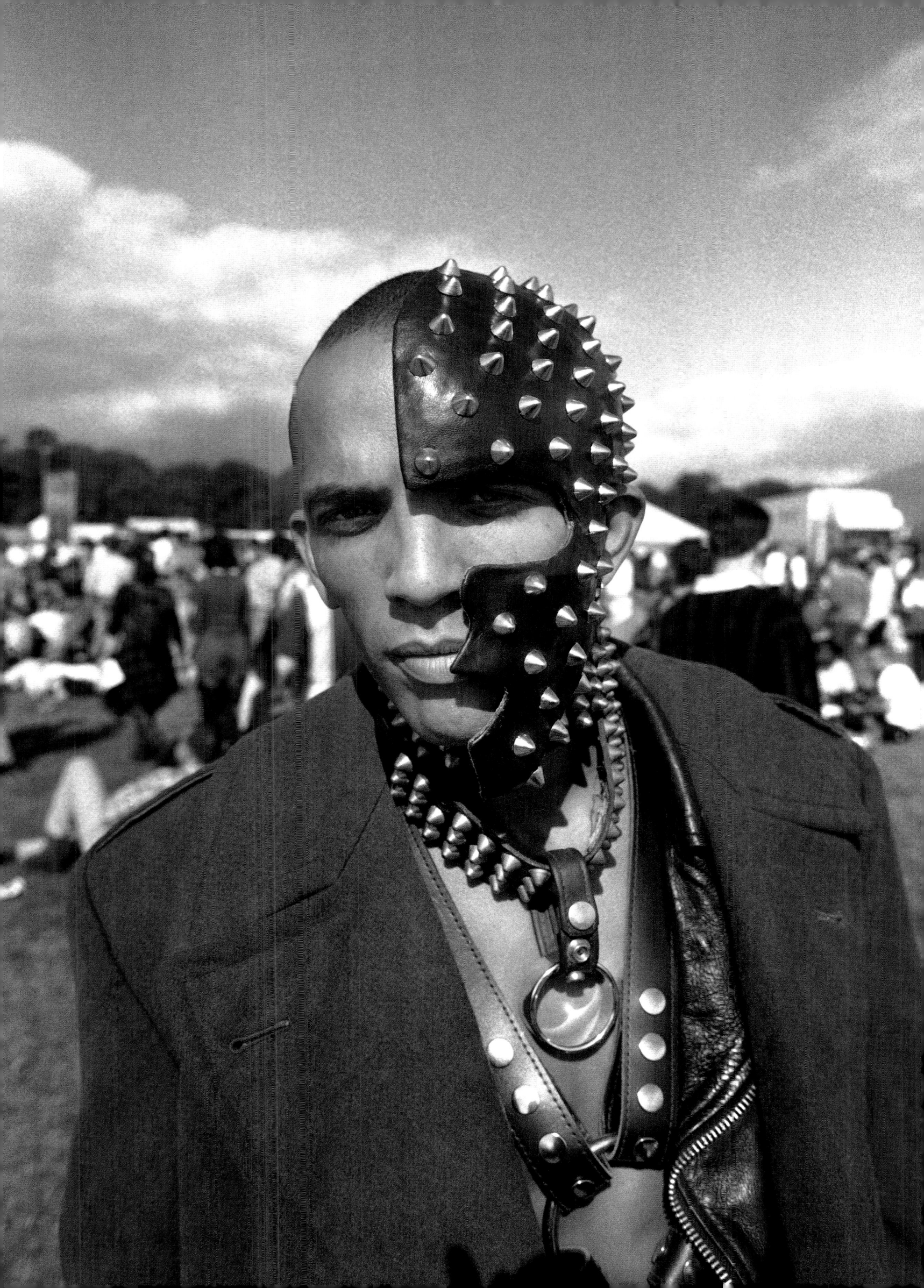

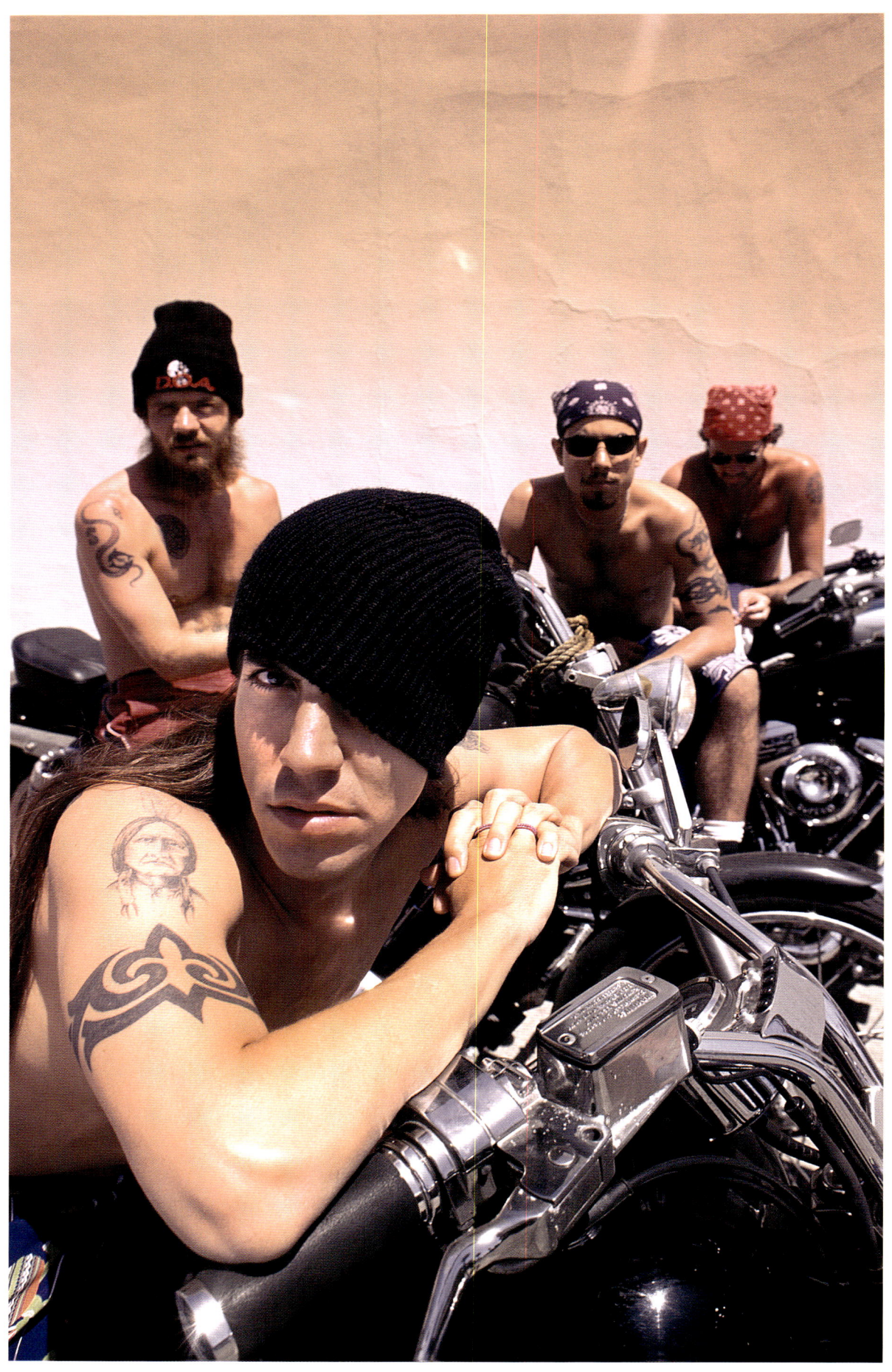

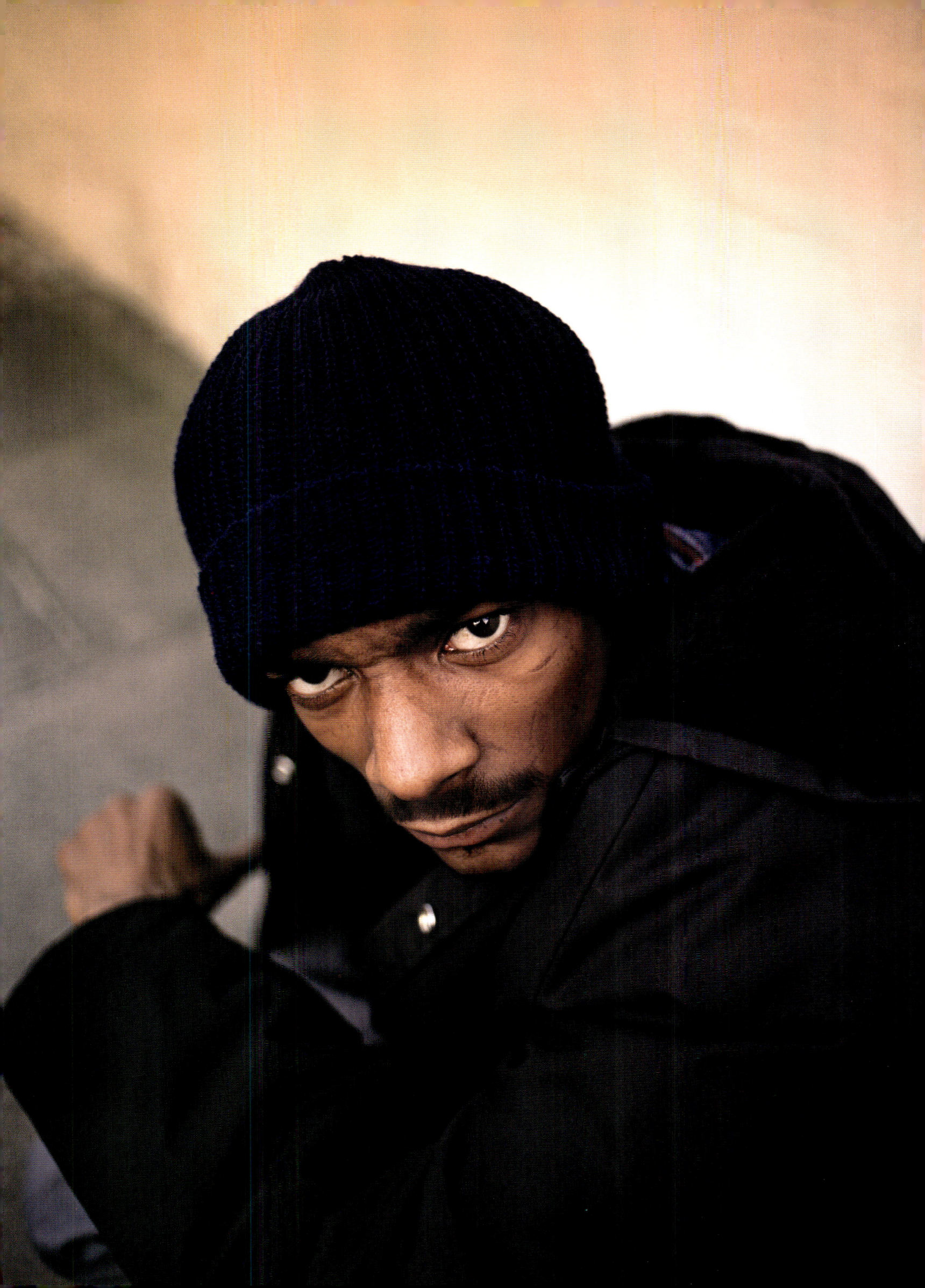

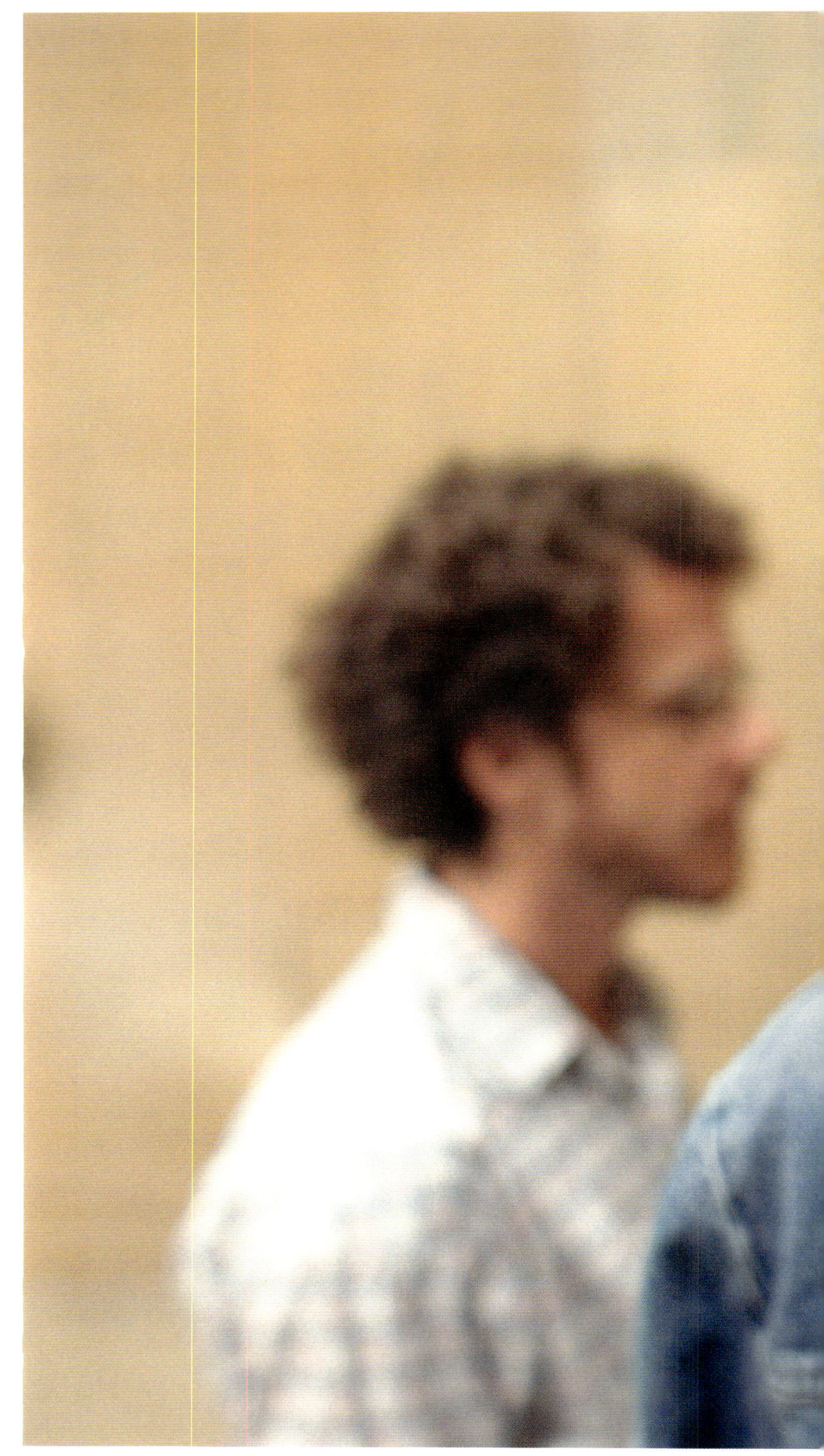

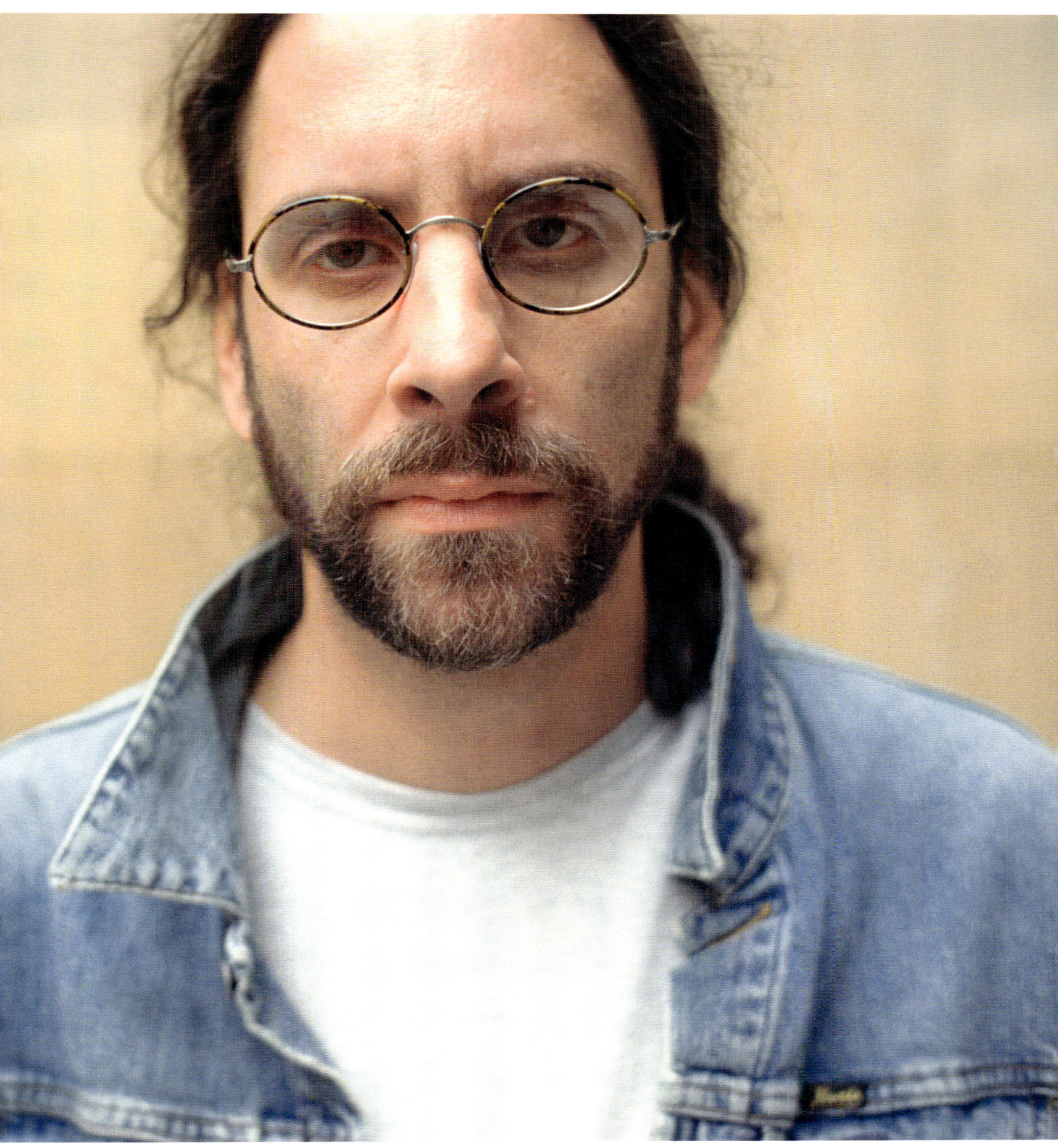

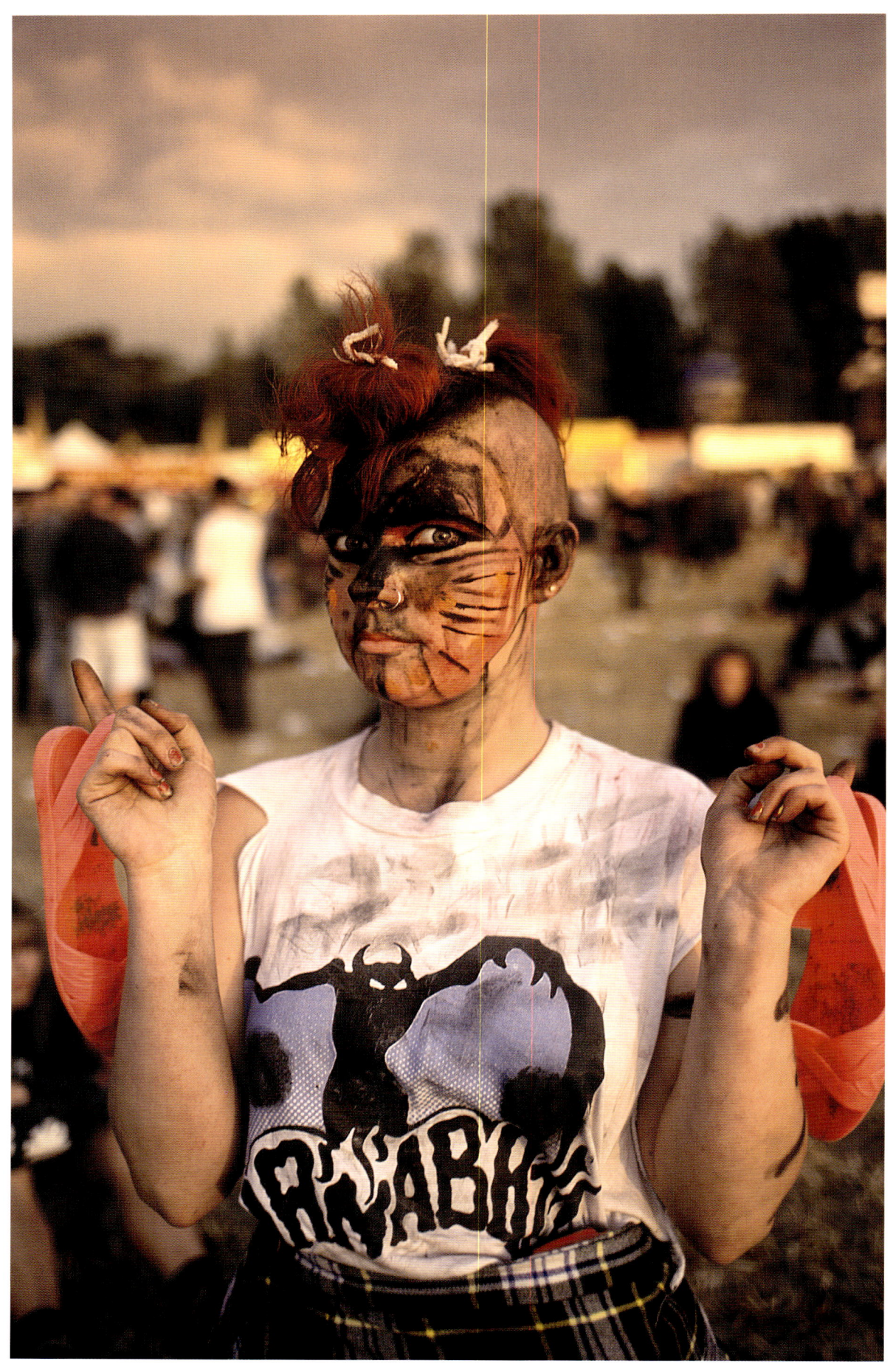

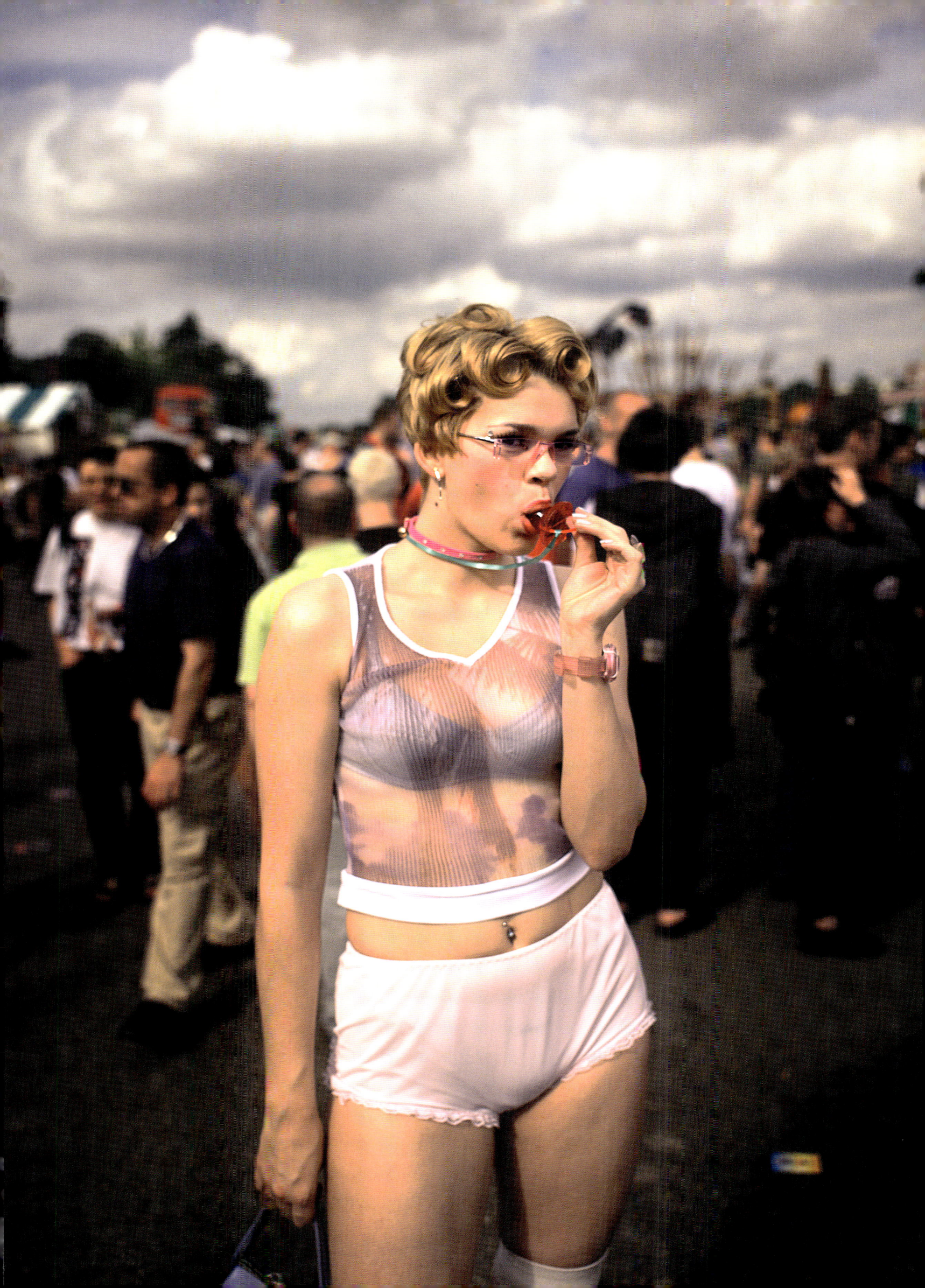

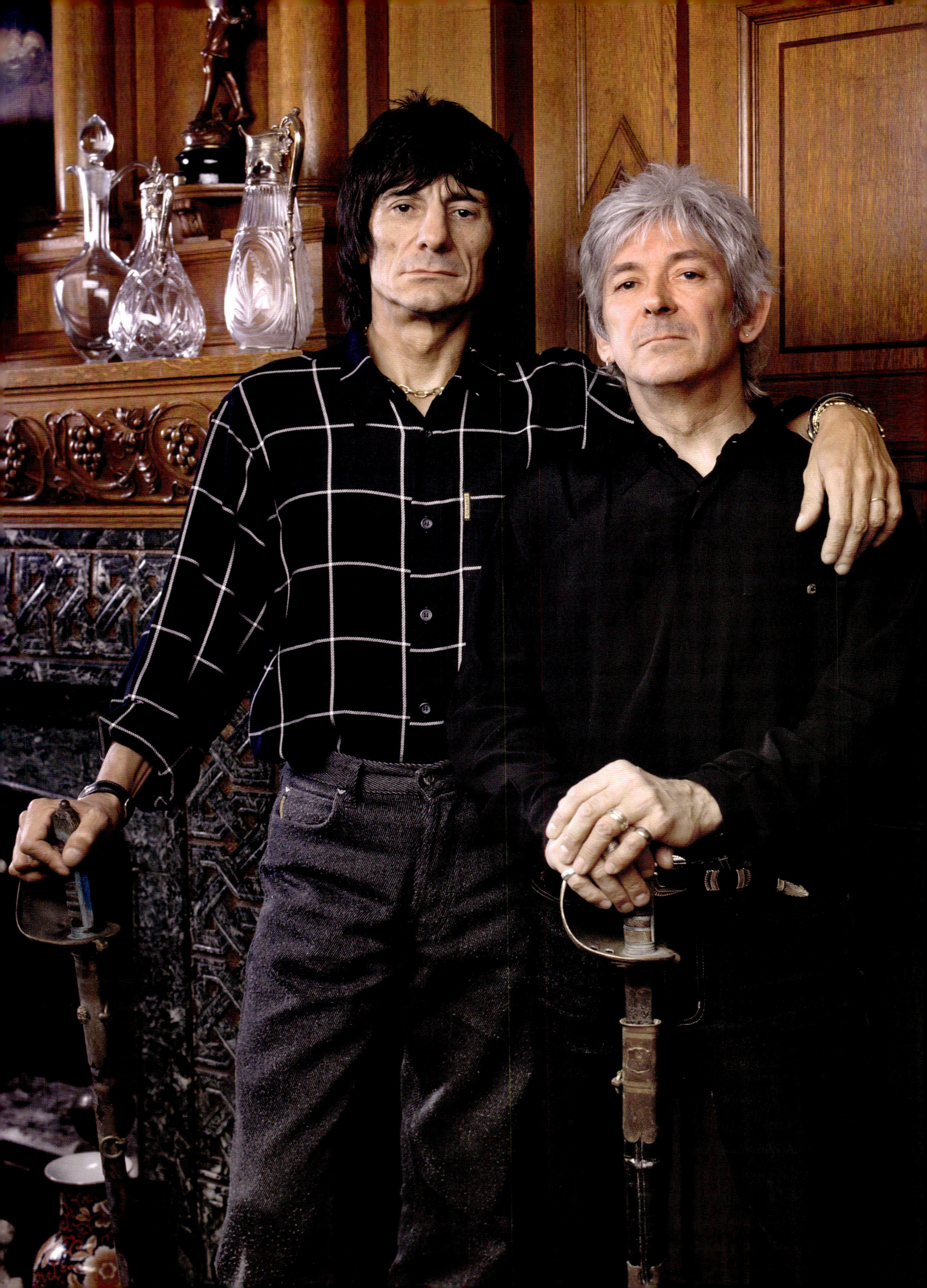

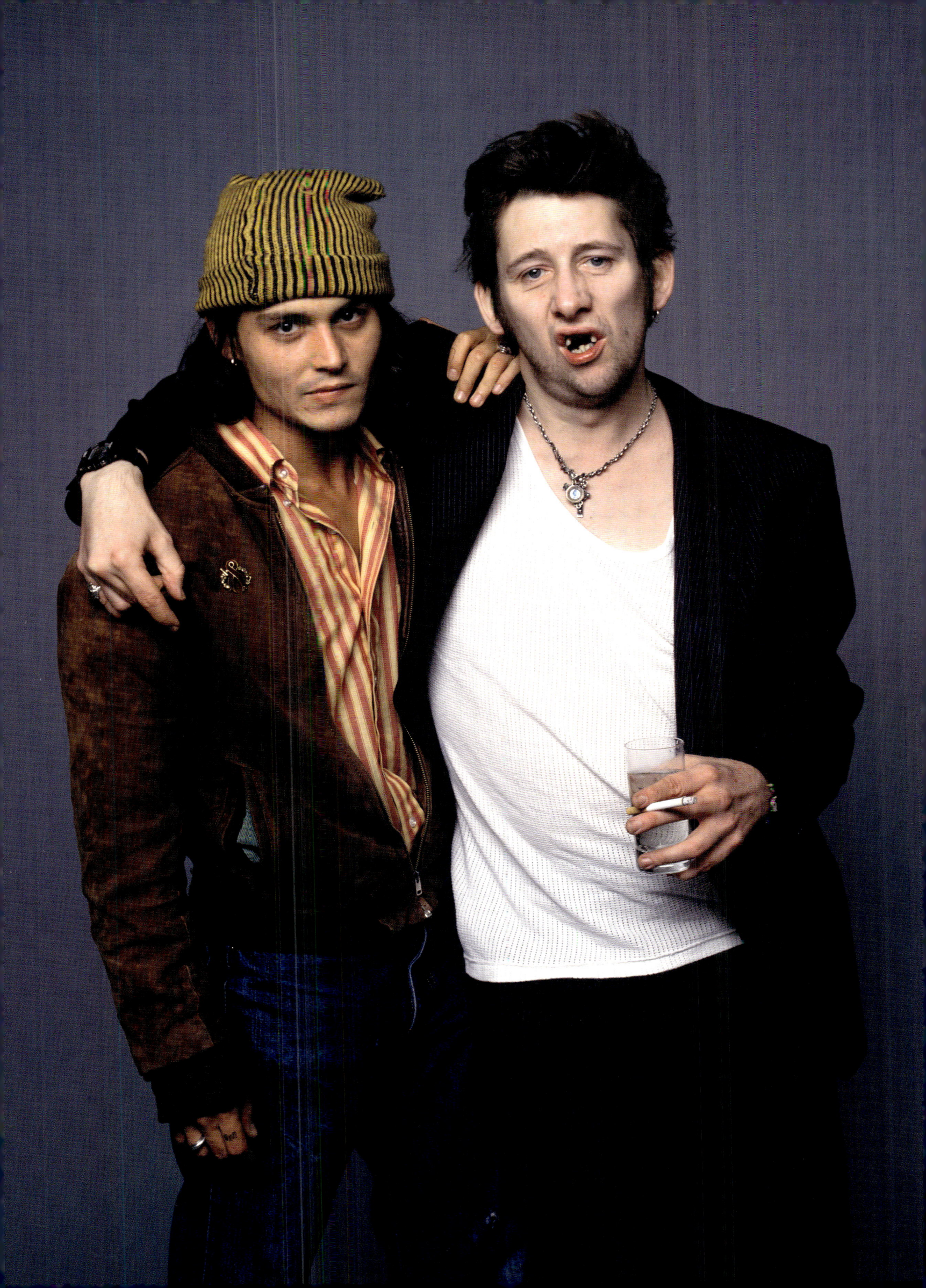

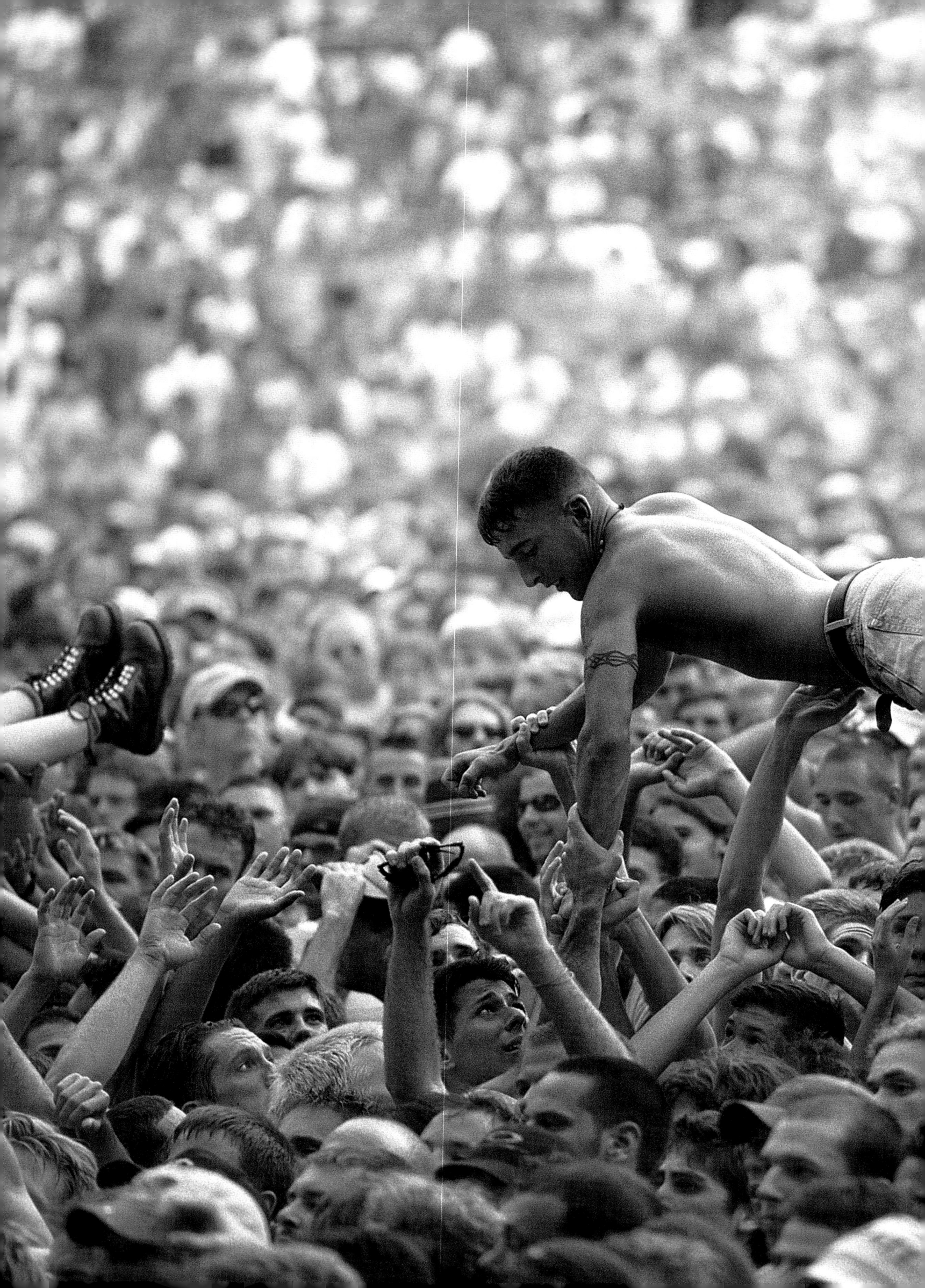

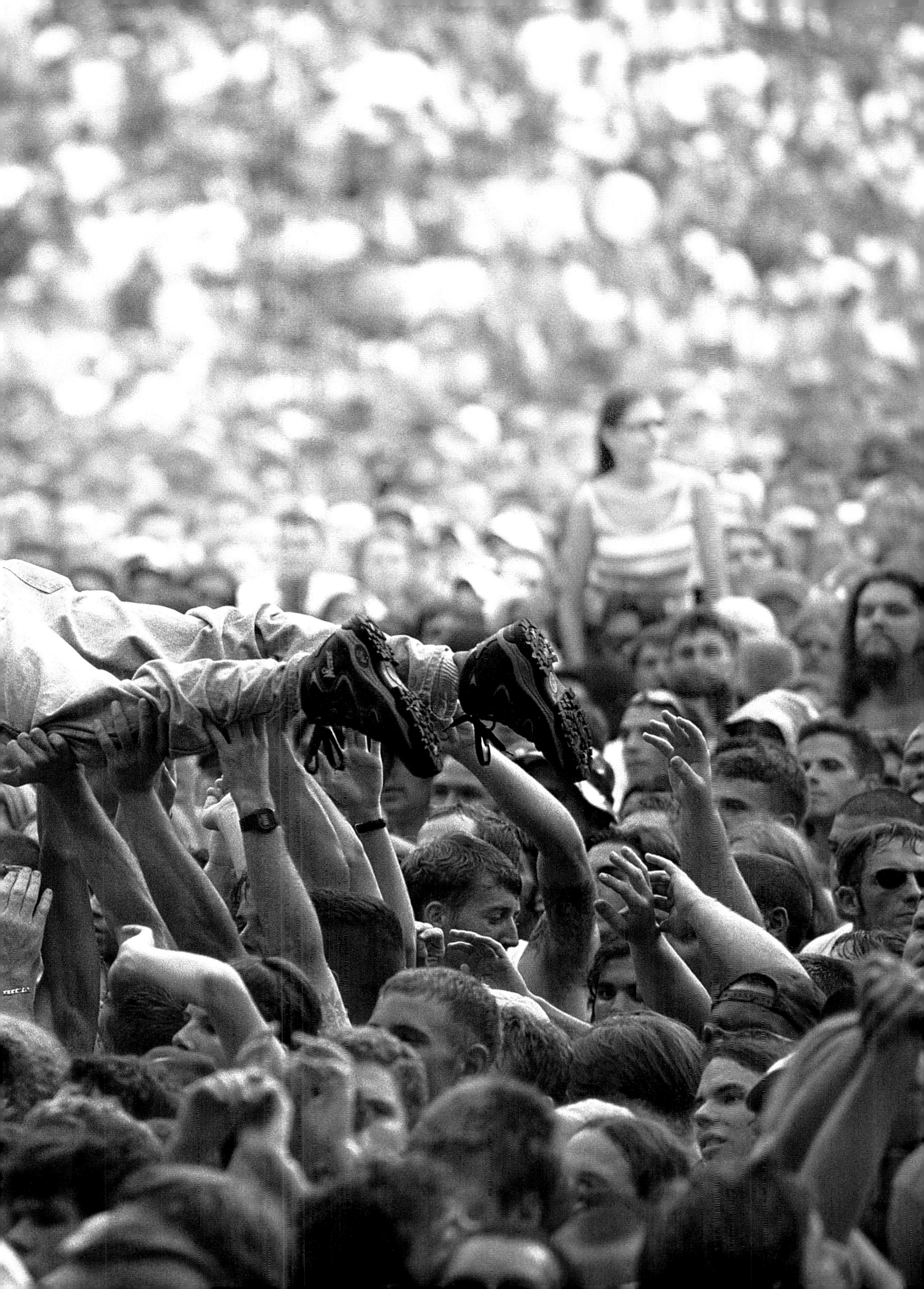

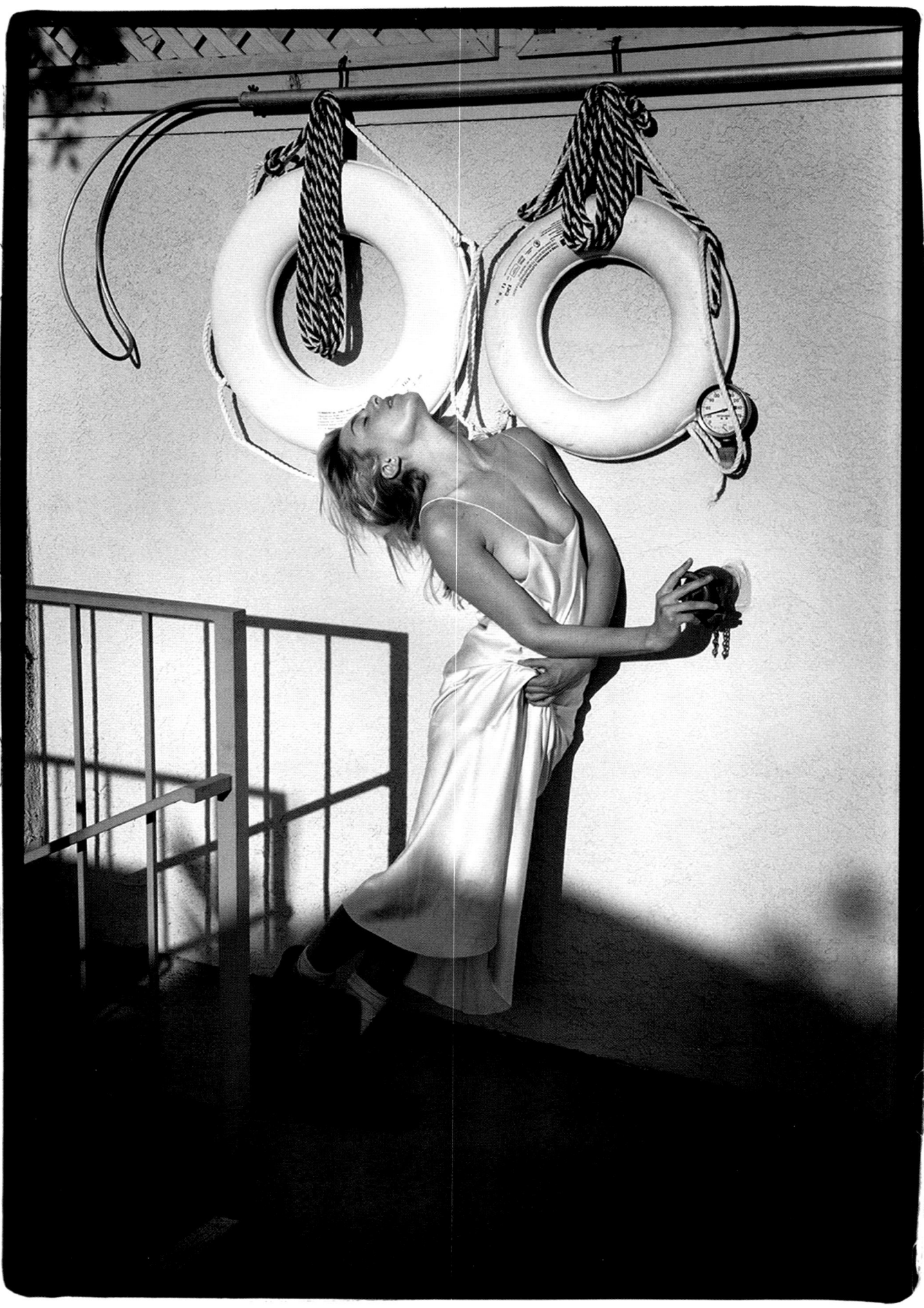

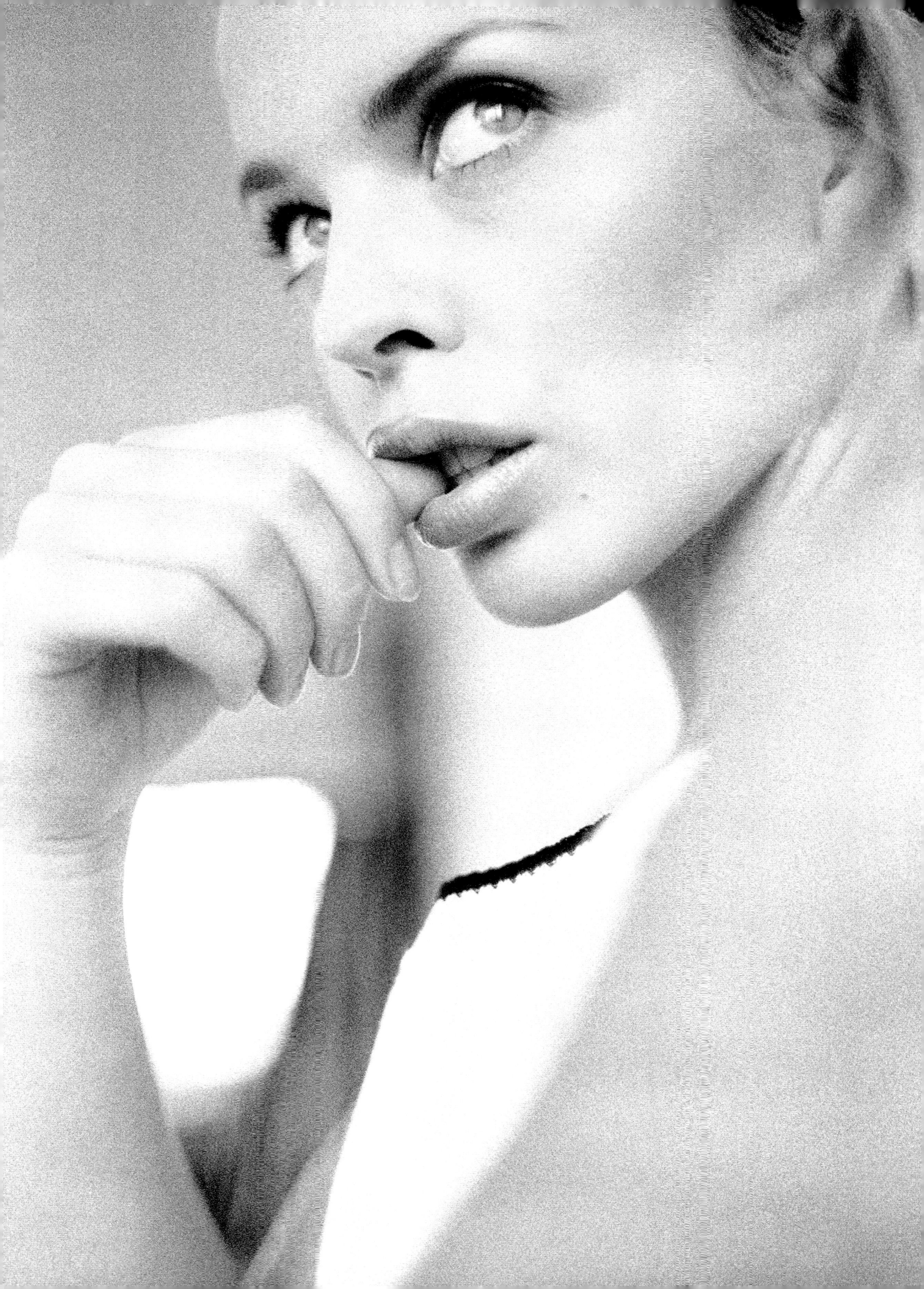

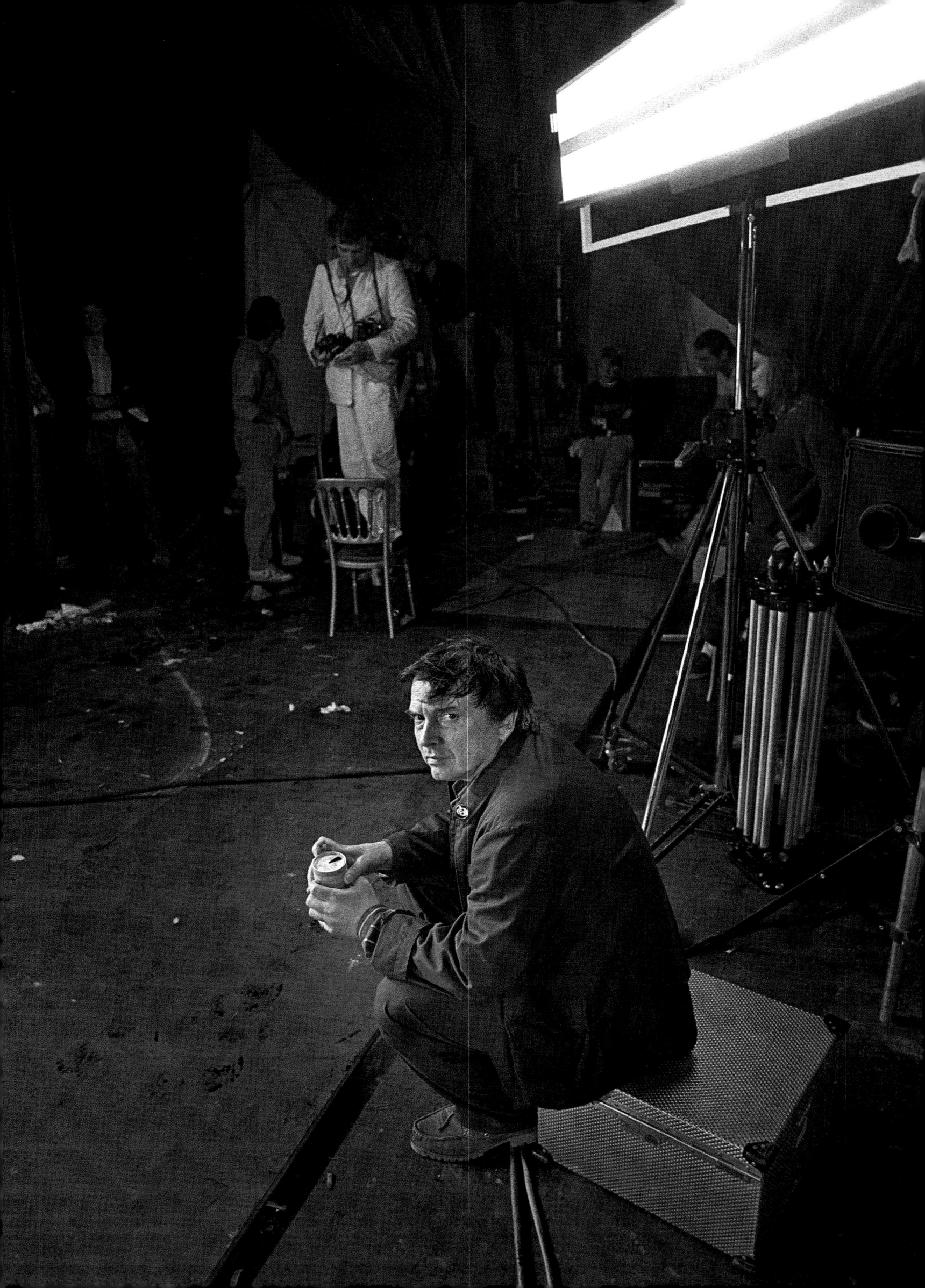

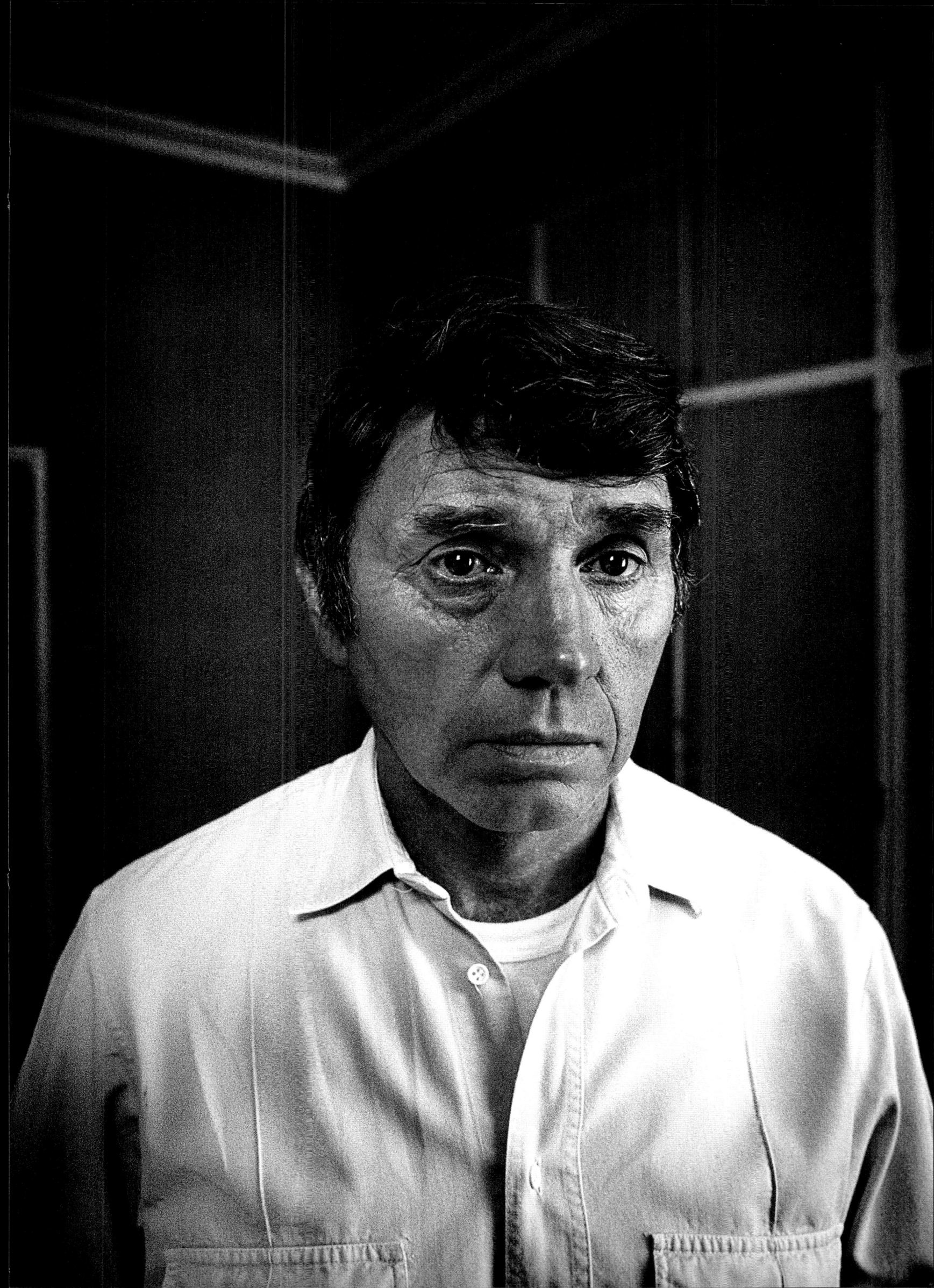

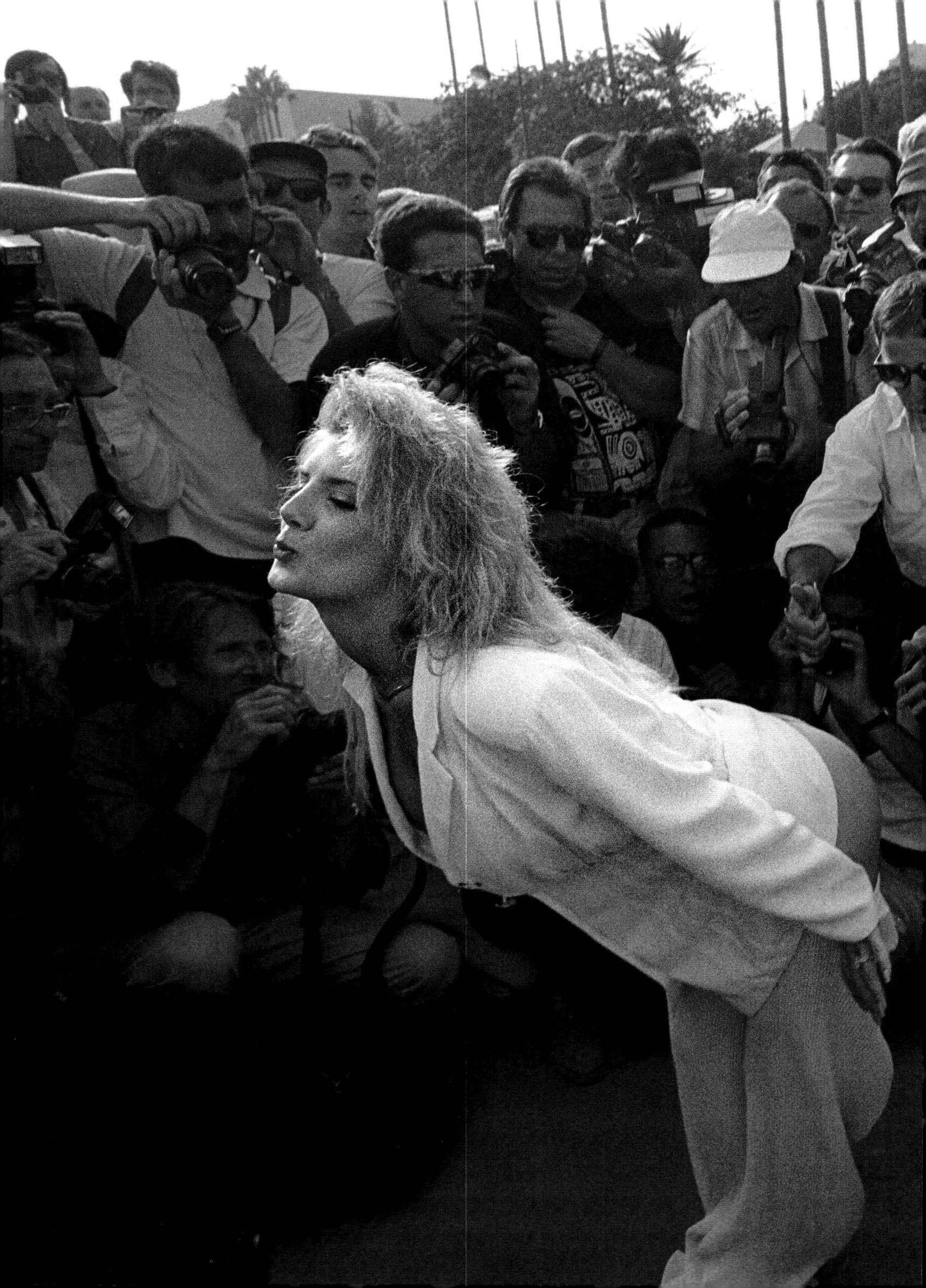

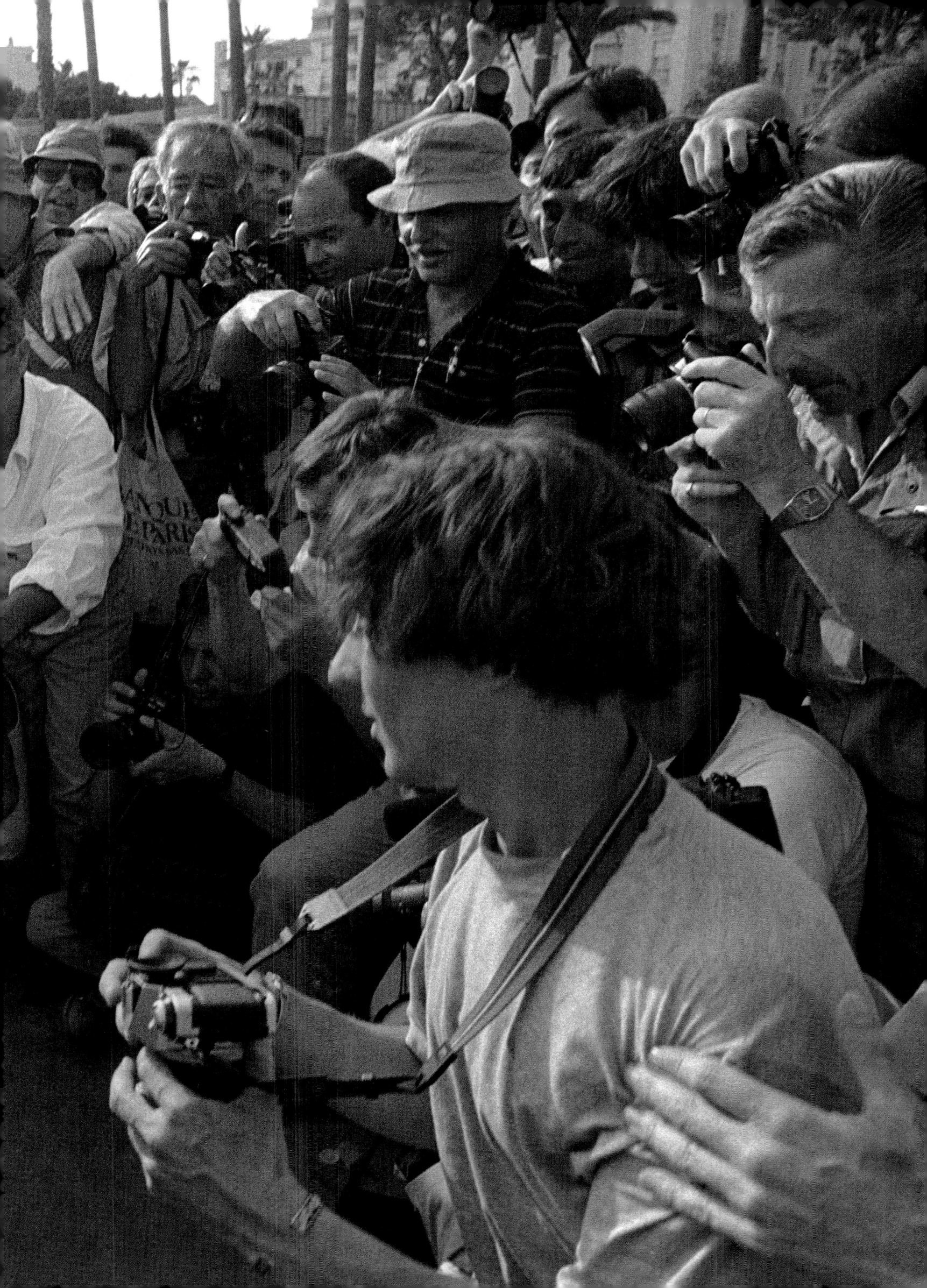

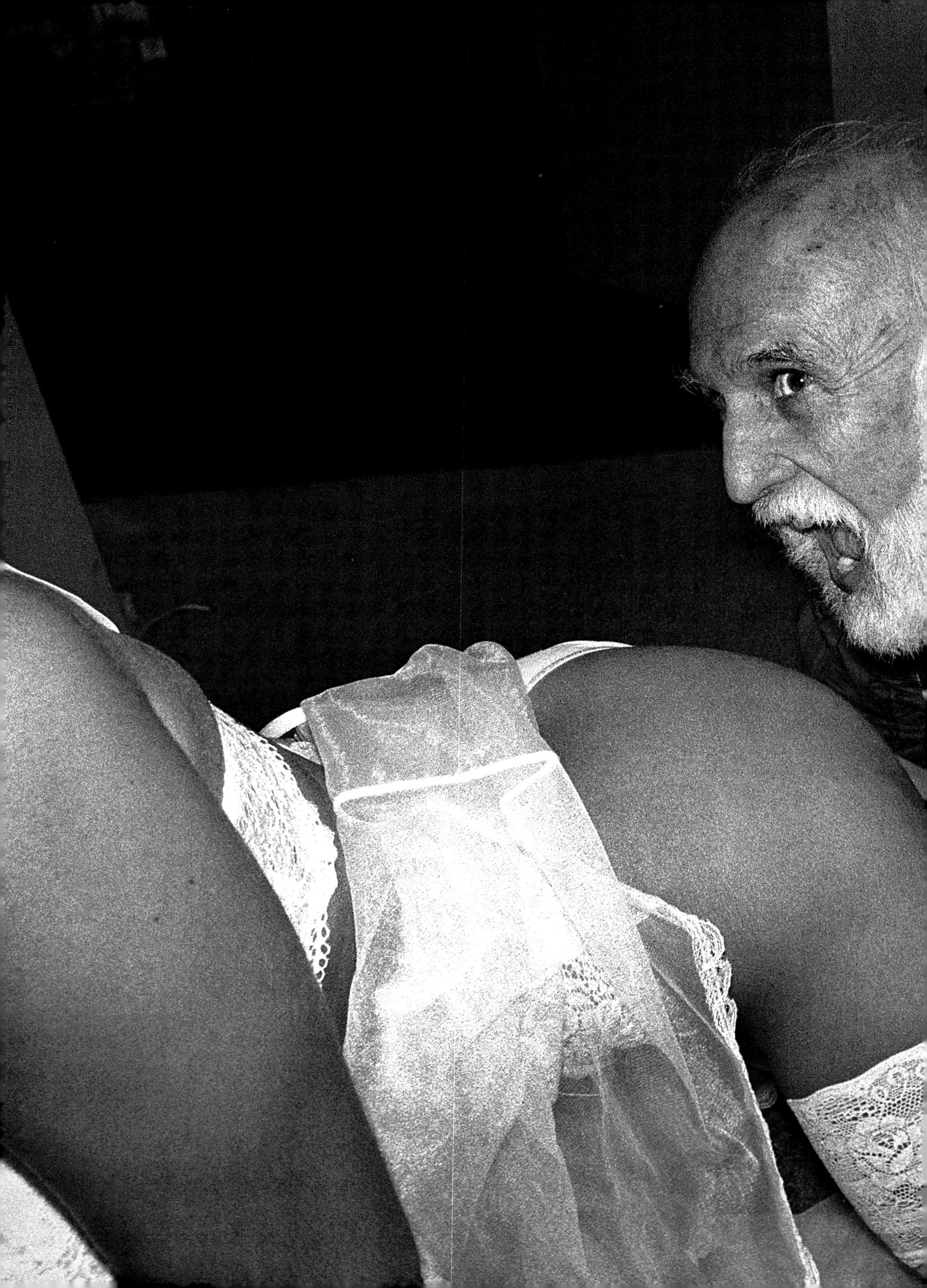

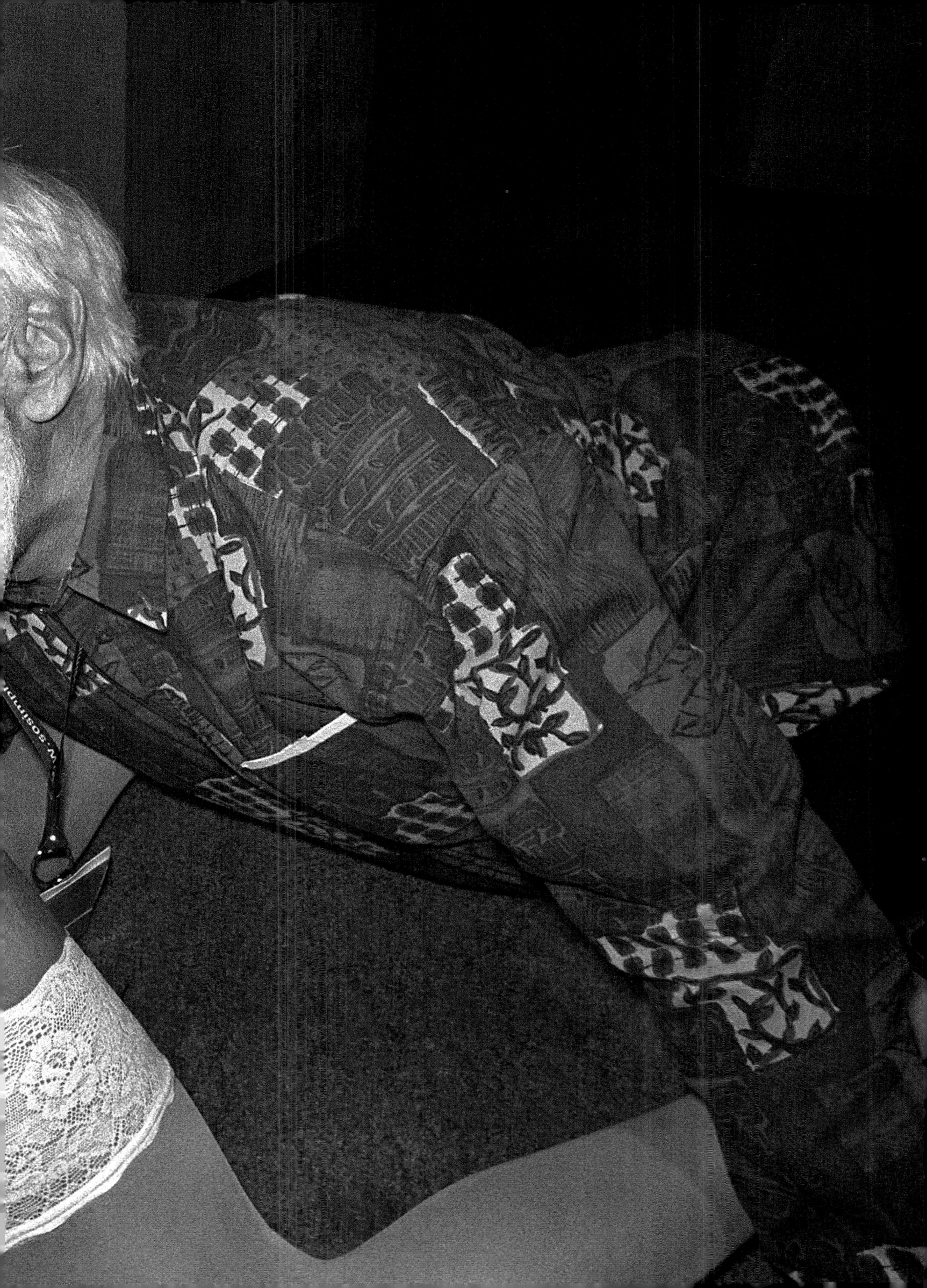

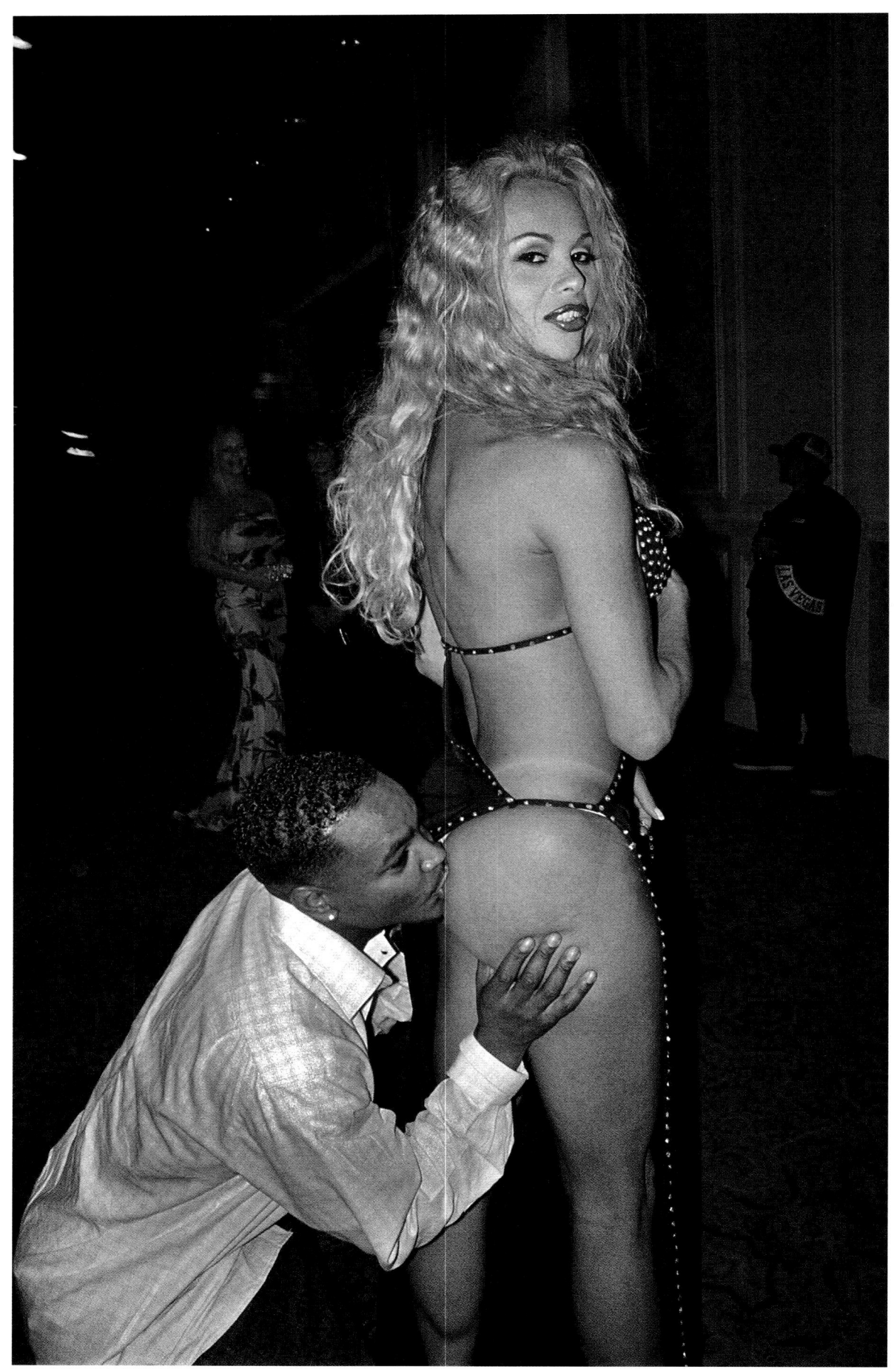

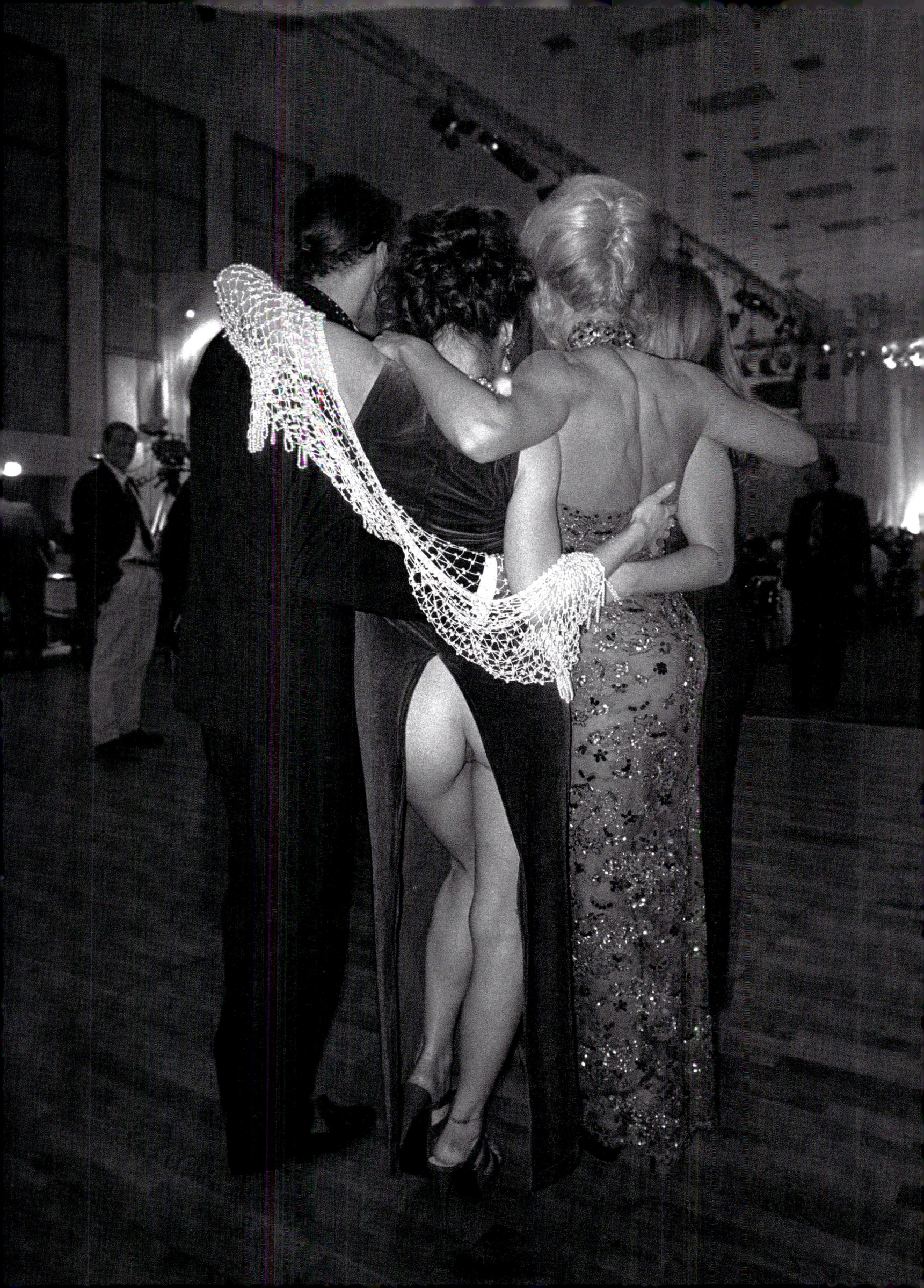

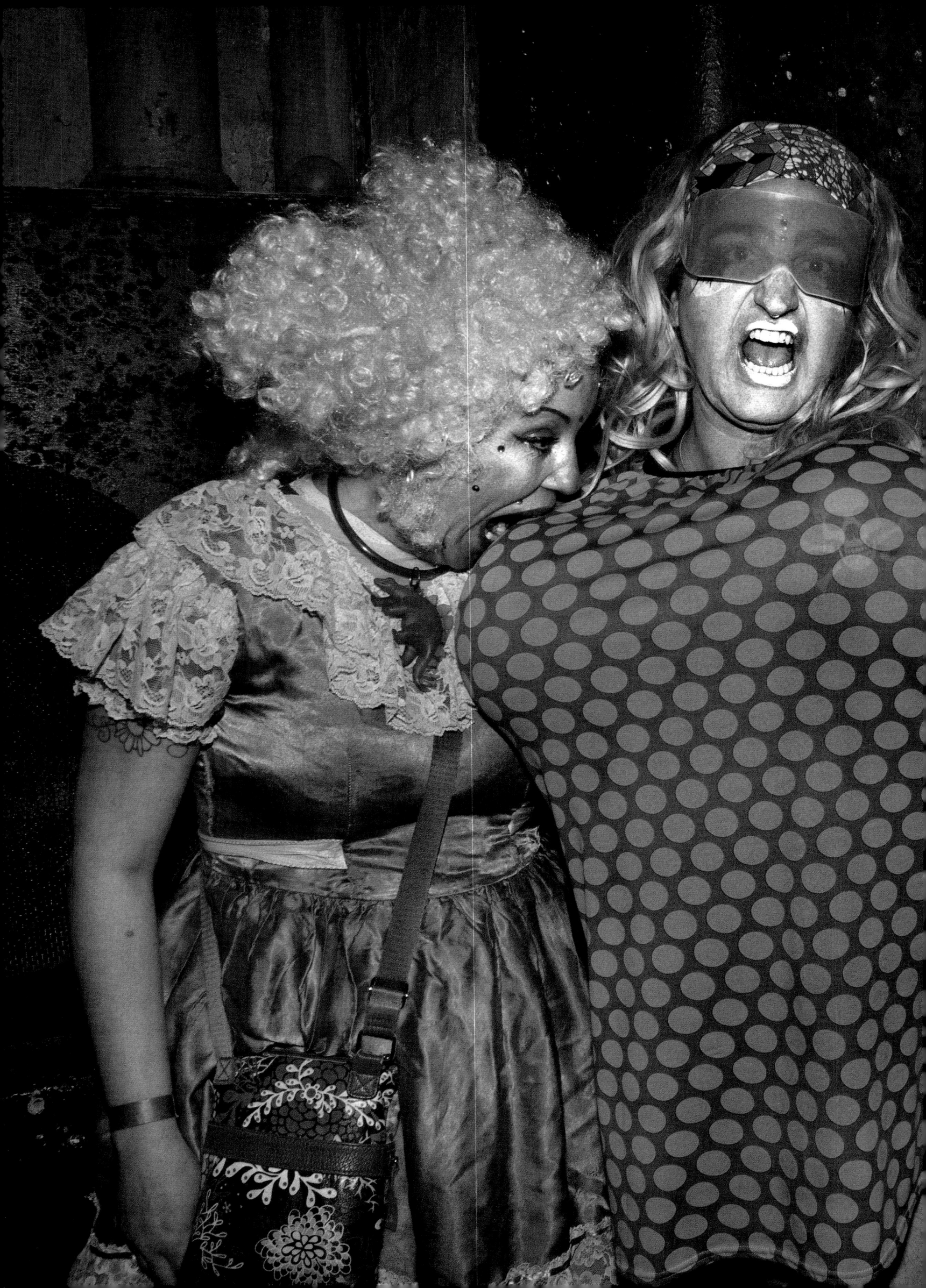

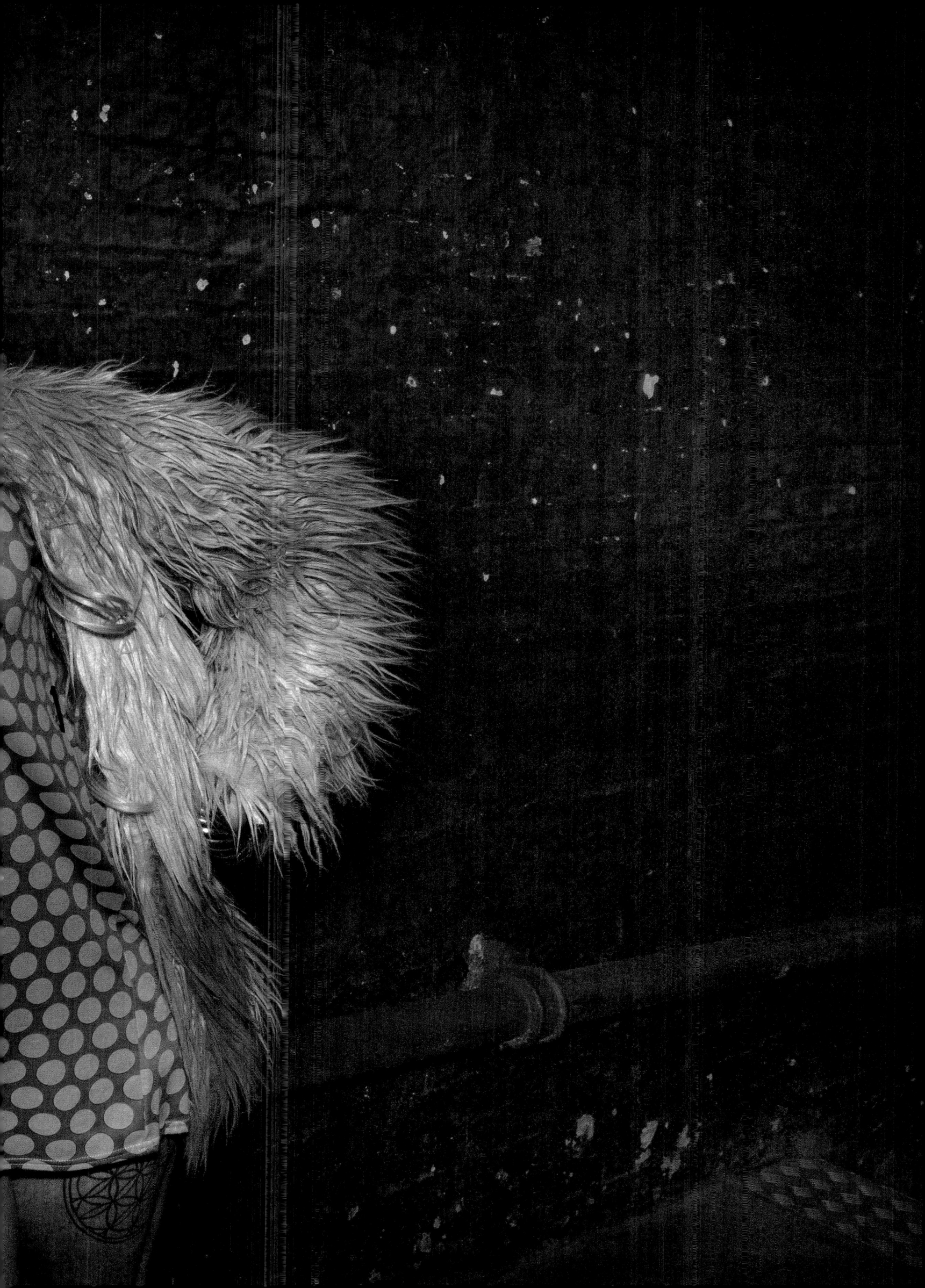

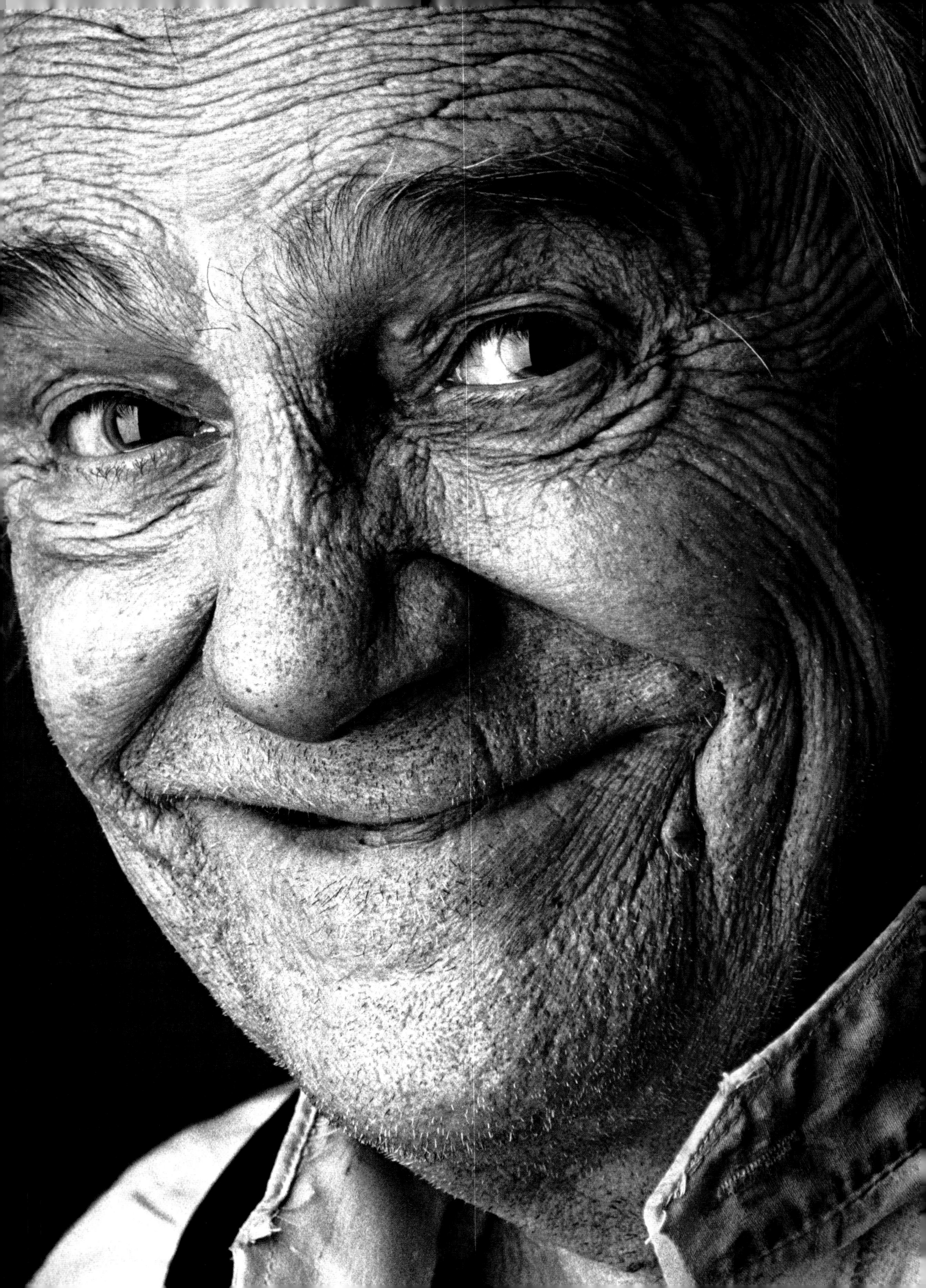

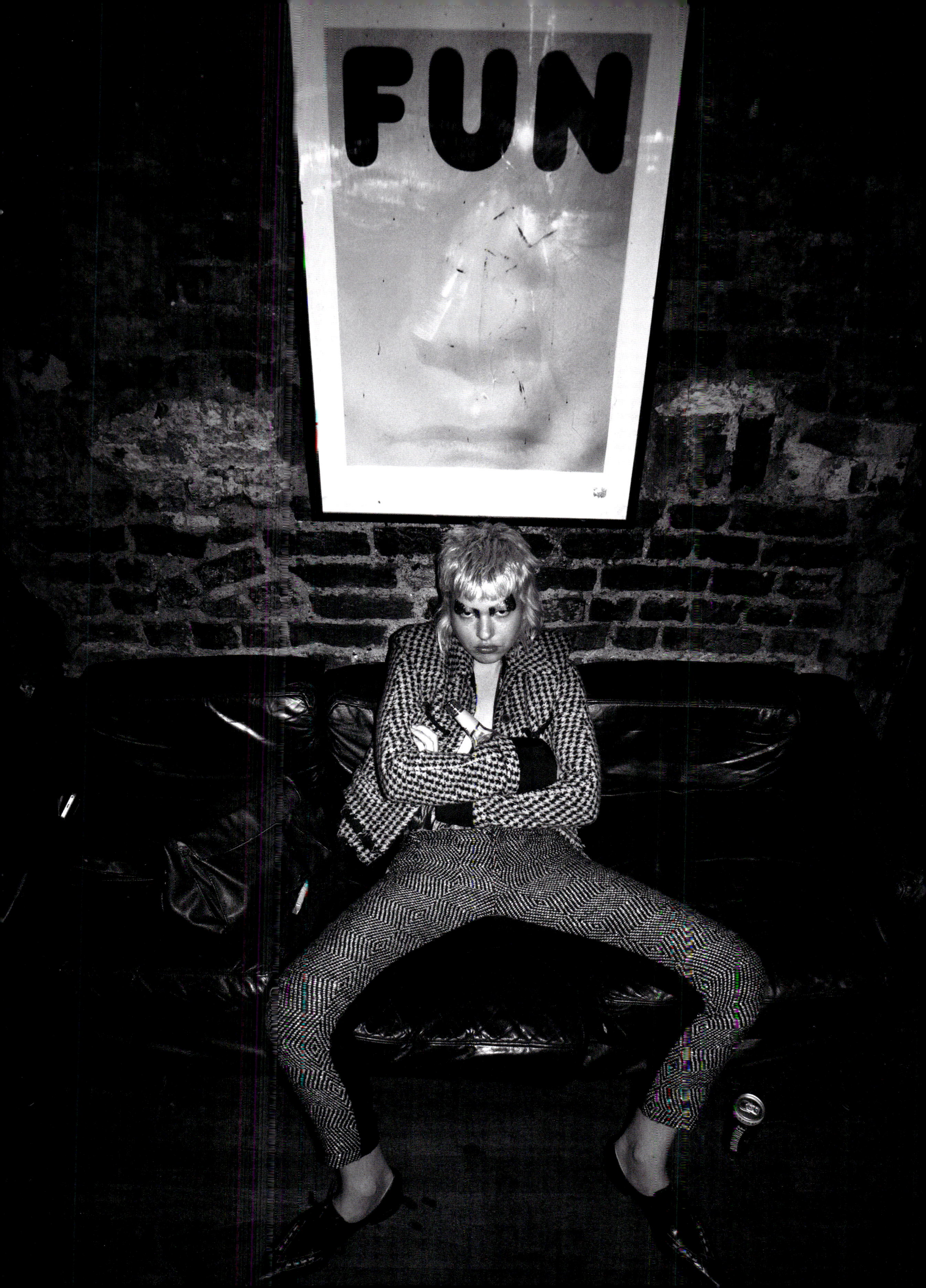

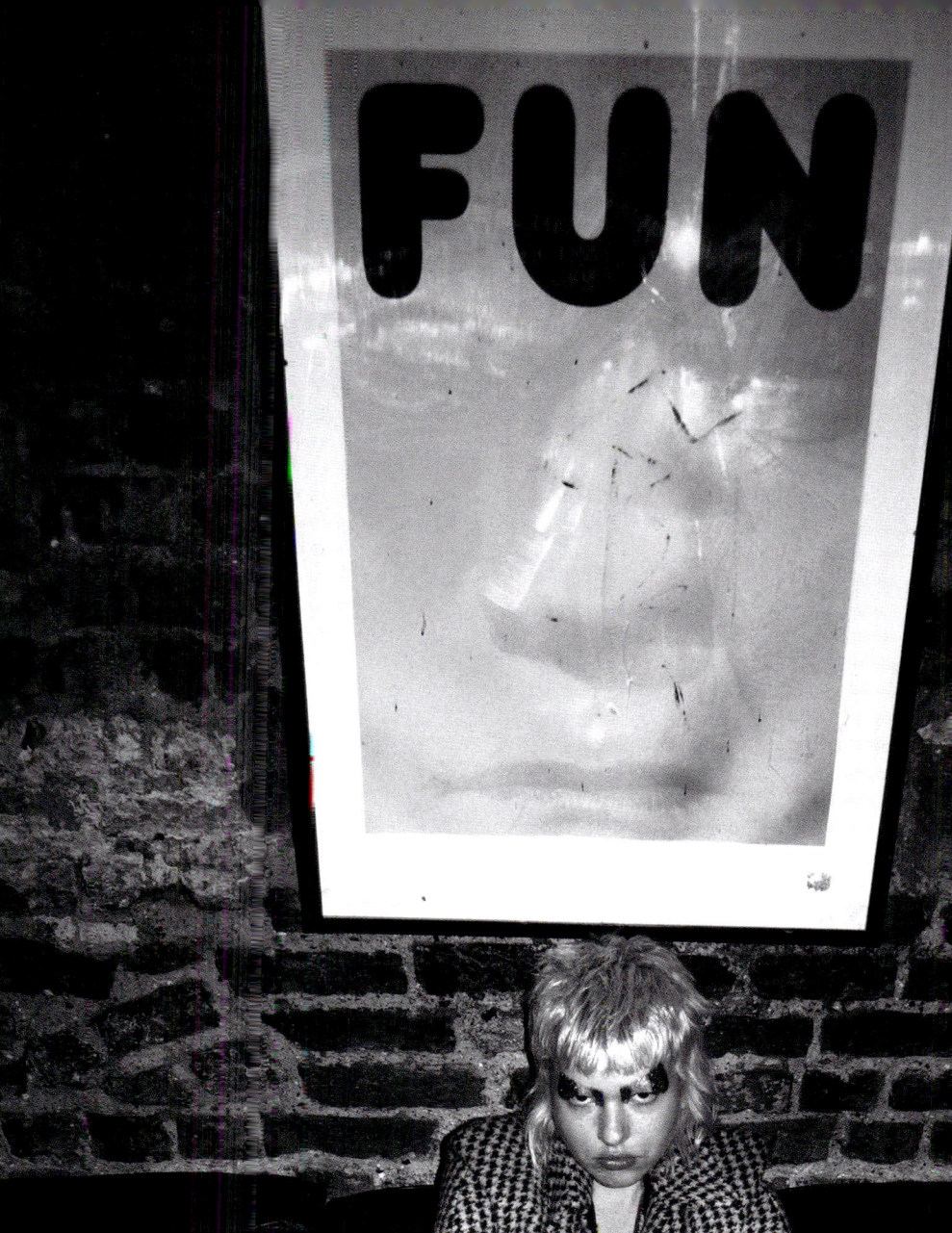

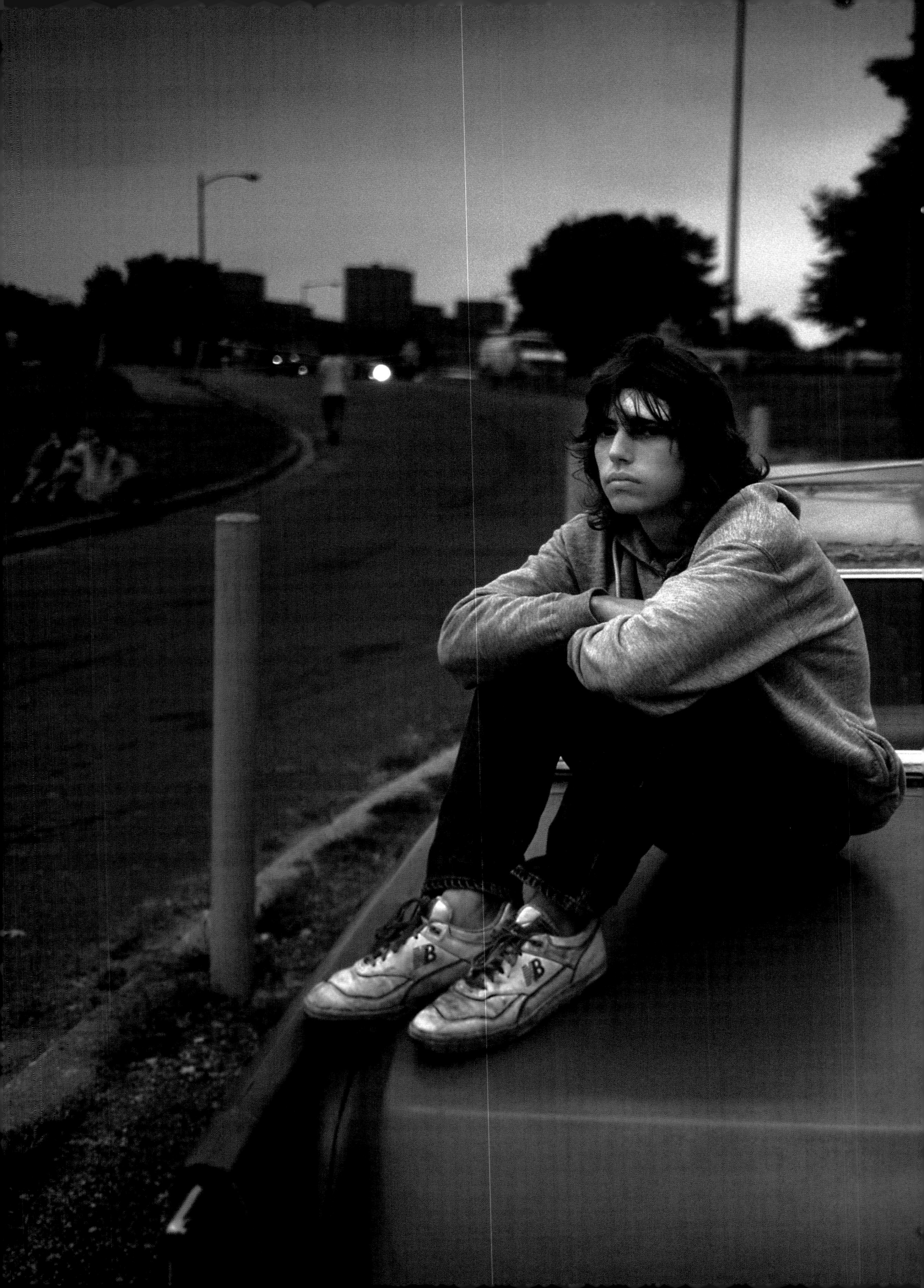

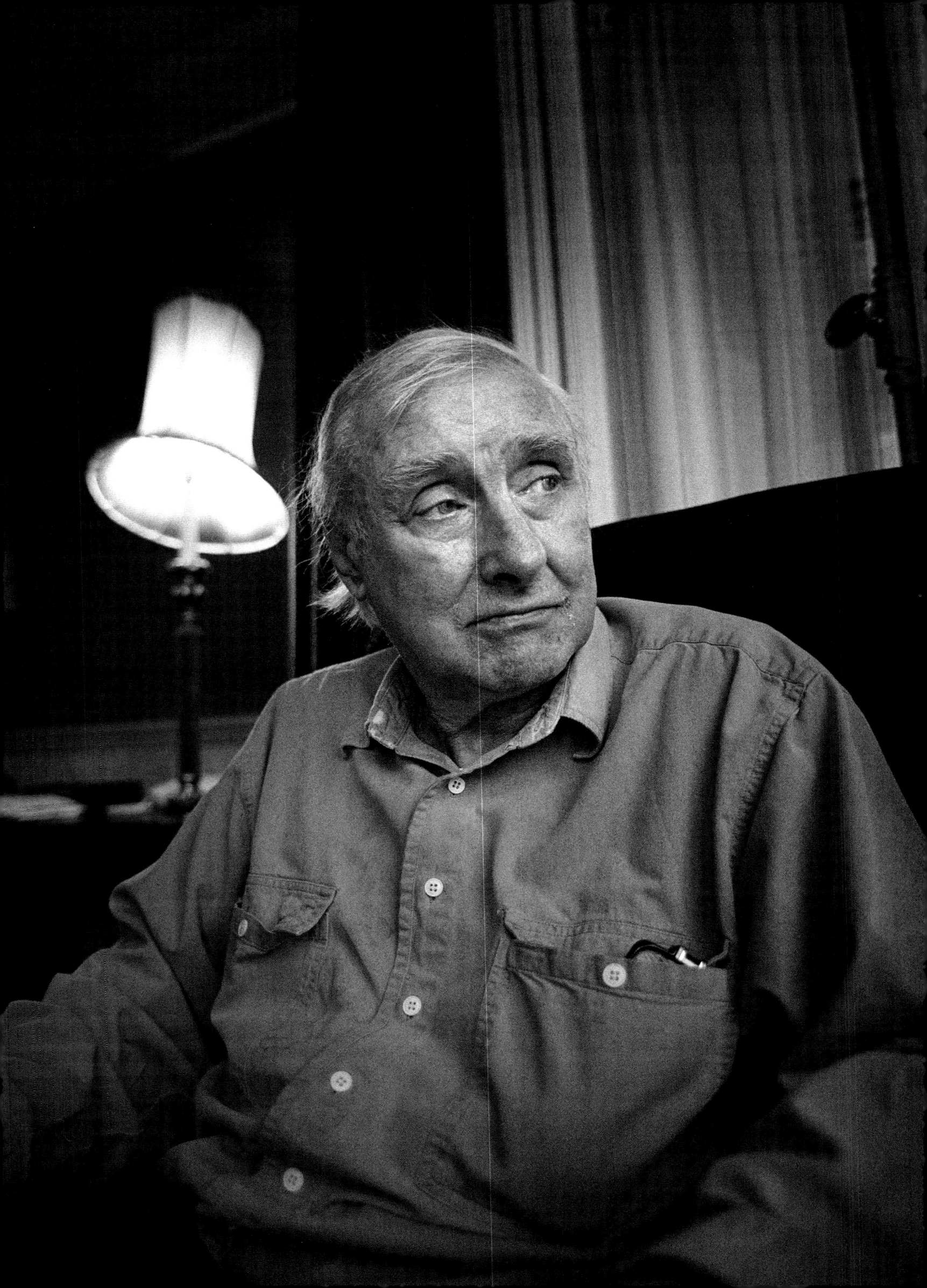

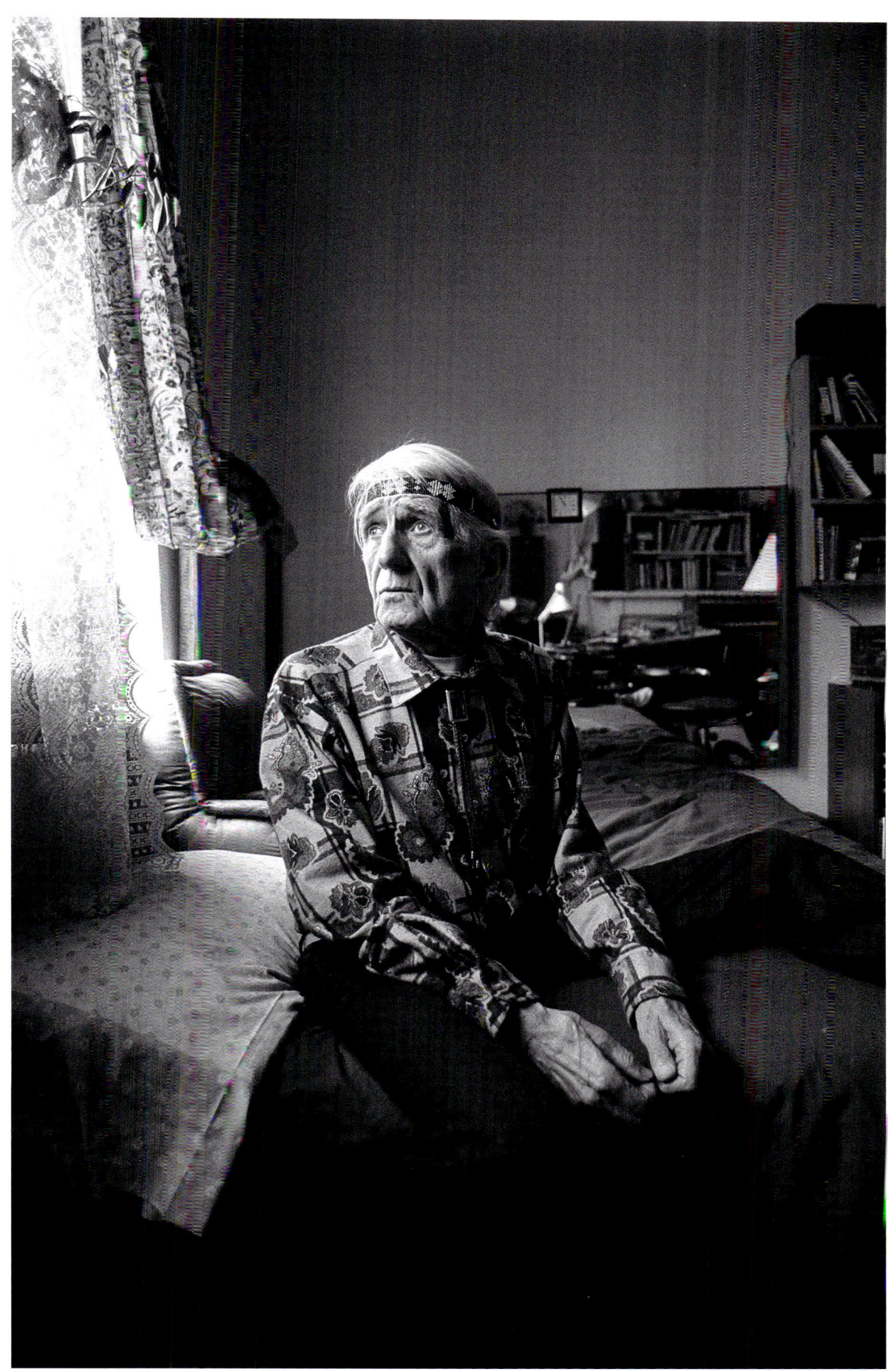

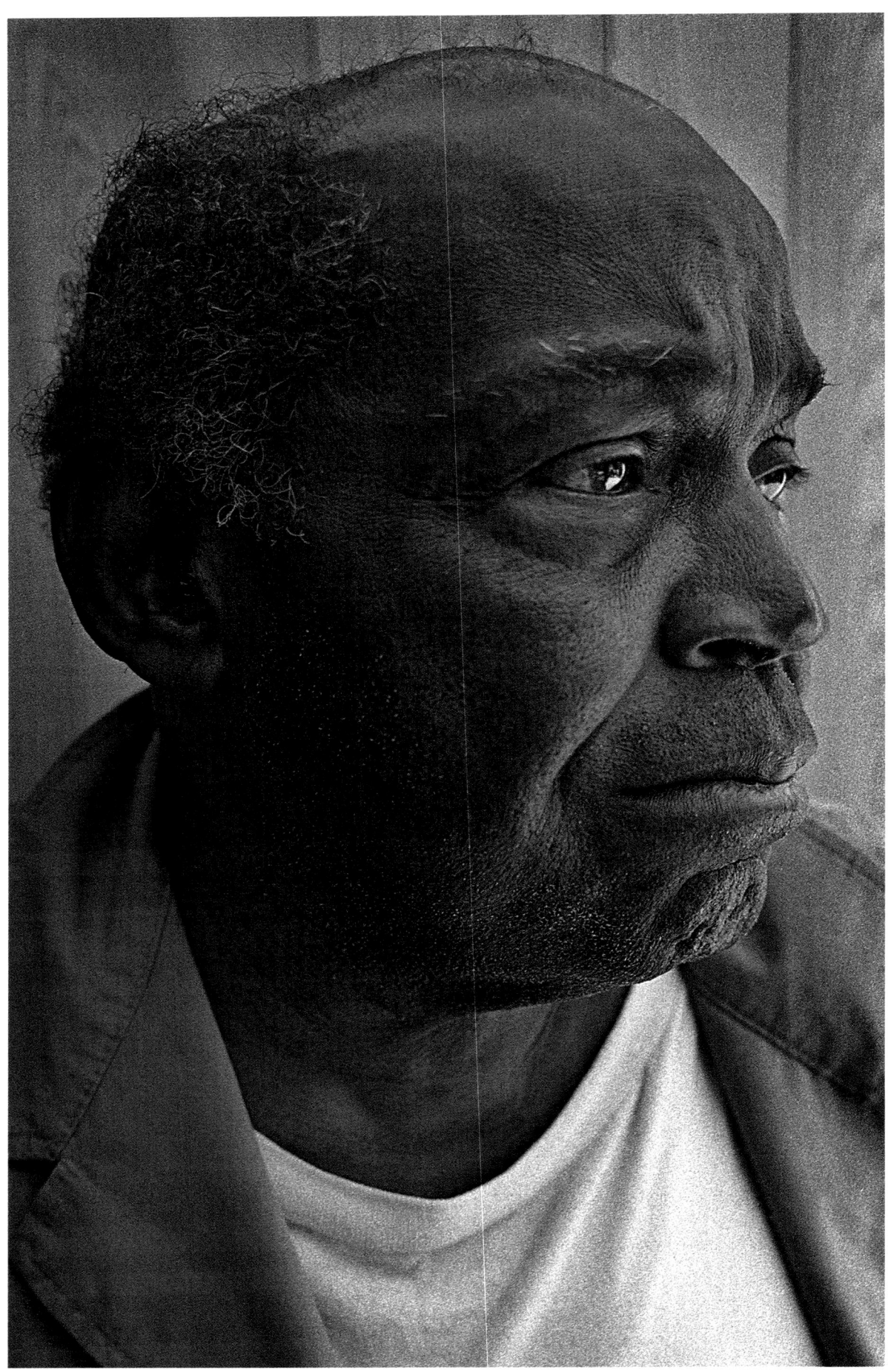

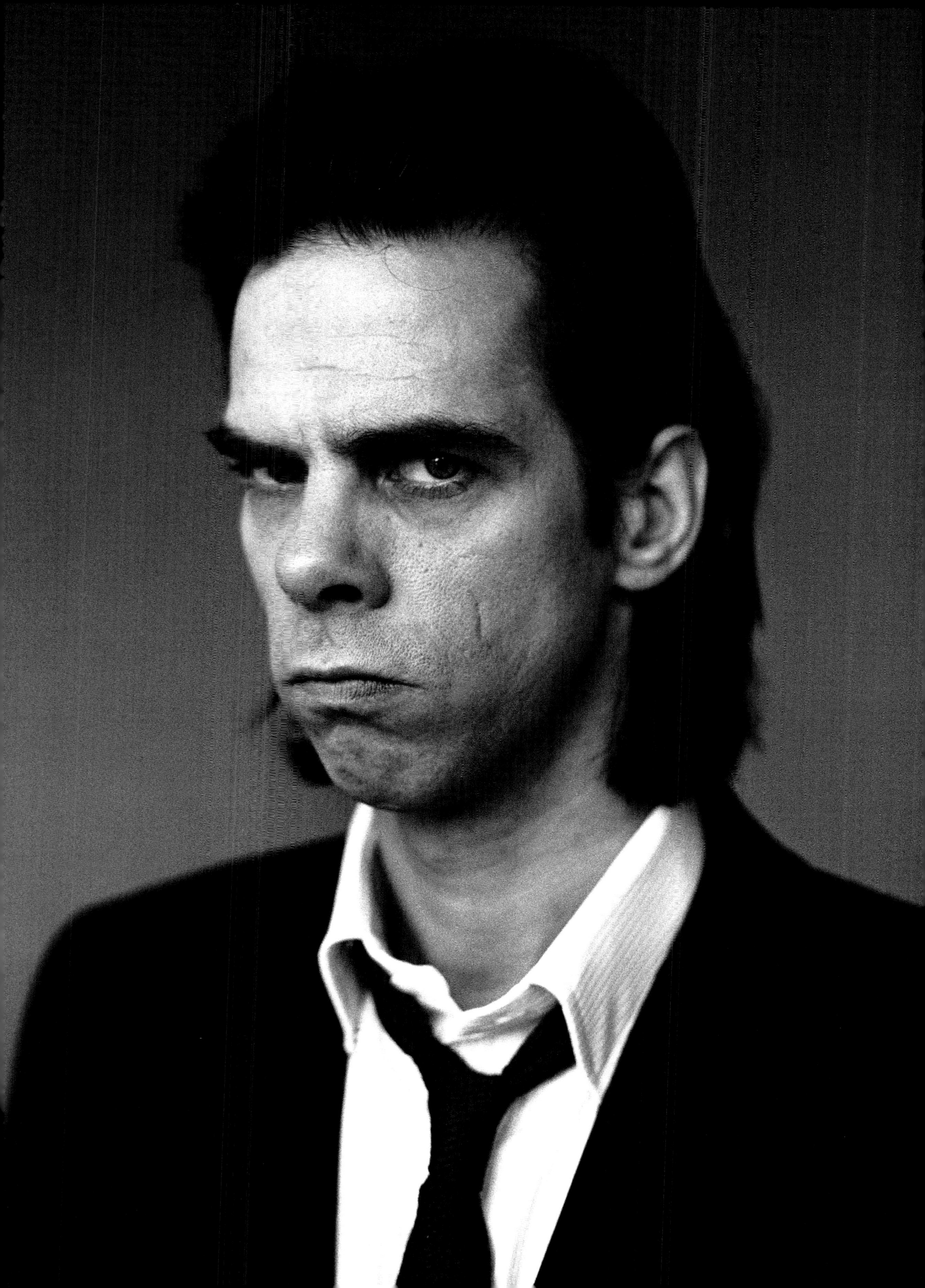

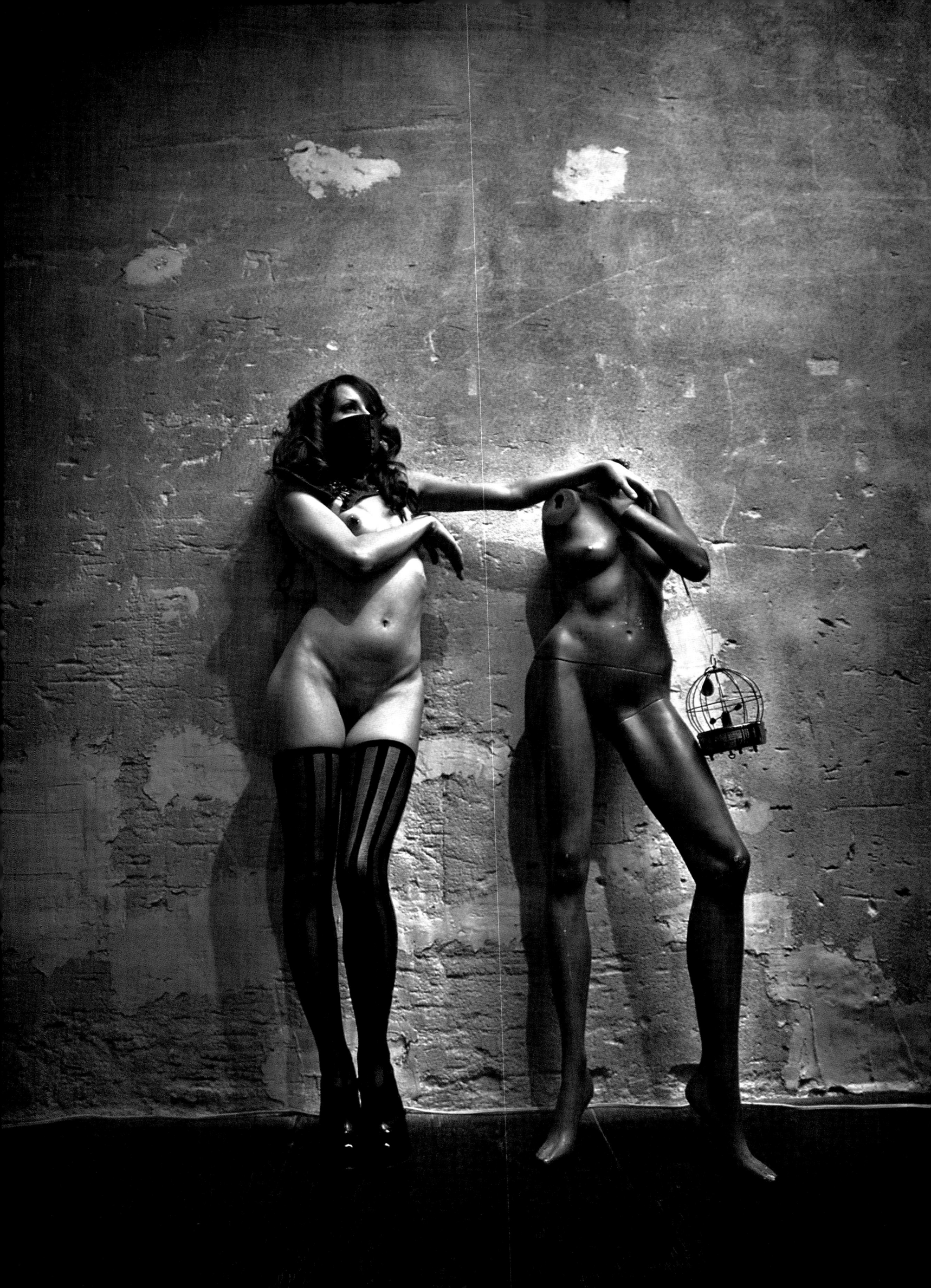

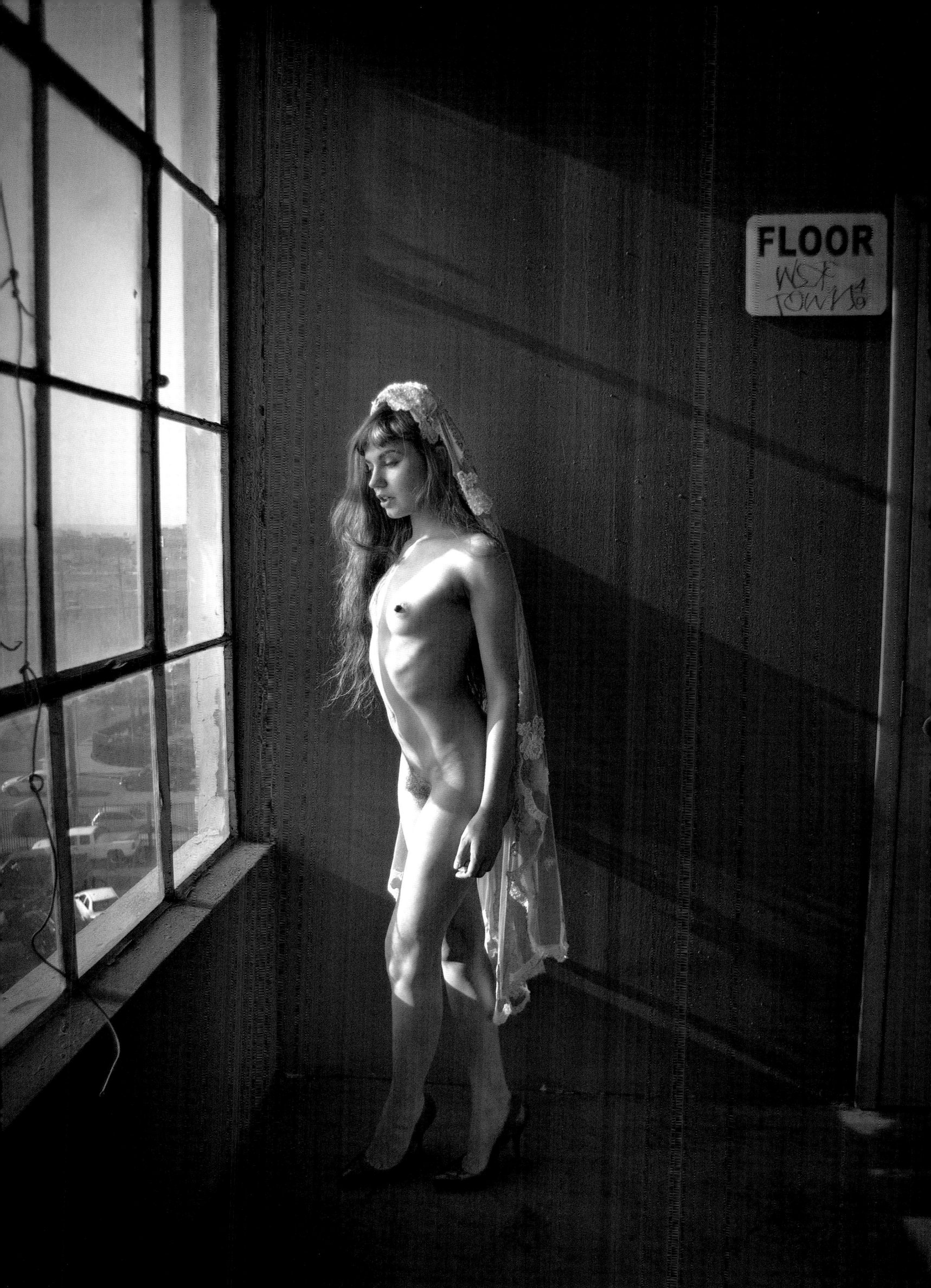

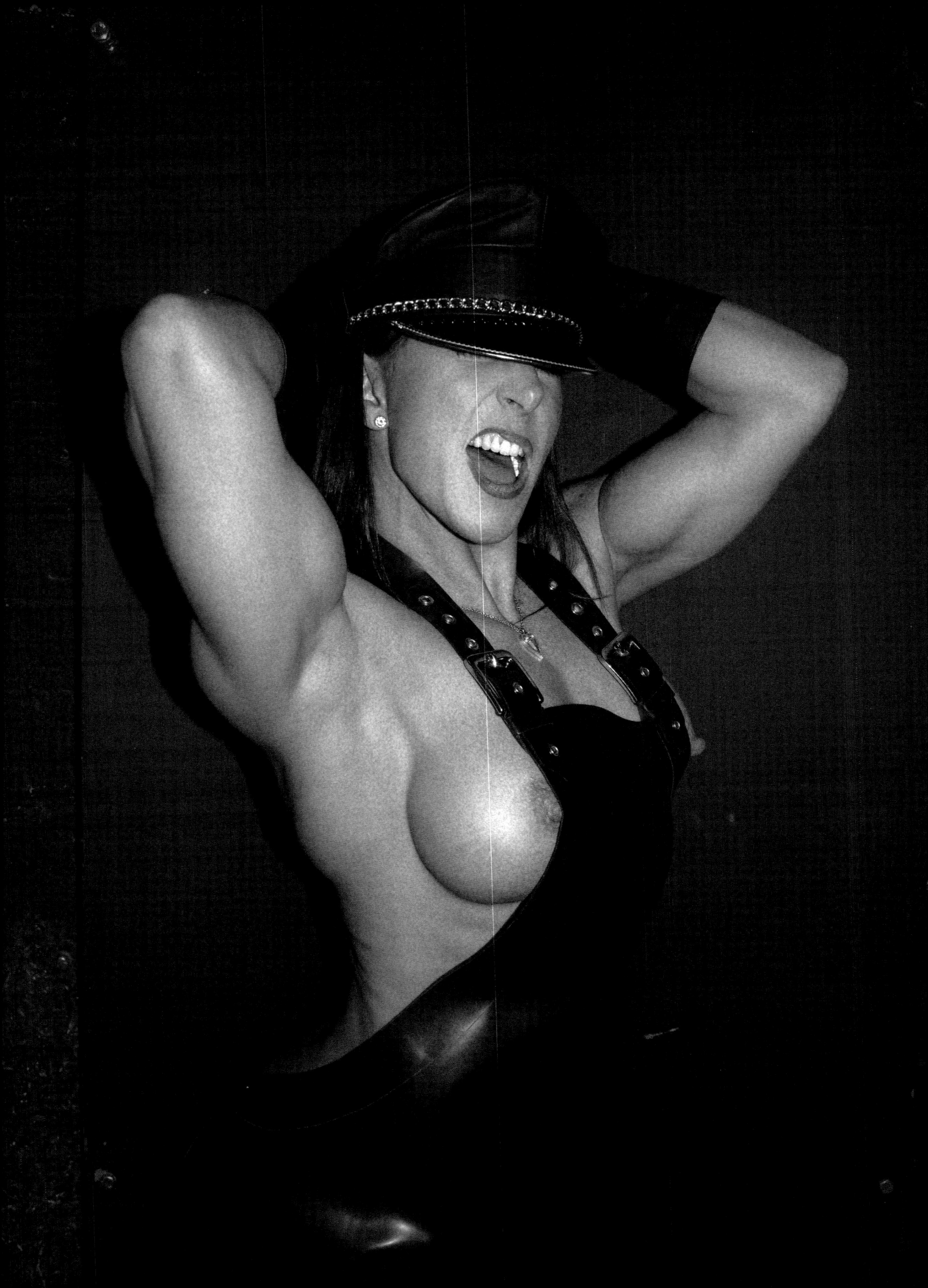

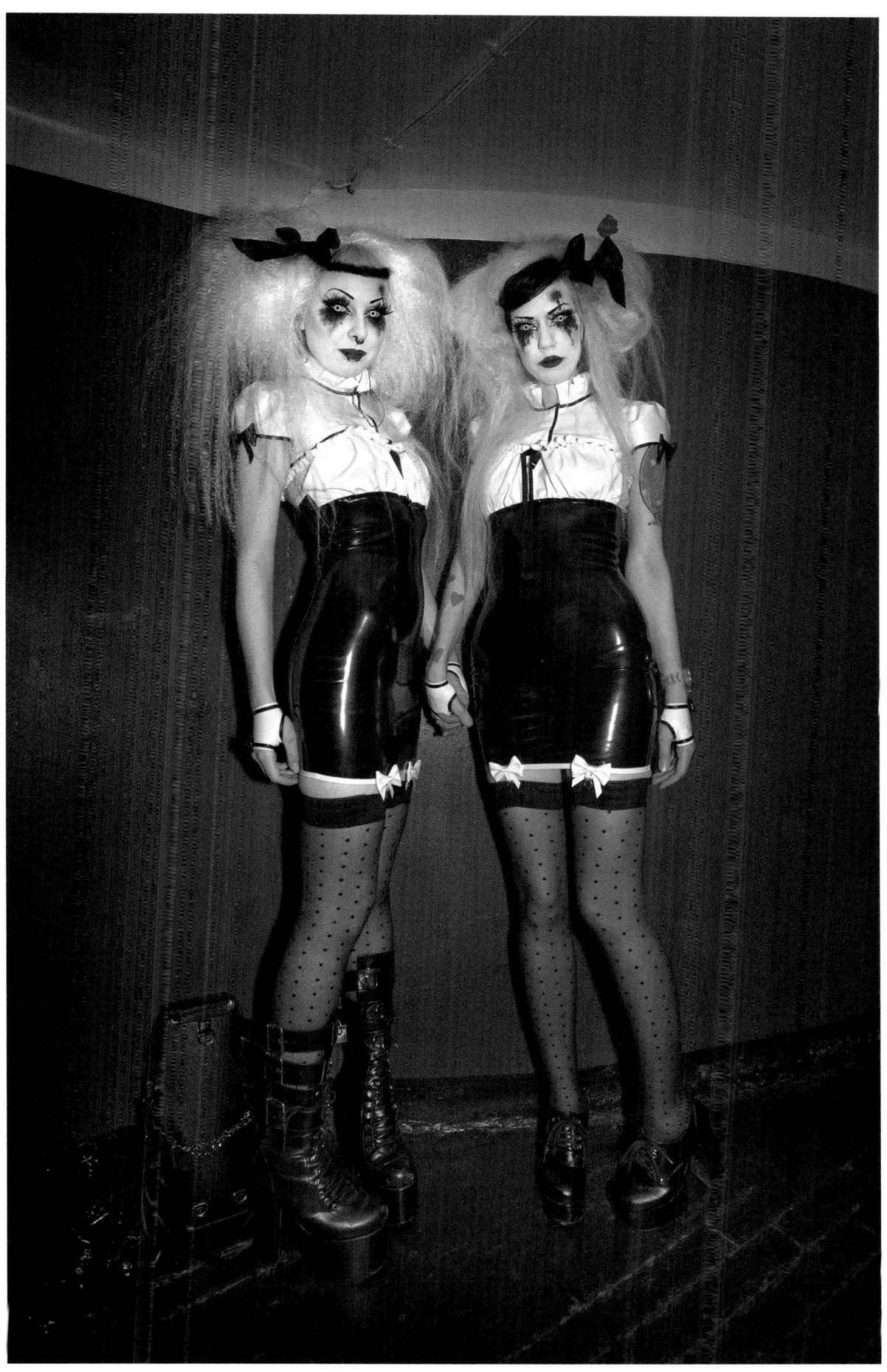

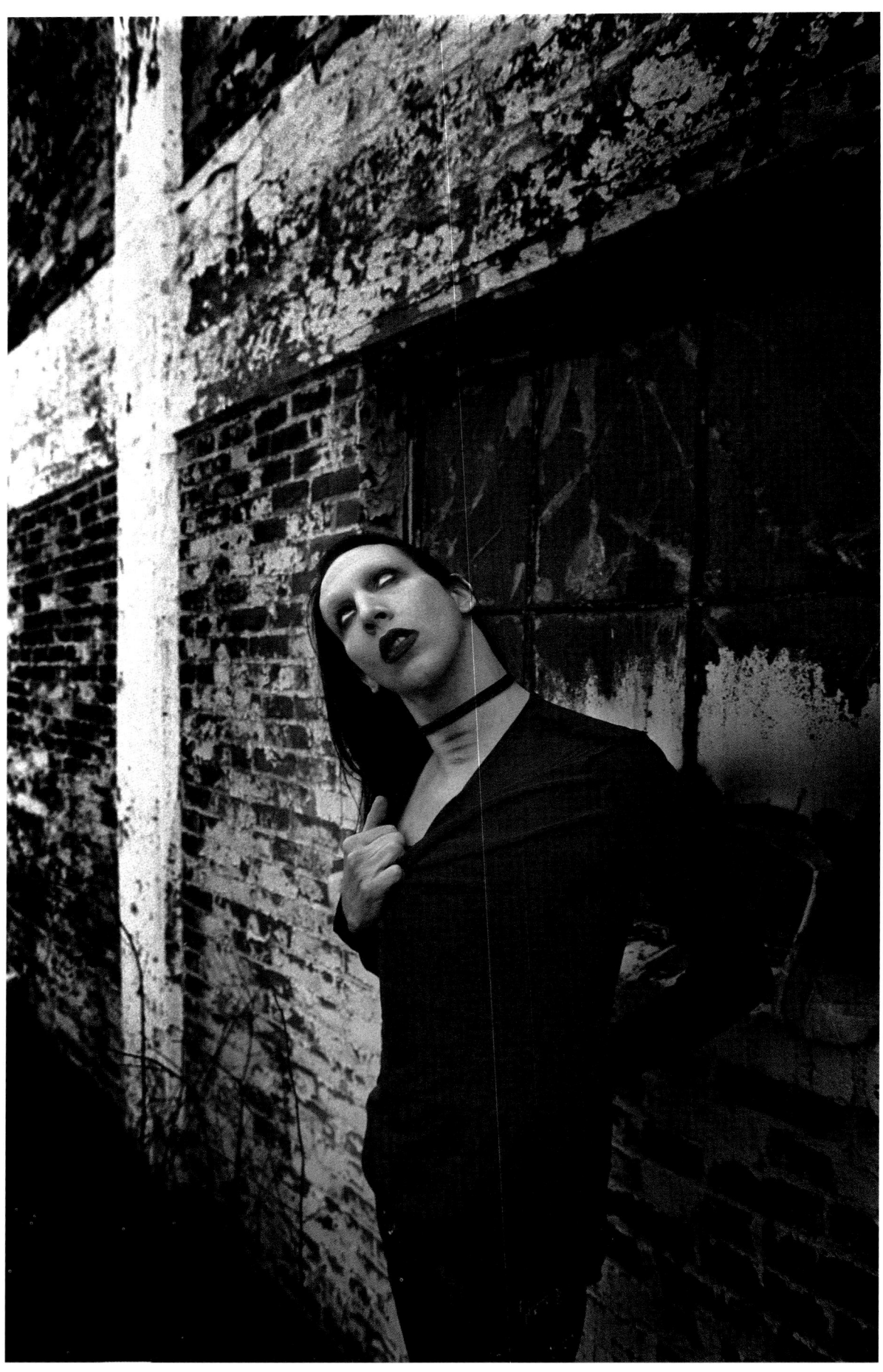

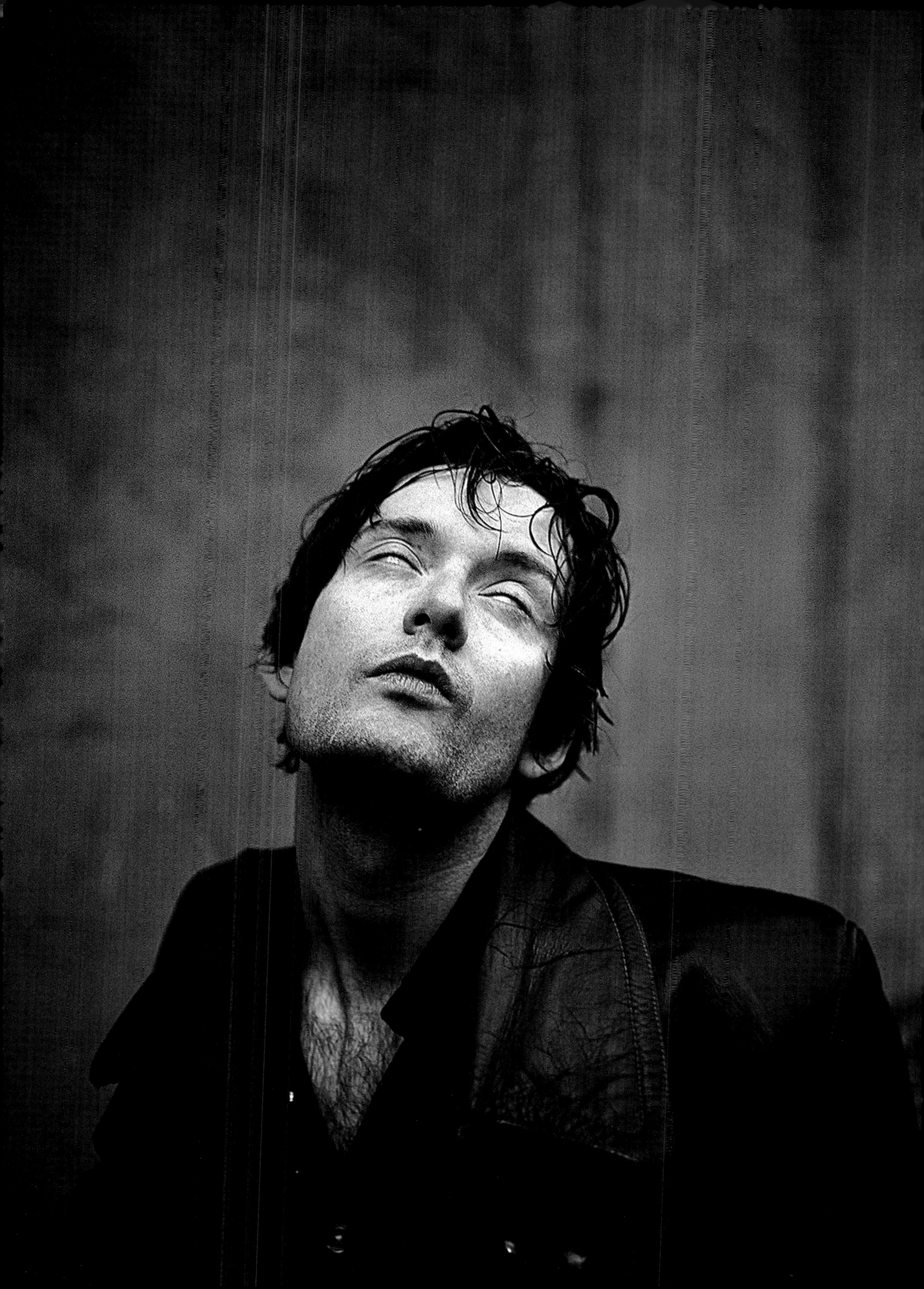

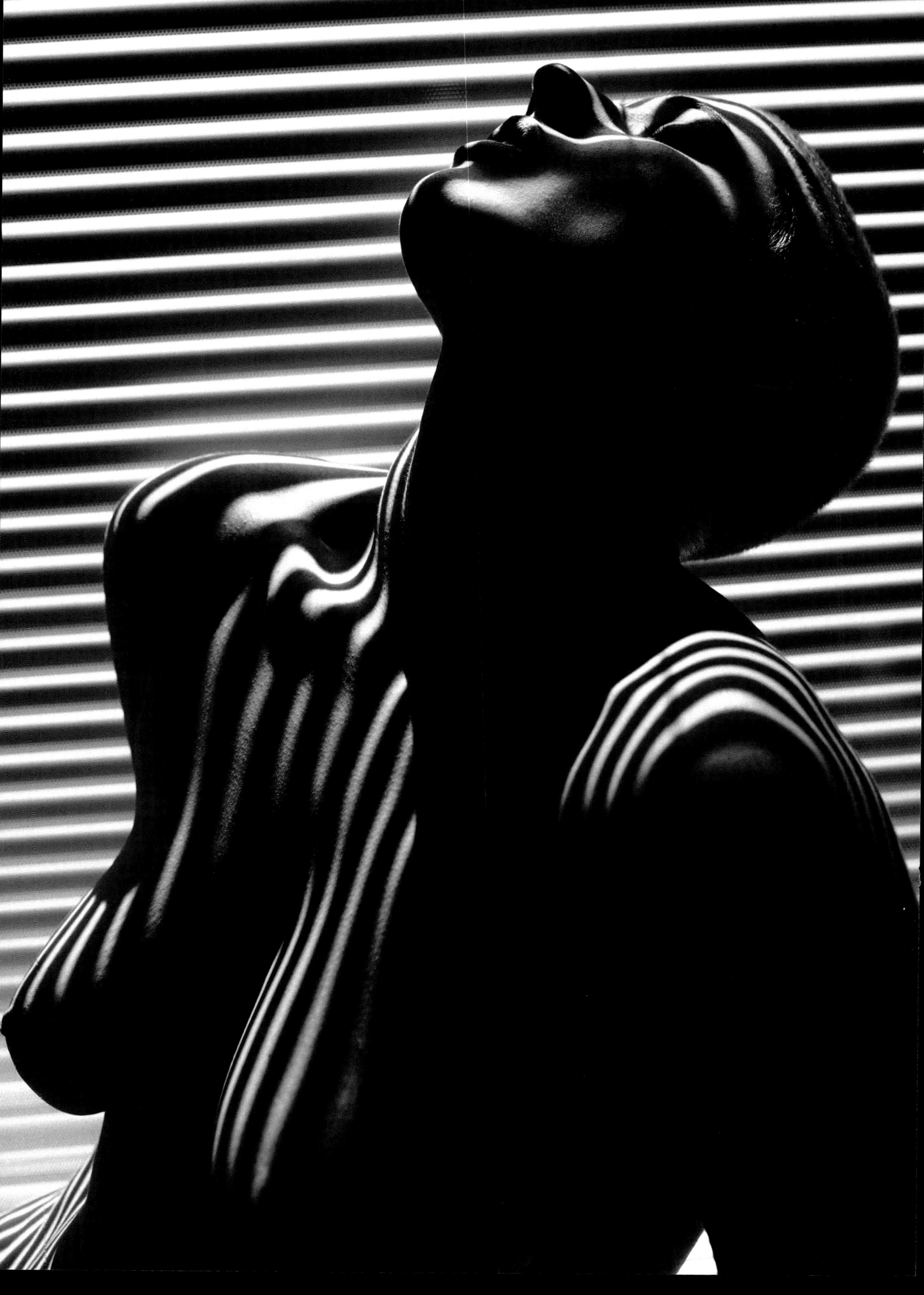

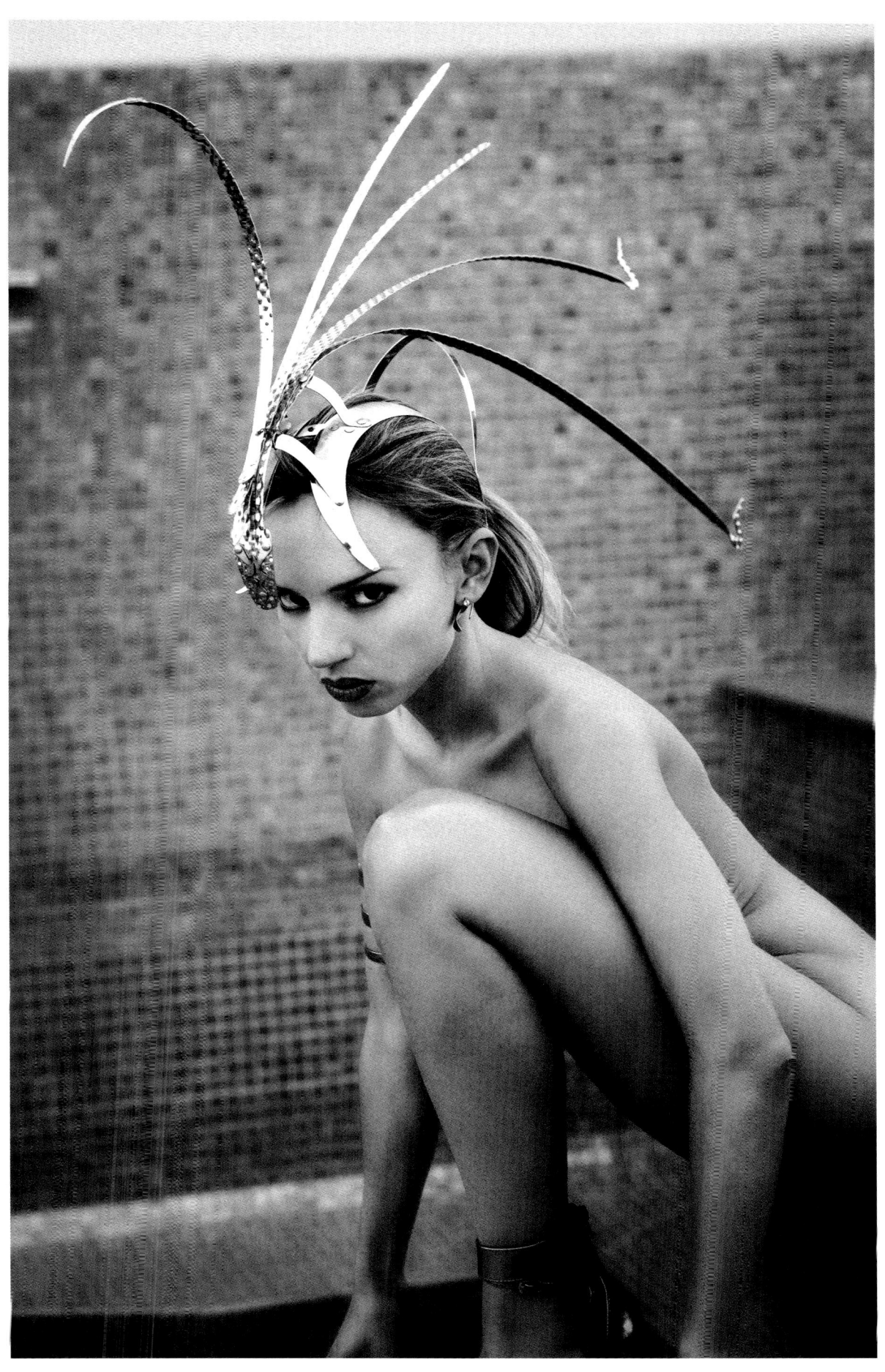

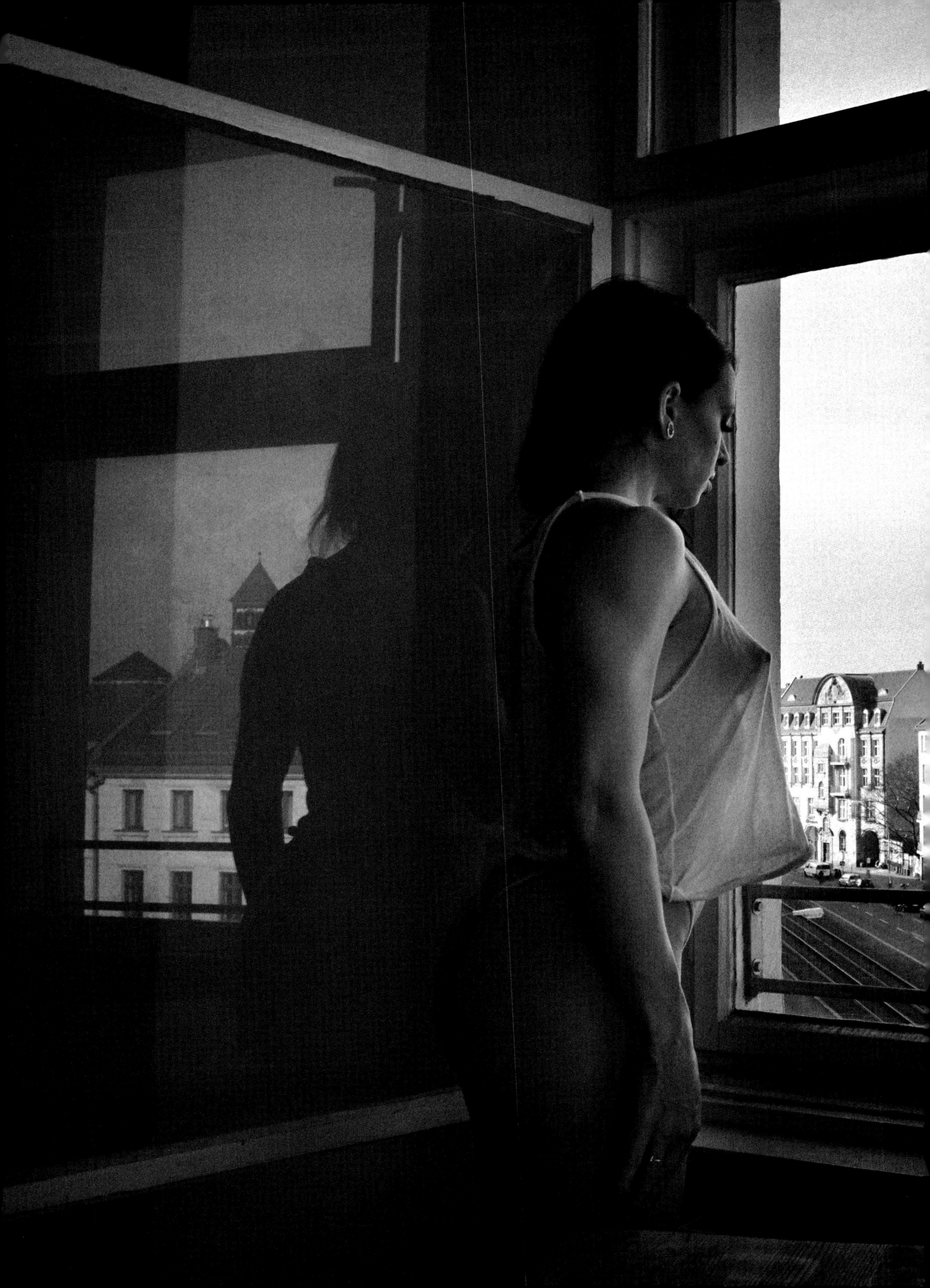

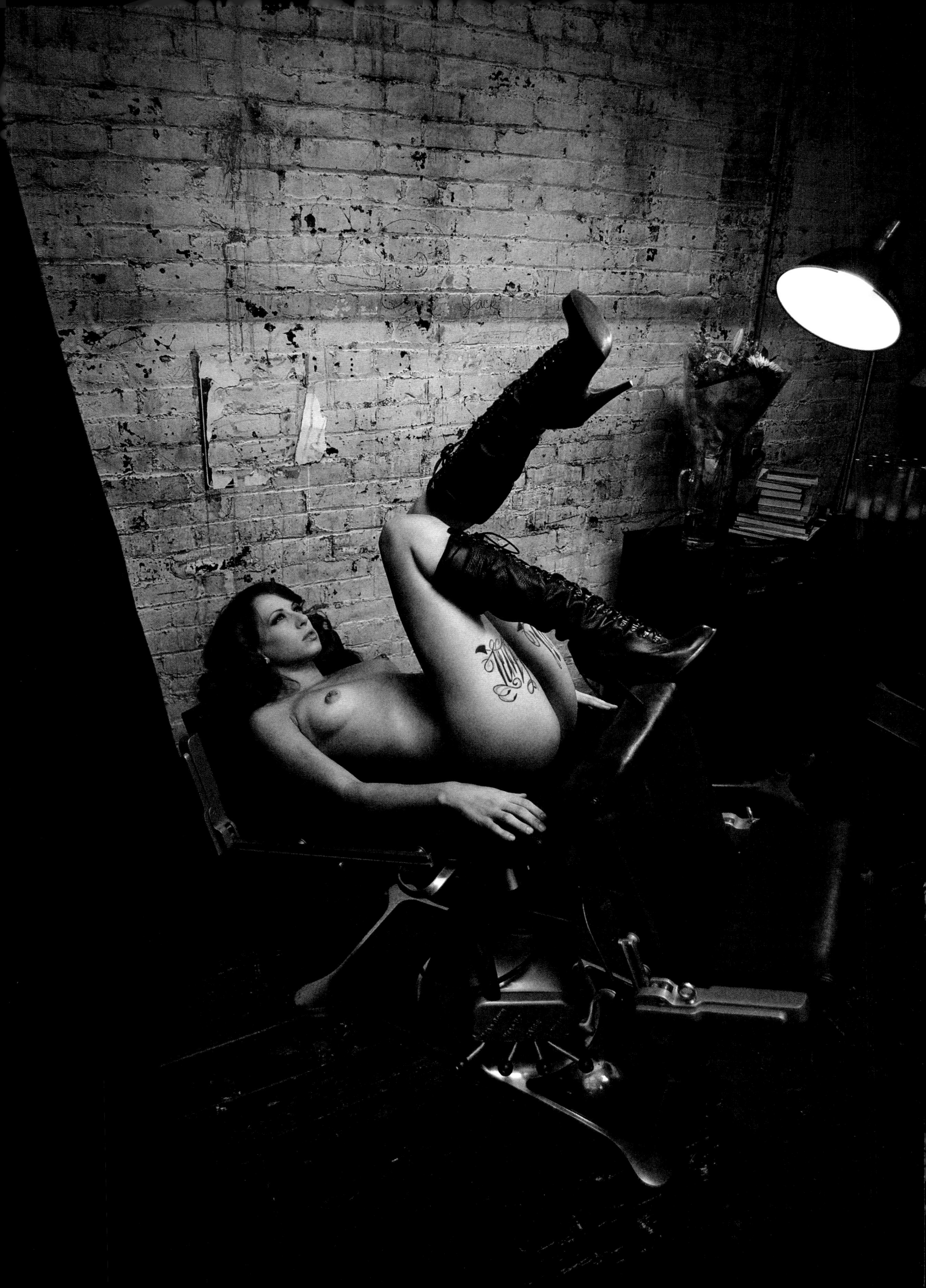

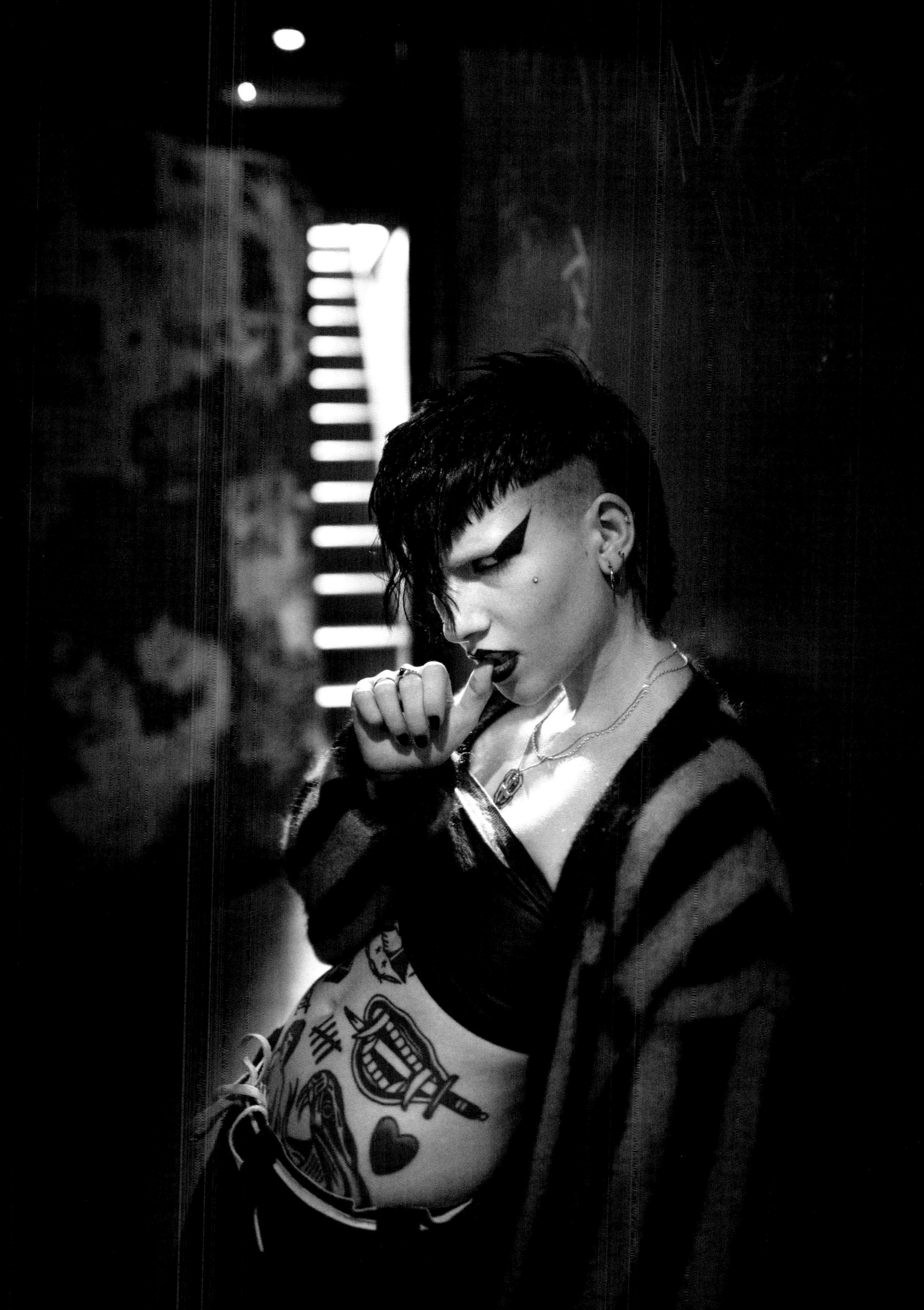

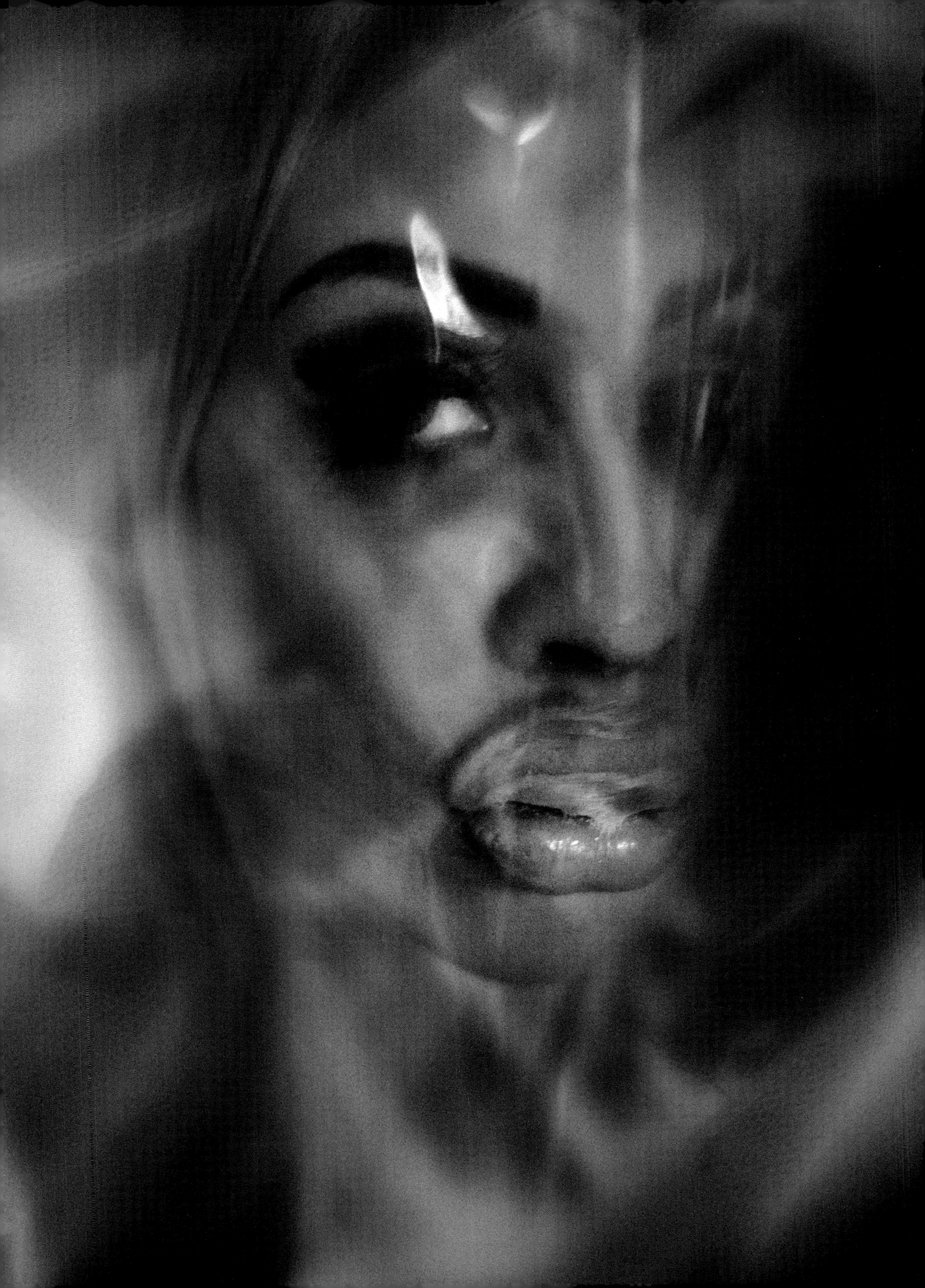

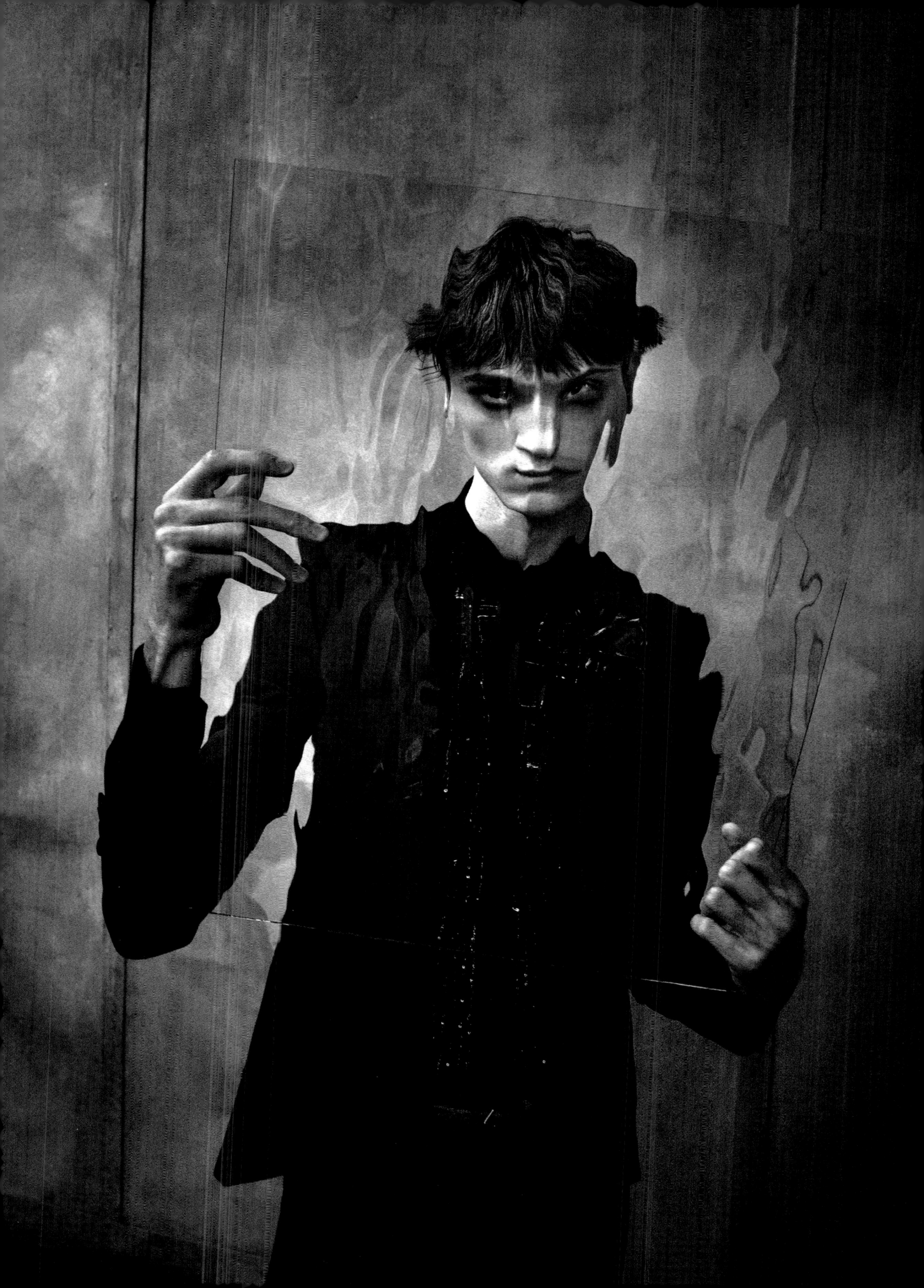

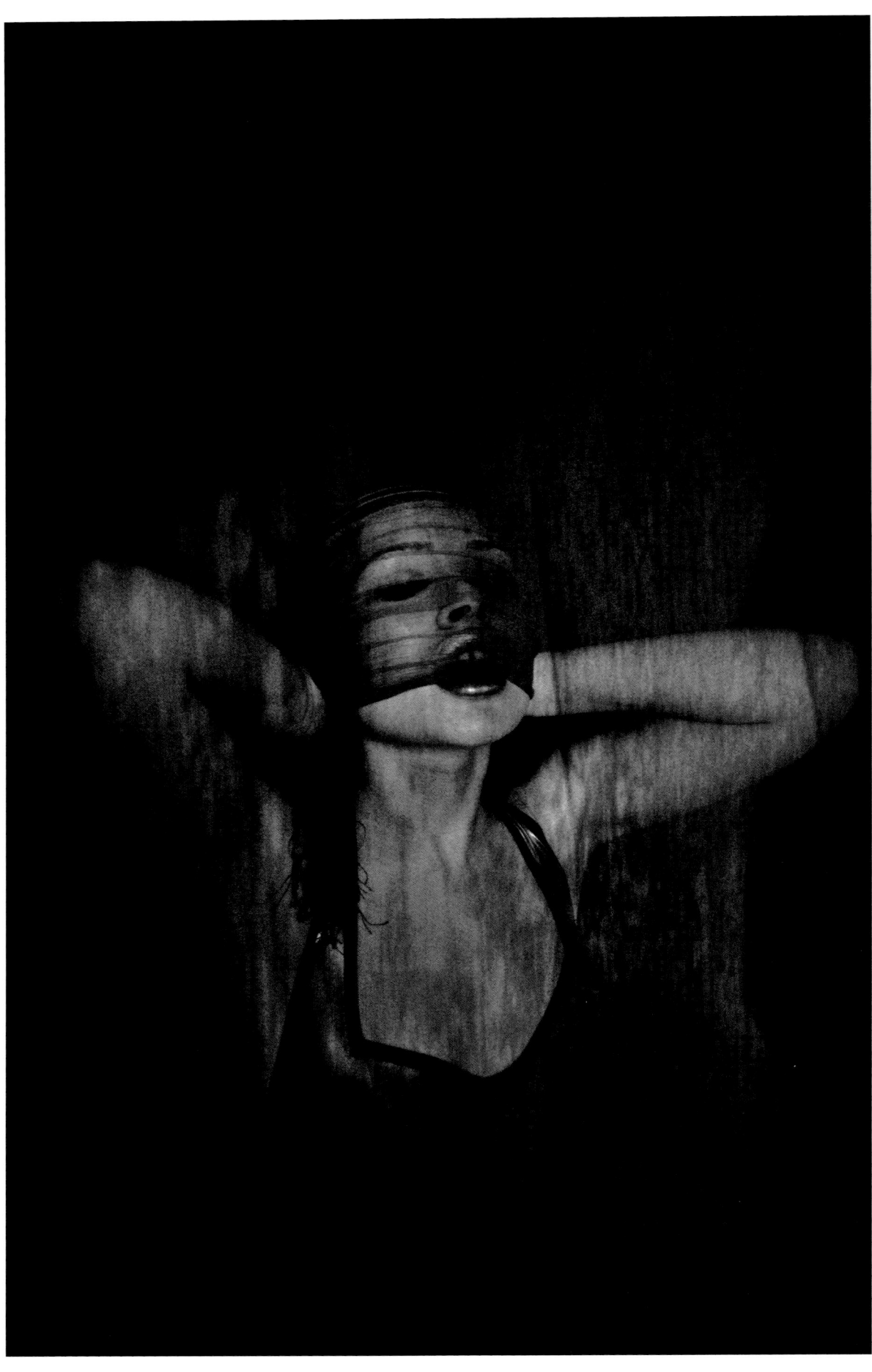

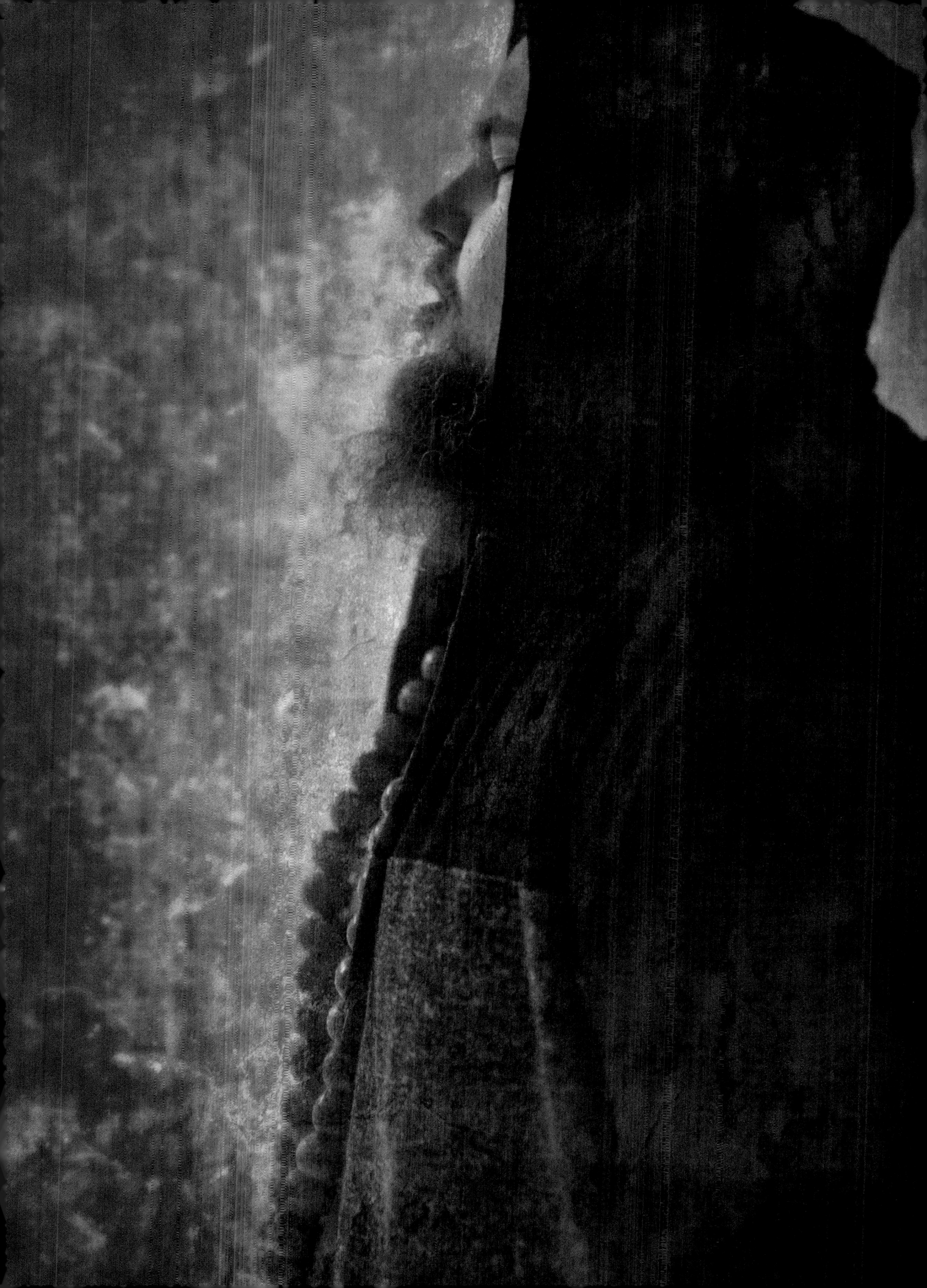

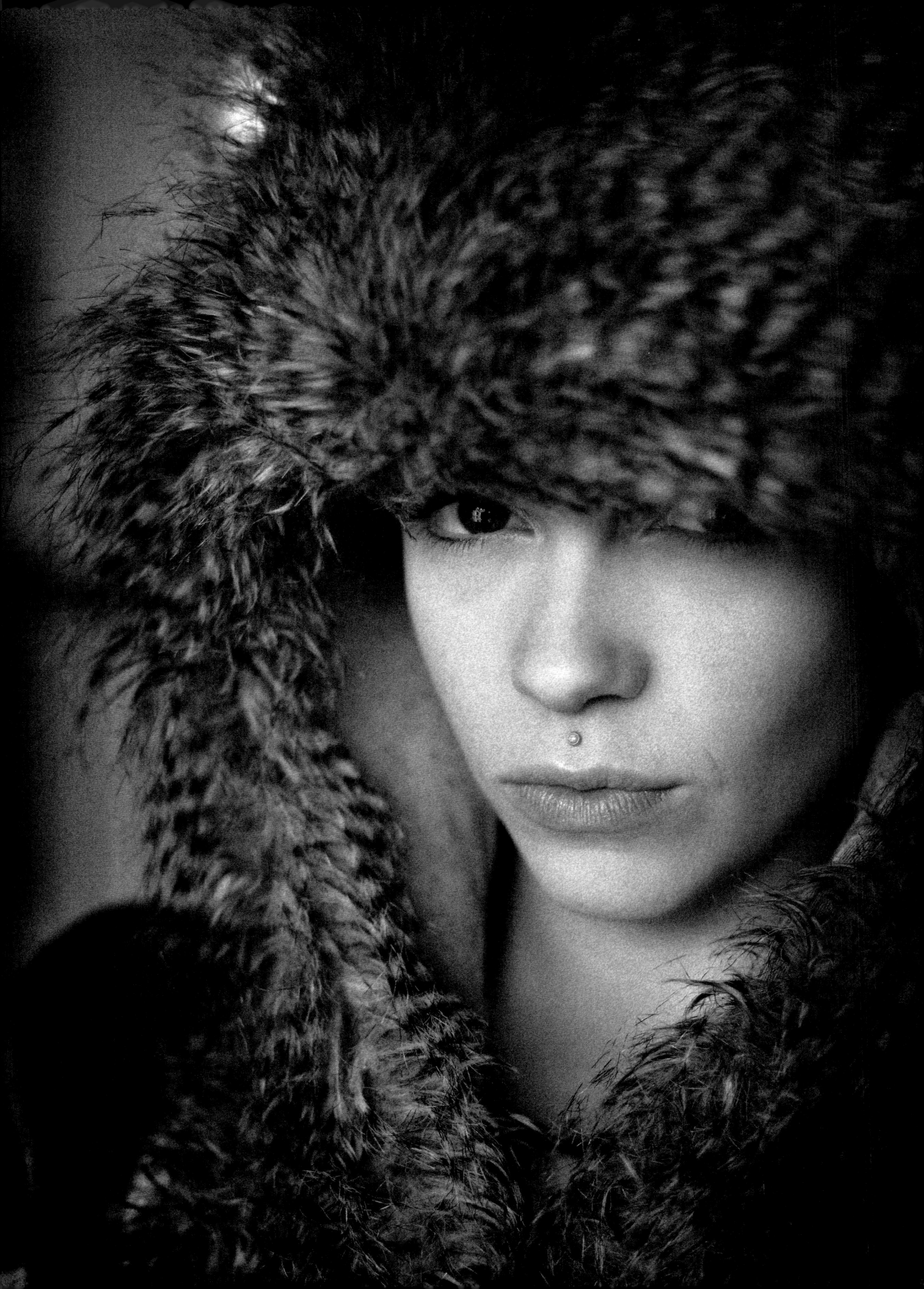

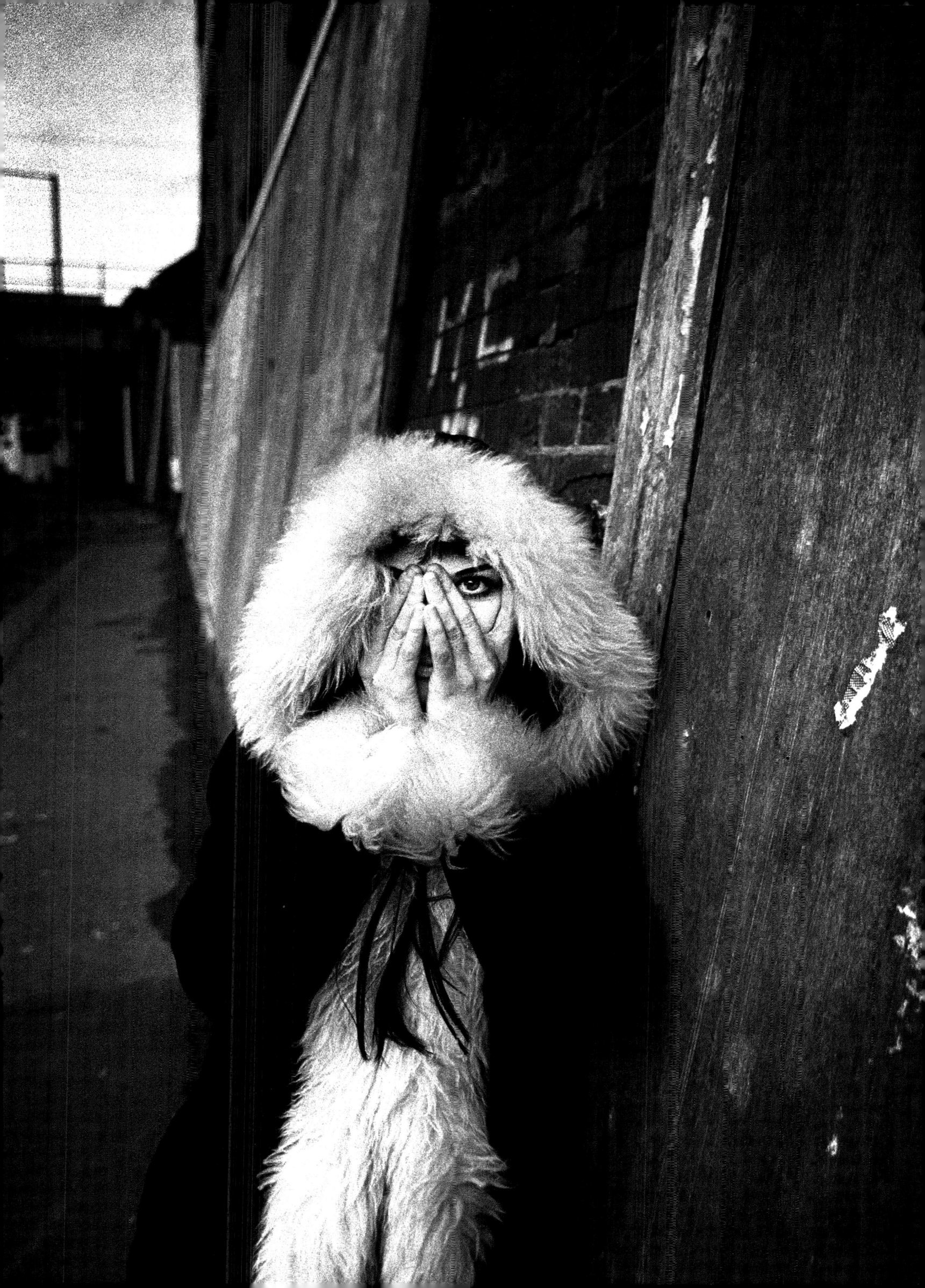

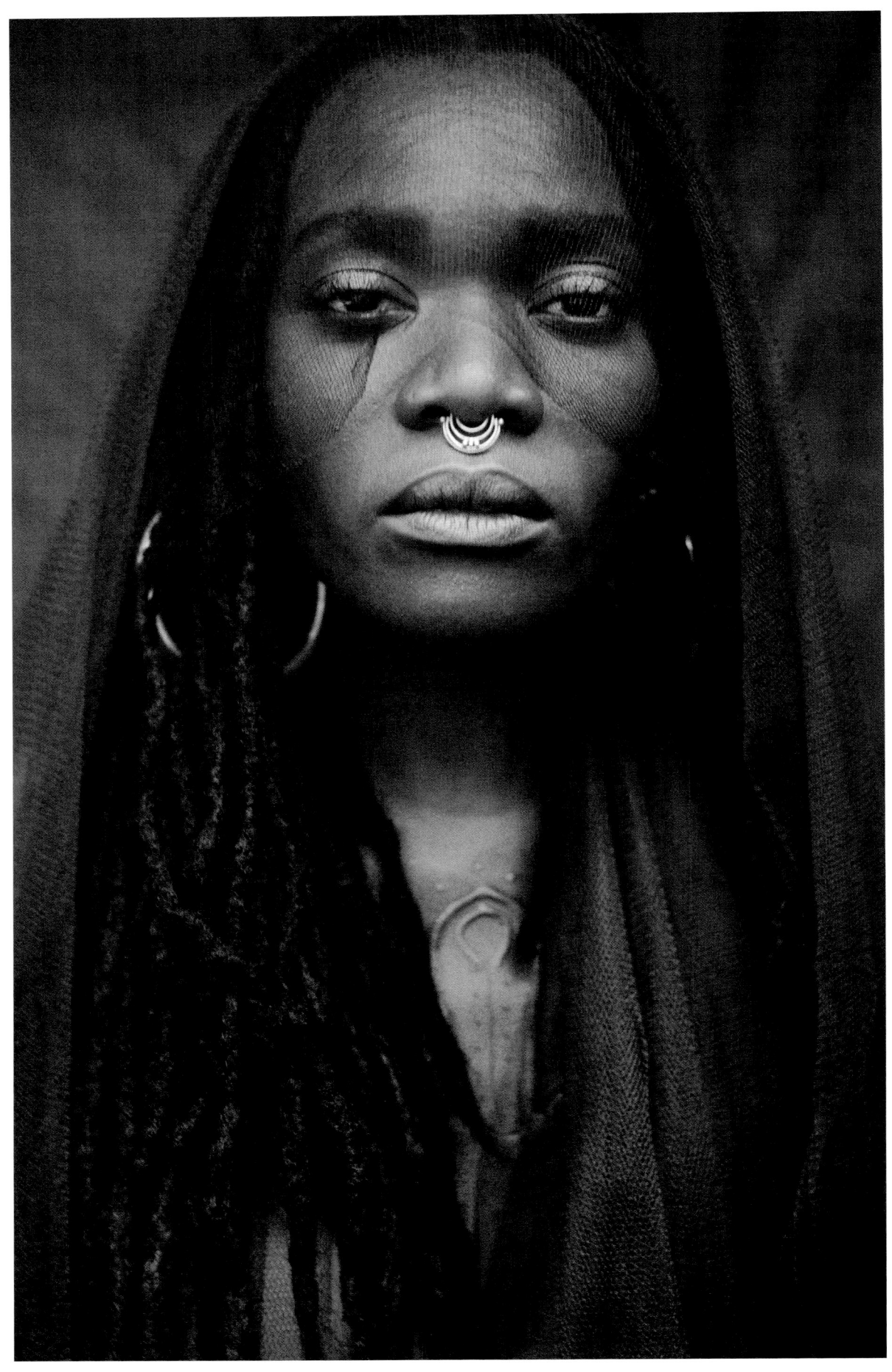

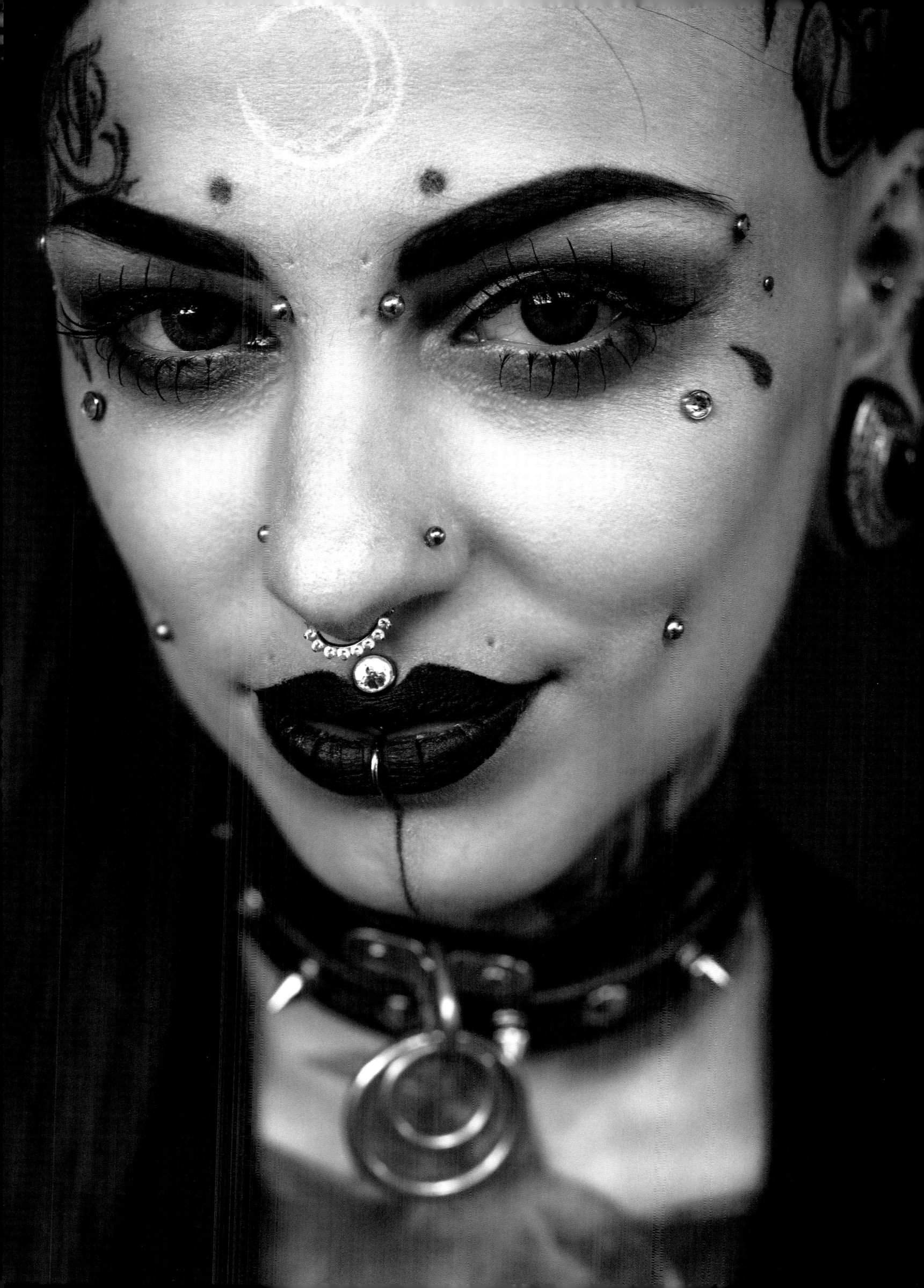

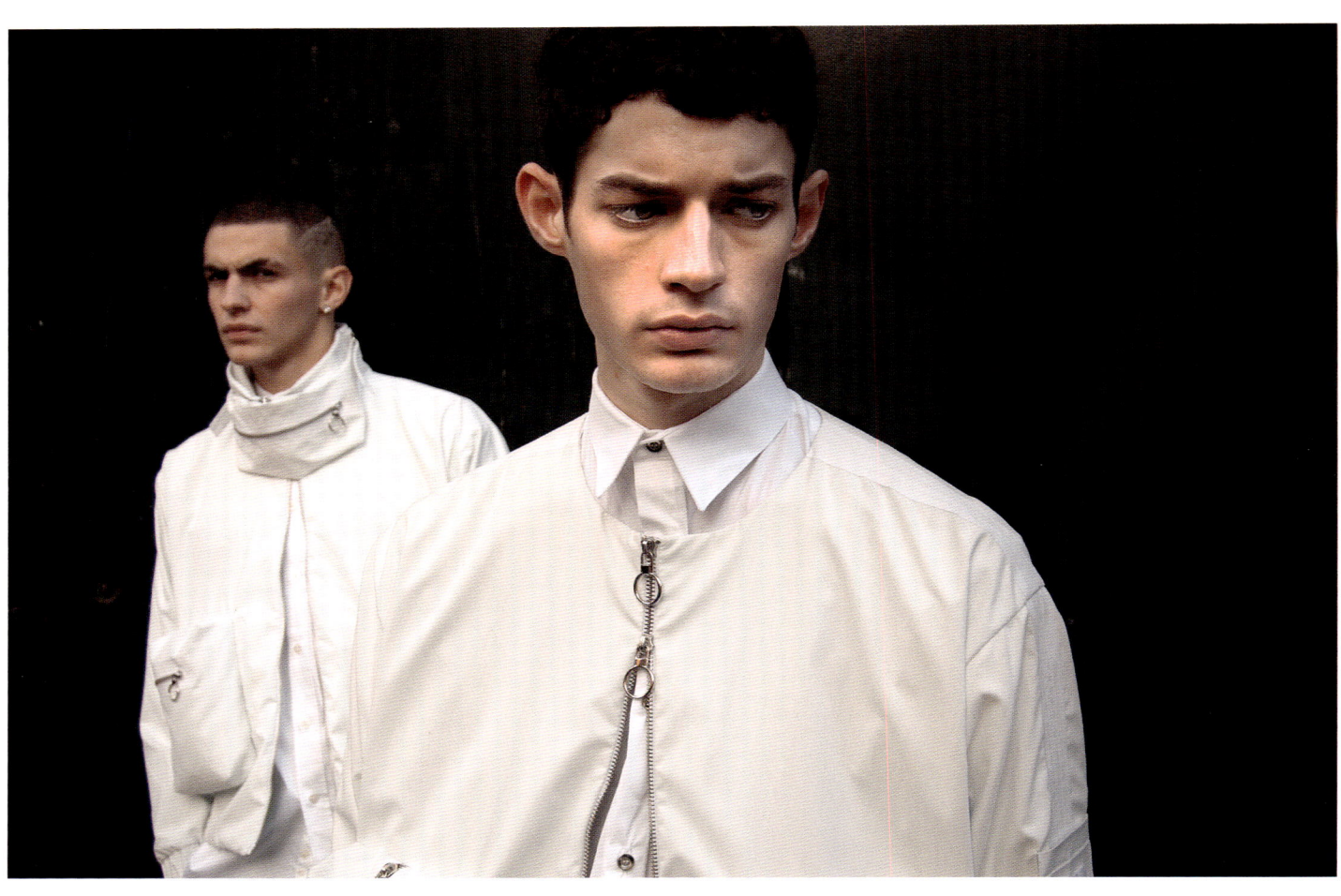

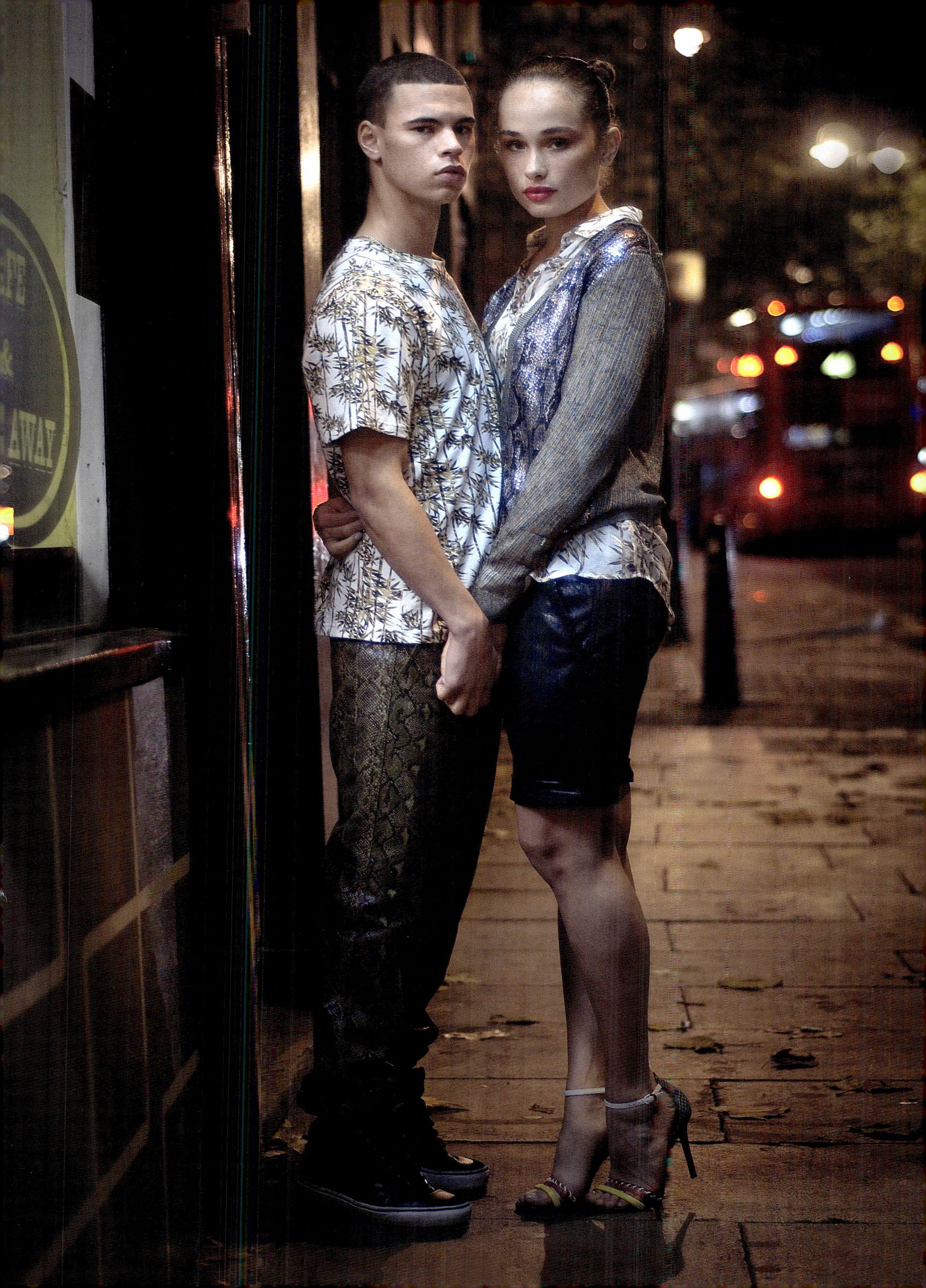

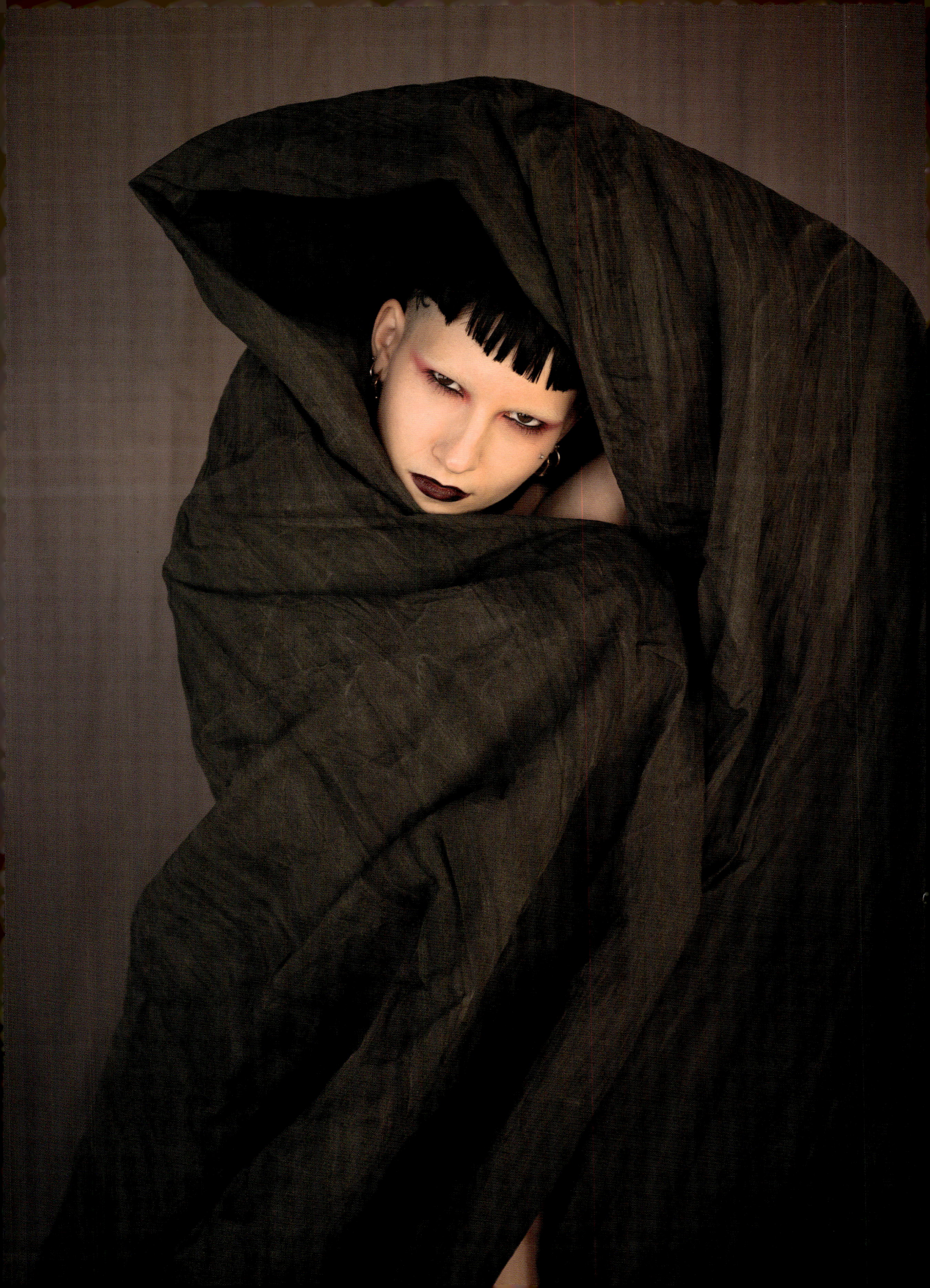

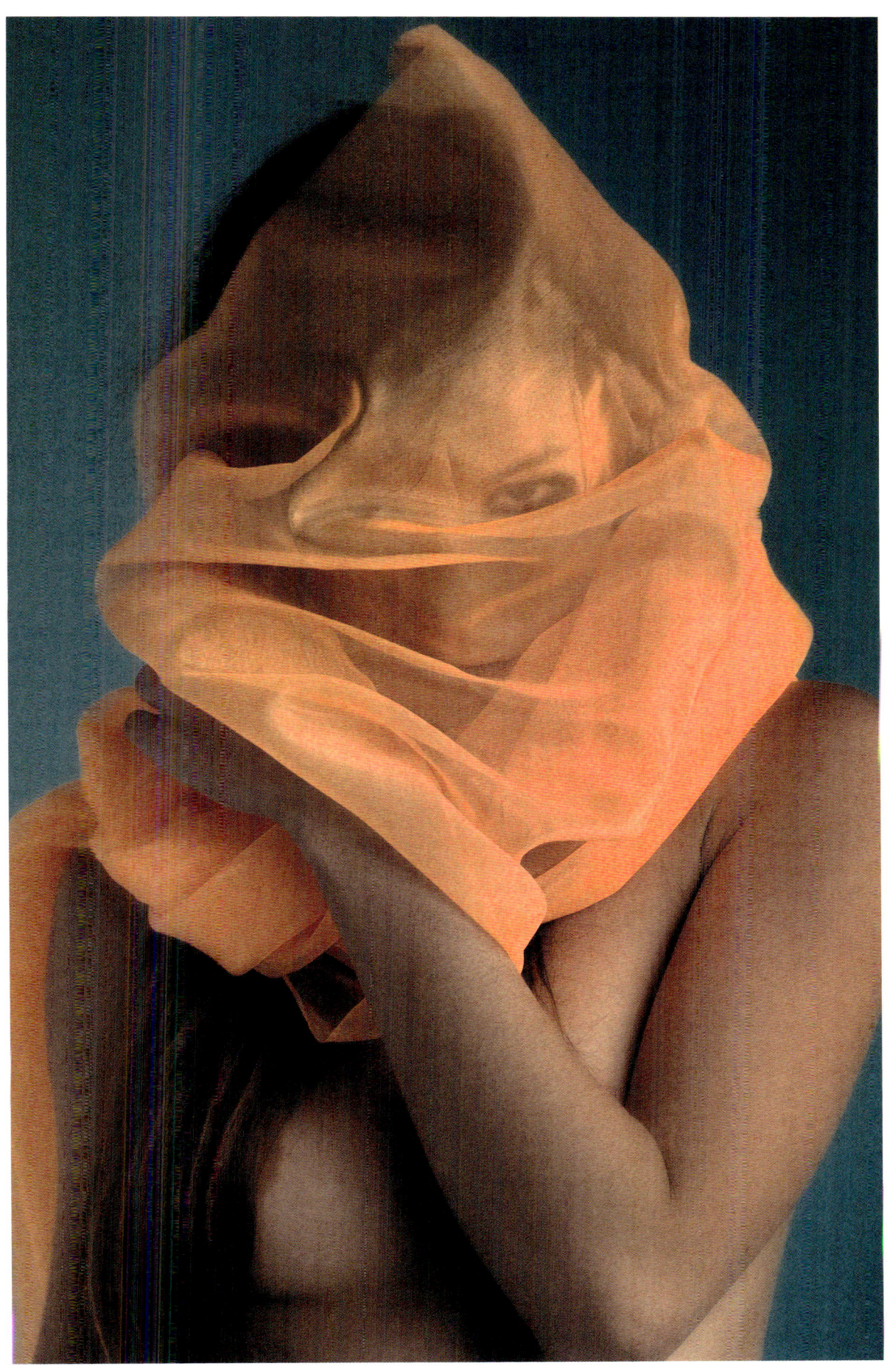

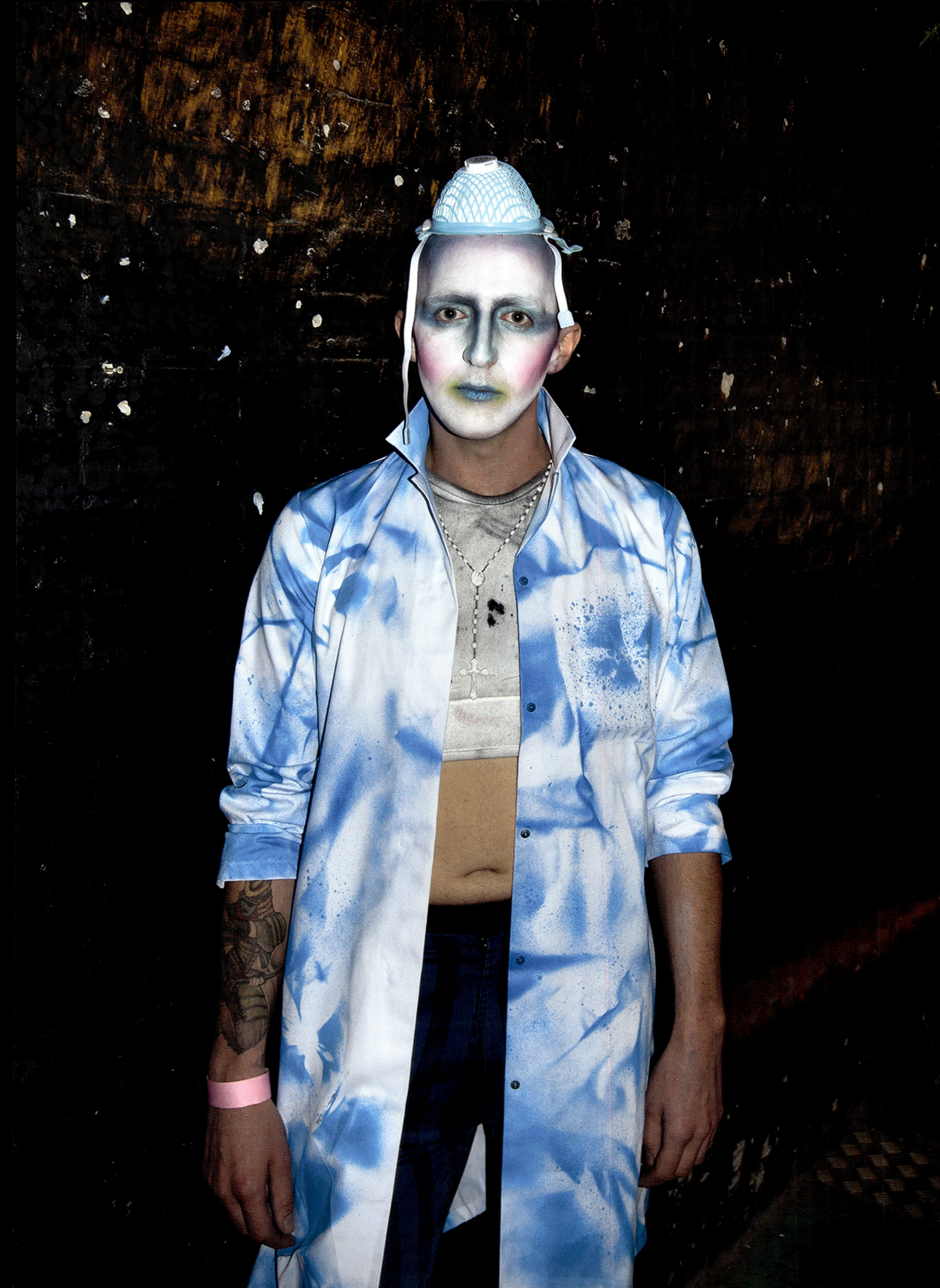

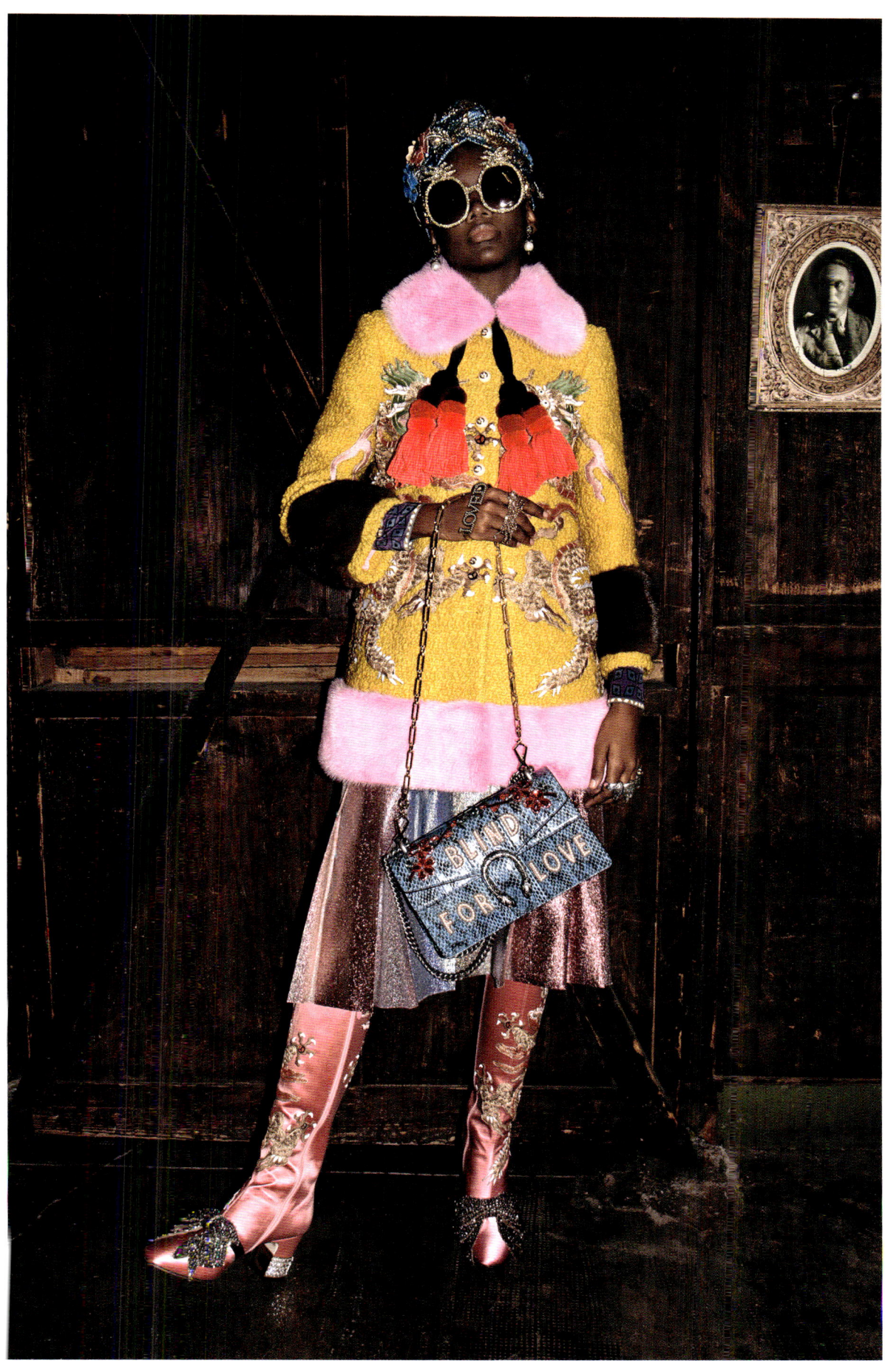

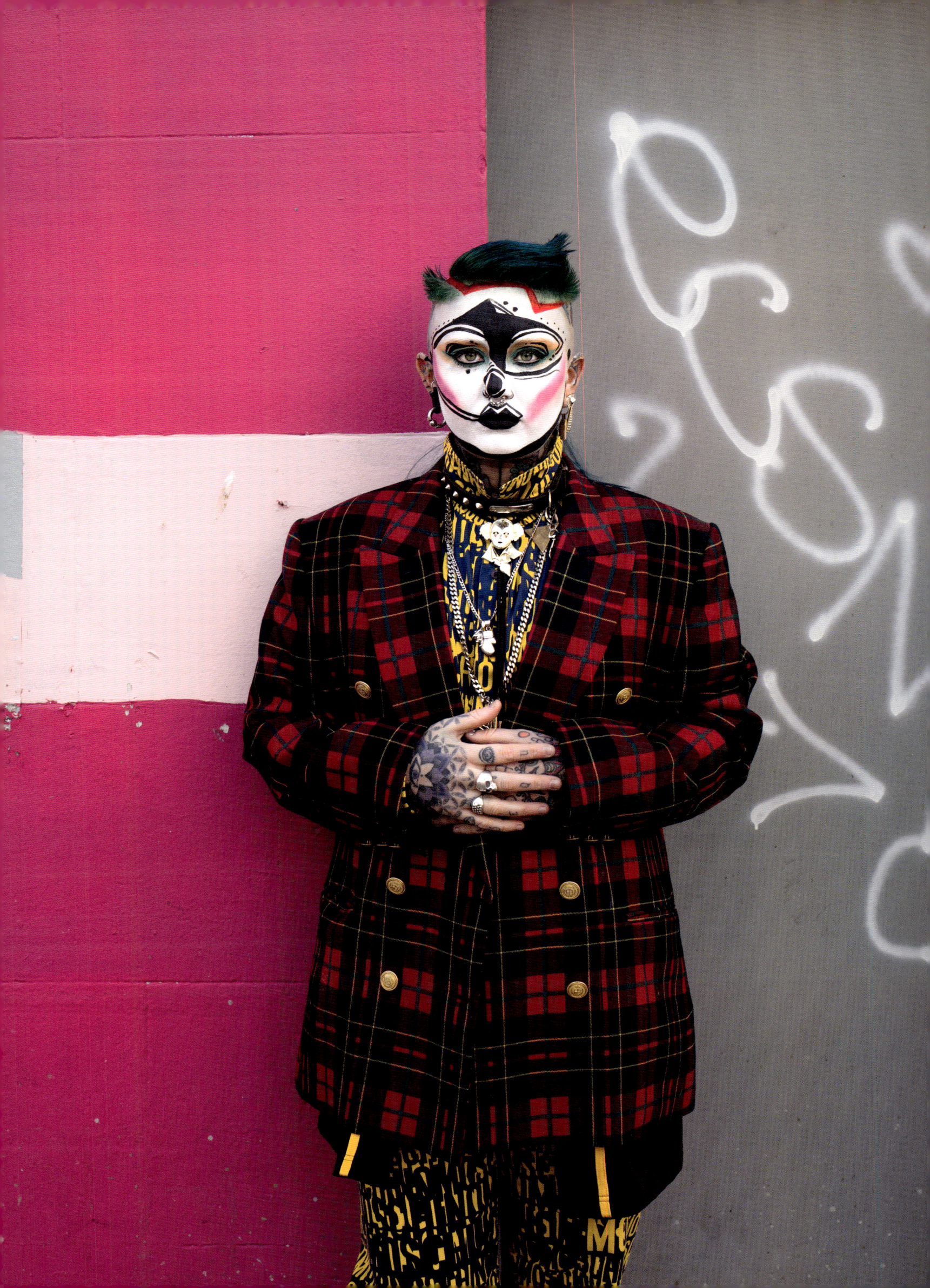

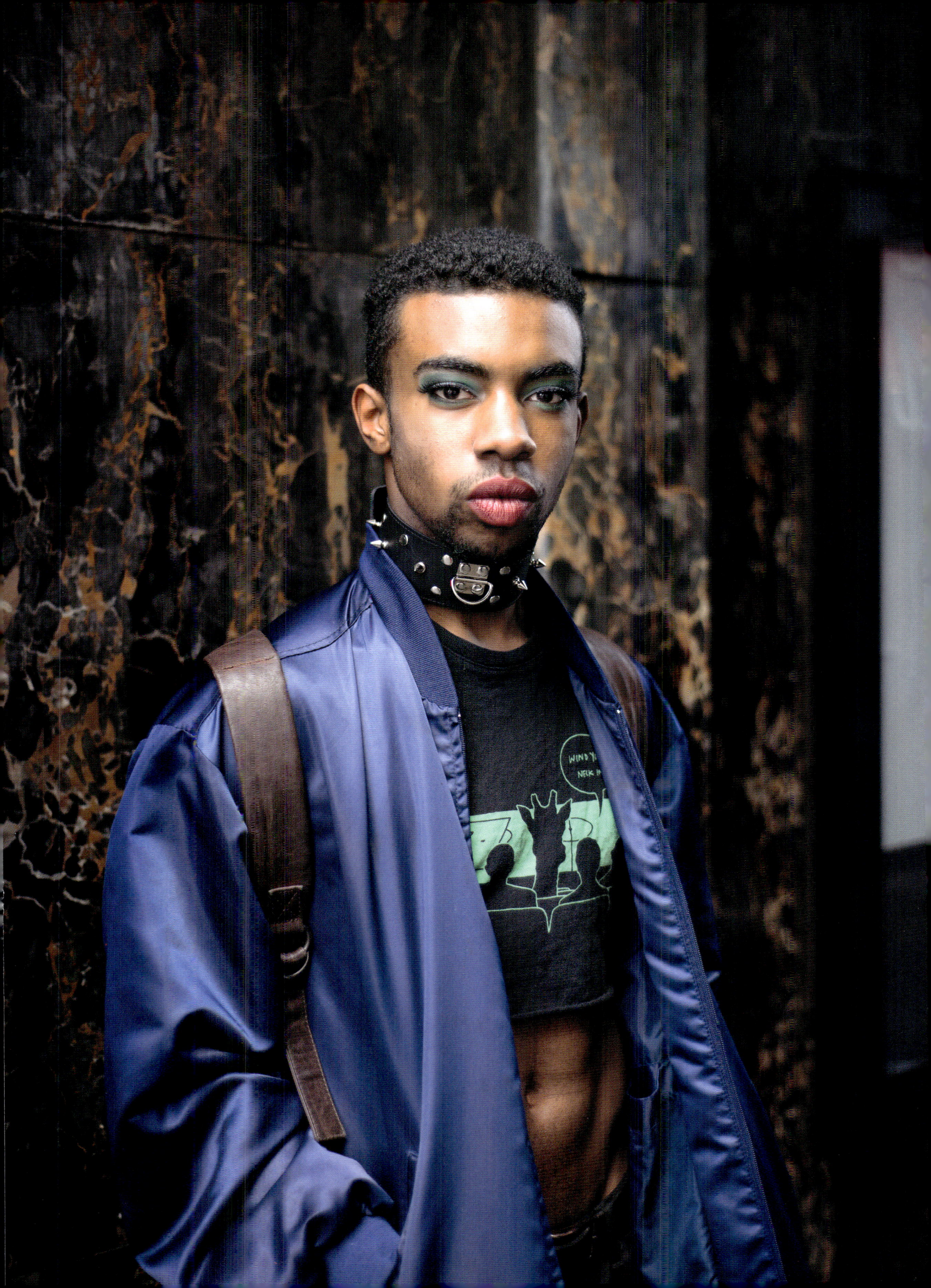

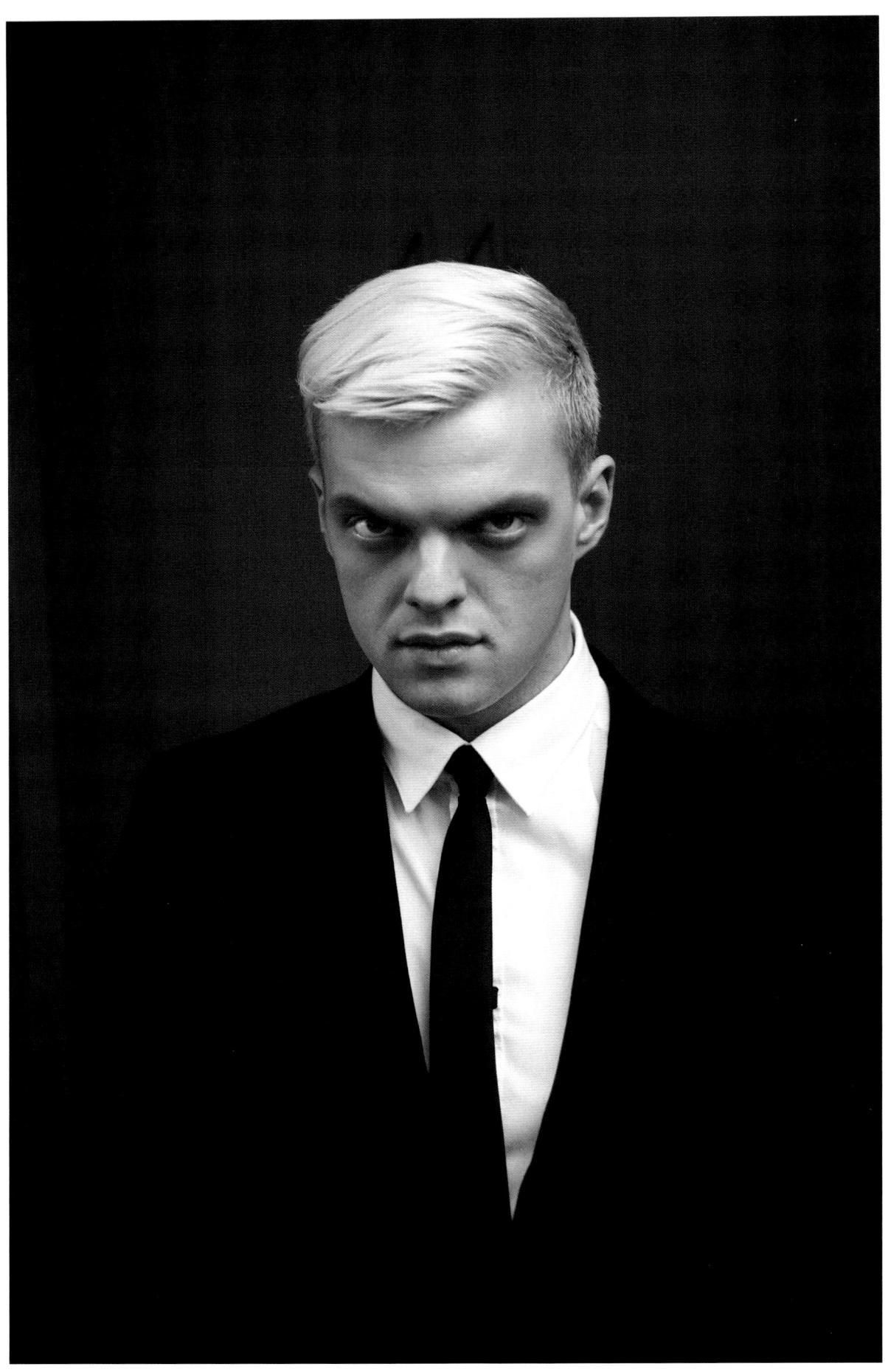

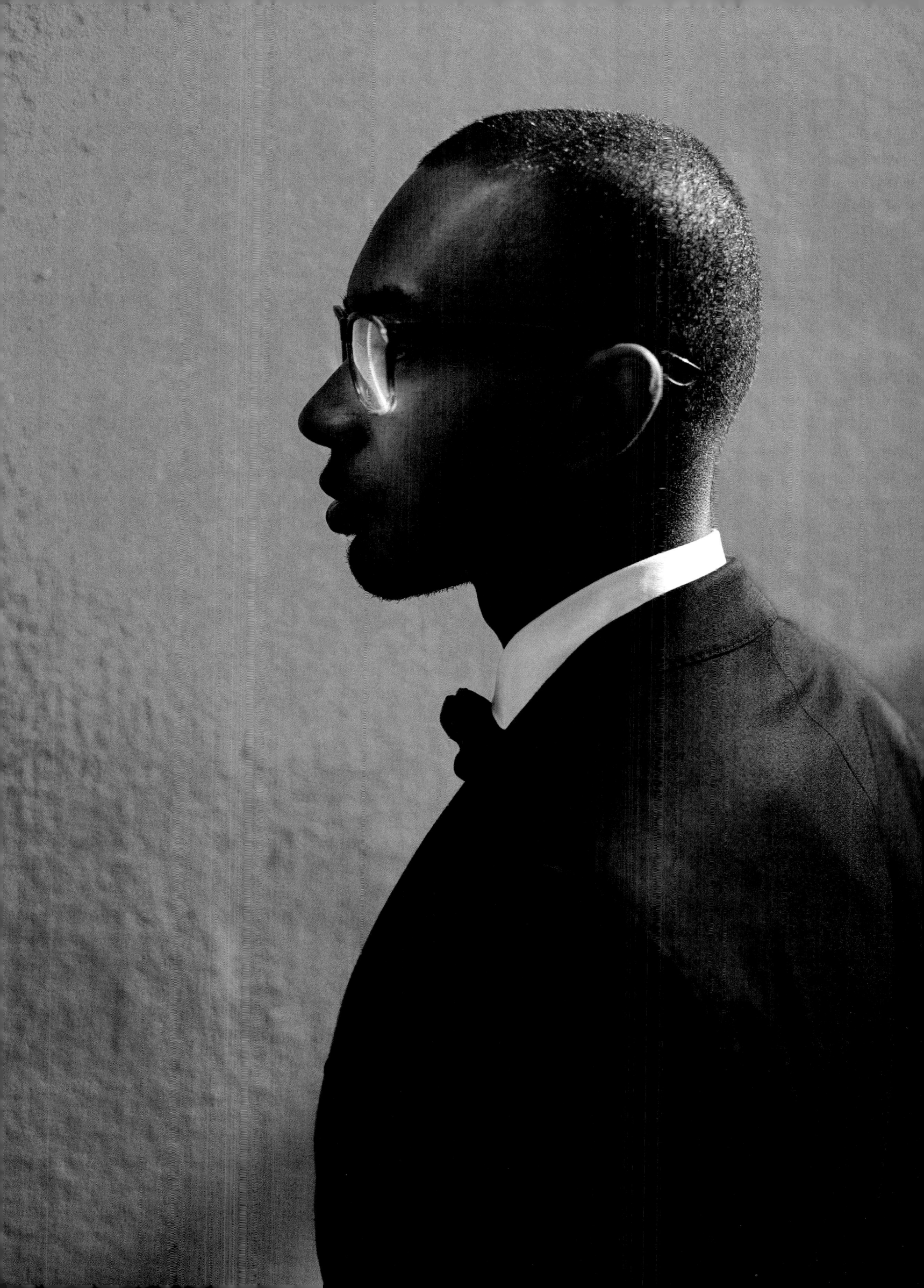

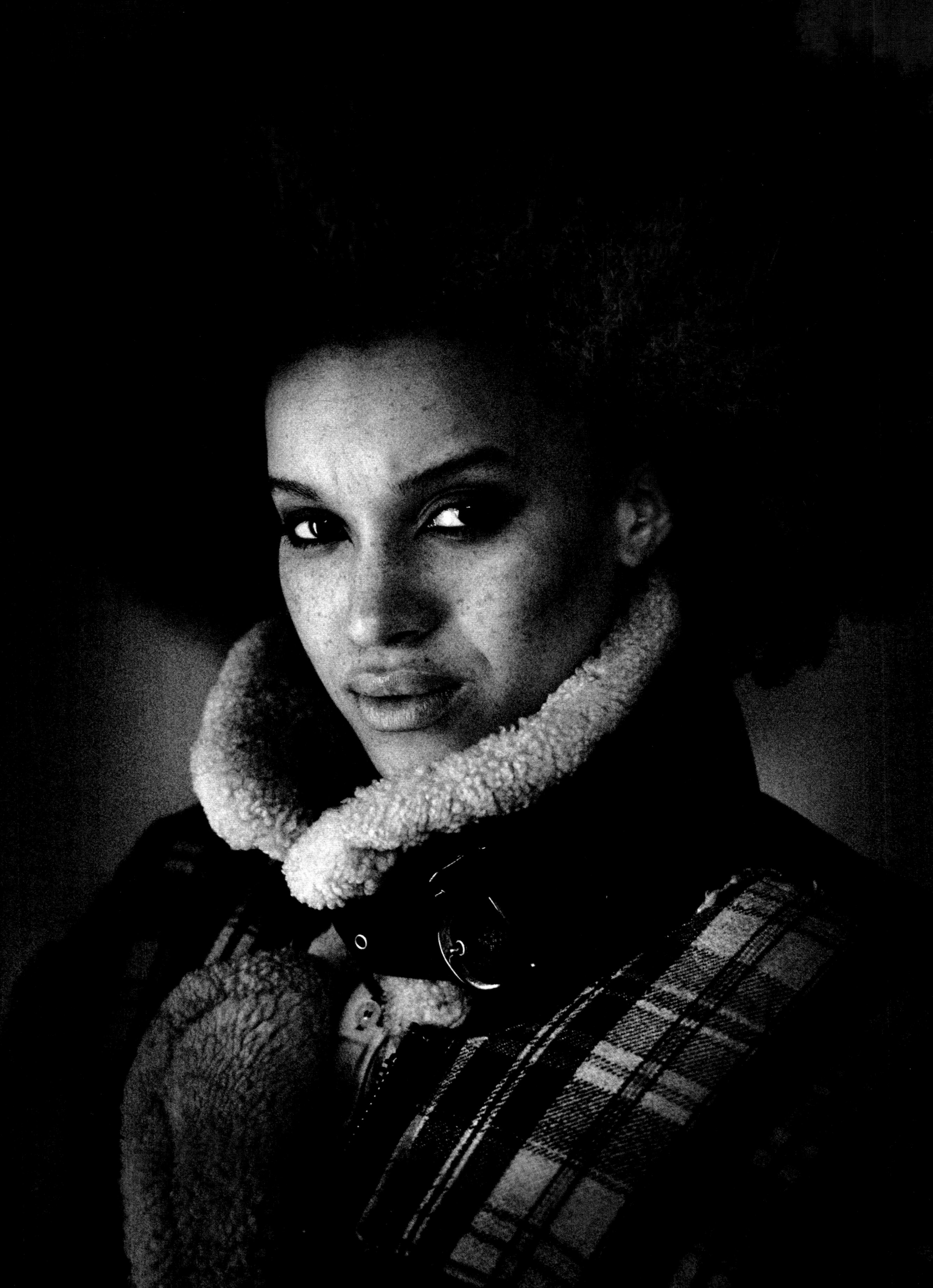

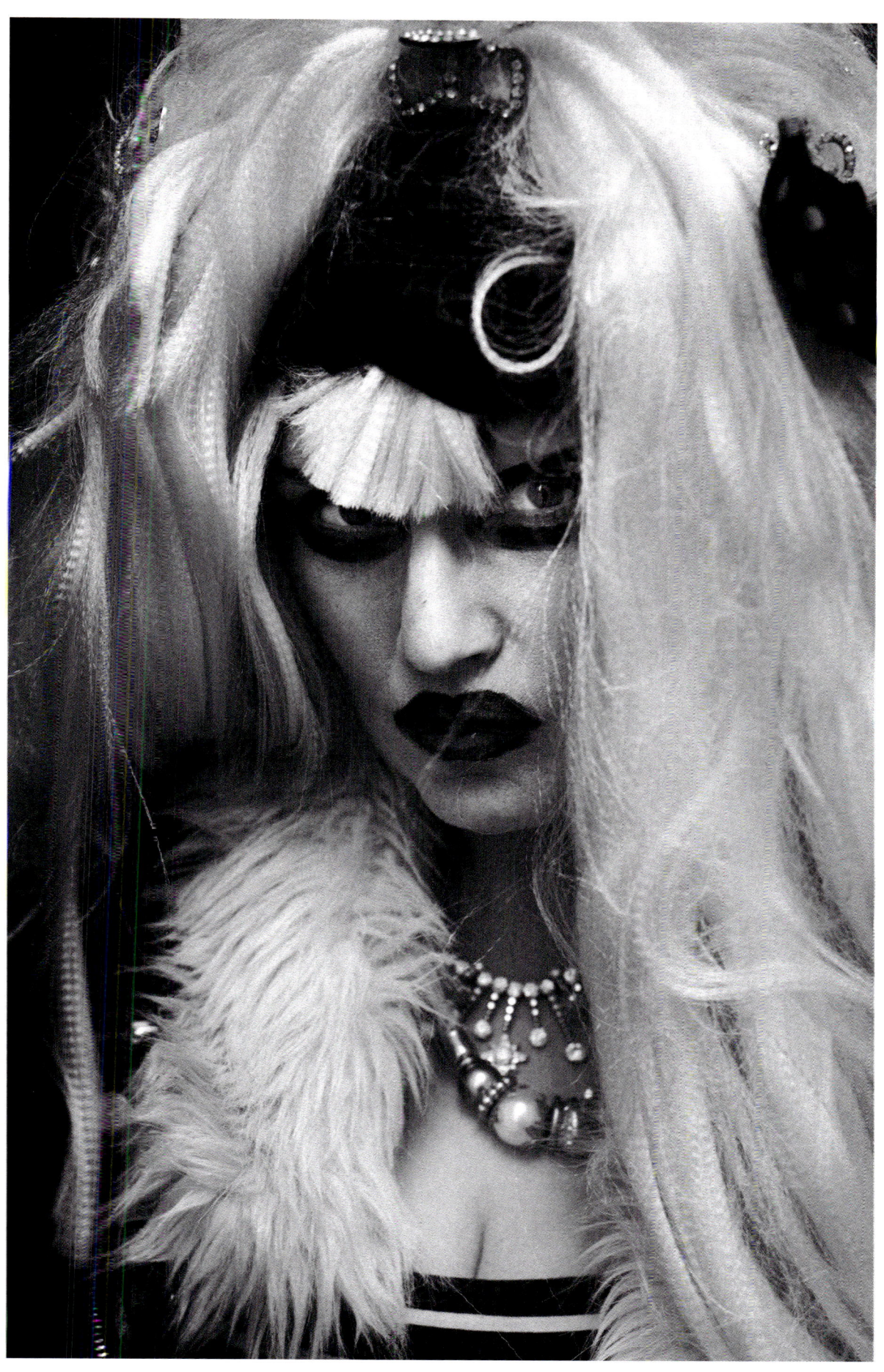

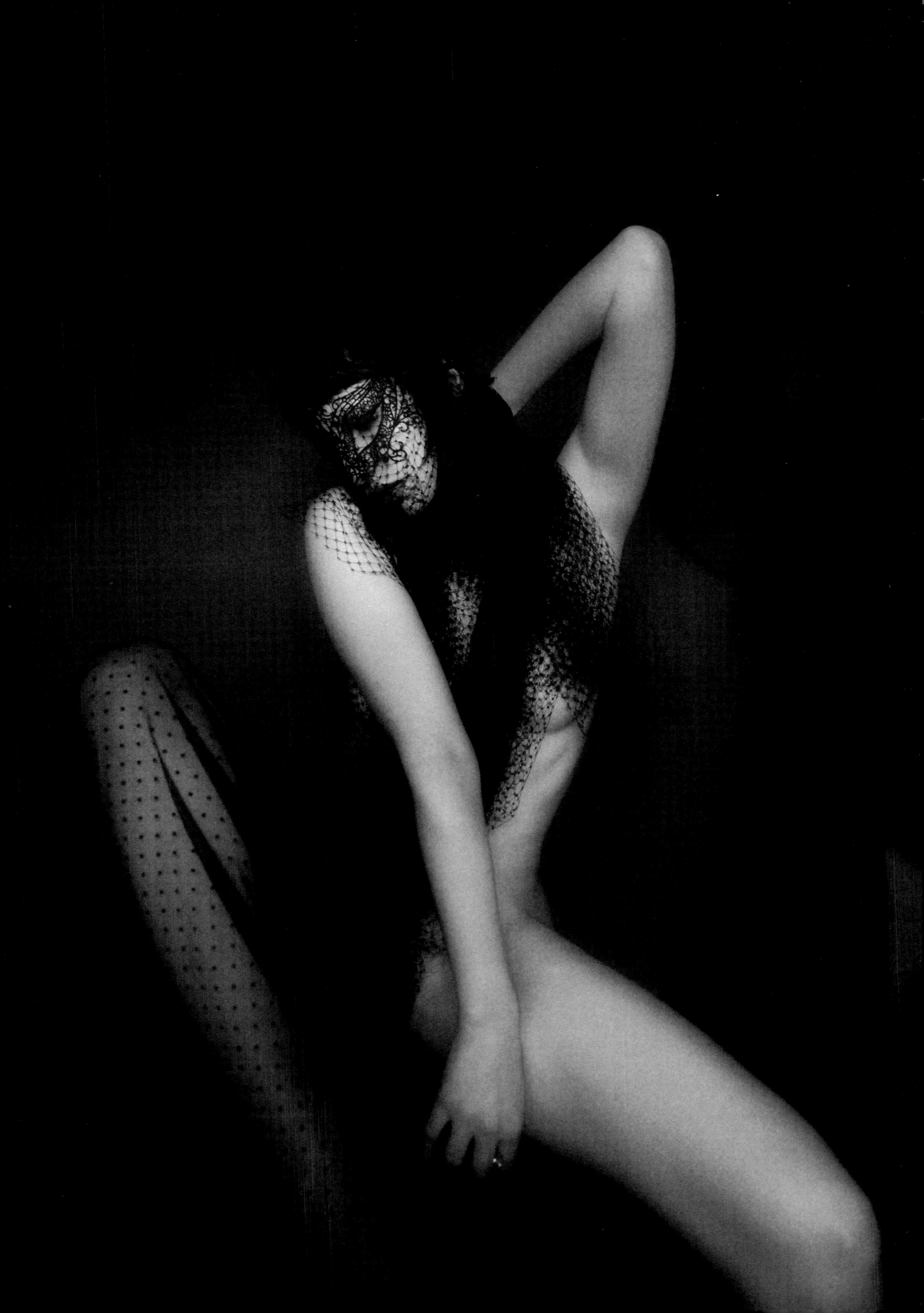

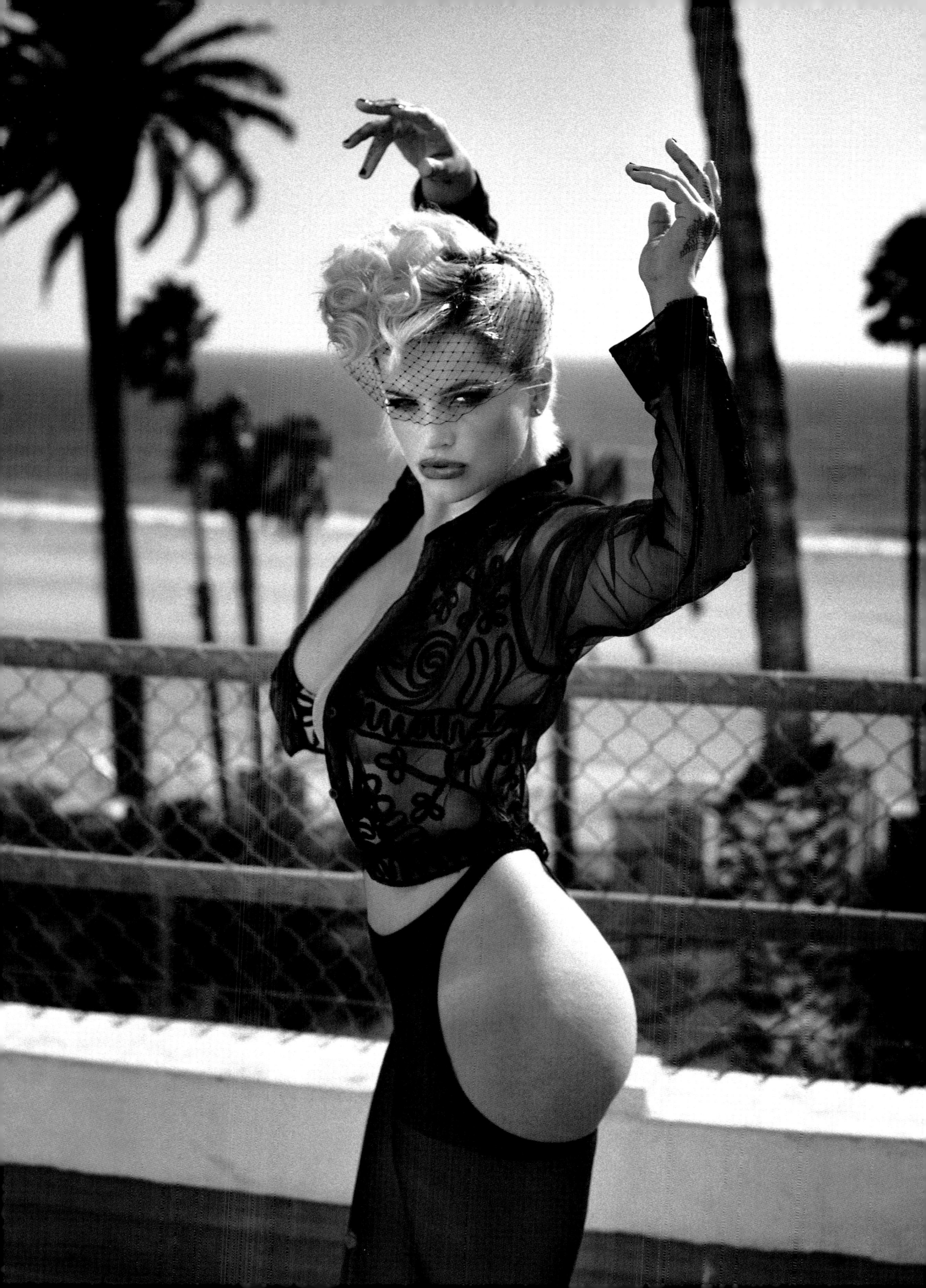

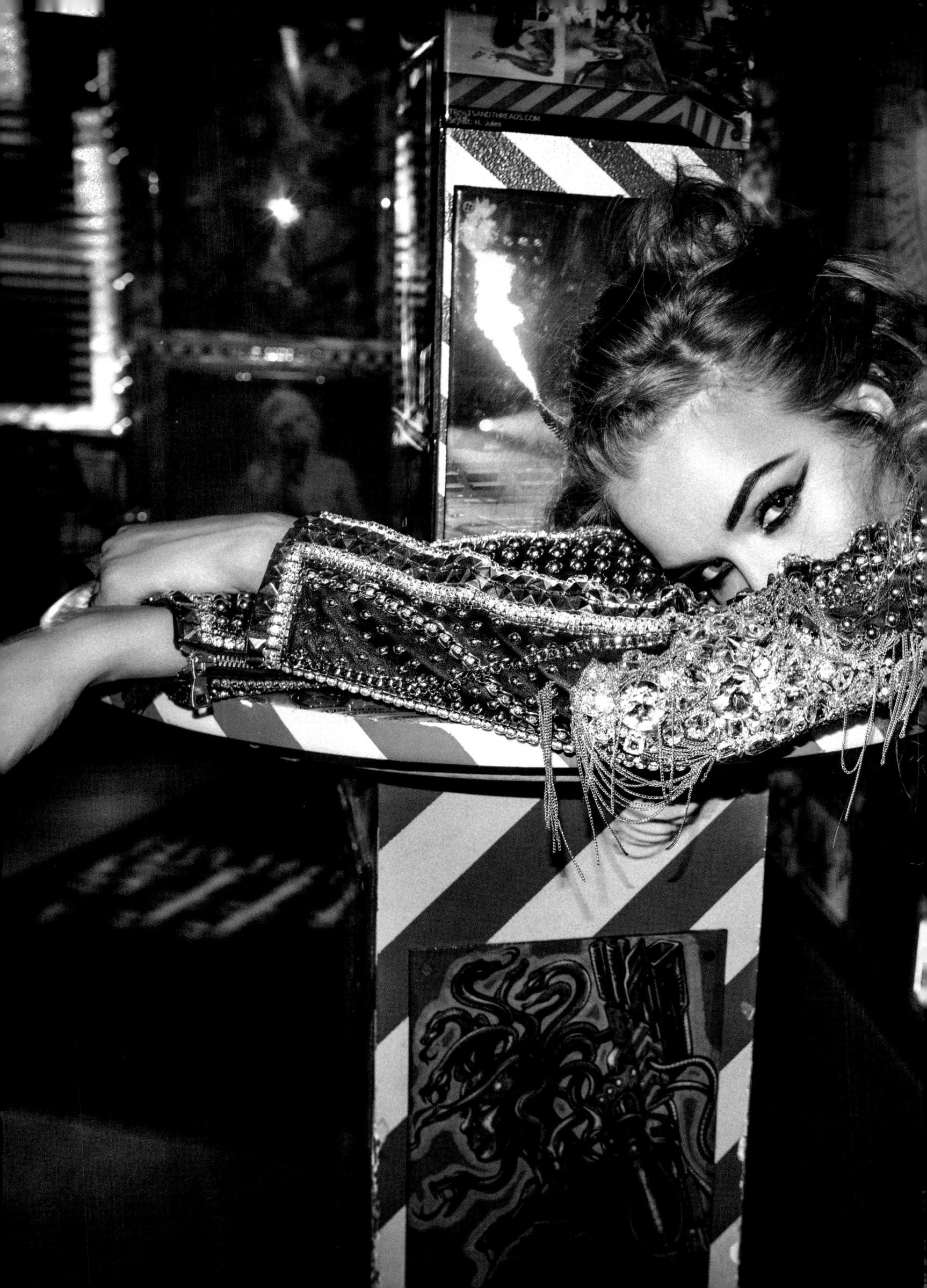

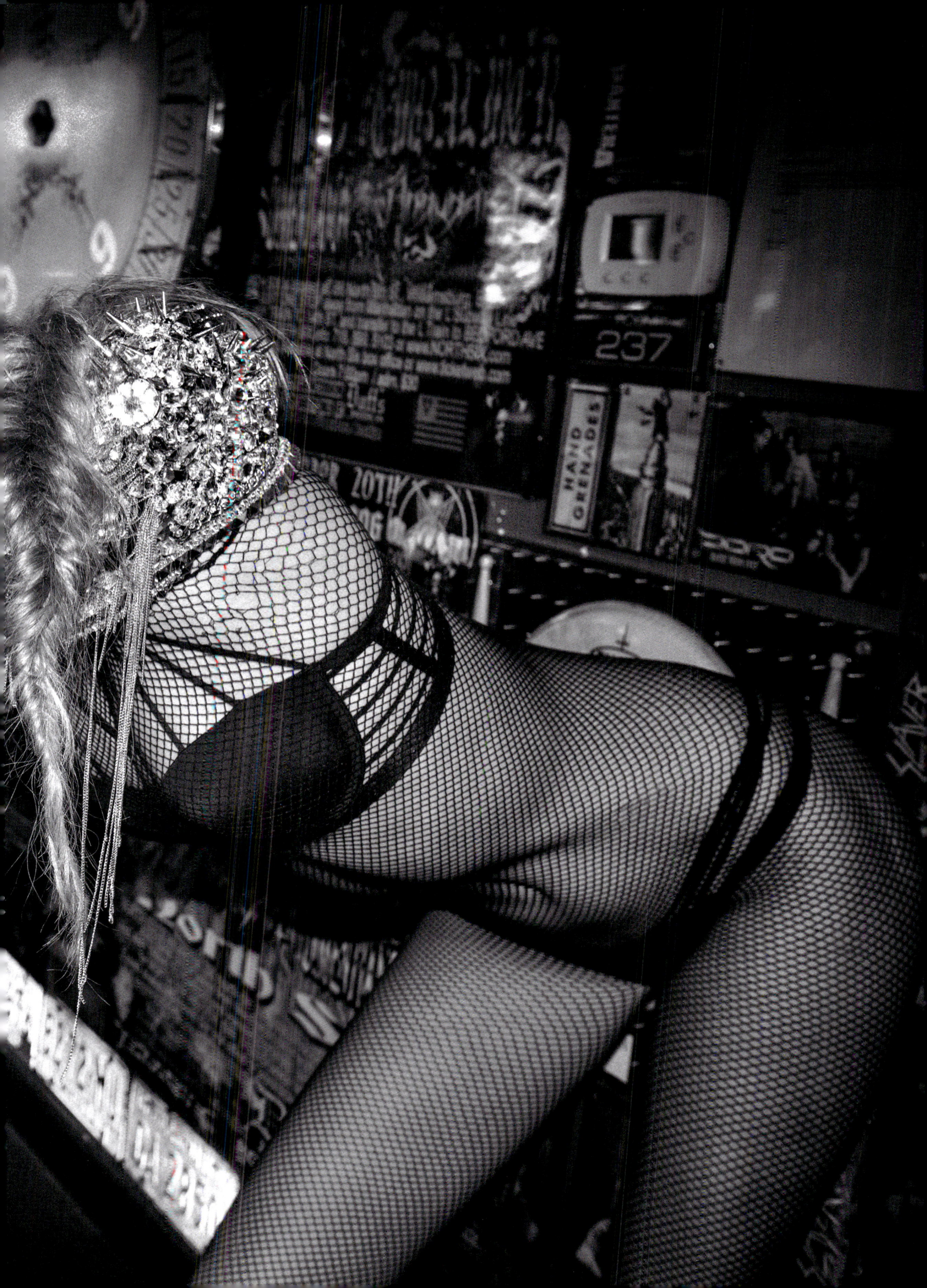

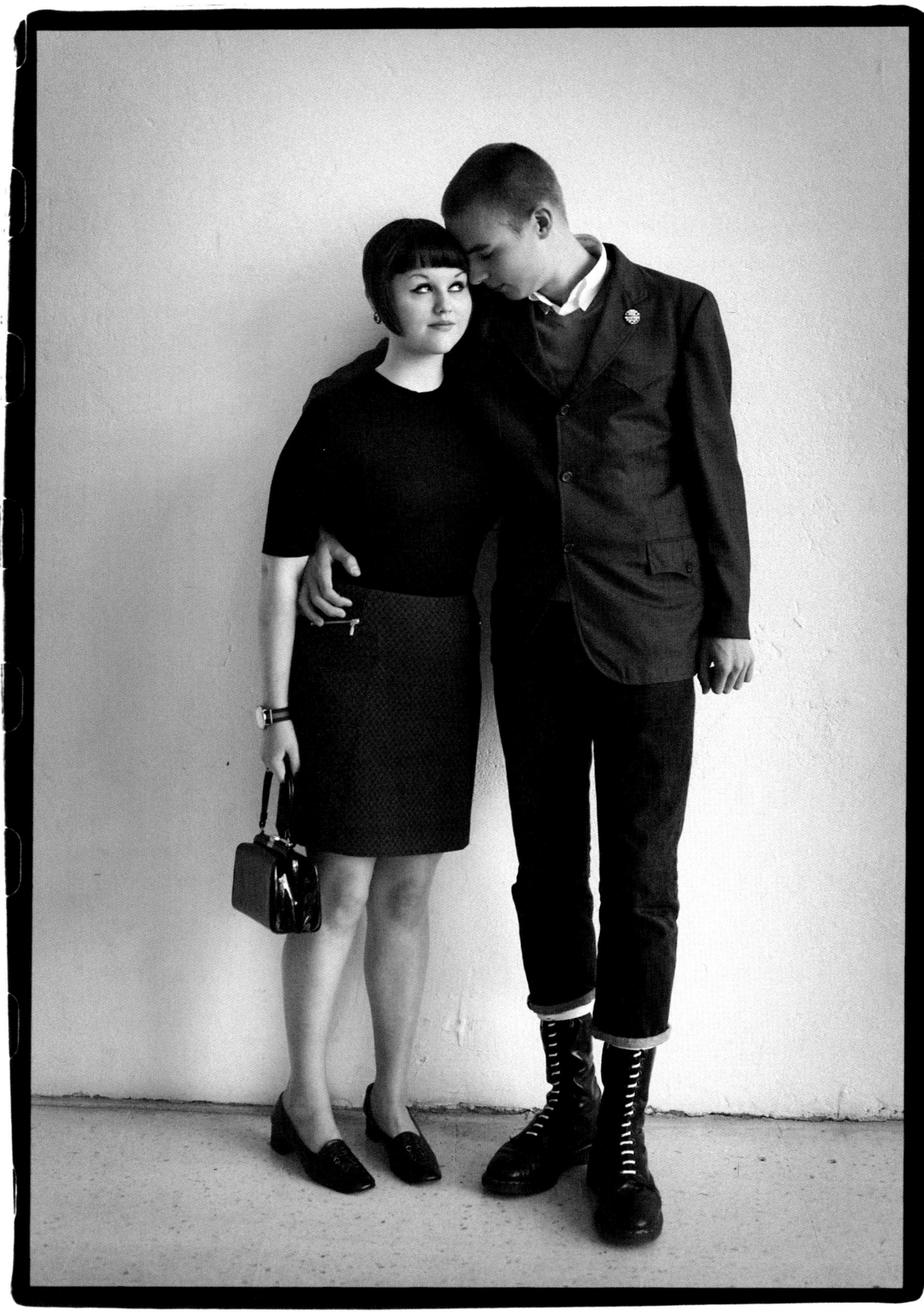

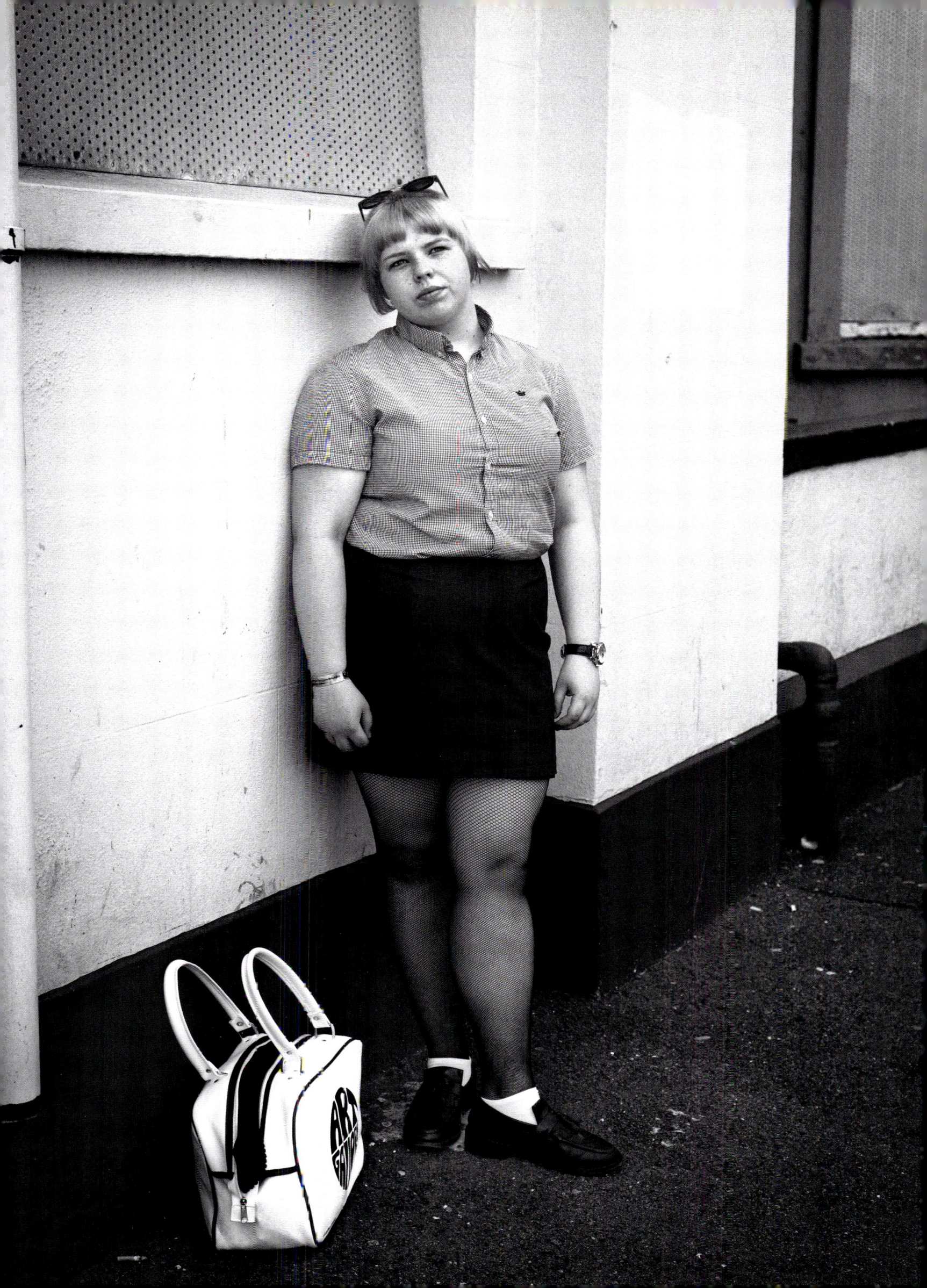

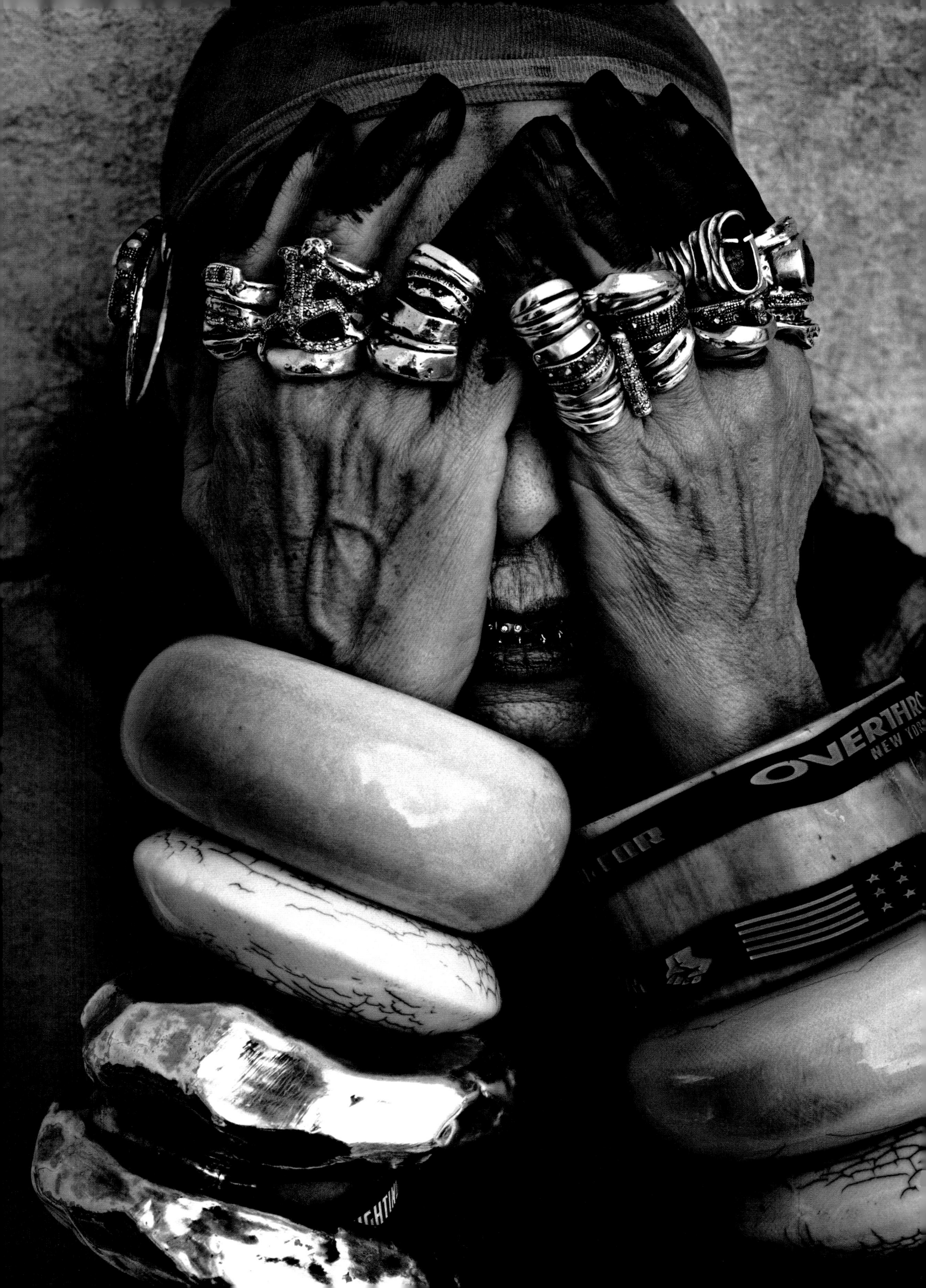

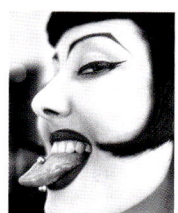

Cover: **Michelle, West Hollywood 1992.** When I took this photograph of Michelle Carr, we'd never met before. I saw her working in the La Luz De Jesus art gallery on Melrose in West Hollywood. We became friends and Michelle later found fame with The Velvet Hammer.

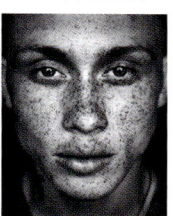

Nicholas Sinclair photographed for Beauty Papers magazine, Acton 2016.

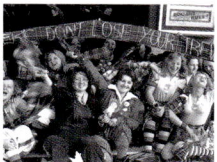

Bay City Rollers fans photographed before one of their gigs at Hammersmith Odeon in 1973. I just happened to be driving by when I saw the commotion all these young women were causing and I thought I would attempt to take some photos.

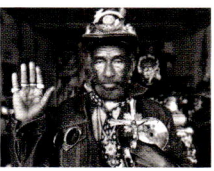

Lee Scratch Perry for Loaded magazine, 1998. Photographed in the recording studio of his home overlooking Lake Geneva.

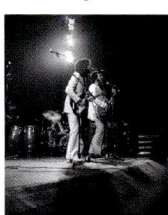

Eric Clapton and Pete Townshend at The Rainbow in January 1973.

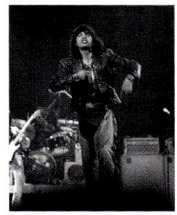

Mick Jagger at Earls Court in 1976. Shot from the audience about five rows back.

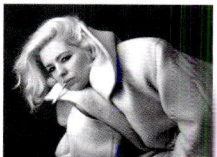

Margi Clarke photographed in her house in Clapham in 1986.

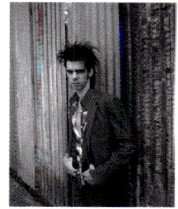

Nick Cave, Southwark 1984.

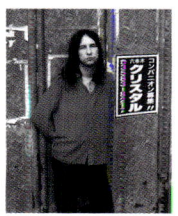

Bobbie Gillespie, Tokyo, Japan 1994.

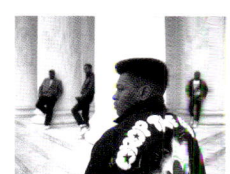

Troublefunk photographed in front of the Lincoln Memorial in Washington in 1987.

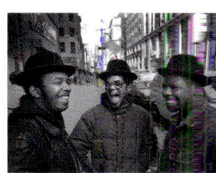

Run DMC photographed close to their record company office at 4th and Broadway, Lower Manhattan, 1985.

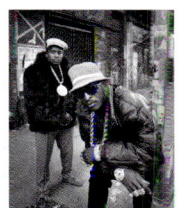

Eric B and Rakim photographed in Eleeke Street, Lower Manhattan 1988. Outside the old Yippie offices.

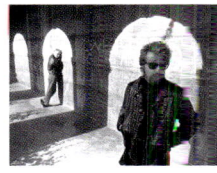

Eurythmics at the Hill Garden and Pergola in Hampstead 1985.

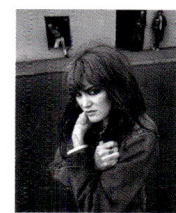

X-ene Cervenka and the Los Angeles band X photographed in Kensal Rise, 1984.

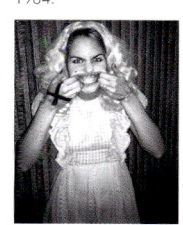

Theo Kogan, lead singer of the Lunachicks photographed backstage at the Reading Festival, 1994.

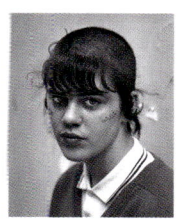

Babs, Soho 1987. I recently found out her real name was Diane.

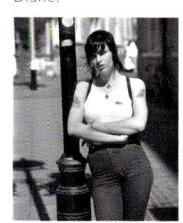

Helen, Carnaby Street 1987.

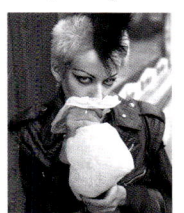

Glue sniffing on Carnaby Street 1981.

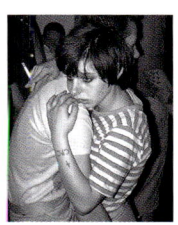

At a Stoke Newington house party 1981.

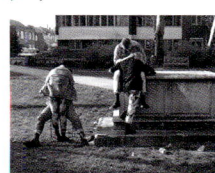

Skinheads kissing on Dovehouse Green, Chelsea 1981.

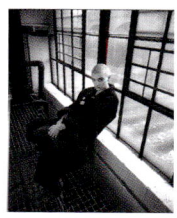

Sinead O'Connor, Wandsworth 1983.

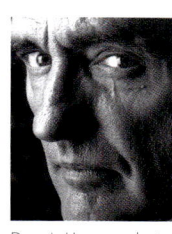

Dennis Hopper photographed at the Savoy Hotel, London in 1990.

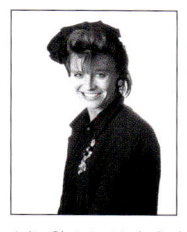

Julie Christie, Hyde Park 1987. This photograph was taken in a tent in the middle of about 100,000 people at a CND / Friends Of The Earth Festival.

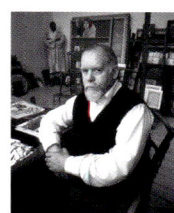

Sir Peter Blake photographed in his studio in Chiswick in 1987. Surrounded by some of the characters from his famous Sgt Pepper LP cover. For The Face magazine.

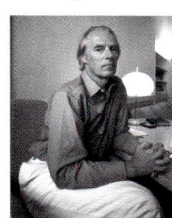

Sir George Martin, photographed at Air Studios, Hampstead 1994. For NME.

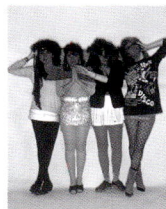

The Slits photographed in 1978 in Lorenz Zatecky's beautiful studio in Sydney Mews, South Kensington. It was the first studio session I'd ever done and I really had no idea what I was doing. I didn't have a commission or anything. Just a lot of chutzpah. Lorenz's assistant David Whyte pretty much did everything for me, except press the camera button.

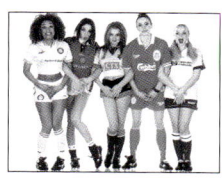

The Spice Girls in Holborn Studios, Hoxton in 1996. For Loaded magazine. In planning this shoot, I was told that Victoria didn't much like football and didn't really have a favourite team. Someone showed her a photo of David Beckham (who she hadn't met at this point) and she became, for the purposes of the shoot, a Manchester United fan. The rest, as they say, is history.

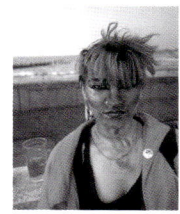

Lowestoft 1986. At dawn after the all-nighter arranged by the London club night, Alice In Wonderland Club.

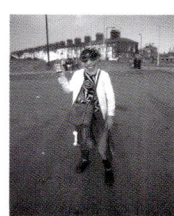

Lowestoft 1986.

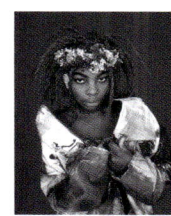

Sherrone, singer with the band Savajazz, photographed at Holborn Studios when it was still in Clerkenwell in 1988. Sherrone was my favourite mid-eighties muse.

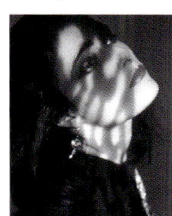

Siouxsie at Holborn Studios when it was still in Clerkenwell in 1991.

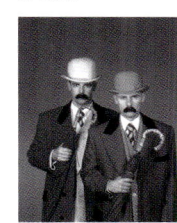

The Pet Shop Boys photographed just before going onstage at Ahoy Rotterdam in 1991. For Time Out.

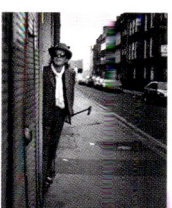

Ian Dury photographed in the Brick Lane area in 1986. During the making of the film King Of The Ghetto.

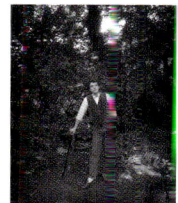

Danny Huston photographed in the back garden of his mother's house in Hampstead in 1984. For Vogue.

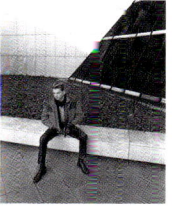

Dave Gahan Berlin 1985. Photographed outside the Intercontinental Hotel.

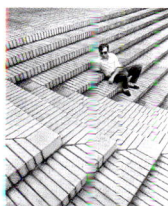

Tim Roth, Fitzrovia 1985.

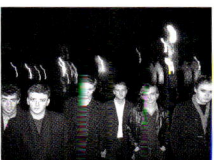

The Fall, Manchester 1982. For NME.

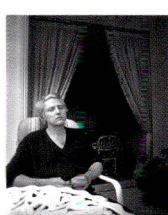

Christopher Walken in the Halcyon Hotel, Holland Park 1985. For The Face magazine.

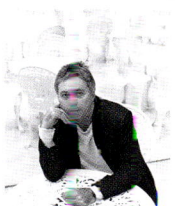

Harold Budd, Covent Garden 1987. For The Face magazine.

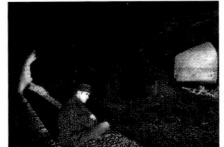

Morrissey photographed in Lambeth in 1985. More or less where St Thomas' Hospital is now.

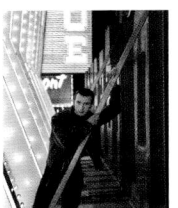

Marc Almond on the awning of the Horseshoe Casino on the old strip in Las Vegas, 1988.

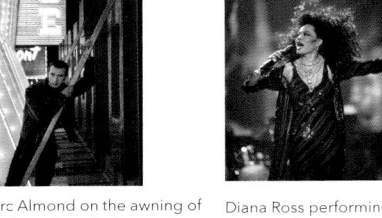

Ian Astbury on the roof of the Whisky a Go Go in West Hollywood in 1991.

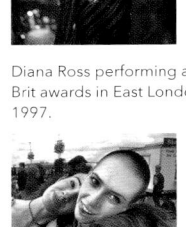

Prima Scream at the Hill Garden and Pergola in Hampstead, 1986.

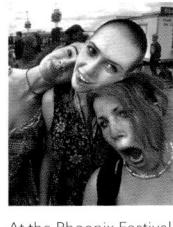

Green Day, St John's Wood 1994.

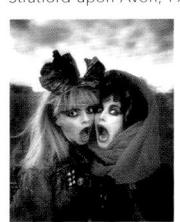

The Cramps in Glendale, California 1990.

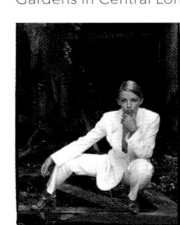

The Beastie Boys photographed in Greenwich Village, New York City 1987.

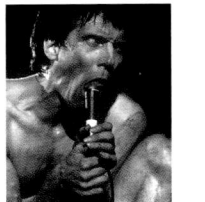

Lux Interior onstage at the Reading Festival 1990.

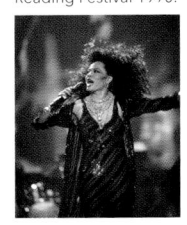

Diana Ross performing at the Brit awards in East London 1997.

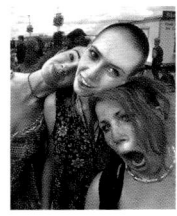

At the Phoenix Festival, near Stratford-upon-Avon, 1997.

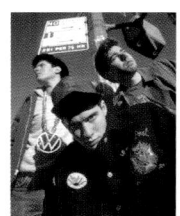

Nina Hagen and Lena Lovich 1987. Photographed for NME on the roof of Arista Records overlooking Cavendish Square Gardens in Central London.

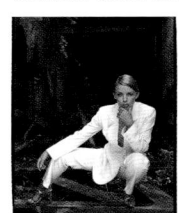

Kylie Mingue, Chalk Farm, London 1994.

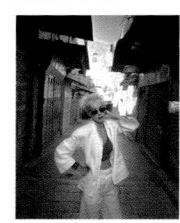

Annie Lennox, Jerusalem 1987.

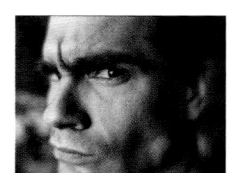

Henry Rollins, Chicago 1990. The life of a rock photographer is not all limos and 5 star hotels. I went straight from the airport to this photoshoot, then got straight back in a cab to O'Hare afterwards. I had an urgent deadline to meet.

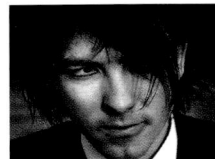

Robert Smith behind Hammersmith Odeon, West London 1984. For The Face magazine.

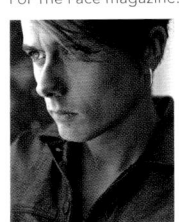

Brett Anderson, Chelsea 1994. For NME.

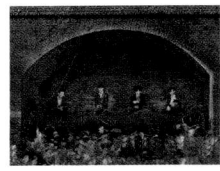

The Jesus And Mary Chain, Tottenham 1984.

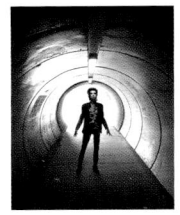

Nick Cave, Wandsworth 1984. This tunnel, which was right next to Wandsworth Town Station, has now been filled in.

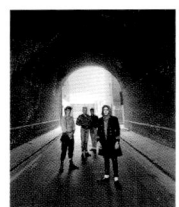

The Cult photographed close to their rehearsal studio in Southwark 1984.

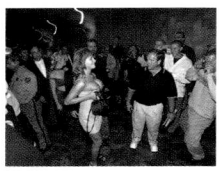

At Ballys before the Adult Video Awards, Las Vegas 1999.

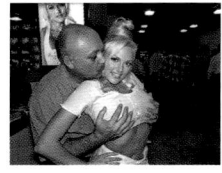

Stacy and friend at the Adult Video News show in Las Vegas 1997. For Loaded Magazine.

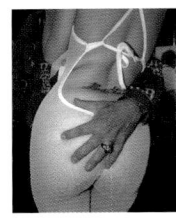

Candy Apples torso and friend's hand at the Adult Video News show in Las Vegas 1999. For The Independent on Sunday.

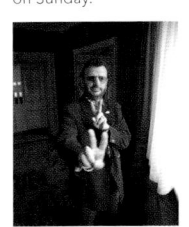

Ringo Starr in the Dorchester Hotel 1992.

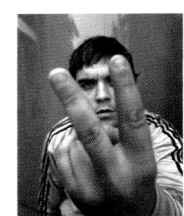

Robbie Williams, Brussels 1996.

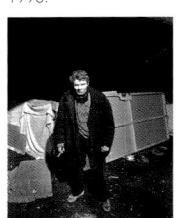

Michael, South Bank London. From The Box People project 1987.

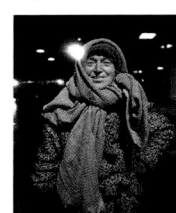

Anon. South Bank London. From The Box People project 1987.

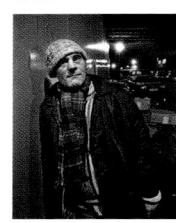

The Embankment, London. From The Box People project 1987.

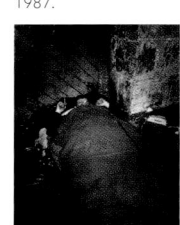

The Embankment, London. From The Box People project 1987.

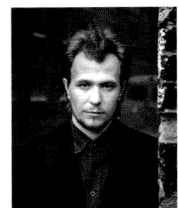

Gary Oldman, Covent Garden 1985.

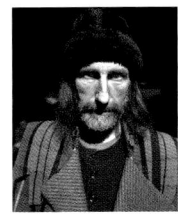

Arthur Brown, Whitby 1998.

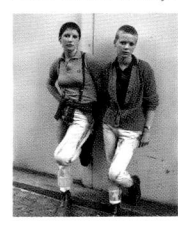

Skinhead girls Debbie and Caroline, Brighton 1980. This photograph became well known after it was extensively used (backdrop, tour brochure, t-shirts, etc), without my prior knowledge on Morrissey's Your Arsenal tour in 1988.

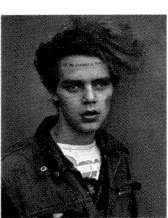

Tuinol Barry, Chelsea 1983.

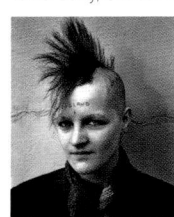

Lita, Soho 1983.

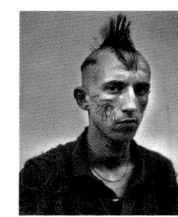

Belsen, Soho 1982.

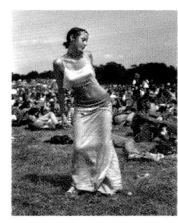

At the Glastonbury Festival 1998.

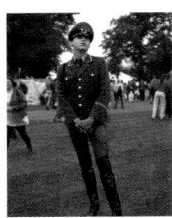

At Gay Pride (as it was then called), Brockwell Park 1994.

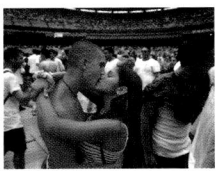

Kissing in the rain, RFK Stadium, Washington 1998. If I remember correctly this was during a weekend benefit concert for Tibetan Freedom. It rained so heavily during the Saturday that a couple of people got struck by lightning and the show for that day ended early.

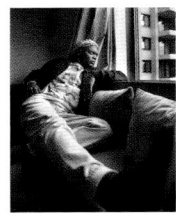

Samuel L Jackson, West London 1997.

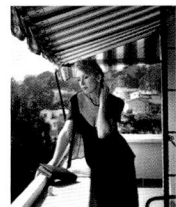

Helen Mirren, Chateau Marmont Hotel, West Hollywood 1994. For Loaded magazine.

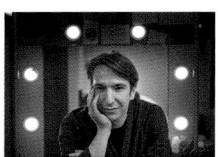

Alan Rickman, Soho 1995.

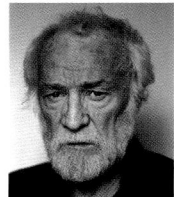

Richard Harris at the The Savoy Hotel

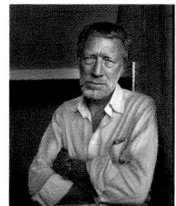

Max Von Sydow at the Old Vic In Southwark 1988. For Time Out.

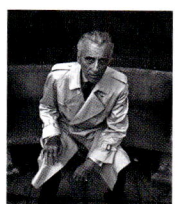

Christopher Lee, Chelsea 1997.

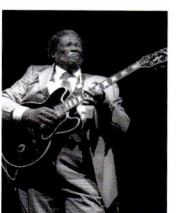

B.B.King in Osaka, Japan. Whilst he was on tour with U2.

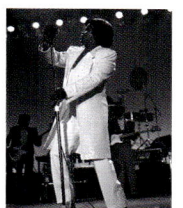

James Brown, Paris 1993.

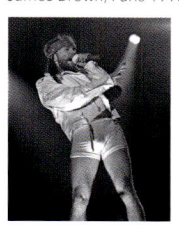

Axl Rose, Oklahoma 1992.

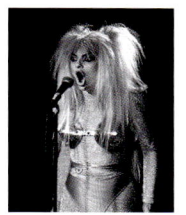

Nina Hagen at the Marquee in London in 1986.

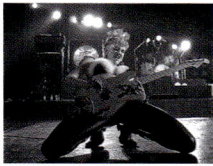

Fur Dixon, bass player with The Cramps, Hammersmith 1986.

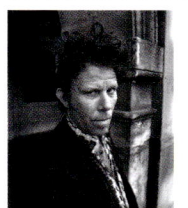

Tom Waits, Paris 1992.

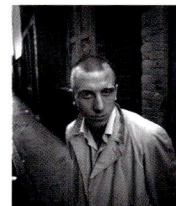

Tim Roth, in the Brick Lane area of East London 1985. During the making of the film King Of The Ghetto.

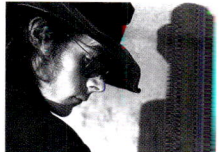

Andrew Eldridge, Leeds 1994.

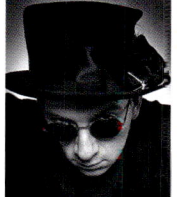

Elvis Costello, Soho 1986. Photographed during the brief period he changed over to his Declan McManus identity.

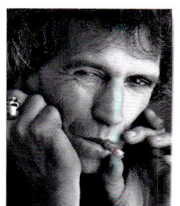

Keith Richards at the Savoy Hotel, 1985. For NME

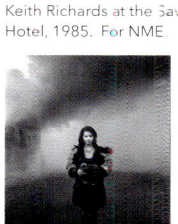

Bjork, Iceland 1991. For NME.

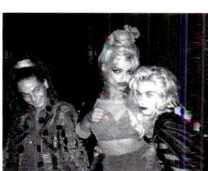

Ari Up, Nina Hagen and Fam Hogg after the Grace Jones show at Brixton Academy 1992.

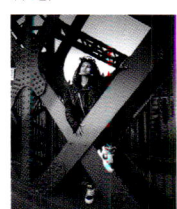

Neneh Cherry, Kensal Rise 1988. For NME.

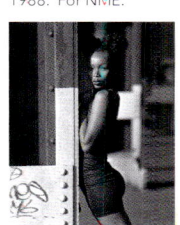

Phina Oruche photographed in the Meatpacking District of Lower Manhattan 1994. For Loaded magazine.

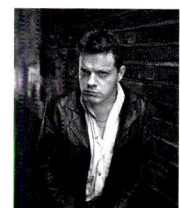

Eddie Izzard, Soho 1994.

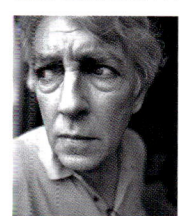

Peter Cook photographed in his house in Hampstead in 1994. For NME.

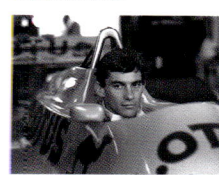

Ayrton Senna, Brands Hatch, Kent 1987.

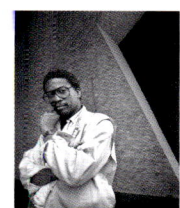

Herbie Hancock photographed beneath the Centrepoint Building in Central London in 1982. For The Face magazine.

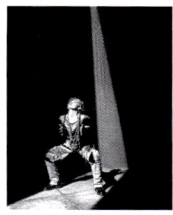

Sarah Shackleton, Liverpool Street 1992.

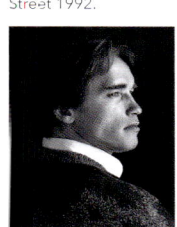

Arnold Schwarzenegger, Dorchester Hotel, London 1995.

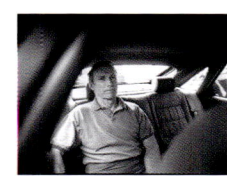

Clint Eastwood, photographed during the Cannes Film Festival in 1994. He was just arriving for a reception at the famous Carlton Hotel. The window was only open about 6 inches but it was just enough for my Nikon FM2 which I'd prefocussed.

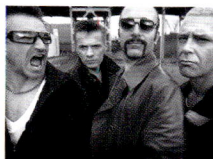

U2, Long Island City 1997. For NME.

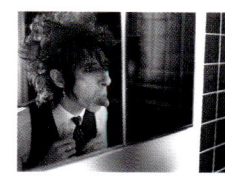

John Cooper Clarke, South London 1981. For The Face magazine.

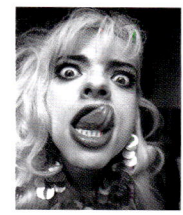

Nina Hagen at home in her flat in Ladbroke Grove, West London 1992.

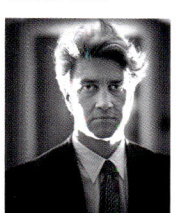

David Lynch at the Savoy Hotel, London 1984.

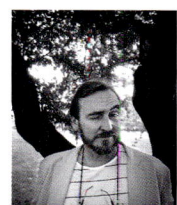

Wes Craven, Green Park, London 1985.

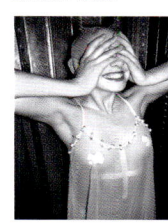

Lucy at Torture Garden, at Ministry of Sound, Southwark 1997.

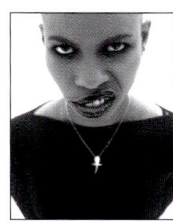

Skin, Chelsea 1996.

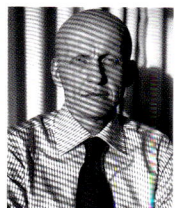

Pierluigi Collina at the St Martins Lane Hotel, London 2004.

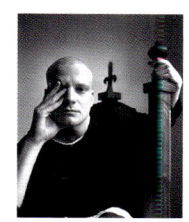

Colin Firth, North London 1987. His head had been shaved for the TV film Tumbledown.

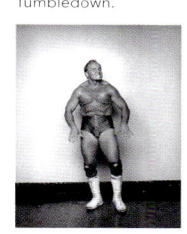

Wrestler Mal Saunders, Wolverhampton 1995. For Simon Garfield's book The Wrestling.

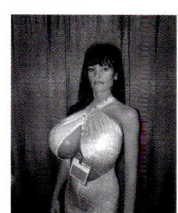

Sofia Staks at the CES Show, Las Vegas 1997.

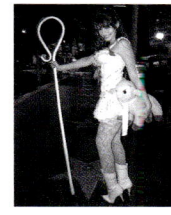

Pornstar Shelby Stevens, Hollywood and Vine, 1998. That night I was with my late friend Tony Biner, just walking along the street when we bumped into Shelby Stevens dressed as Little Bo Peep. Tony and her were good friends. I assumed she was on her way to a party. But on the Hollywood Walk of Fame, who knows?

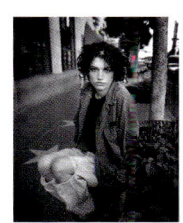

Violence One Love, Hollywood Boulevard 1992. This was taken 6 years earlier and about 800 metres away from the photograph on the facing page. But, in some respects, a million miles apart. I saw her sitting in a planter at Hollywood and Highland. She looked so sad and soulful.

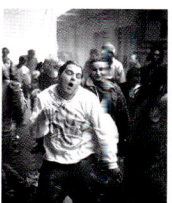

Dancer at the Spiral Tribe all-dayer, Uxbridge 1993.

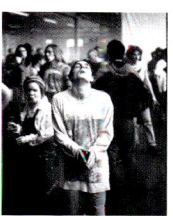

Dancer at the Spiral Tribe all-dayer, Uxbridge 1993.

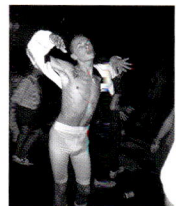

Dancer at The Fridge, Brixton 1990.

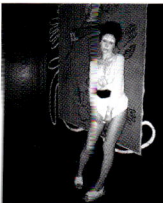

Cat at The Fridge, Brixton 1986.

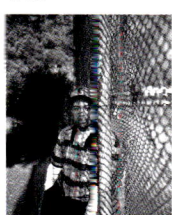

Tiger Woods, near San Diego, California 1994. At age 18 and whilst he was still an amateur.

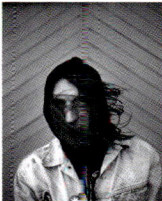

Malcom Treece (of The Wonder Stuff) Brighton, 1988. For NME.

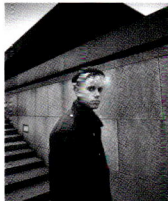

Martin Gore, Berlin 1984. Outside the Neue Nationalgalerie.

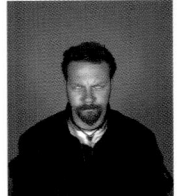

James Hetfield, New York City 1996

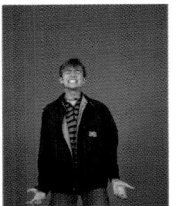

Damon Albarn, Holborn Studio, Hoxton 1997.

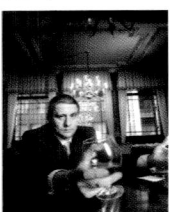

Shaun Ryder, Central London 1995. For Loaded magazine.

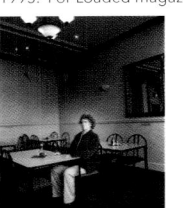

Noddy Holder in the canteen in the Granda TV studios in Manchester 1996.

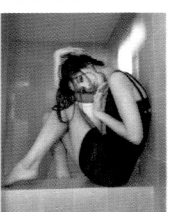

Catherine Zeta-Jones at the Halcyon Hotel, Holland Park 1996. For Loaded magazine.

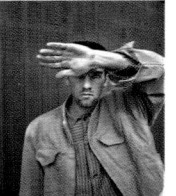

Michael Stipe, Athens, Georgia 1991.

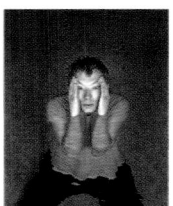

Thom Yorke, Oxford 1995. For Vox magazine.

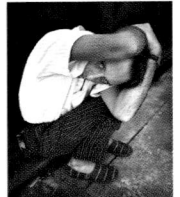

Richard E Grant, East Twickenham (most locals know it as St Margarets) 1997.

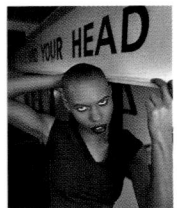

Skin at Chalk Farm Studios in Hoxton 1996.

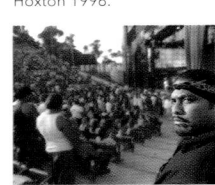

Gawtti (from the Boo-Yaa T.R.I.B.E) at the Irvin Meadows Amphitheatre in California. During the Lollapalooza Festival 1991.

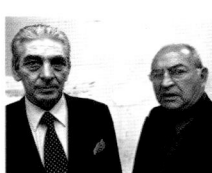

Tony Lambrianou and Freddie Foreman, Southwark 2000. For Vox magazine. They'd both served long prison sentences for involvement in Kray Twins' murders. They were friendly and polite but I'd be lying if I were to say totally devoid of a hint of menace. Freddie's nickname was once 'Brown Bread Fred'.

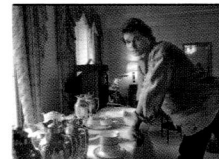

Ray Liotta, The Savoy Hotel, London 1992.

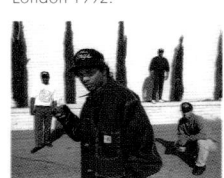

NWA, Compton, Los Angeles 1994.

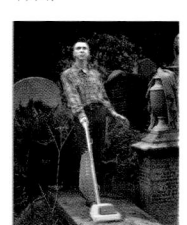

Marc Almond at the Brompton Cemetery in West London. We used an old Hoover that someone had discarded.

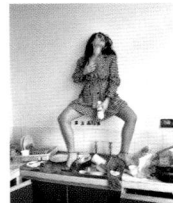

Fifi Dennison at home in her flat in Ladbroke Grove 1993. Washing up; the model's own.

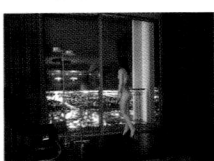

Kristy, North Las Vegas 2012.

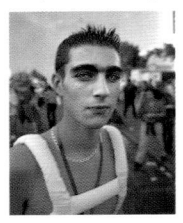

I asked him what his name was and he said "It's classified." Good enough for me.

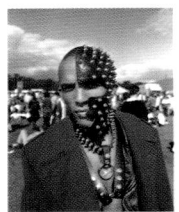

At Mardi Gras, Finsbury Park, North London 2000. Anon, Gay Pride (as it was known then), Clapham Common 1996.

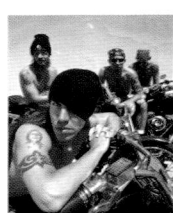

Red Hot Chili Peppers, Hollywood 1994.

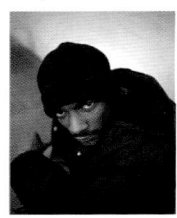

Snoop Dogg, Holland Park, London 1994.

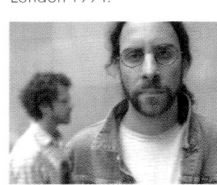

The Coen Brothers, St James's, London.

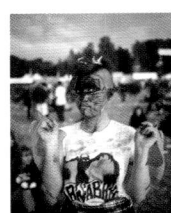

At Glastonbury Festival 1994.

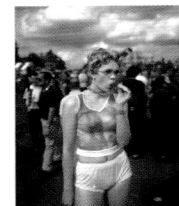

At Mardi Gras, Finsbury Park 2000.

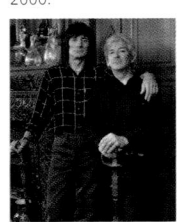

Ron Wood and Kenney Jones at Ron Wood's house on Kingston Hill 2000.

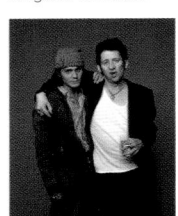

Johnny Depp and Shane MacGowan at Holborn Studios, Hoxton 1996.

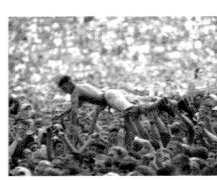

Crowdsurfing at the RFK Stadium, Washington 1998.

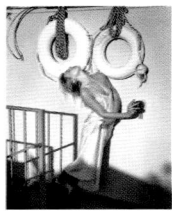

Leonora Scelfo, West Hollywood 1996.

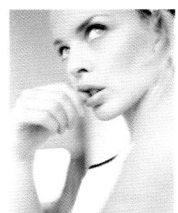

Kylie Minogue at Chalk Farm Studio, North London 1994.

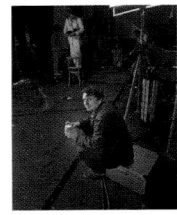

David Bailey whilst shooting the 'Dumb Animals' promotional film for Greenpeace. West London 1985.

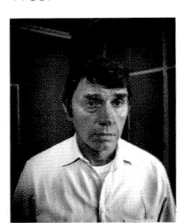

Don McCullin, North London 1987.

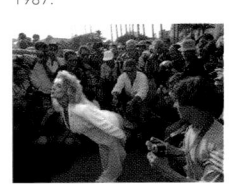

Marissa Malibu photo call during the Cannes Film Festival, 1995.

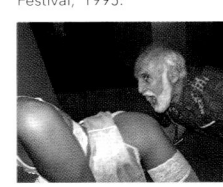

Mila and Marlen at the AVN show in Las Vegas, 1999. For Loaded magazine.

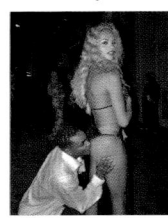

At the AVN show at the Sands Convention Centre, Las Vegas 2004.

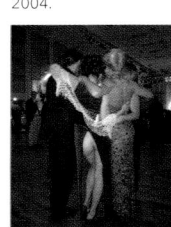

After the Hot D'Or Show, Paris 1998.

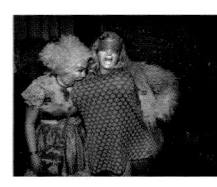

Max and Dementia, Kaos, Islington 2016.

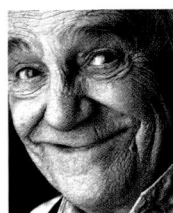

Max Wall, Covent Garden 1984. For Time Out.

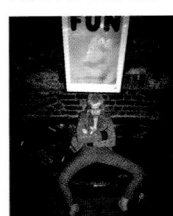

Suzi Leenaars at the Alibi Club in Dalston. Styling Tara St. Hill. Make up Lucy Bridge. Hair Gary Gill. For 10 magazine. Assisted by Natalia Gates.

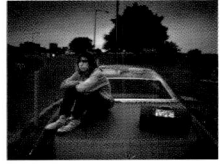

A Deadhead waiting outside a Grateful Dead concert at the RFK Stadium, Washington 1989.

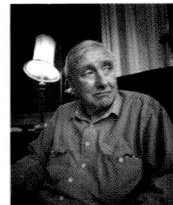

Spike Milligan at his managers office in Bayswater, West London 1995.

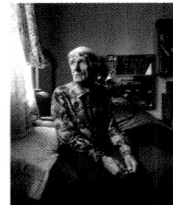

Gil Evans in his tiny flat on the Upper West Side of New York City in 1987. He told me he had a house in Greenwich Village but his ex-wife was living in it. For The Wire magazine.

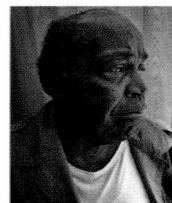

Willie Dixon at his home In Glendale, California 1990.

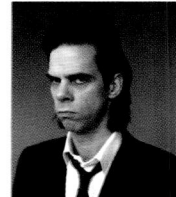

Nick Cave, Chalk Farm Studio 1997.

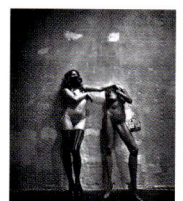

Miss Crash photographed in her apartment in Downton Los Angeles, 2011.

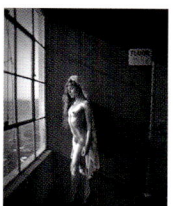

Nettie Harris, Downton Los Angeles 2012.

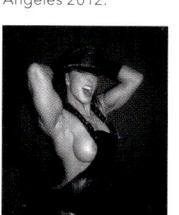

Lisa, Torture Garden, Islington 2015.

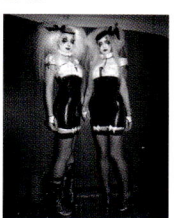

Anne-Sophie and Jenni, Torture Garden, Brixton 2010.

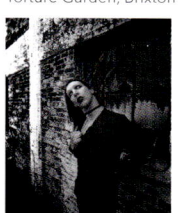

Marilyn Manson, Utica, New York 1997.

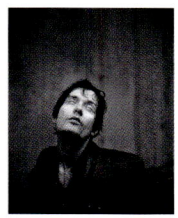

Jarvis Cocker, Fitzrovia, London 1994.

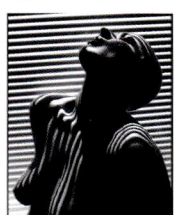

Ray, Downtown LA 2016.

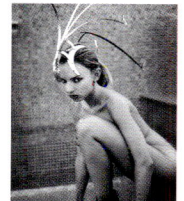

Marie, Cap d'Agde, France. For Michel Coulon.

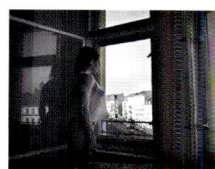

Miss Crash photographed in her apartment in Berlin 2015.

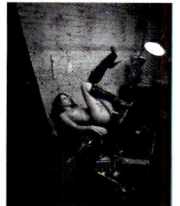

Miss Crash photographed in her apartment in Downton Los Angeles, 2011.

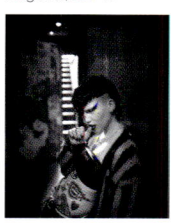

Liz Harris at the Alibi Club in Dalston. Styling Tara St. Hill. Make up Lucy Bridge. Hair Gary Gill. Assisted by Natalie Gates. For 10 magazine.

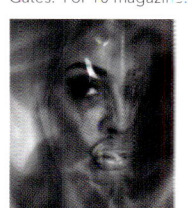

Chessie Kay photographed at her home near Lewes, Sussex 2016.

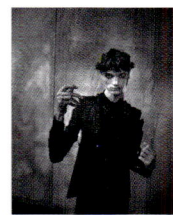

Tom Bird, Aldgate 2017. Styled by Davey Sutton. Makeup by Terry Barber. Hair by Kiyoko Odo. For King Kong magazine.

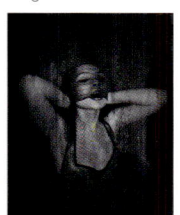

Tomoko, Twickenham 2015.

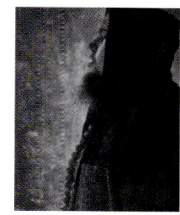

Rag 'n Bone Man, Dalston 2016. For Rollacoaster magazine.

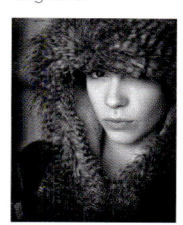

Sparky Sinclair at the Redbury Hotel, Hollywood 2013.

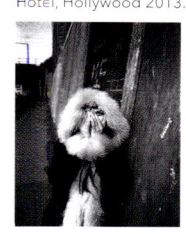

She (Embuggered / Minxus), Camden Town 1993.

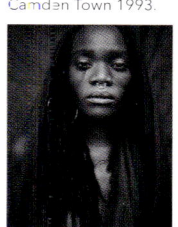

Laurence Sessou shot at Espero Studio in Aldgate 2015.

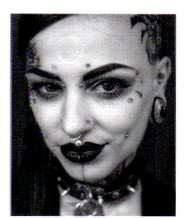

Kokeshi Kuro Neko, Wapping 2017.

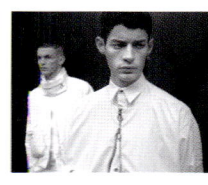

Soho 2012. For GQStyle magazine.

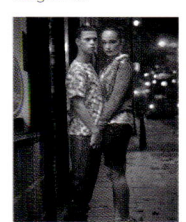

Shoreditch 2012. For GQStyle magazine.

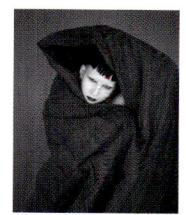

Liz Harris, Beltcraft Studios, Tottenham 2016. Makeup by Susana Mota. Assisted by Natalia Gates.

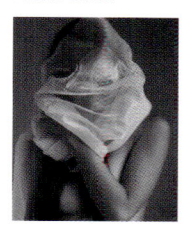

Mia Sollis, Last Shot Studios, April 2016.

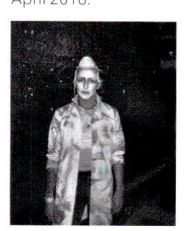

Kane, Kaos, Islington 2016.

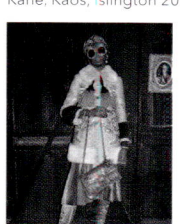

Nicole Atieno, Rome 2016. Art Direction: Christopher Simmonds. Hair Alexandra Brownsell. Makeup Niahm Quinn. Stylist Jonathan Kaye. Assisted by Natalie Gates. For Gucci.

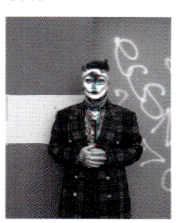

Tuttii Fruttii Gregson, Deptford 2017.

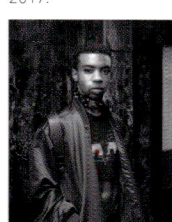

Niall, Soho 2014. From the Soho Street Portraits project.

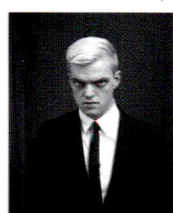

Miguel, Soho 2014. From the Soho Street Portraits project.

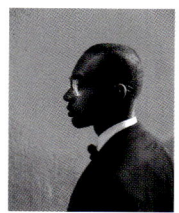

André, Soho 2014. From the Soho Street Portraits project.

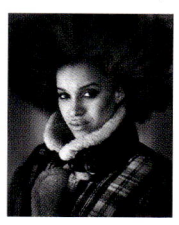

Yasmin, Soho 2014. From the Soho Street Portraits project.

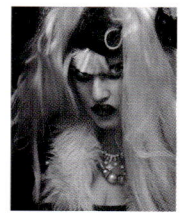

Sissy, Soho 2016. From the Soho Street Portraits project.

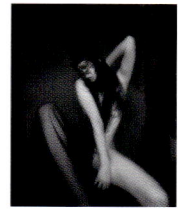

Kayt Webster-Brown, Twickenham 2016.

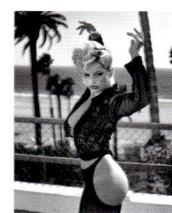

Mariel Gomsrud, Santa Monica, September 2016. Makeup / hair by Yulitzin. Thanks to the Shangri La Hotel

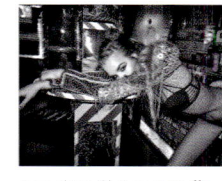

Josephine Skriver at Duff's Brooklyn 2017. Styled by SophiaNeophitou. Hair Tina Outen. Makeup Ayami Nishimura. For 10 magazine. Assisted by by Maya Duan.

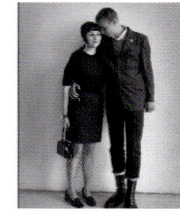

Lara and Jamie, Southbank 2015.

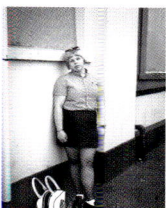

Hanna, Brighton 2016.

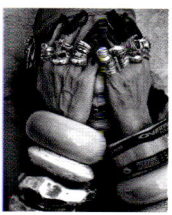

Michele Lamy in the back garden of her house in Paris, 2018. Assisted by Ruby Sanderson.

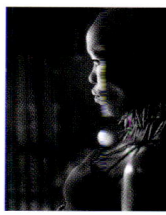

Grace Bol at Duff's, Brooklyn 2017. Styled by Sophia Neophitou. Hair Tina Outen. Makeup Ayami Nishimura. For 10 magazine

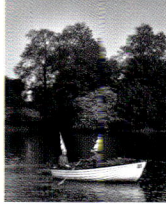

Back cover: Pet Shop Boys whilst filming the 'Can You Forgive Her' video, Battersea 1993.

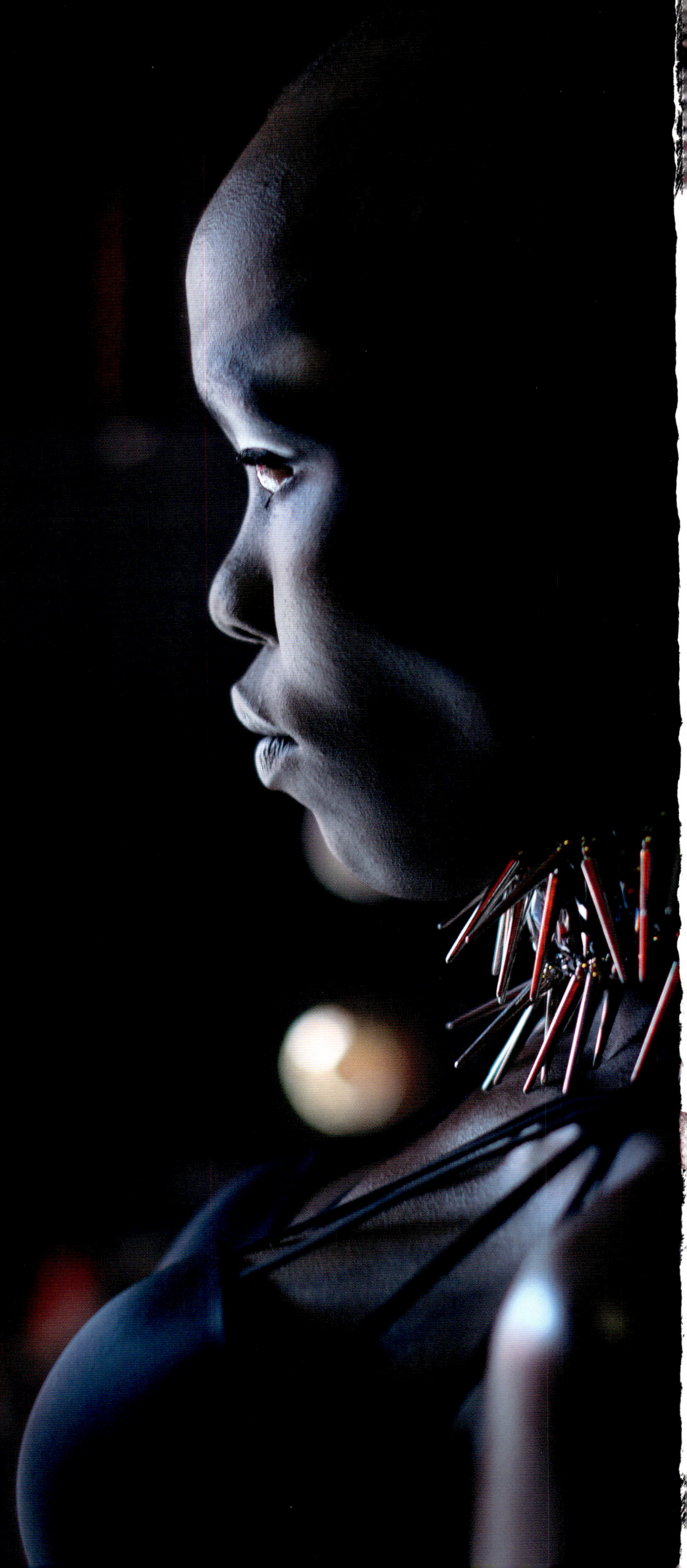

This book is dedicated to my wife Jo-Anne.

I'd also like to say thank you, to all those who helped and supported me over the years. It's a long list, because by now it's become quite a long career, but rather than turn this into another Father Ted Golden Cleric acceptance speech, I will confine myself just to the following.

Sarah Appelhans, Don Ateyo, Mark Bannister, John Best, Tony Biner, Anton Brookes, James Brown, Alex Brunner, Andrew Bunney, Jeffrey Cameron, Murray Chalmers, Susan Compo, Rita D'Albert, Steve Davies, Robbin Derrick, Faye Dowling, Pamela Esterson, Joe Ewart, Suzanne Fitzgerald, Danny Flynn, Amanda Freeman, Katrina Furniss, Jane Garcia, Natalie Gates, Marcus Georgio, Sue Goodacre, Kasper de Graaf, John Halsall, Mary Harron, Angela Hay, Laetitia Hecht, Angela Hill, Tara St. Hill, Fatima Ingraham, Michele Jaffe-Pearce, David Johnson, Kathy Kelly, Carrie Kania, Sarah Kent, Phil King, Hilaneh von Kories, Babette Kulik, Alan Lewis, Rae Lewis, Nick Logan, Victoria Lukens, Celina Lunsford, Gordon Macdonald, Eugene Manzi, Lynda Marshall, Peter Marshall, Gavin Martin, Kas Mercer, David Owen, Rob Partridge, Sue Ready, Cynthia Rose, Andy Ross, Red Saunders, Phil Savage, Jack Schofield, Gary Shove, Sharon Shove, Neil Spencer, Ava Stander, Tony Stewart, Liz Tray, Harv Sunila, Karen Walter, Kayt Webster-Brown, David Whyte, Professor Val Williams, Tim Woodward and Lorenz Zatecky.